Web Development with Apache and Perl

Web Development with Apache and Perl

Theo Petersen

MANNING

Greenwich
(74° w. long.)

For online information and ordering of this and other Manning books,
go to www.manning.com. The publisher offers discounts on this book
when ordered in quantity. For more information, please contact:

Special Sales Department
Manning Publications Co.
209 Bruce Park Avenue   Fax: (203) 661-9018
Greenwich, CT 06830   email: orders@manning.com

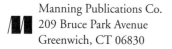
Manning Publications Co.   Copyeditor: Joel Rosenthal
209 Bruce Park Avenue   Typesetter: Dottie Marsico
Greenwich, CT 06830   Cover designer: Leslie Haimes

ISBN 1-930110-06-5
Printed in the United States of America
1 2 3 4 5 6 7 8 9 10 – VHG – 06 05 04 03 02

To Rachel
for saying yes

contents

preface

A quick look at your local bookstore's Internet section will tell you that there are quite a few commercial packages out there for building web sites. What those books often fail to mention is that many of the world's most popular web sites were built using freely available tools, and run on free operating systems (OS). They also tend to be served up by Apache, the world's leading web server, which is also free.

I don't think this omission is due to some vast commercial software conspiracy; there are plenty of books about Linux, one of the free OSs in question. In fact, the success of Linux has drawn much-needed attention to the Open Source software movement, and in turn helped to make this book possible. If anything, the problem is lack of information about free tools, and misconceptions about Open Source solutions.

My goal in writing this book is to make you aware of the amazing richness and quality of Open Source tools for building web sites. I'm not selling anything (other than the book) and I won't profit from your buying decisions. While I will encourage you to consider the advantages of a free OS, chances are good you can use these tools on a commercial OS you already have.

I should also point out that this is an idea book, not a comprehensive reference about any particular programming tool or operating system. As part of the task of making you aware of what products are available and what you can do with them, I'll encourage you to look at online resources and other books for more detailed information.

Who should read this book?

You can take any of several approaches to the material here, depending on what you want or need.

If you are responsible for keeping a web site running, or you are just starting to build one, the early chapters will provide a good checklist for your system; compare my suggestions to your own ideas and see if you have the best tools for your job. The end chapters have guidelines on site maintenance that you might appreciate also.

Site developers and application programmers might be more interested in the middle chapters where I discuss tools for specific needs and explain the advantages of different alternatives. Further on we'll get into designs for specific types of web sites, which may give you ideas as to how to build one of your own.

If you're the person who plans or manages the efforts of the people in the preceding paragraphs, the discussions in all of the chapters may help you with choosing a strategy and architecture for larger sites and more ambitious applications.

Perl provides the glue for tools I'll discuss here. While I intend to explain and illuminate the concepts of various web technologies as I go, I expect the reader to be familiar enough with Perl scripting to follow the examples, with appropriate reference material at hand. Teaching the basics is beyond the scope of this book; and besides, I couldn't do a better job than the many texts already available to help you learn. Leaf through the early chapters and read an example or two, and you'll know if you are ready.

If you implement any of the design plans given here, you are going to get your hands dirty and your feet wet, and you'll slog through other hard-working analogies. Open Source tools are about *source* after all, and you're going to have to look at some to make your way through this world. But don't let that intimidate you; in spite of its geek-oriented, high-tech characterization, the Open Source world is remarkably friendly, and actually provides a much more gentle learning curve than some commercial products I've attempted to use over the years.

I expect you already know that web browsers talk to web servers; that's as much architecture as you'll need to get started. This book is about interesting things to do with servers, and we're going to assume that browsers are the well-behaved, generic clients they really ought to be instead of the crass, ghetto-forming pawns of commercial empires that they've become. (Hey, maybe there *is* a conspiracy!)

But we were talking about you: this book will help you find useful tools and get them to work faster. It's a book for planners, developers, and dreamers of all kinds. As I said before, it's an idea book, aimed at helping you realize how to make your own ideas work using freely available, quality tools.

What's in the book?

The material is separated into four parts:

Part I discusses Open Source tools in general and those that make good choices for a web site in particular. The first chapter talks about the methodology and how to choose good tools from the huge selection available on the Internet. Chapter 2 discusses the selection of an OS, or considerations for the one you already have, along with what to configure for a web site and, more importantly, what to disable; it also explains the basic Apache setup. The third chapter discusses the prevalence of scripting in web applications and introduces simple Perl CGI scripts.

Part II is about tools for serious applications. Chapter 4 covers databases and how to use them from inside a CGI script. Chapter 5 talks about ways to speed up the performance of CGI and go beyond it into the deeper realms that mod_perl provides. Chapter 6 discusses secure communications between the browser and the server, which you'll need for sensitive information such as credit card numbers. Chapter 7 talks about tools for embedding Perl scripts into web pages for better site design.

Part III uses the tools discussed so far to build three basic kinds of web sites. Chapter 8 is about community sites, which focus on news, discussion, and other attractions for a given community. Chapter 9 is for intranet sites, where a variety of applications and information are served up to a protected network. Chapter 10 brings up the issues of e-commerce, such as user profiles, shopping carts, and why we need those security tools from chapter 6.

Part IV goes on to general issues that might come up as any sort of site matures. Chapter 11 covers strategies and tools for managing site content as your simple site grows beyond your initial expectations. Chapter 12 concerns performance management. This includes issues such as how to keep your site online as its popularity grows, especially as it starts receiving multiple servers, and how to keep the hordes of users happy.

There's also a bibliography, or as I prefer to think of it, a suggested book list for people who do this kind of work. As I said earlier, I can't hope to provide everything you need in one book (and if I did, you probably couldn't lift it), so I've gone through my own bookshelves, (both real and virtual), and listed the things that helped me learn to do this job.

Source code

When scattered in with regular text, any code, file names, or other pieces of software will appear in a `fixed width` font. The names of software (i.e., Apache and Perl) appear as normal text.

Code examples are in the same `fixed width` font, and set off from the text:

```
foreach (sort keys %members) {
    print "<TR><TD>$_</TD><TD>$members{$_}</TD></TR>";
}
```

But don't bother typing in the examples—all the code mentioned in this book is also available on the publisher's web site at http://www.manning.com/petersen.

acknowledgments

Anyone who works with programmers or writers learns quickly that both are typically optimistic at the start of a project but late to finish. Imagine what life is like for the managers of these programmers and writers. The patient folks at Manning are a pleasure to work with and gave just the right mix of understanding and expectation to bring this book into being. Marjan Bace took my very different initial concept and developed it into the outline of the present work, refining it further at various stages. Mary Piergies offered her resources and prodding as necessary to get the project moving. When my family's needs became overwhelming, they graciously suspended the schedule, then helped to bring the book back on track when I returned to it.

Technical books, like good software, need plenty of eyes watching for bugs, wrong directions, and shortcomings. Ted Kennedy at Manning brought a host of reviewers to help, doing his own share of the prodding along the way. The reviewers included Bennett Todd, Clinton A. Pierce, D. Jasmine Merced, Dave Cross, Gerald Richter, John Timon, Jonathan Swartz, Martien Verbruggen, Stas Bekman, Randy Kobes, David Cantrell, Joshua Chamas, Vivek Khera, and Dennis Cumro who also did a final technical review of the book shortly before it went to press. My thanks to all of you, and apologies to anyone I've left out.

Writing a book on a subject you love is a wonderful project, and I recommend it wholeheartedly. It's also fun and challenging to move to a new home, raise an infant, and start a new job. I will caution against doing all these in the same year, though, having tried it myself. My wife Rachel did all the above with me, offering commentary on the book from her technical background while spending more than her share of time with our first son, Kai, and bringing our second son, Rowan, into the world. Her faith in the project made possible its conclusion, and I give her my thanks and love.

author online

Purchase of *Web Development with Apache and Perl* includes free access to a private web forum run by Manning Publications where you can make comments about the book, ask technical questions, and receive help from the author and from other users. To access the forum and subscribe to it, point your web browser to http://www.manning.com/petersen. This page provides information on how to get on the forum once you are registered, what kind of help is available, and the rules of conduct on the forum.

Manning's commitment to our readers is to provide a venue where a meaningful dialog between individual readers and between readers and the author can take place. It is not a commitment to any specific amount of participation on the part of the author, whose contribution to the Author Online forum remains voluntary (and unpaid). We suggest you try asking the author some challenging questions lest his interest stray!

The Author Online forum and the archives of previous discussions will be accessible from the publisher's web site as long as the book is in print.

about the cover illustration

The figure on the cover of *Web Development with Apache and Perl* is a "Mandarin de la China" or a Chinese Mandarin, a public official of the Chinese Empire. A Mandarin was a person of position and influence in intellectual or literary circles. The illustration is taken from a Spanish compendium of regional dress customs first published in Madrid in 1799. The book's title page informs us:

> *Coleccion general de los Trages que usan actualmente todas las Nacionas del Mundo desubierto, dibujados y grabados con la mayor exactitud por R.M.V.A.R. Obra muy util y en special para los que tienen la del viajero universal*

Which we loosely translate as:

> *General Collection of Costumes currently used in the Nations of the Known World, designed and printed with great exactitude by R.M.V.A.R. This work is very useful especially for those who hold themselves to be universal travelers.*

Although nothing is known of the designers, engravers, and artists who colored this illustration by hand, the "exactitude" of their execution is evident in this drawing. The "Mandarin de la China" is just one of a colorful variety of figures in this collection which reminds us vividly of how distant and isolated from each other the world's towns and regions were just 200 years ago. Dress codes have changed since then and the diversity by region, so rich at the time, has faded away. It is now often hard to tell the inhabitant of one continent from another. Perhaps we have traded a cultural and visual diversity for a more varied personal life—certainly a more varied and interesting world of technology.

At a time when it can be hard to tell one computer book from another, Manning celebrates the inventiveness and initiative of the computer business with book covers based on the rich diversity of regional life of two centuries ago—brought back to life by the pictures from this collection.

# PART 1

Web site basics

This part deals with basic issues—what is Open Source, what makes a good web server, and why is there so much Perl code involved?

- Chapter 1 discusses why Open Source is a good idea and presents a buyer's guide with some considerations for the long-term aspects of the decision to use a product.
- Chapter 2 is about the web server, starting with the machine and operating system (OS), then the case for using Apache to serve your site content.
- Chapter 3 explains why Perl is a good choice for scripting, and what the alternatives are. We verify that the most recent version of Perl is installed and that it is installed correctly. Then we and write some simple CGI scripts.

After reading these chapters and working out the installations and examples, you can demonstrate a basic site that is ready for more interesting work.

C H A P T E R   1

Open Source

1.1   WHAT IS OPEN SOURCE?

As the Internet grew from a few institutions with dial-up lines to a worldwide information network, a software development methodology and culture grew with it: share code freely, don't charge for it, keep everything in the open. This methodology allowed the Internet's underlying software tools to grow at an amazing speed that caught the commercial software world by surprise; seemingly from nowhere, a set of high-quality tools and protocols emerged that provided for a variety of communications media, including Sendmail (the program which has handled most of the mail traffic on the Internet), BIND (which handles the distributed database of Internet domain names and addresses), and, comparatively recently, the HTTP protocol that makes the web browsers and servers work.

The culture developed as well, largely among devotees of the Unix operating system. They applied the methodology to create tools, languages, and applications that weren't directly related to the Internet, but which couldn't have grown as quickly without the Internet's ubiquitous distribution medium. The members of the culture valued quality programming, for which they used the term hacking, borrowed from another slang. They also valued sharing, and gave high status to those who created or enhanced useful software and gave it back to their community.

During that same period, various companies created good network protocols, good email tools, good news and collaboration programs which either fell into disuse or merged with their Internet cousins. No proprietary system offered the wide access and low cost of entry of the software shared openly by the Internet hackers. Without this culture, and its open development methodology, the reliable, freely available programs which carry the Internet's traffic, and by extension, the Internet, would not exist.

The Internet became high profile as businesses caught on to the potential value of the Web as a medium. Equally important was the advent of Linux, a free implementation of a Unix-like operating system developed by Linus Torvalds and the hacker culture. Linux also seemingly appeared out of nowhere, and by the late '90s gained a high profile as more and more people discovered that it provided a quality alternative to commercial versions of Unix and other OSs. Linux is said to have "snuck into" corporate America as system administrators realized that they could download it free (or purchase a CD distribution for a small fee) and install it without going through the acquisitions process required for an expensive OS license.[1]

In 1998, some prominent members of the hacker culture got together to discuss how to make their kind of development more attractive to corporate America. The results of the meeting were the new label, "Open Source," and an agreement to adopt certain definitions of what constituted an Open Source license. This group styled itself the Open Source Initiative (OSI), and you can read more about them at their web site, http://www.opensource.org/. By sidestepping the issue of what the word "free" meant in what had been called "free software," some in the movement hoped to bring code sharing back to the fore and to encourage licensing that allowed users of a program to see and modify its source and to pass bug fixes and enhancements on to the community.

For our purposes in this book, a software product is Open Source if its license fits the OSI definitions. Some Open Source fans (myself included) complain about licenses that the OSI has approved, and of course there is a large camp that doesn't care for the OSI at all; I hope that my choice doesn't offend them, but I think the value of the now-recognized Open Source label is greater than the political issues surrounding its adoption.

---

[1] Linux was not the first free operating system. Earlier programmers at Berkeley had taken on the task of replacing the copyrighted code in the Unix kernel with free implementations, resulting in three modern offshoots known as "the BSDs" for the original project title, Berkeley Software Distribution. The fact that Linux gets referred to as "the free operating system" is a source of frequent annoyance among *BSD aficionados.

1.1.1　And it's free!

In choosing our jargon and labels, let's not lose track of the fact that Open Source software is also freely available software—you can download it from web sites or copy it from CD distributions and other sources. Of course, CDs and Internet bandwidth have costs, but the price of the software is still 0. For many users, this is the single most important reason to choose Open Source. The budget of a small social organization, a fledgling company, or an individual wanting to publish on the Web can easily be taken up by the cost of hardware and bandwidth. In those cases, software with a low acquisition price can make the difference between being heard or not.

Those who do have money to spend sometimes make the mistake of dismissing Open Source software for this same reason; if you find yourself having that argument, you should read the discussion of quality versus price.

Also, please note that the fact that a product can be downloaded free and/or in source form says nothing about whether you can use it on a commercial web site or sell products based on it. That is a complex issue that requires careful reading of the license. Always read the license!

The complex issue of software cost will be covered in greater detail in section 13.4.

1.2　WHY CHOOSE OPEN SOURCE

Hacker culture, code sharing, Open Source—very interesting topics, but what do they have to do with the real-world concerns of a business, an organization, or an individual creating a web site?

The answer, of course, is: everything. If the cultural phenomenon of Open Source isn't of interest to you, then perhaps one of the following issues is: support, quality, security, and innovation. In my opinion, and that of millions of satisfied downloaders out there, Open Source software is superior on all these counts.

1.2.1　Support

The essential distinction of Open Source software is, of course, source code: the source files for each library and program are distributed with the product, along with documentation (one hopes) and possibly, prebuilt binary executables. This is in comparison to "closed" software, commercial or otherwise, which includes only executables, possibly libraries, and, hopefully, even more documentation.

If you're not the sort of person who makes a hobby of poring through other people's programs, you may be wondering, "so what?" Having to build the program yourself is at best a chore, and at worst an obstacle if you are using an OS different from that of the program's maintainer. Why is carrying all this source baggage important?

Suppose you are using a closed source program—a web server, let's say—and you discover that it has a bug: most files are served correctly, but files in the `foo` directory cause an error. You've checked the documentation and your configuration files and, as far as you can tell, there's nothing wrong with your setup. What do you do?

If you have some support access to the maker of the program, you call them, send them an email, consult your medium, or do whatever is required. Perhaps you also consult newsgroups or web pages about the product in hopes that someone else has encountered the problem. You may get a response from the responsible party or not, and either way you'll probably work around the bug in the meantime.

In contrast, what would happen if in the same situation you were using Apache, an Open Source web server. You've tried everything and can't figure out why it won't serve up your `foo` directory; you've read the fine manual, looked on the Apache web site and sent messages to various newsgroups or your favorite mailing list. What happens next may not sound believable if you've never been through the process, but having gone down this road before (with other products—not Apache) I can say it's a regular occurrence.

You get a response: a reply to your newsgroup posting, an email, or both, depending on how you reported the bug. Someone somewhere has a `foo` directory that behaved just as yours did, and the problem was caused by an obscure configuration file entry that you've looked at a dozen times but didn't realize mattered. Or a message saying "I never tried a `foo` directory before, and I just set one up on my server and it worked; let's compare our sites and see what's different." Or, more likely, a shorter response that goes something like: "Yep, that's a bug. Patches enclosed."

Sometimes you get a less helpful response. Someone may complain to the newsgroup that newbies should be forced to read the FAQ[2] on `foo` in Apache before being allowed to post. Perhaps you get a smug "it works fine for me." Or you might get an acknowledgment that it is in fact a bug, with a good-natured "Patches welcomed."

I've received all of the above in response to intelligent questions about Open Source products, and have even received pleasant replies to more naïve questions. I've gotten rude replies too. It's a big Internet, and the Manners Police are rather overworked. The point, though, is that I never fail to get a helpful response as long as (a) the question is reasonable for the product and the forum, (b) it's apparent from the question that I've checked the documentation and obvious configuration issues beforehand, and (c) the answer is not obvious to a beginner. Generally I know what I need to know within a day, often within an hour.

I'd compare that to the kind of responses I get to problem reports sent to commercial software companies, but for the most part I prefer to repress unpleasant memories. In defense of support staffers everywhere I will admit that they are typically overworked and constantly besieged by questions that (a) aren't reasonable, (b) show no sign of any awareness of documentation, and (c) indicate the questioner hasn't the faintest idea what's on his system. If you have done time at a help desk, I salute you. Nevertheless, I've had almost uniformly negative experiences in going to commercial

---

[2] FAQ is shorthand for Frequently Asked Question file, or sometimes (more irritably) Frequently Answered Question. Popular products often have FAQs that explain solutions to common problems, and you should always check for one before posting a message as I've described here.

support operations for information when I didn't fit those categories; generally they are slow to respond even in the cases where I do get help, to the point where I've worked around the problem or moved on by the time the information arrives.[3]

Professional customer support personnel have some very tough constraints on their jobs: they can't ignore questions from complete idiots, for example. They get paid to answer the phones and are rated on customer satisfaction, so laughing and hanging up are bad for business. Also, the support staff probably doesn't have direct access to the source code of the product, and probably lacks the long-term exposure needed to draw quick answers from it if they did. Instead, if they can't answer a question from their own experiences or a problem database, they go to a higher level engineer, who also may or may not have access to the actual source code.

Contrast that to the situation with an Open Source product. Upon getting an email that reports a possible bug, a reader can do several things. He can delete it; perhaps he's busy or not interested in the problem. He can write a rude response; maybe he's having a bad day and doesn't see why others should get help with their problems. But there is also the excellent probability that he's encountered the same or a similar problem, and has time to write an illuminating response. If the problem is really a bug, perhaps he knows where the bug is and how to fix it, or can point the questioner in the right direction.

Given that variety of responses, you may be thinking that the chance of getting a helpful reply from complete strangers is small. It would be if the number of Open Source enthusiasts were about the same as the number of people who work at help desks, but this is not the case: newsgroups and mailing lists for popular Open Source products are read by hundreds or thousands of smart people, and chances are surprisingly good that one or more of them can help with a question.

The helpful nature of the Open Source community is infectious. Assuming you work through your problems and stay with the program for a while, you will one day find in your mailbox or your news reader a question from some poor soul who's just starting out and is having a problem with his `foo` directory. Even if you never read the source code for a program yourself, chances are good that you can help someone else with a problem based just on your own experience as a fellow user. If your curiosity is greater, you may delve into the code in search of your own answers, and soon you'll find yourself submitting patches.

At the very least, you'll get an opportunity to send rude responses to dumb questions. Just don't let the Manners Police catch you.

---

[3] A humorous "study" posted on Slashdot in 2001 compared the success rate of a commercial technical support company with that of a psychic hotline, and found them to be about equal. I've resolved to try the second approach next time I have a problem.

Commercial support for Open Source products

In spite of my good experiences and optimism, you may not trust this nebulous support organization to work for your needs, or you may work for an organization that requires critical software to have support contracts. In either case you can still choose Open Source products, because there are a number of companies that will be happy to sell you phone, email, or in-person support. I don't want to name some and miss others, so if you are looking for such support, check the web sites and/or magazines that deal with your products of choice; chances are good the support companies advertise there. If you don't see any, ask in the forums that support the product.

1.2.2   Quality

Is Open Source software any good? After all, people give it away, and you get what you pay for!

First of all, let's say what *quality* means in regard to software. I rate the quality of a program mostly on whether it does a good job of what it claims to do, without bugs that keep me from doing what I want it to do. There are other factors of course, documentation high among them, but let's begin the discussion of quality with my main issues.

The first issue is somewhat subjective: does the software do a good job for the user? Does the software provide the features I need, as well as extras that will make my life easier? Does the interface let me use it naturally in its own context? The interface for a database might consist of libraries to link into my code; for a mail reader, the interface probably consists of lists of messages and folders that contain them, with the usual functions of reading, replying, deleting, and so on. A programming tool should provide functions for simple tasks; a database query should involve one library call, or at most a few (prepare, execute, clean up). Software that interacts directly with the user should have simple commands for normal tasks (or single buttons in the case of a graphical interface). I'd be surprised if a mail reader program required more than one step to read a message or switch folders.

The second quality issue is much more objective: how many bug reports are there, and how long do they take to get fixed? Of course, all nontrivial software has bugs, so we can't expect perfection. Let's say rather that good quality software is easy to use and doesn't fail due to bugs in the user's normal work. Poor quality software annoys the user regularly, especially to the point where the user considers some other product. Bugs that stop the user from working should be fixed quickly, while bugs in secondary features might be tolerated longer before we downgrade the quality rating.

To compare the commercial and Open Source worlds on these issues, let's first look at how commercial software achieves good quality. If a commercial software product doesn't have good quality, it won't get positive reviews, it won't make sales projections, and in the grimmest case, programmers won't get paid, so let's assume we don't have to discuss poor quality systems. Software is developed by teams of programmers, guided by knowledgeable team leaders and managers, with goals set by studying market needs and direction. Within the development teams, programmers review each others' code and conduct early testing; when the system achieves certain milestones it is turned over for more rigorous testing by outside reviewers, and when it is approaching the finish line it can be sent out in a prerelease form to eager customers who subject it to real-world conditions. (I know how commercial development works since I've been employed by such companies all of my professional life, and every one of them told their customers that they worked this way.)

After cycles of testing and refinement, the software is released to the general public. When customers report problems, the reports are evaluated in terms of severity and assigned back to the development team or to a maintenance team in the event that the developers are working on the next version or a different product. After clearing the bureaucracy, the bug gets fixed and is part of a new release. Similarly, if someone requests a new feature, the request is evaluated and, if considered worthy, assigned to the programmers for a later version.

The most striking aspect of this model is the isolation of the developers. Looking into the source code is a privilege reserved for the programmers. It is often the only privilege they have, as features, priorities, and overall direction are decided by higher authorities. Features are decided by market researchers; bugs are prioritized by the support managers; the programmers might choose their tools and coding methodology, but even that can be decided for them. Not all commercial companies are such gulags for programmers, of course; in general, the smaller the company, the more influence each programmer has on all of these decisions. But even so, the process remains closed off from the actual users of the product, and the staff is told that this is to shield the developers from distraction.

The "Open" in Open Source provides the key comparison here. It doesn't refer just to the source code, but to the development process. It's not uncommon in repositories of Open Source software to see programs marked with version 0.01, meaning more or less, "this is an outline of a program." One mantra of the movement is "release early, release often,"[4] show your work at every stage to possible users and collaborators. Early releases are not meant for the fainthearted; rather, they provide some publicity for the program, allowing the developers to get feedback and perhaps volunteers to continue the work. These releases may lack key features or interfaces, but can let potential users try out the fledgling software and tell the developers what to work on to make it usable. When version 1.00 is released, expect it to be very solid, though version 1.01 may follow closely on as even more users start working with the "stable" release.

Thus Open Source software is subject to peer review, testing, and refinement from a very early stage. While closed development is reviewed only by the development group and tested by a staff of similar size, an open project can be reviewed by anyone

---

[4] See Eric S. Raymond's "The Cathedral and the Bazaar" for this and other inspirational phrases, at http://www.tuxedo.org/.

interested in the work, and tested thoroughly throughout its life cycle. When reviewers find code that bodes ill for long-term success, or testers find a bug, the matter can be discussed among the wider circle of Open Source developers, and suggestions may come in from other programmers who've faced similar problems. Of course, some of those reviewers and testers may submit fixes for the bugs they find, widening the development pool considerably.

The Open Source movement likes using software that is a work in progress. It turns out that this is a strength of such software. This release often mantra pushes software into the hands of the ready and helpful users as soon as the developer is willing to let it go, often as each new feature is built. While most developers employ some form of regression testing as they go, the user base is far more skilled at trying out features in a wider variety of contexts than is the developer. Open Source projects tend to get released in a "feature, fix" cycle for that reason.

Most projects also mark a solid release as stable, while work on new features and their fixes continues. Users who don't insist on the latest big thing can stay with a stable release while new work is done. Those who need a new feature or like to see what's going on can stay current with the developers. The stable releases correspond roughly to versions of commercial software, since most closed companies don't like showing works in progress. The closed companies that do so limit exposure only to those who sign nondisclosure agreements and beta test licenses.

1.2.3 Security

Before Internet connectivity became common, most administrators' security concerns were restricted mostly to controlling user access to their servers. As more machines became connected, "cracking" became more common and turned into big news.[5] Security is an important concern, whether your site contains sensitive data or just an online brochure—once you are connected, you are available to attack.

The literature of every commercial web product mentions security features—this is a high profile area, and a bad reputation for vulnerability can and should kill an otherwise good product. Less often, that literature will mention how those security features have been verified. Was the code audited by professionals? Was the server bombarded with real breach attempts mixed with regular traffic?

Closed development promotes a notion that code which is seen only by the select is more secure than code which can be read by anyone. In cryptography circles, this is known as the myth of security by obscurity. Some classic examples include encryption protections on word processing documents and spreadsheets and password guards for desktop computer file systems. The files of law enforcement agencies provide any

---

[5] The news media unfortunately refer to computer break-ins as "hacking" when this activity is properly called "cracking," and likewise confuse hackers with crackers, perhaps because hacker sounds more ominous.

number of stories telling how easy it is for a professional to break such encryption when those files have come up as evidence.

Serious computer cryptography researchers and programmers are among the strongest proponents of sharing code. The reason is that they've learned through hard experience that their own clever ideas are often not as clever as they'd like to think, and real security comes only through detailed analysis of every algorithm that touches sensitive data. This is also the reason that there are a small number of accepted encryption algorithms in use today. Very few pass through the analysis unscathed.

The Open Source movement embraces their attitude about code review and analysis, and extends it to whole programs, not just the sensitive bits. Security holes often occur due to a bug in something that seems unrelated to security. For example, in 1999 various mail clients had to be patched to fix so-called "buffer overrun" bugs wherein the software didn't check that an incoming mail header fit into the amount of memory allocated for it. By writing past the end of the buffer, a virus or mail bomb could alter the program's memory and cause it to do something unplanned.

There is also a secondary effect of having the code known to a wide audience: when a vulnerability is discovered in one system, it is not unusual for a developer on another project to say "I saw something similar in the code for Project X; here's a patch." Of course, such familiarity and cross-fixing happens inside the development teams of closed products also, but the sheer number of savvy people involved in Open Source development makes it likely that security holes of similar kind get fixed across projects.

All nice in theory of course, but what about practice? The web sites and magazines of the Open Source movement are full of tirades against closed products and self-congratulation for the quality of their own work, but for confirmation we should turn to other sources.

One study on the matter was conducted in early 2000 by *Security Portal*, a web magazine devoted to security issues and announcements. Its editors gathered data on the time delay between a public announcement of a security advisory to the release of a patch, using reports from three OS vendors: RedHat Linux, Microsoft, and Sun Microsystems. For the data they had, the Linux OS was patched most quickly for a given advisory, followed by Microsoft and then Sun. RedHat Linux should not be assumed to represent the Open Source community, but it provided enough data to form a reasonable comparison and suggest that the movement was living up to its own self-image in this regard.

1.2.4 Innovation

I've mentioned just a few of the achievements of Open Source development—the protocols and programs that make the Web, email, news, and many other Internet services work, plus the Apache web server. These are enough to let anyone rest on their laurels. Those and the many other working systems appear "out of nowhere" from a mix of volunteer programmers, researchers, and commercial enterprises.

It is an interesting facet of the Open Source movement that it draws in the "best and brightest" through its frank openness. Suppose a commercial developer is looking to add FTP services to his product, or a student needs an example of a security algorithm for a class project. Either can find complete, working implementations already built and available for download. Having taken advantage of the work of others, the developer might be moved to contribute his own time to improve the project; or, considering the sort of egos typical among programmers everywhere, he might submit improvement patches just to show off. Many find the cultural aspects of the Open Source movement appealing and start contributing just to get involved.

Whether the ratio of contributors to users is one in five or one in a thousand, the sheer numbers of people involved become amazing. With more companies and institutions than ever connected to the Internet, and the Web taken for granted by the current generation of students, Open Source projects get a large "mindshare" of the world's talent pool. The best of those people become icons of the movement, earning kudos from fellow developers as well as invitations to speak at conferences and business seminars. Regular contributors get job offers from companies which know their talents from working code instead of from a résumé. More recently, companies have been hiring key Open Source developers into positions where they continue their work full time. These developers can advance the company's interests, sometimes by supporting the support staff, while in other instances just giving the company a big name to use in their public relations.

This is not meant to suggest that all the best programmers do Open Source; there is talent everywhere, and closed development companies have strong incentives to keep their best people happy. The great thing is, some of their best people also get a kick out of working on Open Source projects—perhaps as an escape from the constraints of their day job, or for the opportunity to work on something related to their career that doesn't have commercial potential.

All of which paints a very happy picture of contented Open Source developers, but the topic is innovation. Does the Open Source methodology produce the most up-to-date features, headline-grabbing technologies, and best-of-breed solutions?

Sometimes. Open Source development plays the same features game that the closed-product companies play, leading the pack in some areas while lagging in others. Many have complained about the lack of comprehensive and high-quality Open Source desktop. But in the long run, Open Source is a safe bet, for four good reasons, as follows:

Bearing the standard

In many cases, especially with Internet technologies, Open Source products provide reference implementations of protocols, clients, and servers. This has the same meaning as a hardware reference design, where a vendor supplies a working version that others can use in building larger products. The reference implementation of, say, a mail delivery protocol takes the specification and turns it into running code that shows how the various components in a mail system should work.

Some products, including the Apache web server, are distributed with a license that allows all or portions of the code to be used commercially, with the express hope that other vendors will use the correct, accepted implementation.

Long-term development

An Open Source product may be developed by a commercial company, perhaps one that sells support or consulting based on such products, or by individuals in their spare time, or a mixture of both. As such, the market forces are somewhat different. If the software doesn't have reasonable features and a usable interface it won't get used widely, but that doesn't have to mean it leaves the market. If the program is someone's pet project, rather than their livelihood, it may stay available for many years, possibly improving with time. If the developer abandons the project, others may pick up the source code and continue the work. Thus it is not unusual to find obscure, quirky Open Source products in the same market niche as more widely accepted, high profile systems, commercial or otherwise.

This longer development time frame gives products a maturity and richness that are hard to duplicate in a publish-or-perish development methodology. A commercial product that doesn't sell well seldom gets a chance to grow into its potential; the product must be good in nearly all facets of its market to survive. By comparison, an Open Source product can succeed in spite of scant documentation, a poor interface, or both, if it does a valuable job well for its users.

The add-on market

The Open Source world is full of programs that are wrappers for other programs, in part because of the long-term effect mentioned previously. If a tool does its job well but has a poor user interface, another developer may come along and write a better front end for the tool. Probably there will be more than one; the gnuplot graphics generator has interfaces for the major scripting languages, and I can't begin to count the number of mail folder utilities there are for Unix-style mailboxes.

This creates a good division of labor, where the developers of the quirky tool with the poor interface can concentrate on the back-end features that make their tool popular, while others who know how to make a good interface can create wrappers that help the user. In this way a secondary competition can take effect where multiple development teams strive to make the best interfaces.

Feature competition

As we've discussed before, the Open Source world is vast, and given enough contributors it is possible that all of the above happens. In the particular case of Apache, the group of developers managing the official version might respond to feature competition. After all, if it's a good idea, Apache should have it. More likely, any new kind of service or bundling of existing services will be relegated to the module market, the world of developers who write add-ons which aren't part of Apache per se but extend its capabilities. Thus Apache stays relatively small and secure, and those who want a new feature such as script processing are welcome to use add-on modules which provide it.

1.3 A BUYER'S GUIDE TO OPEN SOURCE

In spite of my high opinion of the Open Source movement and general optimism about its potential, I'll admit that being just Open Source doesn't make a product a good choice. When I evaluate a new tool I consider a few factors. Obviously the first is technical quality, as nothing else matters if the tool doesn't do a good job. But what else is important?

In calling this a buyer's guide I want to bring up an important point for business users: Open Source software isn't free in the free beer sense! Every product you install and use has costs beyond acquisition price. The users have to learn it, programmers have to get a sense of what it will do for them, administrators have to keep up with changes and install updates, and so on. Those are the considerations that go into your choice as a buyer—is this tool a good investment of your organization's manpower?

1.3.1 Stable version and ongoing development

My first question is always about the state of the product: has it reached the point of having a stable version that users find useful? If so, how old is that version and is there more being done?

We mentioned version 0 and version 1 in the prior discussion of quality. Though there's no law that says a developer has to follow any particular numbering scheme, the usual arrangement is that version 1 represents the first stable release. That is, the interfaces, underlying file formats and other important details are fixed, and the software is reasonably bug-free and usable. Prior to version 1 the developer may change the names of callable routines, the format for records and documents or other important aspects of the product as he discovers problems or limitations, or just gets a better idea. While the phase leading up to version 1 is often very exciting, you must think twice before using a product that isn't there yet. You could be adding to your own users' or developers' headaches.

If there is a stable version, how old is it? If the answer is more than a year, it could be that the project has stalled out or the developer has moved on. Of course it could also mean that the product works and no one has any complaints, so look into the reasons why nothing is changing.

For the most part, I prefer products that have ongoing development. Even if I don't care about any upcoming features, active development means active support—the programmers have the system fresh in their minds and will respond quickly to bug reports. But let's save the rest of that topic for the next point.

When is it okay to use an unstable product? If a tool fits your needs well and scores highly on other criteria, you can consider ignoring this rule and taking a risk on the possibility of disruptive changes in the software. If you are going to get involved in the development of the tool yourself, feel free to take on the challenge of unpolished software and help move things forward.

1.3.2 Support

As I mentioned previously, active development often means good support, but not always. In the Open Source world, support is usually in the form of mailing lists, newsgroups, web forums, or combinations of these. The developers should be active participants in whatever form of support is chosen, and there should be archives and a FAQ page somewhere to help new users get started without bugging the old hands.

When considering a product, look through the archives and see what sort of problems people have reported and what the responses were like. Helpful and amiable responses from developers are a good sign; unanswered questions are not (even if the answer is "read the FAQ"). You might also take note of who is using the product and how. Someone might be working on the same kind of project that you are, or may have run into an issue which is a show-stopper for your use. You may also get a sense of name recognition as you read through Open Source forums and learn whose opinions you trust.

As a product becomes popular (Open Source or not), its user community often takes on a life of its own. This is a particularly good sign in the Open Source world, because an active user community will have lively mailing list or news postings, plus add-on documentation, front-ends, and other goodies. The existence of a supportive user community is also excellent testimony to the quality of the product.

1.3.3 Leveraging other investments

No product is an island! If this is an end-user tool, how well does it integrate with other products your users regularly employ? If it is a development tool, does it have interfaces to your favorite scripting language? Does it tie in to other tools that will help your programmers?

Few things disappoint me as much as reading about an exciting new product and discovering that the developer has created yet another scripting language, protocol, or widget set. When choosing tools for my own development group, I accept only those that work with Perl for scripting and C for low-level programming. My coworkers don't want to learn another language when we have excellent tools for these already. Similarly, I look for tools that store data (or metadata) in XML formats, supply HTML documentation (or something that converts easily), and work with the other tools we depend on.

1.3.4 Ongoing costs

This aspect of the decision may be difficult to evaluate unless you have experience with software product management. Ongoing costs for a development tool are probably small: time spent upgrading to new versions and performing any conversion necessary (preferably none for a stable product). For a database or other product, ongoing costs can be considerable. Data must be backed up at the very least, and many databases have to be in a special clean state before a backup is useful. Also, every product you install uses system resources: disk space for certain, but probably memory and CPU as well.

A further consideration is upgrade cost: as the product is improved or bugs are fixed, what does it take to get the changes into production? A perverse fact of software is that the most critical systems are often the least maintained, if upgrading and fixing requires downtime and commensurate loss of income. Systems which require shutdowns for routine maintenance can run up a tab very quickly.

All of these factors together contribute to the buzz phrase total cost of ownership, (TCO), which must balance favorably against the expected productivity gains or other values of having the product. For many products, TCO can be evaluated in two phases of ownership: deployment and maintenance.

Since practically any web site of significance will have a database lurking somewhere, let's consider the example of two database products and evaluate TCO. This is an Open Source book, so we'll assume both products are freely available; costs are in people time and system resources. The example database has three tables: users, products, and purchases, and the database engine consists of whatever code is required to perform useful queries on them, such as, finding all the purchases made by a given user. Don't worry if any of the terms here aren't familiar to you; we'll explain them in more detail in appropriate sections of the chapters to follow.

The first product is a flat file database; that is, a set of files on disk, each representing a table. The engine has clever code to make each table look like a Perl hash, providing simple queries. Installation is easy; just drop the Perl modules into the right place, run a script that creates the tables, and start coding CGI interfaces. Access control is handled by the usual file permissions on the tables. Deployment costs consist of that installation time, a quick tutorial session for the programmer who is writing the CGI code, and verification testing.

The second product is a relational database. Although it stores data on disk, we consider it a black box in that we don't know or care exactly how the data is arranged into files. The database engine runs as a separate process which must be started whenever the system reboots. Queries are made via SQL, which is sent to the database server via a special Perl interface. Installation requires getting the server installed correctly, then installing the Perl modules for the query interface, and changing the system startup scripts to get everything going again after a boot. Additional deployment costs are familiarizing the CGI programmers with SQL if they aren't already and verifying that all this works. Also, someone has to create the user, product, and purchase tables and administer user access to them, since relational databases almost inevitably have their own separate internal set of users and permissions.

Deployment cost for the relational database is higher than that for the simpler flat-file database. If the database is small, relatively inactive and unlikely to change much over time, the flat-file database is probably the best choice, but we should consider maintenance costs anyway.

Backing up the flat-file system is simple. A normal system backup will catch the files, although it's possible for the back up process to record a file while it is being updated, which could result in data that isn't consistent. If we need to add a new table, we create a file and run the initialization script again. Adding new data to existing tables might be more complicated, perhaps requiring files to be converted to a new format while the system is offline.

Many relational database products require a special check-point status before backing up the data, ensuring that the disk storage is in a consistent state. In a transactional database this might require storing only completed transactions and ignoring work in progress, so it doesn't have to cause a dramatic pause in the action. Creating tables and modifying existing ones is generally easy once an administrator has learned the appropriate SQL statements, and shouldn't require any other special actions. Relational engines are good at that sort of thing, which is one justification for their use.

While maintenance costs can be somewhat higher for a relational database, the engines provide features that justify the expense for very active databases: superior locking and transaction recovery, for instance, make it unlikely that a crashed process or aborted application will leave the data in a bad state. A flat-file database might require manual correction when things go wrong. In a high-traffic world, things will go wrong quite often, and the tools used should take care of that.

Thus the TCO for a relational database is expected to be higher than for a flat-file database, but it is a better choice for a busy system. For a less critical application, the flat-file database might be acceptable.

1.4 OPEN SOURCE LICENSING

In an earlier section I mentioned licensing as an aspect of Open Source methodology. Deciding on whether to choose an existing license or to create one is an important step for the developer of a product. I'll reiterate my warning to *always read the licenses* of any product you download.

For the most part however, a product license restricts how the licensed code can be redistributed—whether you can charge money for it, in particular, and what sort of notices you must include. Less often the license will restrict how it can be used on your site.

This is in part due to the fact that Open Source developers are accustomed to people downloading software to use it. As the Web increases in popularity however, more and more software gets used through that medium instead of by directly deploying the software on the user's machine. If your web site offers a commercial service, you may be charging your subscribers for the use of Open Source software in spite of licenses that would prevent you from charging for the software itself. When awareness of this change gets through to the majority of developers, we may see changes in Open Source licenses that restrict how the software can be used.

Many Open Source products are distributed with generic licenses. Although you will, of course, read them yourself, I'll cover the three most common types here.

1.4.1   The GPL and LGPL

The GNU Public License (GPL) and its variant, the GNU Lesser General Public License, (LGPL) in many ways define the Free Software movement. Created by Richard Stallman and the Free Software Foundation, the GPL requires that any software licensed under it must either be distributed as source code or with source code either on the same media or made available for reasonable distribution fees.[6] It further specifies that only products which are licensed by the GPL can make use of GPLed code. That is, if you use any code that is licensed in these terms, you "infect" your product with the GPL. The LGPL variant allows licensed libraries to be linked into other programs without infection.

Linux is perhaps the most prominent example of GPL protected code. The operating system kernel and most of its utilities are so licensed. Companies that use altered versions of Linux in their products must post the code for their alterations in prominent places on their web sites, and companies that distribute Linux as a product have to provide the Linux source code and their modifications as well. Linus Torvalds' decision to license Linux under the GPL may be one of the most profound acts in the short history of software.

1.4.2   The BSD/MIT license

These two licenses began separately, but in their modern versions are identical apart from one clause. The license requires that both source and binary distributions of the software must contain the copyrights, notices, and disclaimers given in the license, whether or not the original software is modified to make the present distribution. The BSD license further prevents any claim that the organizations mentioned in the license or the contributors to the software endorse this or any later distribution.

These licenses are no longer used verbatim, as is the GPL. Instead, one copies a template of the license and fills in a few blanks. We'll call such derivative licenses "a BSD license" if it has the original clauses and "BSD-like" if they add anything new.

---

[6]   The confusion over the costs of "free" software was one consideration that lead the Open Source Initiative to move toward "openness" and away from "free" as the main descriptive term for software. The Free Software Foundation disagrees with the move and specifies what it means by "free" in nearly every document.

1.4.3 The Artistic License/"Perl terms"

This license accompanied Perl with version 4 and later. Perl had previously been licensed under the GPL. Perl is currently distributed with a dual license of both the GPL and the Artistic License, and those who download and install the package may choose how they license the product. Many developers who create Perl modules license them "under the terms of Perl itself," by which they mean that dual license.

The Artistic License allows all parties to give away copies of the licensed software, along with bug fixes and modifications for portability. To distribute any other modifications to the software, the licensee must either package them with the original version or make the modifications Open Source. The licensee may also use the licensed software in another product and distribute it in nonsource form so long as they provide the licensed software in original form also.

The license makes the software it protects explicitly available for use in commercial products, so long as the licensee doesn't charge for the protected software itself—that is, you may charge for a product that includes Perl but you cannot charge for Perl. It also has anti-endorsement provisions similar to the BSD license.

1.4.4 The right license?

There is no one right license for Open Source software (or anything else). Choosing a license can be a personal decision or a political one. A given author may feel strongly about commercial software, for example, and so may choose to GPL all of his code to avoid seeing others reselling his work. Others like the fact that Open Source code can be widely used for many purposes, and so choose the Artistic License so as to see the largest possible user base while still keeping the source available.

Developers who are motivated by setting standards often choose the BSD/MIT license; I gave Apache as an example earlier. By publishing standard implementations with few restrictions on reuse, there is a greater chance that new products will comply with those standards.

My only strong recommendation to anyone who is writing Open Source code is: don't create a new license! Variant licenses (or worse, whole new attempts) slow down acceptance of software at best, and at worst waste the community's time by reinvigorating arguments over what is best and right for the world.

Most often a new license is really a commercial license in disguise—"anyone may improve this software, but only I am allowed to sell it for money." These pseudocommercial licenses cause the worst debates about the OSI (which has blessed some of them) and reduce the motivation of contributors to spend their time earning someone else's profits.

Now that I've gotten all my Open Source lecturing out of the way, let's move on to one of the premiere successes of the movement, the Apache web server.

CHAPTER 2

The web server

In this chapter we'll discuss the different aspects of the web server, by which we mean both the physical machine and the program that responds to clients. It may seem somewhat confusing to mean two or more different things at different times, but the usage is normal in the industry. Context should make it clear when we mean hardware or software.

2.1 WHAT MAKES A GOOD WEB SERVER

First we'll start with the physical machine and basic setup. In deciding what is good for the task, we first have to consider what the task is. Is this a server for internal documentation that gets a handful of lookups an hour, or is it a major commercial site that is expecting millions of visitors per day? Obviously those are extremes, so let's consider three scenarios:

- *Community site*—The server is exposed to the Internet and provides news and information to a group of hobbyists, a profession or some similar association. The traffic is mostly reads, with some messages written back to the site. Downtime is annoying but won't result in lawsuits.

- *Intranet site*—This is a server that supports a workgroup within a company's protected network. It has a fast network connection to all the clients, and will host a handful of applications as well as the bulk of the group's online documentation. The server needs to be available during work hours.

- *Store front*—An e-commerce server that hosts a database of product information and creates catalog pages on the fly. Security and constant availability are the highest priority, followed closely by speed.

Those three cases will be used as examples throughout the book, and each gets its own chapter.

2.1.1 Hardware

Obviously the three scenarios have varying hardware needs, depending on the traffic, of course; a popular news site could be the busiest of the three. But in general, traffic level is the first consideration for choosing a machine. A fast CPU makes for a more responsive server; the operators of the e-commerce site might consider a multiprocessor system so that users won't have to fight for computing time.

To decide how much memory our systems need, we have to consider what applications the servers run. By applications we mean both what the web server does to serve up pages, and the other programs running on the machine. The requirements to run a large database might swamp the web server by comparison. If it does, there should probably be a dedicated database server (that will be discussed in chapter 12) If the site offers mostly static pages (HTML files that are sent as-is to the client) then the web server itself won't need as much memory, but if that site also has intense traffic demanding those pages, then, to improve performance, we might need a lot of memory for caches. A site that generates most of its pages dynamically (such as the e-commerce site) will need more memory because each web server process will put greater demand on the system.

Network bandwidth is the next consideration. Consider the size of a typical response to a client and multiply that by the expected number of requests in a time period to figure out your bandwidth requirements. A site that serves large graphics files to a few users per hour might need more bandwidth than a site with intense traffic for textual stock quotes.

Disk space and I/O bandwidth come last, in part because disk space is so cheap these days that only sites with intensive requirements need to even consider that part of the issue. But if your site runs database applications and performance is a chief concern, disk I/O may be the limiting factor. Consider the best SCSI bus and drives for the e-commerce site, and also look into trading memory for application time by caching the results of database queries.

We'll discuss all these issues in more detail later on. If I recommend using a tool that causes memory consumption to soar I'll point out that you need to reconsider your configuration. All of chapter 12 is devoted to performance analysis and problem resolution.

2.1.2 Operating system

Since this is a book about Open Source tools, I'm going to recommend freely available OSs, but let me first say this: beyond certain considerations, the OS doesn't matter that much. If you've already paid for a commercial version of Unix (or your company says you have to use one) or even (horrors!), one of those shrink-wrapped box OSs, you can run almost anything discussed in this book. With that in mind, let's consider what is important in the choice of OS.

Server and application software—Does the necessary and desired software run on this OS? That's the most important consideration, beyond any brand name or feature. Software compatibility is the reason that a mediocre and buggy operating system dominated desktop computing through the '90s, and it will continue to outweigh other factors.

In the case of our example systems, we want an operating system that runs the Apache web server, our scripting language of choice (preferably Perl, although there are others), and the applications that the web clients will run via the server. There also may be a preferred database and other packages that will support the applications developed for the site.

We're in luck here: nearly any OS with a recent release can run Apache and the major utilities. There are caveats for some operating systems, so check the documentation thoroughly before committing to a decision, but we're largely free to choose one based on other factors.

Performance—The OS can be a major factor in system performance. This is a very complex issue, with reams of academic work on the relative merits of such choices as micro versus monolithic kernels and other design factors. To evaluate it in terms that are important to a web server, go back to the same issues used to evaluate hardware: does the operating system support the amount of memory needed by the server? Does it provide for the kind of network connection to be used? What file system options are there and what features do they provide?

Again, nearly any OS that supports the desired software will have the performance features needed for a web server, but some offer goodies worth considering: journaled file systems that recover quickly from crashes, for instance.

Hardware requirements—Didn't we already cover hardware? In this case, we mean any specific requirements for this OS. If some higher power has mandated the use of a particular OS, then we have to use the hardware it supports. If you are making this choice yourself, you may have hardware at hand that you want to use, such as the ever-popular PC that can be recycled into a Linux system.

In either case, make sure that the hardware choice doesn't limit your performance. For instance, an older PC with IDE disk controllers might not support the update speed needed for an e-commerce site, and a prior-generation motherboard could surprise you with the amount of memory it can handle.

Support costs—If downtime will be costly for your site, then you must have adequate support for your operating system. Adequate may be mailing list or newsgroup support for an Open Source OS, if you are comfortable with the rapidity of responses you see when others have emergencies (check the archives). If your OS doesn't have such venues, then you will need commercial support that promises to help you in time of need.

However you choose to arrange your support, figure the ongoing costs in your TCO.

2.1.3   Re-evaluation and installation

Having examined hardware and OSs and made a choice, go back to the beginning and re-evaluate it. The costs for an adequate machine and a commercial operating system may surprise you. If you are purchasing all this for a high-traffic site, you should never buy a machine that is only adequate, because if your site is successful, you will find yourself buying another machine soon.

If your first round of evaluations included a commercial OS, consider Linux or one of the BSDs. The hardware coverage is very broad, as is choice of software for the web server and application languages, and support is free. While the cost of the OS and initial software are not a large fraction of TCO, having more money for memory or disk bandwidth at the start can help you avoid a costly migration early in your server's life.

Install the OS with an eye toward the goal: a fast, secure web site. That means avoiding unneeded services that will have to be disabled later, even if they would be nice to have at the start. Assume that the server will be maintained via file copies and minimal shell access, and don't bother installing your favorite GUI, desktop, and editor. Less is more (more disk space, more security, more peace of mind later).

Where there is a need to assume things, for the rest of the book I'll assume that the web server is running a reasonably modern Linux distribution or Unix operating system, with adequate hardware for the task at hand. In chapter 12 we'll discuss options for improving performance with a marginal system.

2.2 SECURING THE SITE

Whether you have just built a brand new machine or you are recycling an existing server, it's time for a security review. It may seem early in the process to be worrying about this, but in my experience, starting with a secure system is better than trying to lock down a finished installation. The former builds good habits early, while the latter is prone to loose threads.

The particulars are OS-specific, but for most Unix-like systems the procedure is roughly the same:

1 Go to the password file (/etc/passwd or /etc/shadow) and disable shell access for all accounts that aren't necessary for a functioning server. You can take that to mean everything but root, although some people prefer to have one non-privileged account with normal access.

2 If you are running inetd, open /etc/inetd.conf (or whatever the configuration file is on your system) and start commenting out services. Which services do you need? Possibly none, in which case you can just shut down inetd all together: chances are however, that you'll use ftp for maintaining your site, and you'll need telnet to log in and do the rest of the configuration. Consider replacing both of these with ssh; it provides scp to perform secure, password-encrypted file transfers as well as a secure shell that doesn't expose passwords to plain text network traffic. In chapter 11 we'll discuss rsync and other configuration management tools that will ease your site-management tasks.

3 Moving on to tougher tasks, find out what scripts and configuration files your system uses to start other services. Some have a master script (rc.boot), some have a program that executes a series of scripts (often located in /etc/rc.d). On my system, /etc/rc.d has the boot-time scripts: rc.sysinit runs first, then rc executes a series of scripts from one of the subdirectories, then rc.local executes. Examine the scripts to find out what services they start, and which of those services respond to commands from the outside world.

4 Disable services that you don't need for a web server. Some things you should not need are: nfs or other networked file systems; network printer services; SMB or other Windows connectivity services; Yellow Pages (yp) or NIS services; and any remote management utilities you can live without on your system. If you aren't expecting to receive email on this site, you can shut down sendmail, imap, pop, and other such tools. You will probably find inetd's startup somewhere along the line, and you can shut it down also if you aren't using its services.

5 Create a nonprivileged account that the web server will use to own its files, with a name such as www, web, or apache. If anyone other than the system administrator will be putting files on the server, let him use that account; otherwise disable shell access.

6 Change the root password, preferably using mkpasswd or a similar tool to generate a random string of 10–15 letters and numbers. Do the same for any remaining accounts with shell access. I keep such passwords in a small notebook that I can lock in a drawer or cabinet.

Now you are ready to reboot your system and verify that all is well and your system is secure. While booting you may notice other services that should be disabled, so go back to the research step and find out how to remove them. You might also investigate tools such as nessus (http://www.nessus.org) that will help check your security.

Some systems don't need to be locked down this tightly. In particular, an intranet server can be considered secure if it has its own root password and there are no shell accounts that have privileges to change configurations. Since the server is inside a protected network, you can take advantage of nfs and other LAN-level services to make your workgroup's life easier.

If your server has an open connection to the Internet, all these steps are required and should be taken before you proceed with any other installations. From this point on you'll be working with the machine either by logging in directly or via a remote session (preferably protected by ssh). There should be no other way to get to the server's files.

Systems exposed to the Internet get attacked. It is a sad fact of life that crackers are always finding new ways to find and exploit vulnerable systems. But protecting your system isn't as difficult as the media sometimes portrays: remove vulnerabilities by disabling services that your system doesn't need, and tightly secure the rest with passwords that can't be guessed (or generated from a dictionary) and use configurations that make sense.

From here on, I'll assume that the system is secure. As configuration issues or new potential vulnerabilities come up, I'll highlight the steps needed to keep things that way.

2.3 THE CASE FOR APACHE

Now it is time to apply the Open Source value considerations and buyer's guide principles to a real-world choice: what web server should you use for your site?

In the rest of the book I'll present alternatives where possible, but in this case there is only one strong choice: the Apache web server. There are other Open Source choices (including thttpd, which we'll discuss in section 2.9), but most are either experimental or specialized; Apache is hardened by years of use at *millions* of web sites. Of the commercial choices available, many are actually made from Apache itself; the code is offered under a BSD-like license that doesn't constrain commercial use. In fact, the developers encourage other companies to use it as a reference implementation for the HTTP protocol.

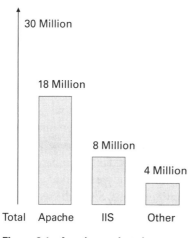

Figure 2.1 Apache market share

The Apache mindshare is one of the largest in Open Source. Estimates of the number of active developers run in the hundreds of thousands, second only to Linux. Development began in 1995, using the code from the original NCSA server (all of which has been replaced in the intervening years). By early 1996 the Apache server was the most popular web server in use by sites polled by Netcraft (http://www.netcraft.com/survey), and in 1998 it gained over 50 percent of the market, making it more popular than all other commercial and Open Source servers combined. Its market share in 2001 has passed 60 percent, running on 18 million servers, more than twice that of Microsoft IIS (the only strong competition). This is illustrated in figure 2.1.

Apache is developed by the Apache Group, a cadre of programmers that was started when a number of web administrators and programmers decided to make an official release of the NCSA server based on their patches. From that beginning they embarked on full-scale redevelopment of the server into their own product, with a stable release in December 1995. The group develops the server and also coordinates the volunteer efforts of countless other contributors, evaluating and accepting patches from outside their number. The membership changes with time as some drop out and other volunteer contributors are invited to join.

2.3.1 Installation

There are a number of options for installing the web server. Prebuilt binary distributions are available for a number of operating systems, and for most sites this is the best way to go. The source distribution is always there of course (this being Open Source), and building Apache from source is quick and easy on most operating systems. Since version 1.3.20, Apache's configuration and build scripts have included support for the free CygWin compiler and tools for Windows operating systems.

The binary distributions on Apache sites (http://www.apache.org) are built with the default set of modules and options. We'll cover what those are in other sections of the book which discuss the need for something that isn't a default. You may need to build from source if your site requires special modules, although it is possible to use a binary distribution with support for dynamically loaded libraries to add in the extras. If you want to strip down Apache by taking out things you won't use or that constitute security risks for your site, make your own binaries. I recommend doing so anyway—it isn't difficult. I'll show you how I built special modules on my system.

Given the number of people who build Apache by hand, it's no surprise that there are programs and tools made just for this purpose. Go to http://www.apache-tools.com/ and search for the Configurator category, where you will find Apache Toolbox, Comanche, and other helpers.

If you download a binary distribution from the Apache site or another distribution site, you will need to find out where it installs the server's main directory. When building from source on Linux or Unix the main directory is `/usr/local/apache` (unless you override the default when setting up the build). I'll refer to that as Apache's home directory from here on, and any relative file paths (those that don't begin with a leading /) are relative to that point.

2.3.2   First tests

Naturally you'll want to see results. Apache works on most systems without any further configuration effort, so let's get started. Your distribution directory contains directions on how to launch the server; for Linux or Unix systems, run this command:

```
bin/apachectl start
```

You should get a response back that says the server started. Fire up your favorite web browser and direct it to your own system. For Linux and Unix users, http://localhost/ or your real host name should work. If all is well, you'll get the default page Apache puts up as part of the installation, directing you to the included online documentation.

If the server doesn't start, or you don't get that page, round up the usual suspects:

1   If `apachectl` didn't start the server, examine the error message. If it reports a problem with the configuration file then the default configuration doesn't work on your system; go on to section 2.4, which is about changing the things you'll probably want to change anyway.

2   Apache may be configured to use another port; try http://localhost:8080/ (or your real host name) instead.

3   Look in the log files, `logs/error_log` and `logs/access_log`. Run-time errors are reported to `error_log`, so if the server started but then had a problem talking to your browser a message will appear there. If there aren't any messages in `error_log`, check `access_log`, which logs every transfer to each connected client. If there aren't any messages in `access_log`, then your browser didn't connect to your server in the first place.

4   Check for other conflicts on your system. Is there already a web server installed that is using the HTTP port? By default, Apache listens for requests on port 80, but it can be configured to use a different port if that's a problem for your system.

2.4 APACHE CONFIGURATION

Like most Open Source programs, Apache gets its knowledge of the system from text files.[1] Get out your favorite text editor and examine the contents of the `conf` directory in Apache's home; it contains a handful of files which are all readable by humans. Lines beginning with '#' (or any text after a '#' that's not in a quoted string) are comments; the rest is information for the server.

The main configuration file for Apache is `conf/httpd.conf`. The other files in the directory are auxiliaries (such as `magic` and `mime.types`) or vestigial configuration files that are left over from the way NCSA did things (`access.conf` and `srm.conf`). The .default files provide the original configuration info shipped with Apache, and can be used as a reference if you want to go back to the way things started.

Note that in discussing configuration here, we mean *run-time configuration*. Apache also has *compile-time configuration*, which uses a separate configuration file (`src/Configuration` in the source distribution) as well as other sources that say how Apache should be put together. One of Apache's strengths is the flexibility each site's management has in deciding what to include in its server. We'll discuss these compile-time options in each section that requires them.

2.4.1 The httpd.conf configuration file

A quick look at `httpd.conf` can be intimidating; it's a big file and it seems very complex. You don't need to digest it all at once, though, and as you've perhaps seen, Apache runs just fine without changing a single line.

The good news is that the file documents all of the defaults and explains which sections you might want to change and why. For further information you can look up each of those options (and the ones not included by default) in the Apache documentation that was installed with the distribution. Assuming you have a working server and browser, go back to the default page and click the documentation link. You'll get a page of documentation topics, including run-time configuration directives; go to that page for a list of everything that can be set.

The configuration file contains comments (any unquoted text after a '#') and *directives*; a directive is either a one-line command or a section containing a set of further directives.

One-line directives begin with the directive name followed by arguments:

```
MinSpareServers 5
MaxSpareServers 10
```

---

[1] Configuration files for Unix utilities are usually plain text delimited by white space. There is a movement toward using XML for configuration information; this format looks more complex at a glance, but it is also very readable once you get used to all the `<brackets>`. XML-based configuration files are easier for programs to parse, which in turn makes it simpler to write configuration helper programs.

These lines contain two directives, setting the values of the `MinSpareServers` and `MaxSpareServers` parameters to 5 and 10 respectively, meaning that Apache will keep at least five servers ready and at most 10 inactive servers). The lines can start and end with white space, and the amount of white space between the directive name and the arguments isn't significant as long as there is some separation. If it reads correctly to you, chances are good it will read fine for Apache.

Sections are bracketed by a pair of tags in the style of XML and HTML:

```
<Location /server-status>
    SetHandler server-status
    Order deny,allow
    Deny from all
    Allow from .your_domain.com
</Location>
```

The Location section starts with `<Location argument>` and ends with `</Location>`; between the < > brackets of the opening tag the directive works as a one-liner, with the directive name followed by arguments. Any number of directives can appear between the opening and closing tags, including other tag pairs that close off further nested directives. By convention we indent the enclosed directives to show that they apply only to surrounding tags, but again the white space isn't significant to Apache.

The most common of these section tags are `<Location>`, `<Directory>`, `<Files>`, and, if you are managing more than one host on a server, `<VirtualHost>`. `<Location>` specifies directives for a particular URL, while `<Directory>` applies to directories on a file system and `<Files>` applies to files that match a pattern. If multiple blocks all match a given file, `<Location>` has the highest importance, so you can set different rules for a file when it is accessed by different URLs. After that, `<Files>` overrules `<Directory>`.

2.4.2 Things you need to change

Actually, Apache doesn't need much configuration. Look for these sections and change them if the conditions apply to your site.

- *ServerRoot "/usr/local/apache"*—Put the home directory for the Apache server here if you aren't using the default. Then search through the rest of the file and change the same string everywhere that it appears.
- *Port 80*—If you have another web server running already, you'll need to tell your new Apache server to use a different port. 8080 is a common alternative.
- *ServerAdmin root@localhost*—Replace the default address with your email address.
- *#ServerName localhost*—This directive is commented out by default, and the server will use the regular host name for reporting its name (in error messages for example). If you'd rather use a different name, uncomment the line by removing the leading '#' and then replace the default with the name you want. Virtual hosts require this directive in each site's configuration section.

2.5 PRODUCTION SERVER

When actively building web sites, a development group often needs a set of servers in different roles: a "toy" server where the developers can experiment with things, a production server where the finished product runs, and perhaps something in between.

If you are working alone and your server isn't exposed to the great wide world, the minimum configuration is fine for getting started and learning what to do next. If, however, you are setting up a group of servers, you should secure your production server immediately. While it's unlikely that some cracker is lurking in the shadows waiting to pounce on your hapless web site, securing the server from the start will establish good habits all around by making developers learn how things need to work in the final installation.

Apache's default configuration has reasonable security practices in place, but not as good as you might like. Read through the Security Tips page in the Apache online documentation, set the protections on your files and directories as shown there, then consider how permissive you want to be with your users.

After deciding on your site's policies, you'll want to look for the following directives in `httpd.conf` and change them accordingly:

- *AllowOverride*—Permits or disables the use of local configuration files (usually called `.htaccess`) in directories, so examine carefully each occurrence in `httpd.conf`. In general, a production server should disable this at the top directory, and then enable it again if needed in specific directories or locations:

```
<Directory />
    AllowOverride None
</Directory>
```

This directive turns off the use of local configuration files in all directories. If you need to enable it again for a given directory—say, the document directory of a trusted user—you can use `AllowOverride` again to enable some features:

```
<Directory /home/sysmgr/public_html>
    AllowOverride FileInfo AuthConfig Limit
</Directory>
```

This allows sysmgr to set some directives in a .htaccess file in `/home/sysmgr/public_html`. Not all directives will be honored; look up `AllowOverride`'s documentation to see exactly what we've permitted.

Note that allowing local configuration files slows down the server, as it has to parse the local file for each request to a URL that permits them. This is not how you want to run your primary applications.

- *Options*—Permits or disables a grab bag of server features, including the execution of CGI scripts and browsing of directories. For a secure server, the top directory should turn off everything:

```
<Directory />
    Options None
</Directory>
```

Options None is as tight as it gets, but you might consider allowing FollowSym-Links or SymLinksIfOwnerMatch. These two permit the use of symbolic links on Linux and Unix, which is convenient as long as users don't have general write permissions to important directories. SymLinksIfOwnerMatch allows links only if the link and the file it points to are owned by the same user. Using just FollowSym-Links is the best option performance-wise, since it doesn't require Apache to do extra look-ups along file paths. See chapter 12 for more information.

Again, the Options directive can be used in specific <Directory> or <Location> sections to open up permissions as needed.

What if we had this section and the previous one setting AllowOverride? They would both apply; Apache neatly merges sections that apply to the same target in the order they occur. The same applies to <Location>, <Files>, and so on. Sane administrators will want to do that merging manually though, so that it is more obvious what directives apply to which sections.

— *UserDir*—This directive controls the mapping of username URLs; that is, http://www.example.site/~user. The default is to enable user directories for all users and map them to public_html, meaning that http://www.example.site/~bob/resume.html gets mapped to /home/bob/public_html/resume.html (assuming /home/bob is Bob's home directory). The argument can either be disabled or enabled (with a list of users following either) or a path can be mapped onto the user's home directory.

If your site doesn't have general user accounts, you can turn this feature off: setting UserDir disabled will turn off the mapping functions. Better yet, if you build Apache from source files you can leave out mod_userdir entirely. See the helpful files on compile-time configuration in the source distribution. If you want to let a few users do this but disable it for the rest, then use:

```
UserDir public_html
UserDir disabled
UserDir enabled bob carol ted alice
```

The more permissive variation is to disable user directories for sensitive accounts and leave it open otherwise:

```
UserDir disabled root www nobody ftp
```

If you allow user directories, then you should also have a <Directory> section that specifies AllowOverride and Options to control what users can do. The default httpd.conf contains such a section (possibly commented out), so modify it accordingly:

```
<Directory /home/*/public_html>
    AllowOverride None
```

```
        Options Indexes SymLinksIfOwnerMatch
</Directory>
```

This section disables the use of local configuration files and allows browsing of directories (that's what Indexes does) and symbolic links that are owned properly.

Mapping ~user URLs to the user's `public_html` directory is a typical scheme, but `UserDir` can also be set to map those requests onto an entirely separate directory tree with a subdirectory for each user. For example, this arrangement directs the requests to appropriate directories under `/www/users`:

```
UserDir /www/users
```

Whether using subdirectories of the user's home or a separate directory tree, each user chooses what files to expose on the web site by moving those files to the appropriate directory. Directory ownership and write permissions should be set accordingly. `UserDir` should never map requests directly to a user's home directory since that could make all subdirectories visible, thus removing the active choice. Another explanation given for this arrangement is that by not exposing the user's home directory, you also don't expose the various hidden files (those beginning with '.' on Linux and Unix) that contain sensitive information such as passwords for mail servers, which are stored by some mail clients. It's not a good idea to use such things on a server that has an open Internet connection.

A third possibility is to direct ~user URLs to another server entirely:

```
UserDir http://another.example.site/home_pages
```

This version causes `UserDir` to redirect requests for http://www.example.site/~user to http://another.example.site/home_pages/user.

ScriptAlias—Specifies a directory that contains executable scripts. This is one way to get the Apache server to execute a script for a URL, and is very secure as long as the administrator controls the scripts. A typical setting is:

```
ScriptAlias /cgi-bin/ /usr/local/cgi/
```

The first argument matches the beginning of a URL, and the second specifies the directory that contains the script for the match. For example, http://www.example.site/cgi-bin/hello_world.cgi would map to `/usr/local/cgi/hello_world.cgi`. Note that directories containing executable scripts should not be viewable by browsers. Set `DocumentRoot` appropriately and don't mingle the two.

That's one way to handle executable scripts. The others are via the `ExecCGI` option in the `Options` directive and by setting special handlers for given files. We'll cover special handlers in later chapters. Think twice about using `ExecCGI`, especially in user directories. In conjunction with `AddHandler`, this option can lead to Apache running arbitrary code. Even if your users are trustworthy, you have to trust that they are taking proper precautions with their directories, passwords, and so forth.

If you have opened up directory permissions, then also use a `<Directory>` section to lock down each script directory:

```
<Directory "/usr/local/cgi">
    AllowOverride None
    Options None
</Directory>
```

The `ScriptAlias` tells Apache that the directory contains executable scripts in spite of `Options None`, so everything is set and ready for testing.

After making all these changes, restart Apache and test the server again. You can even skip to the next chapter and grab a few CGI sample scripts to make sure that works. Your production server is now secure and running!

2.6   DEVELOPMENT SERVER

While it is possible to build a site using a single server, it's often handy to have a separate place for working on new programs and content (a "toy" server where security is loosened and developers can try out their code without a lot of bother). As compared to the production environment, a development server can allow open access to configuration files, documents, and scripts so that programmers can drop in new works quickly. Of course, this assumes that the server is not on an open Internet connection—it should be in a protected network or otherwise configured to refuse requests from outside its LAN.

Here are a few possible configuration scenarios:

2.6.1   Allow everything

The following directives allow Apache to serve documents and scripts from users' directories:

```
UserDir /home
<Directory /home/*>
    AllowOverride All
    Options All
    AddHandler cgi-script .pl .cgi
</Directory>
```

The `UserDir` directive maps ~user URLs to the user's home directory (assuming, of course, your users' directories are under /home), allowing any unprotected document to be read. We then open up permissions in those directories with `AllowOverride All` and `Options All`, and tell Apache to treat any file ending in .pl or .cgi as an executable script.

Each developer can tailor what Apache shows and does by appropriate use of .htaccess files, starting with one in his home directory that will be inherited by each subdirectory.

It's hard to imagine giving the users much more than this, but of course it is possible: we could give each user his own server! If you want to maintain the illusion of a single site but map each user to a different server, look at combining `UserDir` with a `Redirect` for each user to send requests to developer sites.

2.6.2 Allow documents and scripts

This scenario lets users publish documents and run CGI scripts, but only from certain directories:

```
UserDir public_html
ScriptAlias /~user/cgi-bin/ "/home/user/cgi-bin/"
<Directory /home/*/public_html>
    AllowOverride None
    Options Indexes FollowSymLinks
</Directory>
```

The `UserDir` directive maps requests for http://www.example.site/~user to /home/user/public_html, while `ScriptAlias` similarly sends http://www.example.site/~user/cgi-bin/ requests to /home/user/cgi-bin (and tells the server to execute the resulting file—no need for an `AddHandler` directive). Directories are browsable (`Options Indexes`) and users can manage their documents using symbolic links (`FollowSymLinks`), but can't override server configuration or options in general (`AllowOverride None`).

    `ScriptAlias` tells Apache that the given directory contains executable scripts. The previous example works only for a user named "user." For this scenario to work, we need to add a `ScriptAlias` line for each user who is allowed to run CGI scripts. If all users are permitted, we can handle this in one directive using the Match variant of `ScriptAlias`:

```
ScriptAliasMatch ^/~([^/]+)/cgi-bin(.*) /home/$1/cgi-bin$2
```

The parts that look like cartoon characters swearing are *regular expression* matches; see your Apache documentation for more information on the Match variations of directives and how to use regular expressions in them. Briefly, this particular match looks for URLs of the form /~user/cgi-bin/* and translates them to /home/user/cgi-bin/*, where the real user name is substituted for "user" in both cases.

2.6.3 Allow approved documents

As shown in one of the production server configurations, `UserDir` can also be used to map ~user URLs to a separate directory tree. This variation stores users' public documents in subdirectories under /www/users:

```
UserDir /www/users
<Directory "/www/users/*">
    AllowOverride None
    Options None
</Directory>
```

This is as tight as it gets, assuming the directory protections are set properly. If write permission is restricted to the system administrator then only those files permitted by

[^/] matches any character except /. that's to UNIX directory delimiter

the boss will be displayed on the web site. In such a scenario it makes no sense to discuss executing scripts, since a CGI could display arbitrary files (and leads one to wonder if this is actually a development site).

2.7   USING APACHECTL

Having chosen a configuration and set things up properly, test your server again. This is a good idea after any change to a configuration file, even if the changes look trivial. If your configuration allows CGI then take an example from the next chapter and try that out too.

The apachectl program includes helpful code for verifying configuration files. This command checks that things are all proper:

```
/usr/local/apache/bin/apachectl configtest
```

There are three options for restarting the server, in order of severity: graceful, immediate, and hard.

A graceful restart allows Apache to complete work in progress; servers with open connections won't restart until they finish their transfers or time out waiting for clients. A server won't close an open log file until the server shuts down. Your users will appreciate having a chance to finish their business, but you might find it troubling if you are looking for an immediate change.

Trigger this restart using apachectl or kill:

```
/usr/local/apache/bin/apachectl graceful
```

or

```
kill -USR1 httpd
```

If you use apachectl, it will also run a configtest for you automatically, so you can be assured the server will start up again properly.

An immediate restart tells Apache to close log files and open connections and then read the configuration files again:

```
/usr/local/apache/bin/apachectl restart
```

or

```
kill -HUP httpd
```

The apachectl program will confirm the configuration files with configtest before stopping the server. If the server isn't running in the first place, it will just start it for you without an error.

A hard restart is necessary if you have changed the Apache program itself or made system changes that the server won't normally track:

```
/usr/local/apache/bin/apachectl stop
/usr/local/apache/bin/apachectl start
```

or

```
kill -9 httpd
/usr/local/apache/bin/apachectl start
```

Shutting the server down with apachectl is preferable, but not always possible if things are going wrong.

2.8 *SERVING DOCUMENTS*

Your site now has a functional web server that can present static documents and run CGI scripts. Most sites have some static content, and it's easy to manage once you learn how Apache translates a URL into a file path.

We've discussed URL mapping previously in the sections on UserDir. When Apache receives a request for a particular URL, it translates it into a file path and then figures out how to serve up that file. The rules for the latter can be quite complicated. Later chapters will explore them in examples that use handlers to take over this process for certain files or directories. The mapping rules themselves are generally simple:

1. If Apache is configured to handle multiple sites using <VirtualHost> directives, it looks at the site specification to see which set of rules to use. The site is the part of the URL between http:// and the next /. If there aren't any virtual hosts, this part of the URL is ignored and the general rules are applied.

2. The section of the URL after the site specification is the path, composed of words separated by /s; it can end in a file name such as document.html, a trailing path component or just a /. Apache evaluates UserDir, ScriptAlias, <Location>, and other directives to see if they match this path.

3. If the beginning of the path matches a ScriptAlias directive, the rest of the path is mapped onto the given directory and the resulting file is executed as a CGI script. Similarly Alias directives, Redirects, and other rewriting rules are applied.

4. If Apache is built with mod_userdir and UserDir isn't disabled, it checks to see if the path begins with a ~. If so, the first path component is considered to be a user name and the UserDir rules discussed previously are applied to map the rest of the URL as a file path onto the user's document directory.

5. If the rules in number four didn't satisfy the most, the path is considered as a file path relative to the directory given by the DocumentRoot directive, usually the htdocs subdirectory of Apache's home. Any <Directory> directives that match some or all of that file path are applied to the URL.

6. If the path ends in a file name and that file exists, <File> directives are checked and the file is served if permissions allow. The browser receives the file and displays it according to its rules and idiosyncrasies.

7   If the path ends in a trailing /, Apache checks for the existence of a **default file** (usually `index.html`) and serves that if it exists. Otherwise, if directory browsing is allowed (`Options Indexes`), Apache creates a document on the fly that represents a directory listing. Depending on the other options you allow and the number of icons supplied for file types, this directory listing can look like a desktop file browser or an FTP site listing.

8   If Apache hasn't figured out any other way of handling the path, it sends back an error document. These too are configurable; some sites have nice, apologetic error documents that offer an email address for sending complaints, while others reroute the user to a site navigation page. My favorite variations are those that use haiku:

You step into the stream,
but the water has moved on.
Document not found.

There is a bit more to it than that; when Apache decides what file to send to the browser, it also tries to figure out what type of file it is so that it can send along appropriate headers to the browser. These types are managed in the `mime.types` file in Apache's configuration directory. If you are serving up unusual content, you'll need to add types to this file so that browsers know what to do with the documents you send.

Suppose a browser sends a request for http://www.example.site/hello_web.html to our server. The path consists of just a file name, so there isn't much in the way of analysis to do; Apache looks up `hello_web.html` in the `DocumentRoot` directory and sends it back to the browser.

That file contains an IMG tag specifying a relative URL for images/hi.jpg. Assuming the browser is displaying images, it sends a request for that URL back to Apache. The URL has a path, images, and a file name, hi.jpg. Apache looks for directives that apply to the path, and finding none, maps it onto the document root as a simple directory path. It sends the file back with appropriate headers and the image is displayed.

That's static document handling in a nutshell. As I mentioned, there are plenty of ways to make even this process more complicated. Apache has a rich set of directives for rewriting URLs and managing changes of directories, file names, and so on that are inevitable over the lifetime of a site.

If that's all you need, Apache will serve you and your documents well. You might consider an alternative, however, one specially built for speed at just this task.

2.9   THTTPD

thttpd is a small and versatile web server. Its flexibility begins with its name: the 't' stands for tiny, turbo or throttling, take your pick. The author (Jef Poskanzer) offers the software from its web page (http://www.acme.com/software/thttpd/thttpd.html). While thttpd's design goals are much the same as those for Apache—a secure, stable web server that handles static documents and other tasks—thttpd is built for speed, while Apache is meant to be a general platform for many other pieces of software.

thttpd's feature list shows its focus: it serves static documents with a minimal implementation of the HTTP 1.1 protocol, offers a few utilities such as CGI processing, and a unique throttle utility which lets a webmaster allocate bandwidth to different sections of a site. It handles virtual hosts (see chapter 11), an absolute necessity for modern web sites. Other features such as redirection and server-side include (SSI) are given over to external programs, keeping thttpd small.

One reason for its lean size is it runs as a single process, unlike Apache with its separate children. The server listens on its socket for incoming requests and handles each in turn, but it doesn't bog down on any particular client. thttpd uses nonblocking I/O via `select` to fill each waiting socket and move on to the next, so it can feed documents to a large number of browsers concurrently. That single process is smaller than just one normal Apache child (of which a typical configuration has at least several hanging around waiting for work).

Thus by keeping a tight focus and using a minimum of system resources, thttpd provides a very high performance level for servers that run in small spaces. In a race with Apache, thttpd can serve documents faster per second than the larger server can, but the author points out that the bandwidth limitations of most sites limit the performance of either server more than memory or other system resources. Don't expect thttpd to improve on a site that has a network bottleneck.

In chapter 12 we'll discuss how thttpd can be used as a front-end server to handle static documents while a more heavyweight Apache serves dynamic content. Don't consider it just for a secondary role, however; it's a fine server for many workloads.

It is also easy to extend thttpd for more than static documents. PHP users can use the popular mod_php module directly to run their applications, and Freshmeat lists a thttpd variant, pthttpd, which has an embedded Perl interpreter for speeding up the kind of code I'll be talking about in the rest of the book. The web page for thttpd lists add-ons for SSL (see chapter 6) and other frequently needed options.

If you need only to publish static documents, Apache or thttpd will work fine for you. Chances are good you want more from your web server, however, and dynamic content is where the action is, so let's go on to the tools that make the exciting stuff happen.

C H A P T E R 3

CGI scripts

The Common Gateway Interface (CGI) began innocently enough as a way to make the Web interactive through simple fill-in forms and basic controls. Developers soon realized that even with just those simple controls they could create real applications run via a browser in the same way that business applications have worked for decades—the user fills in a form, the computer validates the input, spits back anything that's not right, or moves on to the next form (or completes the transaction, whatever it is). This realization sparked the creation of thousands of web applications, and possibly as many books about CGI programming.

What is almost as amazing is that while in the intervening years HTML and web browsers have increased in complexity by many times, the CGI protocol and its basic tools haven't changed much at all. There are simple text boxes, multiline boxes, selection lists, and a few kinds of buttons—the same basic list of widgets you'd find in the tool kit of most GUI programming libraries. Web application interfaces have certainly become more attractive and more usable, but nearly all those changes have taken place in the addition of HTML features and the use of client-side scripting, primarily through JavaScript.[1]

In this chapter (and most of the rest of the book) we'll discuss server-side scripting, which is visible to the browser only in the documents it sends back in response to requests. Client-side scripting, like advanced HTML, is beyond the scope of this book. There are several web sites with good introductions to JavaScript and another book-shelf worth of detailed guides. The two are often combined, server-side scripts creating client-side scripts embedded in the documents they serve, which in turn prepare the responses sent back to the server.

3.1 WHY SCRIPTING

One of the first things to notice about CGI applications is that nearly everyone talks about "CGI scripts" and few say "CGI programs." In fact, most web applications are written in scripting languages, by which I mean Unix shells, Perl, PHP, Python, Tcl, and others. Of the remainder, a large proportion are written in Java, often using a server specially made to serve Java components, or add-ons such as Apache's JServ, and shockingly few are in C or other compiled languages.

There are good reasons for so many web applications being written in scripting languages, and some poor ones too. Scripts have a rapid development life cycle (important for a medium in which "generation" refers to a year or so of product versions) and are easy to maintain. CGI was created as a means for a web server to run simple programs that parse textual inputs and send more text back in response. Scripting languages are generally good at text manipulation as compared to number crunching, for example.

For every good feature of a technology, there are equal and opposite failings. If a language provides for rapid development and easy maintenance, then it also unfortunately provides for slap-dash development and unreadable code. The CGI world has as many bad examples of programming as any other field of software, but in this case the bad examples are highly visible, such as the various libraries of Perl applications found scattered around. Some programming purists point to these as reasons why web applications should be developed in more strict languages, and while I agree with the desire for better programs, I can't see the pace slowing down any time soon.

Given that we're going to use a scripting language, what characteristics are important for building web applications? How can we emphasize the strengths and diminish the weaknesses? To me, the most important characteristics for a web development language are:

---

[1] A misleadingly named language created by Netscape and made into a casualty of the browser wars; it is as hard to write fancy JavaScript for multiple browsers as it is to write fancy HTML. Still, it's not a bad language and it is worth learning enough of the basics to improve the usability of your sites. Server-side JavaScript is available for some platforms and as an ASP scripting language.

- *Easy to learn*—The language should have a gentle learning curve, since new programmers are entering web development at an amazing pace.

- *Rapid development*—The language should let programmers defer complex tasks while creating the core of a new program, so that the user and developer can work together on high-level features before investing valuable time in lower level coding.

- *Excellent text handling*—CGI programs receive text inputs and often manipulate text files; the output is usually text. The language should have string manipulation, pattern matching, and file handling features that make these tasks simple.

- *More than CGI*—The language of choice (or its utilities) should provide a way for programmers to go beyond the CGI interface and let the script work closely with the server when necessary.

- *Tools for further development*—Given the investment required to master a language, our choice should offer more than just basic CGI. It must scale up to complex web applications, and preferably work as well outside the server in other application programming.

Our choices should also address as well as possible the weaknesses of scripting languages compared to compiled choices:

- *Performance*—Scripting languages run more slowly than C code due to the cost of their high-level data types and memory. Also, scripts have a slow start-up time if they have to be recompiled each time they run.

- *Syntax checking*—While rapid development calls for a forgiving language, maintainable code requires a tool that tells the programmer when he's got problems, preferably before it happens at run time.

- *Resource usage*—Any language with dynamic strings and automatic memory management will take up more system resources than tightly written C code.

3.1.1 Scripting language choices

Obviously a book with Perl in the title isn't going to suggest you use something else, but there are other choices. Tcl and Python are both mature languages with good module-level support for web programming and Apache. Python is built into the popular Zope application server engine, a powerful tool for Apache sites. Vbscript and server-side JavaScript are both popular among ASP programmers. I think that Perl is still the best choice, and the web development community appears to agree, but if you have an investment in either you can certainly do all you wish to do in either language.

A much stronger case can be made for PHP, which was released in 1995 and has grown in both popularity and installed base at a tremendous rate. PHP was created as a tool for generating HTML from templates and evolved into a web programming language; scripts are embedded in HTML in special tags, much like ASP or the embedded

Perl products we'll discuss later. Given its web-centric focus and free availability, it's not surprising that the language took off and now touts an installed base of over one million servers. The generosity of its developers in providing the sources for their own sites helps too.

The PHP community contributes libraries, examples, and support, making it a very good choice for any web developer, especially those who are starting afresh and don't have an investment in another language. For those sites doing web and nonweb development, I still recommend Perl.

3.2   THE CASE FOR PERL

Perl has been the language of choice for CGI programming from almost the beginning, as applications grew beyond what simple shell scripts could easily support. Perl's strengths for the task made it a great fit:

1   Perl's text handling, pattern matching, and simple file management make it a natural for dealing with the text-based medium of the Web. While other languages have come up to speed in this regard, Perl had a huge head start and has improved in the meantime.

2   Perl is easy to learn, in spite of a reputation to the contrary. Developers are rightly concerned about taking on new languages in the face of deadlines, but in my experience and those of my coworkers, Perl lets new users be productive without mastering the whole language at once.

3   Perl has a lot to offer in the long term as well. Perl is a mature language (some would say feature-laden) that has been in development for over a decade. In part due to its success as a web programming language, Perl has received a huge outpouring of contributed modules (the Perl equivalent to add-on programming libraries) for CGI and nearly any other field of programming.

4   Its popularity with system administrators and other utility-oriented programmers has made Perl ubiquitous enough that someone at just about any large site will have experience with it. Even if you don't know Perl yet, chances are good you know someone who does.

On the other side of the balance sheet, Perl has a deserved reputation as a resource hog; as a language that has modules for everything, it is hard to keep Perl programs slim and trim.[2] Plain Perl would be a poor choice for a scripting language if there were nothing we could do about that, but there is:

1   Apache has add-on modules that keep a Perl interpreter running in the server or in a separate process. As scripts are compiled, they are saved in memory and run

---

[2]   Perl's lead developers are discussing the structure of Perl 6 as I write this book. One stated goal is to reduce the size of the interpreter and the memory cost of running programs.

again as needed, avoiding the overhead of compilation time. We'll discuss those modules in chapter 5.

2 Perl can be trimmed down somewhat by building key modules into the interpreter to speed loading time and reduce overhead.

3 Compiled Perl has been high on the list of promises for the last couple of major releases, and could be a reality soon. Of course, if we keep Perl running via the modules mentioned in the first item the release of the compiled version becomes less important, but it will still be a hit if it provides improved optimization.

What about the other issues from the buyer's guide? Given Perl's prevalence in the web programming world it hardly seems necessary to prove the case, but nevertheless, here are more advantages to Perl:

- *Maturity and stability*—Perl 1.0 was released in 1987, and has gone through five major language revisions (where features and meanings of operators changed). Perl 5 came out in 1995, and has undergone annual improvement releases since then. The interpreter comes with most Unix-like operating systems and is available for Windows and Macintosh systems.

- *Continued development*—New versions of Perl are in active development, as are the many hundreds of add-on modules. The Comprehensive Perl Archive Network (CPAN, browsable at http://cpan.perl.org/ and http://search.cpan.org/) has a vast repository of Perl scripts and modules for web programming, system administration, and applications. The CPAN repository is one of Perl's best features; when developing applications I've often gone there to look for help and found a module ready-made for the task at hand.

- *Support*—Perl is actively supported by commercial firms, user groups, web sites, newsgroups, and mailing lists; see http://www.perl.com/ for a guide to free resources as well as commercial organizations that sell training and various levels of support. The Perl Monks at http://www.perlmonks.org/ offer a virtual community site wherein members field questions and discuss Perl in forums and chats, while the Perl Mongers (http://www.pm.org/) run many local user groups. You may have one near you. There are many good books on Perl, some by the language's developers and others by community members. *The Perl Journal* is a print magazine (http://www.tpj.com/). Online magazines include http://www.useperl.org/ and http://www.perlmonth.com/. Perl has a diverse community of users, with books, newsgroups, and mailing lists on various topics including web programming.

- *Good investment*—Having gained proficiency in Perl for one task, you'll find yourself applying it to others. I find it an excellent language for general business application programming, partly because Perl is a good "glue" language for sticking together other products and tools, such as databases and user interface products. Writing reports and system administration tools are both easy.

- *Ongoing costs*—Perl gets a major release about once per year, with two or three maintenance releases following. Modules are released on their own schedules, and the CPAN interface provides easy updates.
- *License*—Perl is released under the Artistic License or the GPL; see the discussion of the "Perl terms" in chapter 1.

Of all the reasons to like Perl, the strongest one for me is the development community. The Support resources I mentioned are some of my favorites, but that list is barely a start. The CPAN archive combined with web sites and mailing lists provide amazing tools for new users and old hands.

3.2.1 Installing Perl

The same options for obtaining and installing Apache apply to Perl: binary distributions, as well as the source distribution, come with many operating systems, and current releases are available on Perl's web site (http://www.perl.com/). The book's web site provides pointers to current distributions.

If Perl was installed with your operating system, consider upgrading or building from source anyway. Some Linux distributions in the late '90s had broken versions of Perl that caused endless headaches and new FAQ entries. If you installed Apache from source, you probably won't have any trouble building Perl.

Binary distributions of Perl have their own notions of where the Perl interpreter and modules reside. The source build on my system puts executables in `/usr/local/bin` (or it links to the executables there from `/usr/bin` or another directory). My examples will assume that location, so correct as necessary if you have a different arrangement. The path to Perl is important due to the way most Unix systems determine how to run a script. The first line can have a comment, sometimes called the *shebang*, telling what interpreter to run, so if your Perl is in a different place, make appropriate changes to the lines that look like this:

```
#!/usr/local/bin/perl -w
```

The location of the modules is less important, but the example explanations can be confusing if you go looking for the files yourself and they aren't where I say they are. Check the output of `perl -V` to find out what directories your installation uses.

3.2.2 Testing a sample script

While CGI scripts are meant to be run from a web server, they are all normal Perl scripts and will run, or at least compile and start, from a regular shell. To test your Perl installation, grab one of the scripts from the CGI samples directory on the book's web site and run it:

```
> ./hello_web.pl
```

If you get an error such as "file not found" and the path to the script is correct, it could be that the shebang line is wrong for your system. Make sure your Perl interpreter is `/usr/local/bin/perl` (or there is a link to it there). If the error says that the file isn't executable, change the permissions or run it as an argument for Perl:

```
> perl CGI/hello_web.pl
```

3.2.3   Updating Perl modules with CPAN

Once you've got Perl running properly, take a few moments to get things up to date. The CPAN module will do this for you somewhat automatically. Invoke it like so from a privileged account:

```
> perl -MCPAN -e shell
```

If this is the first time you've invoked CPAN you will enter a configuration dialog; CPAN will ask you where you want to store its cache of files and the maximum size of the cache. Then it will offer choices for various utility programs—don't worry if you are missing one or more of them, it will compensate. When you get to parameters for various Perl `make` commands, I strongly suggest that you have `make install` run with `UNINST=1`; this tells Perl to remove the previous version of an updated module if the new one is being installed to a different directory, and helps avoid confusion and errors caused by having multiple versions.

After setting up the caching and build process, CPAN will ask you about your network configuration. If you run your server behind a firewall, you'll need the address and port of the FTP and HTTP proxies to get the Perl network modules to run through it; supply each as a URL, such as http://security.example.site:3128/.

Beyond that, CPAN will locate mirror sites near you, and let you specify a set of sites to check for new modules. Once this is finished you are ready to update your installation.

Tell Perl to update all the modules that CPAN uses first (or else it will nag you to do so later):

```
cpan> install Bundle::CPAN
```

Then use the `'r'` command to get a list of modules that came with Perl which are now out-of-date. Chances are good that CGI.pm is on the list, so update it as well:

```
cpan> install CGI
```

The modules on CPAN are often works in progress, and it is not uncommon to find one which doesn't test properly on your system. If so, don't despair; fixes are probably also in progress. If it is a module you need, look at the error and if it appears not to interfere with your intended use, use the `force` command to install it anyway:

```
cpan> force install Bundle::libnet
```

As I was getting a machine up to date for work on this book, I found that the (then) current version of the libnet module didn't test properly because I couldn't give it an FTP site which allowed anonymous uploads to the `/pub` directory. No secure site should allow that, so I didn't let it stop me; I installed anyway as shown, since the rest of the tests passed.

I'll point out other modules as they are needed.

3.3   INSIDE CGI

When Apache gets a request for a URL that maps to a file its configuration says is executable, it runs the file as a program, passing along information about the request as environment variables and possibly also as the program's input. The file's permissions have to be set to allow Apache to run it (that is, script is run as the user you tell Apache to use in your `http.conf` file). The file must also be marked as executable in the configuration file, either by residing in a directory that has a `ScriptAlias` or via the `Option ExecCGI` directive (in which case the file also has to have a handler that says it is executable).

Figure 3.1 shows the flow of control for a simple CGI request:

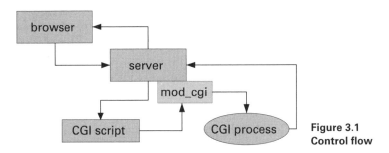

Figure 3.1
Control flow

The browser sends a request to Apache, which maps the request onto a file and notices that the file is designated as a CGI script. Apache passes control to mod_cgi, the internal module which handles CGI requests. mod_cgi first verifies that Apache's user has permission to run the script. Then it sets up an environment to pass information along to the script, and forks off a process to execute it. In the case of a POST request, it also sends input to the new process—see the Interacting section for more information. Then Apache takes the output from the CGI process and passes that to the user.

The default Apache configuration puts CGI programs in a directory separate from documents, typically the `cgi-bin` subdirectory of Apache's home. This is partly for ease of configuration, and partly to keep overly curious web surfers from reading programs.[3]

A `ScriptAlias` directive such as this one marks all of the files in `/usr/local/apache/cgi-bin` as executable:

---

[3] If you'd rather keep scripts and documents together, it's easy enough and doesn't compromise your security. Use the `AddHandler` directive to tell Apache which files are scripts, and it will always treat them as scripts, never as documents to send to a browser. This method avoids the use of `Script-Alias` also.

```
ScriptAlias /cgi-bin/ "/usr/local/apache/cgi-bin/"
```

Any URL of the form http://www.example.site/cgi-bin/hello-web.pl gets mapped onto that directory, and, assuming the correct file permissions and no script errors, `/usr/local/apache/cgi-bin/hello-web.pl` gets run in response. The program's output is sent back to the requesting browser, just as a file would be if Apache were serving a static document—except that Apache has rules for sending standard headers along with documents. CGI programs have to do this on their own.

First-time CGI programmers have to learn more about HTTP interactions than do writers of static pages. In particular, CGI scripts have to send correct headers before their output. The web server takes care of headers for static pages using rules based on the content.

The minimum required header is the Content-Type declaration which tells the browser what sort of document it is receiving. Make this the first output of a shell script and then the rest of the script can send whatever it wants:

```
echo "Content-Type: text/plain"
echo ""
```

The content type "text/plain" tells the browser that it is receiving a plain text file and should display it as is. The blank line after the header tells the browser that it has received all headers and what follows should be interpreted as the displayable text.

Here is a very minimal example of a CGI script:

```
#!/bin/bash
echo "Content-Type: text/plain"
echo ""
ps axw
```

The script sends the plain text header, then runs the `ps` command. Since all script output is sent to the browser, the browser gets a list of processes running on the web server.

The content type can be any valid MIME type (and you have a list of them in `conf/mime.types`), but in practice, CGI scripts are most likely to send text/plain or text/html; a script that sends back a graph might use one of the image types. While plain text is convenient, it isn't terribly interesting. In sending back HTML however, a script can make use of any of the features of modern web documents that the browser is likely to understand. Unless otherwise specified, all programs from here on will send back text/html.

The problem with sending back HTML, of course, is that one has to know how to write HTML-tagged text. Fortunately, Perl programmers have the help of an exceptionally talented module that will do all of the tagging for them: the aforementioned CGI.pm, which is the basic programming library for uncounted thousands of web applications.

If you haven't updated CGI.pm via CPAN yet as explained previously, do so now, then take a brief look at its built-in documentation via the perldoc command:

```
perldoc CGI
```

You'll get a short example program, followed by quite a lot of information. Like most things in Perl, you don't need to learn it all at once. Let's start on some examples of our own. (You'll find them all waiting for you on the book's web site, so don't waste your time typing and learn it in pieces.)

3.3.1 Hello, Web!

In keeping with programming traditions, we should start by saying hello:

```
1  #!/usr/local/bin/perl -wT

   # Check for undeclared variables.
2  use strict;

   # Load the CGI module.
3  use CGI;

   # Make a query object for calling HTML output functions.
4  my $q = CGI->new;

   # Print the standard HTML headers:
5  print $q->header;

   # Send the opening <HTML>, a <HEAD>, and <TITLE> block,
   # then the opening <BODY>.
6  print $q->start_html('My first CGI');

   # Put some text in an <H1> block.
7  print $q->h1('Hello, Web!');

   # Print the closing </BODY> and </HTML>.
8  print $q->end_html;
```

That looks like a lot of work, especially compared to the plain text equivalent:

```
#!/bin/bash
echo "Content-Type: text/plain"
echo ""
echo "Hello, Web!"
```

The Perl version is written to be a good example, not a tight script, so it is more verbose and clumsy than it needs to be. Let's break it down line by line:

1 This is the shebang line that tells what shell to run; in this case Perl, with the -wT switches to activate warnings and taint checking. While taint checks aren't actually needed here, it's a good habit to get into for CGI programs. We'll explain taint checking later in this chapter.

2 The warning switch (-w) and use strict activate further error checking and compiler feedback. Though optional, every Perl program that's worth storing on a disk should run with both. Programs that don't run when these checks are turned on are rather suspicious. With Perl 5.6 and later you can replace the warning switch with the pragma use warnings, and be more selective, if necessary, about what actions generate messages.

3 `use CGI` loads CGI.pm, the module that will write the HTML tags for us. The documentation for CGI.pm (see the previous section) explains how to use the functional interface as well as the object-oriented interface. I'm going to demonstrate only the latter, in part because it will be the only way to use CGI.pm if we invoke other modules later, as we'll see in chapter 7. Don't let object-oriented scare you off, though. There is nothing particularly difficult about Perl objects when used in moderation.

4 `CGI->new` creates a query object as the comment says. For our immediate purposes, the only matter of importance is that all the CGI functions are called via this object, called `$q` in this example and the others. Rather a lot goes on behind the scenes in this statement, as we'll discuss later in this chapter.

5 `$q->header` prints the standard header: Content-Type text/html as mentioned earlier. You can pass parameters to this function to have it print other headers for cases where the script isn't going to send HTML output.

6 `$q->start_html('My first CGI')` outputs a flurry of tags necessary before sending any actual document text. First, it sends a `<!DOCTYPE>` tag that declares the document to be HTML (in case any XML parsers are listening), followed by the opening `<HTML>` and `<HEAD>` tags, then the `<TITLE>` tag with the argument text (which most GUI-based browsers will display in the window title bar). It then prints closing `</TITLE>` and `</HEAD>` tags and opens the `<BODY>` section, meaning that we can send the document text.

7 `$q->h1('Hello, Web!')` is the document text. The h1 function is a good example of how CGI.pm handles HTML tags: the argument text is placed between `<H1>` and `</H1>` tags, so that it will be displayed in the browser's big header font.

8 `$q->end_html` prints the closing tags. The script ends here and the browser displays the document it sent, shown in figure 3.2

Once you understand what it does, it's clear that the script can be tightened up considerably. It could be reduced to one print statement (after loading CGI.pm). If you run the script from the command line, you can see the output yourself:

```
$ ./hello-web.pl
Content-Type: text/html; charset=ISO-8859-1

<?xml version="1.0" encoding="utf-8"?>
<!DOCTYPE html
        PUBLIC "-//W3C//DTD XHTML Basic 1.0//EN"
        "http://www.w3.org/TR/xhtml-basic/xhtml-basic10.dtd">
<html xmlns="http://www.w3.org/1999/xhtml" lang="en-US"><head>
<title>My first CGI</title>
</head><body><h1>Hello, Web!</h1></body></html>
```

While CGI.pm is certainly overkill for this example (as is any script at all), the HTML functions become handy in any program that sends a lot of tagged text back to a browser. CGI.pm won't forget closing tags, won't misspell tags, or perform other common errors

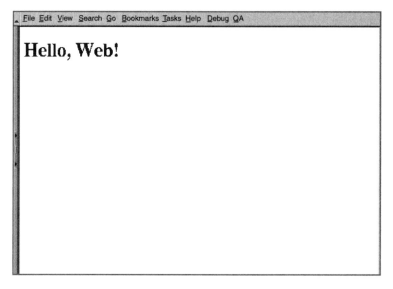

Figure 3.2   hello-web.pl output

of HTML text generated by humans. With a few exceptions noted in the documentation, it has functions for all the HTML tags that work as the h1 example.

For instance, if you want to print text in the browser's bold font, you can do that by using the "strong" tag:

```
print $q->strong('my emphasis');
```

This results in a pair of tags with the argument text in between:

```
<STRONG>my emphasis</STRONG>
```

CGI.pm even does paragraph tags correctly, which few humans and fewer HTML editors seem to do. Text passed to the p() function is marked off with <P> and </P>. The function strings together multiple arguments with spaces, and other HTML functions are welcome as inputs, so it's easy to manage paragraphs:

```
print $q->p('Now is the time',
            $q->strong('for all good programmers'),
            'to come to the aid of their party.');
```

CGI.pm is particularly clever with array reference arguments. See the `tableform` examples in section 3.3.4 for a demonstration.

Of course, this script serves static content, so it could be replaced with just a `hello.html` document.[4] Let's move on to a more interesting script.

---

[4]   Some Perl coders use CGI.pm outside of web programs, just for its helper functions in writing correct HTML. Load CGI with the -nodebug pragma, don't print the Content-Type header, and terminate output with an extra newline for ease of (human) reading. See the `html-output.pl` script for an example.

3.3.2   Dynamic content

The arguments to the HTML output functions in the previous example were all constant strings, but any Perl function or variable will work just as well:

```perl
#!/usr/local/bin/perl -wT

use strict;
use CGI;
my $q = CGI->new;

# Set up the headers and stuff.
print $q->header, $q->start_html('Web Clock');

# Print the program name in an H1 block.
print $q->h1('The time according to', $0);

# Print the time in bold.
print $q->p('The date and time is:', $q->strong(scalar(localtime)));

# End the document.
print $q->end_html;
```

In this example, dynamic.pl, we include the program name in the H1 block via the Perl variable $0, then print the time via the localtime function. Notice how the HTML functions string their arguments together by connecting them with white space in the output, and the use of nested functions to put some text in the browser's bold font.

If you run this same script from the command line instead of a browser, you'll see all the tags for the formatting. It's rather hard to read, though; most of the document is on one line because CGI.pm doesn't write extra white space into its output. The browser will ignore the white space anyway, so it only slows down the transmission.

Often though, you'll want to read the script output when debugging problems. For such occasions there is a variant of CGI that creates more human-readable HTML: use CGI::Pretty instead of use CGI at the beginning of the script.

Here's an example of the output when we change CGI modules:

```
Content-Type: text/html; charset=ISO-8859-1

<?xml version="1.0" encoding="utf-8"?>
<!DOCTYPE html
          PUBLIC "-//W3C//DTD XHTML Basic 1.0//EN"
          "http://www.w3.org/TR/xhtml-basic/xhtml-basic10.dtd">
<html xmlns="http://www.w3.org/1999/xhtml" lang="en-US"><head><title>Web
Clock</title>
</head><body><h1>
          The time according to cgi-bin/dynamic.pl
</h1>
<p>
          The date and time is: <strong>
                    Sat Aug 11 14:36:01 2001
          </strong>
</p>
</body></html>
```

You may already have realized the potential of CGI scripting: if you can write Perl variables and functions back to the browser, you can send anything else that Perl can do. Reports, searches, and all the other things that are easy to do with Perl scripts are easy to do with Perl CGI scripts. In general, the Perl part is easy; the challenge is in creating HTML that looks good to users. You'll need to combine some HTML expertise with your Perl programming to make a good web site.[5]

Many organizations have a message of the day file containing messages displayed to users upon logging in. Writing a message of the day script is easy: just use CGI.pm to write the HTML setup, then open the file in Perl and print the lines to the browser, adding any HTML tags that are appropriate. Similarly, a script that fetches lines from the beginning or end of a file, or reformats the output of another command is easily translated into CGI.

Here's a simple script, `printself.pl`, that attempts to print itself on the browser:

```
#!/usr/local/bin/perl -wT

use strict;
use CGI;
my $q = CGI->new;

# HTML header and starter.
print $q->header, $q->start_html($0);

# Print the program in a PRE block.
open SELF, "<$0";
print $q->pre(<SELF>);
close SELF;

# End the document.
print $q->end_html;
```

The script opens itself as a file (using $0 again), then uses the special property of the file IO operator <> in a list context to read the whole file in as arguments to $q->pre(). Remember that the HTML functions string together their arguments, so the file contents will be printed with extra spaces at the beginning of each line. The HTML <PRE> tag tells browsers to print the marked text as-is, including newlines and white space. Other than that, the output, shown in figure 3.3, is correct—apart from one small problem!

Even in a PRE block, HTML tags are HTML tags (otherwise the browser wouldn't notice the ending </PRE>), and browsers are supposed to ignore tags that they don't understand. The Perl code in this line looks (to the browser) like it has a tag in it:

---

[5] CGI.pm has helper functions for all the HTML tags. What it lacks is documentation for them! You need to know what HTML you want to write first. Having decided that, CGI.pm will make it easy for you to write. The reason for this is mostly pragmatic; HTML is a large and growing specification, and is better documented by its own experts than by Perl programmers.

Figure 3.3   printself.pl output

```
print $q->pre(<SELF>);
```

The browser ignores the mysterious `<SELF>` tag and displays the output as:

```
print $q->pre();
```

This is a problem for any CGI program that gets its output from files, databases, or any other source that it doesn't create itself. If the output contains something that looks like HTML but isn't, the browser won't display it correctly.

There are a few workarounds to this problem. We could rewrite the code to avoid `<SELF>` or break it up so that the browser doesn't see it as a tag. It's better to not send anything HTML-like at all, however. CGI.pm supplies an escaping[6] function for just such occasions, `escapeHTML`, which takes care of the problem. Here's `printself2.pl` which works around that and the extra white space issue:

```
#!/usr/local/bin/perl -wT

use strict;
use CGI;
my $q = CGI->new;

# HTML header and starter.
print $q->header, $q->start_html($0);

# Print the program in a PRE block.
```

---

[6] Escape is an unfortunate bit of computer jargon that means "adding strange additional characters to get the characters you wanted in the first place."

```
open SELF, "<$0";
print $q->pre($q->escapeHTML(join('',<SELF>)));
close SELF;

# End the document.
print $q->end_html;
```

The Perl `join` function is used to gather the file contents via `<SELF>` and concatenate the lines together without extra white space. This is not just to get around the problem of leading spaces in the original script. Unlike HTML helper functions, `escapeHTML` works only on its first argument and ignores the rest, so we have to feed it the whole file at once. Perl has other clever ways of reading a file into a single string, such as changing the special `$/` variable:

```
undef $/;
print $q->pre($q->escapeHTML(<SELF>));
```

`printself3.pl` demonstrates this technique, commonly called a slurp. Note that it is not a good practice to use this method of reading a file into a variable if the size of the file isn't known with confidence to be reasonable; slurping a several megabyte file into a scalar is inefficient at best and may cause mysterious script failures.

In this example we used `escapeHTML` to work around output that accidentally resembled HTML tags. It is just as important to avoid letting users put arbitrary HTML or JavaScript into text that will be displayed in a browser. Malicious users can break applications or even steal information from unsuspecting sites, as seen in the uproar over the so-called "Cross Site Scripting" bugs widely reported at the end of 1999.

It's time to move on to examples that are closer to real applications. CGI scripts become interactive when they use HTML forms and controls as we'll see next.

3.3.3 Interacting

Interactive scripts use HTML forms, which are sections of a document bracketed by a `<FORM> </FORM>` pair. A form contains normal HTML as well as tags that are allowed only inside form sections and which create the input elements and controls which are familiar to anyone who has entered data at a web site.

Forms have their own special section in documents because, traditionally, browsers ignore tags they don't understand. A browser that doesn't implement forms just ignores everything from the opening `<FORM>` to the closing `</FORM>`, displaying the rest of the document normally. This used to be a major issue in site design, so one would see pages with warnings that said they required a forms-capable browser. These days, however, it's not much of a worry.

Forms have been greatly enhanced via JavaScript to the point where a well-designed web application looks as good and can be as useful as a desktop application. In the original implementation, though, a form had various input elements (text, check buttons, etc.) and three controls: a submit button that sends the form data to the server (to be processed by a CGI script), a reset button that sets all inputs to the values they had when sent to the browser, and a default button that sets the inputs to their default values (which could be different than the starting values). The only required control was the submit button, and only that button causes the browser to send data back to the server.

For yet another trivial CGI example we can create a form which has only a submit button. The example is called `pressnow.pl`:

```
#!/usr/local/bin/perl -wT

use strict;
use CGI;
my $q = CGI->new;

# HTML header and starter.
print $q->header, $q->start_html('Press now and win!');

# Make a simple form containing only a button.
print $q->start_form,
  $q->submit('button','Press now and win!'),
  $q->end_form;

# End the document.
print $q->end_html;
```

This script starts out like the others, until we get to $q->start_form. As you may have guessed, this function prints the opening <FORM> tag. The next line uses $q->submit() to create a submit button—the first argument is the name of the parameter, which I'll explain shortly, and the second is the value and also the text of the button. $q->end_form closes the form section. Run the example to see the form, as shown in figure 3.4.

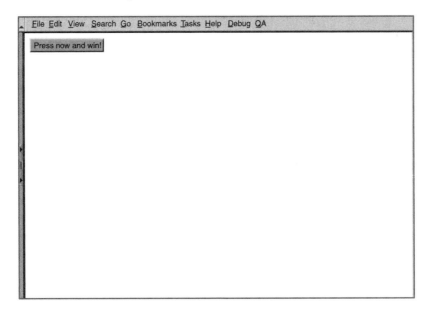

Figure 3.4   pressnow.pl

Clicking the button doesn't appear to accomplish much; the browser refreshes and shows the same form. The reason, however, is that the default action of a form when completed via the submit button is to call the same CGI script that invoked it, passing along the current values of the inputs. In this case the only value to pass along is the value of the button, and the script doesn't check that anyway.

The browser sends data back by requesting the URL of the receiving script and putting the data either on the end of the URL or in a special header that is sent with the request. The first method is called a *get* and results in URLs that include ? and &; the ? signals the beginning of the data, which is written as "name=value" pairs separated by &. The second method is called a *post* and is invisible to the user since the data is not shown in the URL, but is sent along quietly as "name=value" pairs in the request header.

One of CGI.pm's best features is that it gathers the form data for you when the query object is created. The script doesn't have to know whether data was sent via a get or a post, and doesn't have to do any decoding on its own. All of the form data is available via the param function:

```
$q = CGI->new;    # gather all form data.
print $q->param; # print the names of all parameters.
```

To get the value of a particular parameter, pass its name to the function. Without any arguments, param returns a list of all parameter names, so it's easy to write a script that prints its parameters even if you don't know them in advance:

```
foreach my $name ($q->param) {
    print $name, ' = ', $q->param($name), $q->br;
}
```

Furthermore, a script that invokes itself can tell if it is being run for the first time or via a submit button by checking whether or not param returns any values. An empty list means that the script is running without any form data; otherwise the script has been invoked with parameters, so it must be the second or later invocation.

We can use that trick to add some positive reinforcement to our previous example, as shown in pressnow2.pl:

```
#!/usr/local/bin/perl -wT

use strict;
use CGI;
my $q = CGI->new;

# HTML header and starter.
print $q->header, $q->start_html('Press now and win!');

# Print a very simple form with just a button.
print $q->start_form,
    $q->submit('button','Press now and win!'),
    $q->end_form;

# Give positive reinforcement for clicking it.
if ($q->param()) {
```

```
        print $q->h1('You won!');
}

# End the document.
print $q->end_html;
```

When run the first time, the script displays only the button; on subsequent runs it adds the victory text.

Let's expand the use of inputs and also show more of the capabilities of the submit button with a more interesting example.

3.3.4 HTML forms with CGI.pm

As the name suggests, HTML forms were created for fill-in forms. Here's a CGI script called `textform.pl` that makes simple form with text fields:

```
#!/usr/local/bin/perl -wT

use strict;
use CGI;
my $q = CGI->new;

# Starters.
print $q->header, $q->start_html('Address info');

# Create a form with text entry fields.
print $q->start_form,
    $q->h1('Please enter your address below.'),$q->p,
    'Name:',$q->textfield(-name => 'name'),$q->br,
    'Address:',$q->textfield(-name => 'address1'),$q->br,
    'Address:',$q->textfield(-name => 'address2'),$q->br,
    'City:',$q->textfield(-name => 'city'),
    'State/Province:',$q->textfield(-name => 'state'),
    'Zip/Postal code:',$q->textfield(-name => 'zip'),$q->br,
    'Country:',$q->textfield(-name => 'country'),$q->p,
    $q->submit('button','Enter'),
    $q->end_form;

# End the document.
print $q->end_html;
```

The `textfield` function creates a text input field. The argument is given as a Perl `key => value` pair to specify the name of the input. Those names will become important later when we look at scripts that get input data back from the browser. Request the script to see how the form is set up, as shown in figure 3.5.

Though admittedly this works, it's not very attractive—we'd expect the fields to be lined up at the very least. It also annoys users who don't live in a state or province, but that's a bit beyond the scope of this example. All the fields are the same length, but we'd expect to enter more characters into a street address than into a state or province name. And of course the script doesn't actually do anything with the data (a problem we'll leave for the next chapter).

Figure 3.5   textform.pl

Let's address the layout of the form first. One of the interesting challenges of HTML layout is that the browser is in charge of displaying the document, and does so according to its knowledge of fonts, window size, and other parameters that the server and the HTML designer can't know. A common mistake among new web designers is to attempt to force a layout on the browser by aligning characters, using nonbreaking spaces, or other font tricks. Even if they succeed in making something look good on their own browser, the result probably looks silly and amateurish on any other configuration.

HTML form layout and most any other kind of document layout are managed via tables, which let the designer place elements on a grid and apply justification and other rules within cells. Though at first it seems like a clumsy mechanism, tables can produce sophisticated documents. Most of those spiffy sites with sidebars, columns, and headers use nested tables to create their layouts. Once you've learned a trick or two you can guess the table grids for a site just by looking at how elements flow over the screen.

A table begins with a <TABLE> tag as you'd probably guess, and ends with the closing </TABLE>. Each row of the table is set off by a <TR> </TR> pair, and each cell is marked by <TD> </TD>. There are also header cells marked by <TH> </TH>. Browsers will render headers differently from normal cells,[7] usually with a bold font.

---

[7] Assuming they render them at all. Remember that when a browser encounters a tag it doesn't understand it ignores it. If you find your table headers are missing, you're dealing with a browser that doesn't like them.

CGI.pm provides helper functions for tables and their elements. A table begins with the `table` function, whose arguments are usually `Tr` functions corresponding to table rows, containing `td` functions for elements in turn. Note that `Tr` is capitalized to avoid conflicting with the Perl `tr` operator. We could lay out our form using the table functions like so, from `tableform.pl`:

```
$q->table(
        $q->Tr(
                $q->td('Name:'),
                $q->td($q->textfield(-name => 'name'))
                ),
        $q->Tr(
                $q->td('Address:'),
                $q->td($q->textfield(-name => 'address1'))
                ),
        $q->Tr(
                $q->td('Address:'),
                $q->td($q->textfield(-name => 'address2'))
                ),
        $q->Tr(
                $q->td('City:'),
                $q->td($q->textfield(-name => 'city')),
                $q->td('State/Province:'),
                $q->td($q->textfield(-name => 'state')),
                $q->td('Zip/Postal code:'),
                $q->td($q->textfield(-name => 'zip'))
                ),
        $q->Tr(
                $q->td('Country:'),
                $q->td($q->textfield(-name => 'country'))
                ),
        )
```

This works just fine, and the resulting form certainly looks better than the first one, as you can see in figure 3.6.

CGI.pm has a nice feature that simplifies table layout: if an HTML function receives an array reference as an argument, it applies the requested tags to each element of the array. Thus the following pieces of code create the same tags:

```
print $q->td('A'), $q->td('B'), $q->td('C');

print $q->td(['A', 'B', 'C']),

my @letters = ('A' .. 'C');
print $q->td(\@letters);
```

Here's the same form layout using the trick from `tableform2.pl`:

```
print $q->start_form,
    $q->h1('Please enter your address below.'),$q->p,
    $q->table(
              $q->Tr([
```

```
                    $q->td(['Name:',
                            $q->textfield(-name => 'name')]),
                    $q->td(['Address:',
                            $q->textfield(-name => 'address1')]),
                    $q->td(['Address:',
                            $q->textfield(-name => 'address2')]),
                    $q->td(['City:',
                            $q->textfield(-name => 'city'),
                            'State/Province:',
                            $q->textfield(-name => 'state'),
                            'Zip/Postal code:',
                            $q->textfield(-name => 'zip')]),
                    $q->td(['Country:',
                            $q->textfield(-name => 'country')])
                ]),
            ),
    $q->submit('button','Enter'),
    $q->end_form;
```

The code is more compact, but the table comes out the same. Now we need to address the layout issues. We'll do so using attributes for the HTML tags.

Form input fields have attributes that alter the way the browser displays them, such as the font or width of a text field. Attribute names and values correspond to the key => value pairs of the hash, which we've used so far to specify the names of the inputs. To set the width of the country text field, we would call the function like so:

```
$q->textfield(-name =>  'country', -size => 5)
```

Figure 3.6 tableform.pl

The size attribute sets the size of an input in characters. Figure 3.7 shows the output of `tableform3.pl` with all the fields set to reasonable sizes:

Figure 3.7   tableform3.pl

Notice how the State/Province field is pushed far to the right, due to the width of the address fields. We can tell the browser to let long fields like the addresses span multiple columns using the COLSPAN attribute, set like so:

```
$q->td({-colspan => 3},
        $q->textfield(-name => 'address1', -size => 40))
```

Note the important difference: td is an HTML helper function that displays content, so to tell it that we also want to set attribute values, we have to pass the attributes in a hash reference as the first argument. The content in this case is the output of the textfield function, which doesn't display content itself, so it takes its attributes as regular arguments.

To set the attributes of individual table cells, we'll have to call td for each one. That makes using the array reference feature a little trickier, since each element of Tr's array reference is a table row. Here's how I did it in `tableform4.pl`:

```
$q->table
(
 $q->Tr
 ([
   $q->td(['Name:',
           $q->textfield(-name => 'name', -size => 20)]),
   $q->td('Address:') .
   $q->td({-colspan => 3},
```

```
                $q->textfield(-name => 'address1', -size => 40)),
        $q->td .
        $q->td({-colspan => 3},
                $q->textfield(-name => 'address2', -size => 40)),
        $q->td(['City:',
                $q->textfield(-name => 'city', -size => 20),
                'State/Province:',
                $q->textfield(-name => 'state', -size => 3),
                'Zip/Postal code:',
                $q->textfield(-name => 'zip', -size => 10)]),
        $q->td(['Country:',
                $q->textfield(-name => 'country', -size => 5)])
        ]),
    ),
```

The cell with the `'Address:'` label is concatenated to the long text field using Perl's . operator, rather than just stringing them together with commas. That combines the two `td` calls into a single element of `Tr`'s array and so they end up on one row. The same trick works on the row after that. And figure 3.8 shows the result, which is somewhat more pleasing to the eye:

Figure 3.8   tableform4.pl output

Note the use of an empty table cell in the third row, created by an empty call to `td`. There are plenty of useful attributes we could assign to fields. For instance, we could set a black background on fields that are required by using the BGCOLOR attribute:

```
$q->td({-colspan => 3, -bgcolor => 'black'},
        $q->textfield(-name => 'name', -size => 20))
```

It's beyond the scope of this book to provide a full list of HTML tags and attributes. Check an online or printed resource. There are several good books on the subject, but with the speed of change in this business it's worth knowing some good web sites too. The authoritative specification is on the World Wide Web Consortium's page; look for pointers on http://www.w3.org/MarkUp/. The specification is rather formal, though, and hard for a beginner to interpret. There is a link to a starter guide on the same page, and more can be found elsewhere with a few clicks on your favorite web search site. I found a good HTML tag library on ZDNet's developer page at http://www.zdnet.com/developer, and another on United Webmasters' site at http://www.unitedwebmasters.com/rehtml.htm.

I hope that with a little digging and a good reading of CGI.pm's documentation you'll be able to generate any of the tags you want. Practice and exploration will teach you what works.

3.3.5 Taking action

Up to now, our scripts haven't done anything with their inputs. The most obvious thing to do would be to store data in a file and retrieve it on some other form. Since the next chapter is about databases I'll save that topic for later. But we need to know something more basic first: how does a script get the information that it is sent? And how can a script direct that information to the appropriate application?

I gave a preview of the answer to the first question in the examples for submit buttons: The script uses CGI.pm's `param` function to receive values and also to set them to be displayed in the form. If you recall, I showed a simple way for a script to know if it had been invoked with input data:

```
if ($q->param()) {
    print $q->h1('You won!');
}
```

If the `param` function returns anything at all, it means the script received input data. In fact, what it is returning is a list of all the parameter names. If invoked with a single argument, it is assumed to be a parameter name and the value of that parameter is returned. If invoked with multiple arguments, those after the first are assigned as values to the parameter.

As for how to direct input data to another script: an HTML form has an `ACTION` attribute that specifies the URL of a CGI program that is to receive the data when the user clicks Submit. The default action is to invoke the current script again. This makes it easy to write a single script that processes multiple pages of data, checking for various parameters along the way to know which page to send to the browser. The action can be any URL, however, and it's not unreasonable to have different scripts for different parts of an application.

Here's yet another variation of the address entry form script `checkdata.pl` that demonstrates checking for input data:

```
#!/usr/local/bin/perl -wT

use strict;
use CGI;
my $q = CGI->new;  # all input data loaded to $q

# If we have data, display the confirmation.
if ($q->param) {
    print
      $q->header, $q->start_html('Confirmation'),
      $q->h1('Please verify that this is correct:'),$q->p,
      $q->table
        (
         $q->Tr
         ([
           $q->td(['Name:',$q->param('name')]),
           $q->td(['Address:',$q->param('address1')]),
           $q->td(['',$q->param('address2')]),
           $q->td(['City:',$q->param('city')]),
           $q->td(['State/Pr:',$q->param('state')]),
           $q->td(['Zip/Postal:',$q->param('zip')]),
           $q->td(['Country',$q->param('country')])
          ])
        );
    print
      'Please click the button below if this is correct ',
      'or use your browser\'s Back button to return to ',
      'the form and make corrections.',
      $q->start_form(-action => 'savedata.pl'),
      map ({$q->hidden($_)} $q->param),
      $q->submit('button','Enter'),
      $q->end_form;
}
else { # No data, so print the form.
    print $q->header, $q->start_html('Address info'),
    $q->start_form,
    $q->h1('Please enter your address below.'),$q->p,
    $q->table
        (
         $q->Tr
         ([
           $q->td(['Name:',
                   $q->textfield(-name => 'name', -size => 20)]),
           $q->td('Address:') .
           $q->td({-colspan => 3},
                   $q->textfield(-name => 'address1', -size => 40)),
           $q->td .
           $q->td({-colspan => 3},
                   $q->textfield(-name => 'address2', -size => 40)),
           $q->td(['City:',
                   $q->textfield(-name => 'city', -size => 20),
                   'State/Province:',
                   $q->textfield(-name => 'state', -size => 3),
```

```
                      'Zip/Postal code:',
                      $q->textfield(-name => 'zip', -size => 10)]),
              $q->td(['Country:',
                      $q->textfield(-name => 'country', -size => 5)])
              ]),
            ),
       $q->submit('button','Enter'),
       $q->end_form;
}

# End the document.
print $q->end_html;
```

The script uses `param` to check whether or not it is receiving input. If it is, it uses further calls to the same function to display the input values in a table and ask for confirmation. When the script is called without input it displays the now familiar form.

Note that in the section that displays the form, `start_form` is called without arguments. That means the form will use the default action when Submit is clicked. The default action is to invoke the same script (the same URL, actually) and pass it the input data, thus making the `param` trick work.

In the confirmation section, however, `start_form` is called like so:

```
$q->startform(-action => 'savedata.pl'),
```

The action is given explicitly, and when the submit button is clicked the data will be sent to a different script, `savedata.pl`, an example from the next chapter. We could specify a complete URL here, including a different site. Most commonly, however, we want a different application in the same relative location, and this specification works fine.

Also notice the line toward the end of that form:

```
    map ({$q->hidden($_)} $q->param),
```

This line creates *hidden* fields for all the parameters received by the script. Each hidden field is named for a parameter, but this code doesn't obviously assign a value. Running the script shows that the values get carried forward, so how does it work?

The answer is that CGI.pm implements *sticky* parameters. If a parameter is present when the script is invoked, any input named for the parameter will take that parameter's value automatically. Thus for each parameter (listed by `$q->param`) the code creates a hidden field, and CGI.pm puts the parameter value in the field without being told.

Sticky parameters often surprise programmers when they try to set a value for an input. When a script is invoked without parameters, this code will create a text field named 'Username' displaying a value of 'bob':

```
print $q->textfield('Username', 'bob');
```

If the script is invoked with a parameter string of 'Username=carole' then that same code will display 'carole' in spite of the fact that it appears to set the value. That's because the parameter value sticks to the input.

The way to override a parameter's value is to call `param` explicitly, as in:

```
$q->param('Username','bob');
print $q->textfield('Username');
```

But why did the example script need hidden fields in the first place? The browser will send CGI data only for its current set of inputs. In order to pass along the form data from the first invocation, we have to store that data in some kind of input. In this case we use hidden fields to keep the data out of the user's view.

This trick is not implemented well here for a general CGI application. In particular, it doesn't take into account an input with multiple values, which would have to be copied separately, and it creates a hidden field for the button input. But it will serve the needs of the current example, which are only to pass along the contents of the form to `savedata.pl`.

We could have used other tricks, such as tacking the form data onto the URL given in the `start_form` function, but this variation is compact and also provides debugging information. With the confirmation screen loaded, use the `"show page source"` function of your browser to display the HTML code. You'll find the hidden fields there with the contents that we're passing along.

3.4 STRICTNESS, WARNINGS, AND TAINT CHECKING

The most common admonitions given by experienced Perl programmers to new CGI coders are:

1 use `strict`

2 Turn on warnings with `-w` or use `warnings`

3 Any script that accepts user input needs taint checking (`-T`)

Many folks who are just learning Perl assume that since these features are optional, programs don't require them. (The usual excuse that a short or simple script doesn't need extra error checking is belied by the fact that any program under maintenance tends to stop being short and simple.) Not so; they are optional partly for historic reasons, and partly practical, since many sites use "one liner" scripts that are written entirely on the command line to implement simple utilities. Perl tries to get out of the way of such simple programs, but that's no reason to turn down its help for larger matters.

There is no significant run-time penalty for using Perl's maximal error checking. I've encountered programmers who think they are getting more from their scripts by turning off strictness and warnings in production, but in fact they are probably spending any such savings in the time used to edit the script and make the change. There is a significant penalty in development time when a programmer tracks down a bug caused by misspelled variable names and other typo errors which are easily caught by turning on the error checks.

For taint checking, Perl turns this on automatically for any script which runs under an effective user or group that is different from the user who started the script (i.e., setuser and setgroup scripts). The value of taint checking extends far beyond those special cases, though, and should be used by any script that takes user input or processes data previously input by the user and stored in a file or database. Taint checks prevent a program from taking external actions based on user input—opening a file named by the user, say, or running a command via the backtick operator containing user values. Before such tainted values can be used, a script must process them through a regular expression to verify it is getting what it expects.

Perl explains all these issues in the appropriate perldoc entries—`strict` and `warnings` (or `perlrun` if you aren't using version 5.6 or later) for those pragmas and the `perlsec` page to explain taint checks and other security issues. Please see those pages for more details, especially if you still think you can do without them.

3.5 CGI MODULES

This chapter hardly scratches the surface of CGI programming or Perl's helpful CGI aides. While there are plenty of other good resources for learning the ins and outs of CGI, new programmers generally have to fend for themselves in finding good tools.

While I don't have space here to present or evaluate all of the variety of Perl's web programming modules, there are a handful available on CPAN that you may find useful:

- *Validation tools*—CGI::ArgChecker helps verify input parameters; register a test function for each parameter, then call it with the query object to check all inputs at once. CGI::Validate performs type checking and other tests in the style of Getopt::Long, which may be familiar to Perl programmers who write command-line scripts.

- *Caching*—CGI::Cache stores the output of CGI scripts, along with the parameters that generated the output. If it receives a request with parameters matching a cached value, it sends back the associated HTML without running the script again. It understands expiration time and other conditions for dropping HTML from the cache.

- *Form generation*—CGI::QuickForm will build a form based on a hash of input descriptions and other criteria. Developers who are familiar with 4GL form manager programming might really like this module. CGI::Screen provides an easy way to generate multipage forms with consistent controls.

- *HTML templates/embedded scripting*—There are so many Perl modules on this theme that I've devoted a whole chapter to the subject.

CGI.pm is also bundled with other modules that are likely to feature in larger CGI programs. I've mentioned CGI::Pretty for making more readable HTML output.

There is also CGI::Carp, which makes Perl's error message functions (`warn` and `die`, as well as `confess`, `croak`, etc. from Carp.pm) write to the server error log with time stamps and the name of the script logging the error. CGI::Cookie provides a comprehensive API for managing cookies (see chapter 5).

Now that we have working CGI scripts, let's investigate giving them something to work on. The next chapter brings databases into the script tool set.

# PART 2

Tools for
web applications

Now that we have a web server and language in place, we can think about how to build our site. This section is all about tools that will help you create your applications:

- Chapter 4 covers databases, starting with files and working up through relational engines.
- Chapter 5 brings mod_perl into Apache to combine the web server and language interpreter into a powerful package.
- Chapter 6 discusses security issues, starting with encrypting web traffic via SSL and continuing through techniques of user management.
- Chapter 7 shows how to merge Perl scripting into HTML documents for dynamic web pages.

After you've worked through these chapters, you'll have a good set of tools for building your site.

C H A P T E R 4

Databases

Now that we have a way to build web applications, we need to store and retrieve data for them too. Fortunately the Open Source world is well-stocked with tools for this, ranging from simple file managers to full-blown relational databases.

Database software is far more mature than web technology; SQL, the most commonly used relational database language, is over 20 years old, and that makes it a relative newcomer compared to some mainframe products that are still in use. Commercial products dominate the scene, unlike the case of web servers and programming languages. Mention SQL or relational database to other programmers and you're likely to hear of experience with Oracle, Sybase, Informix, or other big players. If you are building a commercial web site, chances are you've already chosen one of these. These are fine products, and I won't try to dissuade anyone who can afford them. However, there are alternatives which don't involve huge licensing fees.

4.1 FILES

The first choice to consider for data storage is the simple, reliable file. Many applications can get by with plain file interfaces, especially if the load is light and there won't be much contention for file access.

The problem with using a file interface is that the application has to do everything: build the record, lock the file, write the record, and check for errors. When retrieving data, the application either searches files sequentially for records or implements some indexing scheme of its own to speed things along.

Many beginning programmers don't consider the maintenance issues of their code when making this kind of choice. If the needs of the application change, record layouts or indexing systems might have to change with them. Code that depends on those will then break unless everything is changed correctly at once. The hours spent writing conversion scripts and testing changes to sensitive code might give the developer time to consider another choice.

That said, files are perfectly fine for many needs. Data that is written in chronological order and seldom updated, such as logs, guest books, and other sequential information can be handled easily. Perl is especially good at handling flexible text formats for such data, though it can handle binary records as well.

4.2 ADDRESS BOOK

Our CGI address-gathering form in chapter 3 left off with `checkdata.pl`, a script that presents a form for information input and then offers a confirmation screen that passes the data along to `savedata.pl`. It's time to look at that script, which uses basic Perl file I/O. The structure of the script is the same as the previous examples—if it receives input it stores it, and if not it directs the user to enter the data.

```perl
#!/usr/local/bin/perl -wT

use strict;
use CGI;
my $q = CGI->new;  # all input data loaded to $q

# File for the addresses -- make sure Apache can write here.
my $addrs = '/usr/local/apache/data/address.dat';

print $q->header;

# If we have data, save it to a file.
if ($q->param) {
    if (open(ADDRESSES, ">>$addrs")) {
        print ADDRESSES
          join("\t",
                $q->param('name'),
                $q->param('address1'),
                $q->param('address2'),
                $q->param('city'),
```

```
                    $q->param('state'),
                    $q->param('zip'),
                    $q->param('country')
                    ),"\n";
        close ADDRESSES;
        print $q->start_html('Thank you'),
        $q->p('Your address has been entered.  Go to the',
                $q->a({-href => 'showaddr.pl'}, 'show address'),
                'page to see the current address book.'
                );
    }
    else {
        print $q->start_html('File error'),
        $q->h1("Error in $0"),$q->p,
        "Couldn't open $addrs: $!";
    }
}
else { # No data, so tell the user to start from scratch.
    print $q->start_html('Address required'),
    $q->h1('Please enter the data first.'),$q->p,
    'Please go to the ',
    $q->a({-href => 'checkdata.pl'}, 'address entry page'),
    ' and enter your address there.';
}

# End the document.
print $q->end_html;
```

Note the use of $q->a (for anchor) to create links in either section; the href attribute provides the URL for the link, and the remaining arguments form the link text.

As with any program that uses files, the script must ascertain whether it really opened the address file. If not, it should take action to tell the system what went wrong. Typically this is done with the Perl die or warn functions, which will print a message to the error output device—the error_log file in the case of a CGI script. For an end-user application you should probably not print error messages in HTML. In the case of these examples though, you are the end user, so I kept matters simple.

Assuming the file was opened, we print a line containing all the input parameters from the form, separated by the tab character. This makes it easy to use Perl's split function to turn a record back to a list of fields. Any character that is unlikely to be in the input would do; browsers generally interpret tabs as meaning to go to the next field, so it is difficult to put one in a text box. A robust implementation would still escape the delimiter properly.

After writing the record, the script closes the file and prints a thank you, along with a link to the script, showaddr.pl, that will display the data. That example follows:

```
#!/usr/local/bin/perl -wT

use strict;
use CGI;
```

```
my $q = CGI->new;
my $addrs = '/usr/local/apache/data/address.dat';

# Open the address book.
if (open(ADDRESSES, "<$addrs")) {
    # Print the address book as a table.
    print $q->header, $q->start_html('Address book'),
    $q->h1('Addresses as of ' . localtime);
    my @headers =
      qw(Name Address1 Address2 City State Zip Country);
    my @rows;
    while (<ADDRESSES>) {
        push @rows, $q->td([split /\t/]);
    }
    print $q->table(
                    $q->Tr([$q->th(\@headers), @rows])
                   );
    close ADDRESSES;
}
else { # Couldn't open the file.
    print $q->start_html('Error'),
    $q->h1("Error in $0"),$q->p,
    "Couldn't open $addrs: $!";
}

# End the document.
print $q->end_html;
```

This example reads the address file and builds a table with a row for each record. This is handled by the `while` loop:

```
while (<ADDRESSES>) {
    push @rows, $q->td([split /\|/]);
}
```

Perl's `<>` operator reads a line from the given file and puts it in `$_` if it isn't assigned otherwise. That's the same variable that `split` operates on by default, as shown in the next line. For each record in the file, the script creates an entry in the `@rows` array, created by feeding an array reference to the `td` function. That's a lot of short-cuts for one task. If it isn't obvious to you on a first or second reading, look at it this way:

```
my $line, @fields;
while ($line = <ADDRESSES>) {
    @fields = split /\t/, $line;
    push @row, $q->td(\@fields);
}
```

It may seem odd that the script builds the rows of the table and then passes the results to the `table` function later to create the HTML. In fact, this is a common tactic, since `table` has to get its arguments all at once; a CGI.pm script commonly builds temporary arrays and passes them along to the HTML functions.

That makes the file example complete enough for argument's sake. It uses three scripts which gather input, save it, and display a simple report. But the application isn't very usable, since we can't look up an address without printing the whole file, and we can't update any information at all. (Raise your hand if your address book doesn't have any out-of-date listings.)

In the next example we'll make a more functional address book using a different storage system.

4.3 HASH FILES

In the middle of the complexity scale between simple text files and relational databases one finds various simple store and fetch systems. Some OSs have special indexed files that store data along with a key that can be used to retrieve a particular record quickly. Unix has various flavors of dbm (gdbm, sdbm, ndbm, odbm, and the Berkeley DB) which use a hashing algorithm to transform the key into a record number. The various implementations differ on how the key is hashed and whether they store hash tables and record data in one file or two, but the ingrained notion of key hashing and record retrieval put the dbm family and other such software under the umbrella of *hash files*.

There are a few important constraints to consider when using hash files for data storage. The first is that these systems implement a single, unique key; data is associated with one tag, if you will, that can be used to pull it out of the file. If we store two different records with the same tag, the second will be retained and the first will be lost. If we need more than one tag for a record, we have to implement secondary keys of our own in some fashion.

Another aspect comes from the use of hashing, whereby a string is converted to an integer used to look up a stored record. Good hashing algorithms spread their results across the full range of integer values, so keys won't clump together even if their string values are similar. As a result, the lexical value of a key (the way you'd sort it alphabetically) has nothing to do with its hash value, and records are stored in a seemingly random order in the file. Hash files don't provide sorted or chronological retrieval. If you need either, you again have to implement it yourself.

The other considerations are specific to the implementation. dbm and its early variants had small limits on the size of a record and the total size of data stored at a particular hash value, making them poor choices for applications with a lot of unpredictable data. gdbm is superior for data that is mostly read, but requires that writes to the file be exclusive—all other applications have to close the file and reopen it afterward. The Berkeley DB implementation is very robust, and handles the locking required for simultaneous reads and writes; many OSs ship with an older Open Source version of the product, though the current version has a unique license that requires royalty payments under certain circumstances. Check with the owner, Sleepycat

Software at http://www.sleepycat.com/, to find out how the license works, or stick with the old version.[1]

4.3.1 Perl's tie and hash files

The programming interfaces for hash file implementations aren't terribly complicated—not much worse than for regular files. The program opens the hash file, then calls routines to look up keys, retrieve records, and update them, not unlike the steps for opening, reading, and writing a text file (except for the look up part).

Perl provides modules for hash files that make them so easy to use that most of the code disappears. You've probably already considered that a hash file and a Perl hash have the same conceptual interface and limitations. Perl hashes have a single unique key that is used to store and retrieve arbitrary data, and don't provide sorting or in-order retrieval. Perl also has tie, a function that lets a specially written object pretend to be a Perl scalar, array, or hash. Put those two together and you have the various DBM_File modules that provide a Perl hash interface to a hash file.[2]

Here is an example using DB_File, the Perl module that ties to the Berkeley DB interface. The program calls tie, which invokes the appropriate code in DB_File to open the hash file:

```
use DB_File;

# DB_File database of addresses.
my $addrs = '/usr/local/apache/data/addresses';
my %db;  # This hash will stand for the database.

# Open the data file or write an error to the log.
tie %db, 'DB_File', $addrs
    or die "Couldn't open db file $addrs, $!";
```

The arguments to tie are the hash or other Perl variable that is associated with the file, the name of the module which contains the interface code, and the path to the file.[3] We can pass additional arguments to give the file's mode and set other parameters, but the defaults allow for reading and writing and will create the database if it doesn't exist.

DB_File is a standard Perl module which gets compiled only if your system has some version of Berkeley DB. The code loads it via use just as it does with the CGI

---

[1] Berkeley DB implements more than just straight hashing; you can use it to build sorted indexes or map onto flat files indexed by record number as well. I use it extensively, and my comments about its license shouldn't be taken as a warning against the product. You should of course read the license yourself.

[2] There is also the AnyDBM_File module which will select from the DBM_File modules available from your system based on its or your own ordering modules. If you are writing code for unknown systems, use AnyDBM_File rather than a specific implementation for maximum portability. You'll also have to implement file locking and other services at the lowest common denominator.

[3] That's how you tie hash files, at least. tie can be used to bind most any kind of Perl variable to some other object. Read the perltie documentation for more details.

module. If you're curious, locate `DB_File.pm` and browse through the code. You'll notice functions that Perl will call to emulate all of the operations on a hash—storing a value for a key, deleting entries, and so on. Creating a tied hash or other Perl object isn't a trivial coding task, but it's reasonably straightforward once you've seen it done and read the `perltie` documentation.

After setting up the tied hash, the program treats it just as it would a normal Perl hash, as you'll see in the example code in the next section. When you release the hash (by using `untie`, or just letting the hash variable go out of scope) you also close the file and release any locks or other resources.

4.3.2 Hash file address book

Let's revisit our address book application with a hash file implementation in mind. One limitation of the previous version was the lack of a query function to look up a single address. Since hash files are very good at this task, we'll focus on that improvement in reworking the code.

Also, unlike the previous example, all the code for this application is in one file, `addrbook.pl`. Writing it this way makes some things easier; all of the initialization is done in one spot, for instance. On the other hand, Perl has to compile the code for all of the pages of the application, even though only one will be used for any given invocation. We'll address this problem in chapter 5.

My commentary is sprinkled through the example, but the code appears here in the same order as it does in the file. Read the file directly if you want to see just the code.

We start with the usual set of `use` statements, adding `use DB_File` to get the tied interface:

```
#!/usr/local/bin/perl -wT

use strict;
use CGI;
use DB_File;

# Load the CGI input data.
my $q = CGI->new;

# List the inputs that correspond to form fields.
my @fields = qw(name address1 address2 city state zip country);

# DB_File database of addresses.
my $addrs = '/usr/local/apache/data/addresses';
my %db;  # This hash will stand for the database.

# Open the data file or write an error to the log.
tie %db, 'DB_File', $addrs
    or die "Couldn't open db file $addrs, $!";
```

Now the hash file database is ready to use. It is somewhat inefficient to do this for every invocation given that some pages won't read the database at all, but putting the initialization here prevents anything else from working if for some reason the program can't open the hash file.

Next we have a couple of utility functions:

```
# Print a navigation bar of submit buttons.
sub navbar {
    return join('',
                map {$q->submit('page',$_)}
                @_, 'Entry', 'Display', 'Query'
               );
}
```

This function creates a row of buttons. If called with any arguments (which Perl keeps in the special @_ array), it creates buttons for those first, then adds in Entry, Display, and Query. Note that all of these buttons are named 'page' to make it easy to find out which button was pressed—the code will call $q->param('page') and the answer will be the name of the page to display next.

```
# Print the entry/update form.
sub entry_form {
    return
      $q->table
        (
         $q->Tr
         ([
           $q->td(['Full name:',
                   $q->textfield(-name => 'name', -size => 20)]),
           $q->td('Address:') .
           $q->td({-colspan => 3},
                   $q->textfield(-name => 'address1', -size => 40)),
           $q->td .
           $q->td({-colspan => 3},
                   $q->textfield(-name => 'address2', -size => 40)),
           $q->td(['City:',
                   $q->textfield(-name => 'city', -size => 20),
                   'State/Province:',
                   $q->textfield(-name => 'state', -size => 3),
                   'Zip/Postal code:',
                   $q->textfield(-name => 'zip', -size => 10)]),
           $q->td(['Country:',
                   $q->textfield(-name => 'country', -size => 5)])
          ]),
         );
}
```

This function creates the form for entering or modifying an address. While this example doesn't actually have an update page, adding one is a simple matter as we'll see in the next example.

```
# Display the appropriate form, depending on input.
my $page = $q->param('page');
```

```
my $find = $q->param('find');
if (!$page || $page eq 'Query' || $find && !$page) {
    print $q->header, $q->start_html('Query page'),
    $q->h1('Query address book'),$q->p;
    if ($find) {
        my @values = split(/\|/,$db{$find});
        if (@values) {
            print $q->table
                (
                  $q->Tr
                  ([
                    $q->td(['Full name:',$values[0]]),
                    $q->td(['Address:',$values[1]]),
                    $q->td(['',$values[2]]),
                    $q->td(['City:',$values[3]]),
                    $q->td(['State/Pr:',$values[4]]),
                    $q->td(['Zip/Postal:',$values[5]]),
                    $q->td(['Country',$values[6]])
                    ])
                );
        }
        else {
            print "$find not found";
        }
    }
    print $q->start_form,"Enter a name:",
    $q->textfield(-name => 'find', -size => 20),
    $q->p,navbar,$q->end_form;
}
```

This section handles queries. The tangle of conditions in the `if` statement display this page by default if the script is invoked without parameters. This is a good choice, since queries are the most used function in database applications. We also get here if the Query button is pressed or the script is invoked with a `find` parameter but no page; here's how that works.

Skip past the `if ($find) {` section and look at the end. At the bottom of the page, the script creates a text entry box labeled "Enter a name:". This input is called `'find'` and is used to search for names in the database. If the user enters text there and presses Enter, the browser will send that input back to the server. Thus the script will have a `find` parameter but no page. The user could also fill in the field and click Query, so we need to check for both cases.

Moving back up to the beginning, if the script did get a `find` parameter, it looks up that string in the database, but if you don't look carefully you'll miss it: `$db{$find}` is the lookup code. Since the `db` hash is tied to the hash file, reading a value in `db` causes DB_File to do the lookup for us and return the string stored in the database.

If there was a string stored for that key, the script displays a table with the values that it retrieved. If not, it prints a message to that effect. In either case it lets the user do another lookup.

A more robust script would let the user enter changes here and update the database. You can work out how to do that yourself, or skip ahead to a later example.

```
elsif ($page eq 'Entry') {
    print $q->header, $q->start_html('Entry page'),
    $q->h1('Address book'),$q->p,
    'Enter an address:',$q->p,
    $q->start_form, entry_form,
    $q->hidden('function','Entry'),
    navbar('Confirm'), $q->end_form;
}
```

This section is invoked when the user clicks the Entry button. It puts up the entry form, then calls navbar('Confirm') to put in the standard set of buttons plus an additional confirmation button. The confirmation mechanism should be familiar from the previous examples. The hidden field function is used to store the fact that this is a new entry.

```
elsif ($page eq 'Display') {
    print $q->header, $q->start_html('Display page'),
    $q->h1('Address book'),$q->p,
    'Address book listing:',$q->p;
    my @headers =
        qw(Name Address1 Address2 City State Zip Country);
    my @rows = map {$q->td([split /\|/])} values %db;
    print $q->table(
                $q->Tr([$q->th(\@headers), @rows])
                );
    print $q->start_form,
    navbar, $q->end_form;
}
```

The Display page shows a report of all the addresses in the database. This is similar to the file example's report, except that all the data is retrieved by this call: values %db. Perl's values function returns a list of all the values stored in a hash; db is tied to a hash file, and DB_File obediently retrieves all the records from the file and returns them as a list. One could get spoiled with such service.

The code is simple enough that the @rows array isn't really needed; the map call could be embedded in the call to $q->Tr.

```
elsif ($page eq 'Confirm') {
    print $q->header, $q->start_html('Confirmation page'),
    $q->h1('Confirm', $q->param('function'), ':'),$q->p,
    $q->start_form,
    $q->table
      (
       $q->Tr
```

```
       ([
         $q->td(['Name:',$q->param('name')]),
         $q->td(['Address:',$q->param('address1')]),
         $q->td(['',$q->param('address2')]),
         $q->td(['City:',$q->param('city')]),
         $q->td(['State/Pr:',$q->param('state')]),
         $q->td(['Zip/Postal:',$q->param('zip')]),
         $q->td(['Country',$q->param('country')])
       ])
     );
     print 'If this is correct, press Update; if not, use ',
     'the Back button on your browser to return to the form.',
     map ({$q->hidden($_)} @fields),
     $q->p,navbar('Update'), $q->end_form;
}
```

The confirmation page is essentially the same as it was in the file example. The
parameters listed in the @fields array are preserved for the next invocation of the
script by storing them in hidden fields. The function parameter is used to print a
confirmation message that tells the user what will happen.

```
elsif ($page eq 'Update') {
    my $name = $q->param('name');
    my $value = join('|',map {$q->param($_)} @fields);
    $db{$name} = $value;
    print $q->header, $q->start_html('Success'),
    $q->h1('Update completed');
    print $q->start_form, navbar, $q->end_form;
}
```

This section stores a record in the hash file. It creates a string by concatenating all of
the input fields with a separator character, then stores the string via the simple line:

```
    $db{$name} = $value;
```

This shows again how remarkably easy Perl can make our lives. Behind the scenes,
DB_File is called to store the string in $value at the key of $name.

```
else {
    print $q->header, $q->start_html('Error'),
    $q->h1('No input function'),$q->p,
    $q->start_form, navbar, $q->end_form;
}

# Through with the hash file.
untie %db;

# End the document.
print $q->end_html;
```

The rest of the script prints an error message as a catch-all case and ends the document. The hash file will be closed automatically by the end of the script, so there isn't
any special code for it here.

`tie` and DB_File make hash files so easy to use that one can get carried away. In a larger program it would be important to conserve operations on the `db` hash so that code isn't constantly running back to the hash file for keys and records.

Perl's `tie` magic has been applied to other sorts of databases and functions. In fact, there is a module that lets a relational database table act as a Perl hash, similarly to the hash file implementation we've used here. CPAN lists `tie` implementations for clocks, network services, encryption packages, and many other uses, so if you have a need for such a module, check CPAN first.

4.4 RELATIONAL DATABASES

While hash files have a number of good applications, a complex web application will soon find itself bumping up against their limitations. If you find yourself tempted to add your own secondary indexing scheme to a hash file or to add other features, it's time to take a step back and look at a better solution.

Relational databases are the next step up in both resource cost and development complexity. For application development purposes they should also be the final step—relational databases have all the features an application needs. The relational model is the child of the hierarchical and network models used in mainframe application development in the 1960s and '70s. Although some new models have been developed (notably object-relational, used by PostgreSQL), the application world has stuck to the relational model since it became entrenched in the '80s.

Most of the argument since then has been over what features to add to SQL, the query language used by relational databases. The widely adopted SQL92 standard provides a benchmark for compliance, somewhat simplifying the complex task of comparing and evaluating different database products.

As I mentioned at the beginning of the chapter, the commercial database market is quite crowded, with major players jostling each other by adding new features and services while newcomers attempt to carve out niche markets. The Open Source market is smaller, with two widely used implementations: MySQL (http://www.mysql.com/) and PostgreSQL (http://www.postgresql.org/). There are also new arrivals such as Interbase (http://www.interbase.com), somewhat free products like Mini-SQL (which was mSQL) (http://www.hughes.com.au/), and ongoing experiments including a proposal to write an entirely new database server all in Perl, making it worth a look around to see what has been released.

4.4.1 What's relational?

From an application developer's point of view, the primary characteristic of a relational database is the fact that it organizes data into tables that can be queried and merged on the fly to produce compound data sets.

For example, suppose we have a personal information database that stores a contact name and address in one table and phone numbers in another table. A given contact can have one or more phone numbers, and by storing them separately the application doesn't have to anticipate in advance how many are needed.

The following SQL statements would work in most databases to create the tables:

```
CREATE TABLE Contacts (
    Name VARCHAR(20) NOT NULL,
     Address1 VARCHAR(40),
     Address2 VARCHAR(40),
     City VARCHAR(20),
     State VARCHAR(3),
     Zip VARCHAR(10),
     Country VARCHAR(5),
     PRIMARY KEY (Name)
     );

CREATE TABLE Phones (
     PNumber VARCHAR(12) NOT NULL,
     Name VARCHAR(20) NOT NULL,
     PRIMARY KEY(PNUMBER)
     );
```

After loading the tables with data, we could query the Contacts table to search for a given name or city:

```
SELECT * FROM Contacts WHERE Name = "Theo Petersen";
SELECT Name, Address1 FROM Contacts WHERE City = "Denver";
```

Of course, we could accomplish the same sort of thing with a set of flat files or hash files. The relational part comes in when we use SELECT to join tables:

```
SELECT Name, City, PNumber FROM Contacts C, Phones P
    WHERE C.Name = P.Name;
```

This query creates a dataset that combines the Name and City fields from Contacts and the PNumber field from Phones for all records where the Name fields match.

From the application's point of view, the complexity of the query doesn't increase the complexity of the code that uses it. We could have the database merge additional tables, sort and group the data, and perform calculations based on the fields and it would still work pretty much the same. To do the same query with a pair of flat files, we would at least have to write nested retrieval loops; adding any more constraints would add correspondingly to the code.

Thus for the application developer, a relational database is a sort of data "black box" that handles a great many implementation tasks. The application is correspondingly simpler, while the cost in system resources is greater.

The application also doesn't include the database code; most relational databases are built on a client/server model in which the real database work is done in a separate process (which can also be on a separate machine, as was mentioned in previous chapters and will come up again in chapter 12). This allows the database engine to cache pages and perform other optimizations across queries. Some databases do run entirely in the application, saving connection and data transfer overhead for higher performance.

Relational databases have some security features in common. In particular, users have to identify themselves to the database server before they are allowed to get at the data. Most servers keep their own list of users and permissions, although some will use the OS's user database. Thus when making the decision to use a relational database, bear in mind that each application will have to log in to the database before it can retrieve or update anything, adding a further layer of user administration to the overall maintenance cost.

4.4.2 Choosing a relational database

The choice of which commercial database product to use often comes down to budget and politics. While we'd like to think that technical merit is the key issue, anyone who has worked in business application development for long knows better. These products are expensive, and so the choosing and licensing process happens high up on the organization chart, whether for web applications or central accounting systems.

Chances are good then that a commercial web site designer already has a database product in mind before development starts, either because the organization already uses that database elsewhere or because the sales process has already occurred. But that's okay—chances are equally good that the choice will work fine for web applications. Long-term competition has forced the vendors to produce products that are more or less alike from the point of view of typical usage. If your business has extreme needs, such as tremendous size or amazing transaction counts, then evaluate your choices more carefully.

If you have the luxury of making your own choice, consider one of the Open Source implementations listed in the next section. You'll be pleased with the support you get from fellow developers and the number of free scripts and examples on various web sites. If your budget forces you in this direction, don't feel that you are settling for poor man's best, as these databases are in use at thousands of busy public and private web sites, competing very well with their commercial cousins.

When you consider the technical issues for a database, check whether Perl's DBI package supports it; this is a crucial factor for any Perl-based applications, web or otherwise. The two discussed next are both part of the DBI family, as are most of the commercial products.

4.4.3 MySQL

Like many Open Source products, MySQL began life as a tool for one company's internal applications, spread to its customers, and then took on a life of its own. TcX was the original developer, and continues to contribute code and support although the name has changed to MySQL AB, reflecting the emphasis on the product.

The original design goals for MySQL were speed and robustness for large databases. In exchange, the developers sacrificed some features of the relational model that many critics feel are too important to lose, including the ability to roll back uncommitted updates. This trade-off led to a seemingly endless discussion in various forums over whether MySQL is a "real" database, which did not end when MySQL implemented many of the features in questions (it's hard to kill a good flame war).

I've studied the issues carefully, and have concluded that anyone who gets involved in ending the argument wastes a lot of time that is better spent on more fruitful pursuits. Meanwhile, thousands of satisfied customers use MySQL every day for small to very large databases, including some very high traffic, well-regarded web sites such as Slashdot (http://slashdot.org), the news site renowned for the "SlashDot Effect" of causing other web servers to become unavailable after linking to them in a story.

Until 2000 MySQL had been released with its own license, which caused more debate among Open Source developers than its database features did. MySQL is now licensed under the GPL for the server and the LGPL for client libraries, making it free to use in commercial and Open Source software. In the same move, MySQL made alliances with commercial firms to offer a wider selection of support plans, as explained on the web site.

How does it rate on the other buyer's guide issues?

- MySQL has had stable releases since 1996. The web site clearly marks the current development and stable releases, and the developers patch the stable release often as they find and fix bugs while continuing work on newer versions.

- MySQL has excellent support via its mailing list. Typical new user questions are answered quickly, and the lead developer often responds in person to more challenging bug reports.

- The product ships with adequate documentation and has pointers to add-on tutorials and manuals on the Web. There are also several published books on MySQL, and other books on Perl programming include MySQL examples.

- Most web programming languages and tools have interfaces to MySQL, including Perl, PHP, Java, and C. Some commercial development products support it directly as well.

- MySQL has export abilities for saving copies of tables for backup, and a suite of utilities for other maintenance tasks, so long-term cost of managing the database shouldn't be much different from that of commercial databases.

4.4.4 PostgreSQL

PostgreSQL turns up alongside MySQL in so many discussions that one would think they are related. However, the main factor they have in common is their free availability. PostgreSQL contrasts nicely with MySQL and often serves as the purists' alternative in discussions of database merits.

The history of PostgreSQL spans over 20 years and includes luminaries of database modeling, but the most important events for our purposes are more recent. The current PostgreSQL Global Development Team took over what was then called

Postgres95 and began working it into a manageable, maintainable product while holding to the goals of releasing a full-featured database. In a remarkably short time given the size of the code base and the cast-of-thousands list of previous maintainers, they were turning out bug fixes at first and then new features, returning PostgreSQL to its proper place in the A-list of database choices.

2000 proved an interesting year for Open Source databases. A few months before MySQL allied and changed licenses, the PostgreSQL developers announced a deal with Landmark Communications to form a new company, Great Bridge. The purpose of the merger was to offer commercial support and focus to PostgreSQL, and to provide support from Great Bridge and PostgreSQL, Inc. In 2001 RedHat announced it would sell its own commercial version of the product.

Developers coming from a commercial database background will feel at home with PostgreSQL. It supports most of SQL92, including the more complex SELECT options such as subselects that MySQL lacks. PostgreSQL has full transaction support, meaning that an application can perform updates inside of a transaction and roll it back if anything goes wrong; until the transaction is committed, no other process will see the changes in the data.

Naturally these features have a performance cost, fueling the endless comparison discussions I mentioned earlier. Chances are good, though, that PostgreSQL will meet your needs for reasonable application workloads on reasonable hardware.

Comparing PostgreSQL to other databases misses many points of interest, however; I mentioned previously that PostgreSQL follows an object-relational model that has many features which are lacking in relational databases. The one I like most is its array type, which lets a record hold lists of values under one name and access them using a syntax similar to that of C and Perl.

PostgreSQL scores very high on the buyer's guide:

- Stable releases are updated 3–4 times a year from a mature code base.

- PostgreSQL has free support via a variety of mailing lists, including a list just for novices. Some language interfaces and utilities have their own mailing lists as well. Commercial support is also available as mentioned previously.

- The PostgreSQL Documentation Project has created an excellent set of manuals that are the envy of most other Open Source products. The text of Bruce Momjian's book on PostgreSQL is also online (http:\\www.ca.postgresql.org/docs/awbook.html).

- PostgreSQL is widely supported by programming languages and utilities, although it trails MySQL at least in the products I evaluated for this book.

- PostgreSQL has backup and archiving utilities that come with the distribution, and others are available via Open Source web sites.

4.4.5 Which to choose

Choosing between MySQL and PostgreSQL might seem simple—make a list of features you need and see which product is best. As the two products mature however the distinctions blur and the choice becomes more arbitrary.

My examples for the rest of the book will use MySQL, largely because certain products used in later chapters require it. Apart from those cases, however, PostgreSQL can replace MySQL with only a few changes in the code.

4.5 INSTALLING MySQL

MySQL is nicely self-contained, making it a good choice for installation from binary distributions if there is one for your platform. By comparison, I find myself rebuilding Apache with updates to various modules that I want built-in, so binary distributions don't do anything for me there. The download site (http://www.mysql.com) offers distributions for Linux and many Unix flavors, and the aforementioned Microsoft versions that come with a price tag.

Building MySQL from source is easy on Linux, but more challenging for some Unix-variants due to MySQL's reliance on threads, so read the documentation on configuration requirements carefully. Once you've mastered a configuration however, you should find it easy to keep your installation up to date new versions are released.

By either road, you should be able to get the server working quickly. Be sure to add it to your system startup procedures as well so that MySQL will be waiting for you after a reboot.

4.5.1 Set the root password

The installation procedure will admonish you to set a password for root, the account with the highest level of privileges in the database. Do this before going onto the next step, using a string you'll be able to remember (preferably without writing it down).

```
$ /usr/local/bin/mysqladmin -u root password 'mysqlrocks'
```

4.5.2 Create a database

Your applications will need at least one database in which to create tables and store data. You can use multiple databases to organize your tables more closely. My examples use a database called `Info`:

```
$ mysqladmin --user=root --password='mysqlrocks' create Info
Database "Info" created.
```

4.5.3 Add users and permissions

As I mentioned previously, you'll need to create at least one database user before any applications can connect to the database. Do *not* use the root account for applications!

```
$ mysql --user=root --password='mysqlrocks'
Welcome to the MySQL monitor.  Commands end with ; or \g.
Your MySQL connection id is 143 to server version: 3.22.32
```

```
Type 'help' for help.

mysql> GRANT SELECT,INSERT,UPDATE,DELETE ON Info.* TO web@localhost
    -> IDENTIFIED BY 'nouser';
Query OK, 0 rows affected (0.11 sec)
```

In this sample, the root account is used to log in to the database and create another user called web with a password of nouser. The new user is allowed to retrieve and update all of the tables in the Info database.

4.5.4 Create tables

While you're logged in as root, add the table used by the example:

```
mysql> use Info
Database changed
mysql> CREATE TABLE Addresses (
    -> Nickname VARCHAR(20) NOT NULL,
    -> Name VARCHAR(20) NOT NULL,
    -> Address1 VARCHAR(40),
    -> Address2 VARCHAR(40),
    -> City VARCHAR(20),
    -> State VARCHAR(3),
    -> Zip VARCHAR(10),
    -> Country VARCHAR(5),
    -> PRIMARY KEY (Nickname)
    -> );
Query OK, 0 rows affected (0.00 sec)

mysql> quit
```

4.5.5 Testing the server

If you've managed to perform the installation steps, you've already connected to the database server successfully. You'll want the application user to be able to connect too.

```
$ mysql --user=web --password=nouser
mysql> INSERT INTO Addresses VALUES ('Theo', 'Theo Petersen',
    -> '35 Home Address Lane', '', 'Hometown', 'CO', '80111', 'USA');
Query OK, 1 row affected (0.00 sec)

mysql> SELECT Name, City FROM Addresses;
+---------------+----------+
| Name          | City     |
+---------------+----------+
| Theo Petersen | Hometown |
+---------------+----------+
1 row in set (0.00 sec)
```

If your results look anything like this, your server is working fine.

4.5.6   Learning more

MySQL's distribution includes a manual that is comprehensive but not aimed at beginners. If you need help getting started with SQL, look for "SQL tutorial" on your favorite web search site.

See the bibliography for suggestions to add to your bookshelf.

4.6   DBI, PERL'S DATABASE INTERFACE

In touting the strengths of Perl I mentioned its role as a glue language for sticking other pieces of software together. One of the best examples of that gluing is the DBI module.

DBI, (database interface), is similar in nature to other database connector products such as ODBC and JDBC. Perl programs use DBI to connect a driver module called a DBD (database driver) to a database server and send and receive data.

DBI is considered a "thin" interface because it does not attempt to completely abstract the underlying databases. It provides generic functions for connecting to the database, sending commands, and retrieving results, but those commands are given in the native SQL dialect of the database server. DBI's role is not to conceal database peculiarities, but to provide a simple and common means of connecting Perl to servers.

As such, the key to DBI's success has been the quality of its interface and the driver modules. DBI provides very efficient methods for retrieving the results of queries, as you'll see in the examples to follow. The DBD modules are provided by experts in their respective databases who use Perl and DBI constantly in their own work and have every reason to want the best linkage between the two.

Prior to DBI, database connectivity with Perl was a matter of creating specially linked versions of the language or using an interface module specially created for that database. Those solutions worked, but choosing one was a big commitment since changing databases could potentially mean changing all of the code as well. With DBI, the code that connects the application to the database is largely generic; if the application sticks to generic SQL as well, it's possible to switch databases without too much code being lost.

Since applications don't often switch databases, that portability is nice but not a crucial concern. What's more important is that the generic, but efficient DBI methods make coding an application easy without sacrificing too much performance.

After looking through the examples here, you'll probably want to learn more about DBI's capabilities. See the module's built-in documentation, as well as the driver modules. There is also a separate DBI_FAQ module that contains pointers to further information, including a book just on programming with DBI.

4.6.1   Installing the Perl modules

DBI and the driver modules are installed via CPAN. From a privileged account, invoke the CPAN shell and tell it to grab the DBI module bundle for you:

```
# perl -MCPAN -e shell

cpan shell -- CPAN exploration and modules installation (v1.54)
ReadLine support enabled

cpan> install Bundle::DBI
```

Then install the DBD module for your database of choice:

```
cpan> install Bundle::DBD::mysql    # MySQL

cpan> install DBD::Pg               # PostgreSQL
```

While you're running CPAN, get the FAQ module:

```
cpan> install DBI::FAQ
```

Then read it via `perldoc`:

```
$ perldoc DBI::FAQ
```

There are also a variety of helper modules in the DBIx:: namespace. Look for them at http://search.cpan.org/.

4.6.2   Making a connection

Perl scripts invoke the DBI module with the usual `use` syntax, but do not touch the underlying DBD directly. DBI will call up the appropriate driver module when the script calls `connect`, as shown here:

```
use DBI;

# Open a MySQL database.
my ($dbname, $host, $user, $password) =
  qw(Info localhost web nouser);
my $dbh = DBI->connect("DBI:mysql:$dbname:$host",$user,$password)
  or die "Can't connect user $user to database $host:$dbname";
```

While this example has the database name, host, user, and password hard-coded, it demonstrates passing them to `connect` via variables. Your own code might obtain the user and password from a login form, or may use a generic user for all database connections as my CGI examples do.

The connect function returns a *database handle*, which traditionally goes by the name $dbh, although your code can call it anything you wish. This handle is used to make further queries of the database, and to close the connection to the database when the script is finished. DBI functions create other kinds of handles also; in particular, *statement handles* are used to get data back from SQL statements that return results which don't fit easily into a Perl variable.

If your system is set up to run the book's example scripts as-is, you can use `addrdb.pl` to test your DBI installation; it connects as shown in the example.

4.6.3 CGI scripts with DBI

The last CGI example used a hash file to implement an address book. It's time to revisit that example using DBI and the table and user created via the commands given previously. This version has a few other changes also; it provides a way to update an address, and drops the confirmation page when making changes.

The code is in addrdb.pl. It starts with the familiar opening:

```
#!/usr/local/bin/perl -wT

use strict;
use CGI;
use CGI::Carp;
use DBI;

# Load the CGI input data.
my $q = CGI->new;

# List the inputs that correspond to form fields.
my @fields =
  qw(Nickname Name Address1 Address2 City State Zip Country);
```

Next, the script has to open the database, or exit if it can't. This is somewhat inefficient, as I commented before with the hash file example, since not every invocation will use the database. It does make the code cleaner however, and I'll address the inefficiency later.

```
# Open the MySQL database.
my ($dbname, $host, $user, $password) =
  qw(Info localhost web nouser);
my $dbh = DBI->connect("DBI:mysql:$dbname:$host",$user,$password)
  or die "Can't connect user $user to database $host:$dbname";
```

In a more robust application we'd get the user and password from a prior form and pass them in here. Until we have a way to get the password securely, though, I'll leave that step out of the example.

Then we have helper functions, more or less the same as the previous example, although this time the data entry form is used more often:

```
# Print a navigation bar of submit buttons.
sub navbar {
    return join('',
                map {$q->submit('page',$_)}
                @_, 'New', 'List all', 'Query'
                );
}

# Print the entry/update form.
sub address_form {
    my $modify = shift;
```

```
my $nick = shift;
if ($modify) {
    $nick = $q->textfield(-name => 'Nickname',
                          -default => $nick,
                          -override => 1,
                          -size => 20);
}
else {
    $nick = $nick . $q->hidden('Nickname', $nick);
}
return
  $q->table
    (
     $q->Tr
     ([
       $q->td(['Nickname:',$nick]),
       $q->td(['Full name:',
               $q->textfield(-name => 'Name',
                             -default => shift,
                             -override => 1,
                             -size => 20)]),
       $q->td('Address:') .
       $q->td({-colspan => 3},
               $q->textfield(-name => 'Address1',
                             -default => shift,
                             -override => 1,
                             -size => 40)),
       $q->td .
       $q->td({-colspan => 3},
               $q->textfield(-name => 'Address2',
                             -default => shift,
                             -override => 1,
                             -size => 40)),
       $q->td(['City:',
               $q->textfield(-name => 'City',
                             -default => shift,
                             -override => 1,
                             -size => 20),
               'State/Province:',
               $q->textfield(-name => 'State',
                             -default => shift,
                             -override => 1,
                             -size => 3),
               'Zip/Postal code:',
               $q->textfield(-name => 'Zip',
                             -default => shift,
                             -override => 1,
                             -size => 10)]),
      $q->td(['Country:',
              $q->textfield(-name => 'Country',
```

```
                                          -default => shift,
                                          -override => 1,
                                          -size => 5)])
                 ]),
             );
    }
```

Note that `address_form` now takes parameters. `$modify` indicates whether the nickname can be changed. If not, it's displayed in normal text and also stored in a hidden field so that the browser will pass it back unmodified. The rest of the parameters are values for each field, supplied by Perl's `shift` function; if `address_form` is called without those parameters the fields will be filled with blanks. This allows the script to call the function to display an existing address and use the same form to modify it.

The code drops into sections for each page, again following the previous example. The first is for queries (the default page if no parameters were received or only the `find` parameter was passed along). If the `find` parameter was passed in, it also queries the database via DBI:

```
# Display the appropriate form, depending on input.
my $page = $q->param('page');
my $find = $q->param('find');
if (!$page || $page eq 'Query' || $find && !$page) {
    print $q->header, $q->start_html('Query by nickname'),
    $q->h1('Query address book'),$q->p,$q->start_form;
    if ($find) {
        my @values =
          $dbh->selectrow_array
            ('SELECT * FROM Addresses WHERE Nickname = ?',
             undef, $find);
        if (@values) {
            print address_form(0,@values),$q->p,
            'Make any changes, then click',
            $q->submit('page','Update'),$q->p,
            'Or click',$q->submit('page','Delete'),
            'to delete this addres',$q->p;
        }
        else {
            print "$find not found", $q->p;
        }
    }
    print "Enter a nickname:",
    $q->textfield(-name => 'find', -size => 20),
    $q->p,navbar,$q->end_form;
}
```

The call to `$dbh->selectrow_array` is the database query. It takes an SQL `SELECT` statement and sends it to the database, then retrieves one row of output and puts the fields into an array. This is convenient for queries that return only one row, such as those which look up a single address.

Note the odd WHERE clause in the query:

```
'SELECT * FROM Addresses WHERE Nickname = ?'
```

The '?' tells DBI to expect a *bind parameter*, a Perl variable that will replace it in the statement. $find then follows as a parameter to selectrow_array and is dropped into place when the query executes.

Since the SELECT statement is passed along as text to selectrow_array, we could have gotten the same effect by putting the value of $find into the query directly:

```
"SELECT * FROM Addresses WHERE Nickname = '$find'"
```

By putting the query string in double quotes, Perl will interpolate $find into the string and pass the result along to the function. This is fine as long as the interpolated variable won't contain quotes, which would disrupt the SQL syntax. In my own code I tend to use interpolated strings as long as they are convenient and safe, since it is more readable to me later.

Bind parameters have a strong advantage over interpolated strings: DBI automatically escapes any characters in a bind parameter that would bother SQL. To do this properly though, DBI needs to know what sort of value a parameter is. Note that in the code, selectrow_array receives a second parameter of undef; that is a placeholder for driver-specific *query attributes*, a hash of information you can pass in to help the underlying database handle the parameters. (See the DBI documentation for more information.) Lacking that information, DBI assumes the parameter is text, which works fine for this example and most databases.

There is one other point to note here. Since I used SELECT * the fields of the row are in the order that they are defined in the table, and selectrow_array maintains that order. I've conveniently defined the table and the address form with the same fields in the same order. However, a change to either would cause this code to break. A safer version would specify the desired fields in the proper order.

The code passes the retrieved data along to address_form to be displayed to the user, and also provides buttons for updating or deleting the data. This conveniently ties all the functions that require retrieved data onto one page.

The next section lets the user add an address:

```
elsif ($page eq 'New') {
    print $q->header, $q->start_html('New address'),
    $q->h1('Address book'),$q->p,
    'Enter an address:',$q->p,
    $q->start_form, address_form(1),
    navbar('Add'), $q->end_form;
}
```

It doesn't do much other than call `address_form` again. Since no data is passed in to display, the form will be blank.

The next section stores the data passed along when the user clicks the Add button:

```
elsif ($page eq 'Add') {
    $dbh->do('INSERT INTO Addresses VALUES (?,?,?,?,?,?,?,?)',
            undef, map({$q->param($_)} @fields))
      or die $dbh->errstr;
    print $q->header, $q->start_html('Success'),
    $q->h1('New address entered');
    print $q->start_form, navbar, $q->end_form;
}
```

The SQL INSERT statement adds a row to a table. Note the use of bind parameters in the VALUES() clause. This version is somewhat fragile, since the fields have to be defined in the table in the same order given by the @fields array. VALUES() could be preceded by the list of field names in this form:

```
'INSERT INTO Addresses (Nickname, Name, Address1, Address2,
        City, State, Zip, Country) VALUES (?,?,?,?,?,?,?,?)'
```

An even more clever version would construct the field list from the @fields array, as I'll do in the update code which follows.

The function $dbh->do is used to execute any SQL statement which doesn't retrieve data. It uses the same order of parameters as the select functions: statement first, then attributes, followed by bind parameters. do also returns a false value if something goes wrong in executing the statement, so we check for that possibility with the or die Perl idiom and get the error message using $dbh->errstr.

The next two bits of code handle updates and deletes:

```
elsif ($page eq 'Update') {
    my @modify = @fields[1 .. $#fields];
    my $sql = 'UPDATE Addresses SET ' .
      join(',', map {"$_ = ?"} @modify) .
        " WHERE Nickname = '" . $q->param('Nickname') . "'";
    $dbh->do($sql, undef, map {$q->param($_)} @modify)
      or die $dbh->errstr;
    print $q->header, $q->start_html('Success'),
    $q->h1('Updates entered');
    print $q->start_form, navbar, $q->end_form;
}
elsif ($page eq 'Delete') {
    $dbh->do('DELETE FROM Addresses WHERE Nickname = ?',
            undef, $q->param('Nickname'))
      or die $dbh->errstr;
    print $q->header, $q->start_html('Success'),
    $q->h1('Address for', $q->param('Nickname'), 'deleted');
    print $q->start_form, navbar, $q->end_form;
}
```

As promised, the Update section builds its SQL UPDATE statement from the @fields array, after first dropping out the Nickname field. The statement is then passed as the first parameter to do as before. The Delete section is similar enough, and both statements have a WHERE clause in common (though they pass in the nickname in different ways). When updating or deleting, you must tell the database which record (or records) to affect by supplying a WHERE clause that would retrieve the desired data in a SELECT statement.

The next section of the script displays all the records in a table format:

```
elsif ($page eq 'List all') {
    print $q->header, $q->start_html('Display address book'),
    $q->h1('Address book'),$q->p,
    'Address book listing:',$q->p;
    my $rows = $dbh->selectall_arrayref('SELECT * FROM Addresses');
    if ($rows) {
        print $q->table($q->Tr([map {$q->td($_)} @$rows]));
    }
    else {
        print $dbh->errstr;
    }
    print $q->start_form,
    navbar, $q->end_form;
}
```

This example shows another DBI select function, selectall_arrayref. This function takes a SELECT statement and retrieves all the rows it matches, then gives them back to the program as a reference to an array of arrays. That is, it returns $rows, which is an array reference; each element of @$rows is also an array reference, and those arrays contain the fields of each row. If selectall_arrayref returns a false value then something went wrong in executing the statement.

The references to rows and fields may seem a bit deep there, but actually work out to be very convenient, since CGI.pm's HTML helper functions do clever things with array references: $q->td makes each field into a table cell and $q->Tr makes each returned record into a row of the table. This allows for the very compact call to $q->table which displays all the data.

The closing portion of the script isn't all that interesting:

```
else {
    print $q->header, $q->start_html('Error'),
    $q->h1('No input function'),$q->p,
    $q->start_form, navbar, $q->end_form;
}

# End the document.
print $q->end_html;
$dbh->disconnect;
```

The main thing to note here is the call to $dbh->disconnect, which closes the database connection.

While there is still much to be desired for an address database, this script provides a quick tour of DBI in a small space. It's time to drop the example for now and look at other tools.

4.7 DATA MAINTENANCE VIA CGI

Putting Perl's DBI and CGI modules together shows off much that is good about the language. Perl has clever tools that make short work out of complicated tasks, once you learn how to use them.

A common theme in web database applications is the generic web interface: given the definition of a table, have Perl (or another language of choice) create CGI forms and controls for displaying and maintaining the table. In fact, there are several such tools available to the public, and probably more of them lurking privately. Perl implementations include WDBI and HTMLViews.

4.7.1 WDBI

The Web Database Interface started out as Bo Frese Rasmussen's WDB, then was expanded and rewritten by Jeff Rowe (and later other contributors) into a very complete toolkit for generating and running database query and update forms via CGI. It is built on top of DBI, and uses an adapter module for each DBD that provides administrative functions for the database that are beyond the scope of normal DBI operations. Adapters are provided for many DBDs, including those for MySQL and PostgreSQL.

WDBI is mature with an active user base. The home site (http://www.wdbi.net/) offers the latest version, documentation, tutorials, and subscription to the mailing list. The installation documentation is sparse, and getting WDBI to work initially required a bit of trial and error. After getting the product in place, the online documentation is very helpful in guiding users through the basics of queries and updates.

The product's web site indicates that WDBI is in the process of a major overhaul, so a modernized version may be available by the time you read this. If not, the version I used makes a fine utility for database managers. With more effort it can be used as a tool for general users.

4.7.2 HTMLView, an alternative to WDBI

DBIx::HTMLView is another Perl-based solution for creating CGI forms for tables. It takes an object-oriented approach to the task, supplying object classes for almost every entity one can imagine in a database interface—various field types, tables, databases, and so on. One nice effect of this approach is that collections of data, such as rows selected from a table, can be used wherever fields are allowed, making it easy to construct master/detail forms where a record in one table is associated with a set of rows from another.

While I like the architecture of HTMLView, I find it to be more of an application-building tool than a quick way to display and update records. For simple tasks I prefer WDBI, so that's what I'll show in the examples to follow.

4.7.3   Installing WDBI

After downloading and unpacking the distribution, go to your Apache root directory (`/usr/local/apache` in my examples) and create a `wdbi` subdirectory under both `cgi-bin` and `htdocs`. Then copy the files from WDBI's `html_docs` and `images` directories into `htdocs/wdbi`; they will provide graphics and online help for the generated forms.

Next, copy the `wdbi.cgi` script from WDBI's `cgi-bin` directory to Apache's `cgi-bin`. Go to `cgi-bin/wdbi` (under Apache's root) and create a subdirectory, `conf`, and copy in the distribution's `conf/wdbi.conf` and the adapter for your database (`mysql_dbi.pl` in my case).

WDBI uses form definition files (FDF) to describe database tables and set permitted actions on their data. We'll create an FDF shortly, but before that we need a place for the files to live. In `cgi-bin/wdbi` create an `fdf` subdirectory, then give it a subdirectory for each database which will have WDBI interfaces. In my example I'll use the Info database again, so I'll create `cgi-bin/wdbi/fdf/Info`.

Under Apache's root directory you'll now have a set of files and directories like the following:

- *htdocs/wdbi*—contains image files and HTML help
- *cgi-bin/wdbi/fdf*—directory for database subdirectories
- *cgi-bin/wdbi/fdf/Info*—example database subdirectory
- *cgi-bin/wdbi/conf*—directory for configuration files
- *cgi-bin/wdbi/conf/mysql_dbi.pl*—DBD adapter
- *cgi-bin/wdbi/conf/wdbi.conf*—WDBI configuration
- *cgi-bin/wdbi.cgi*—main CGI script

Now it's time to do the configuration. Edit `wdbi.cgi` and look for the variable `$CONFIG_DIR`, then change the path to the full path of the `conf` directory—`/usr/local/apache/cgi-bin/wdbi/conf` in my example. Then edit `wdbi.conf` and read the documentation for each variable, setting the values appropriately. For my example, these are the values that I changed from the defaults:

```
$WDBI = ( $ENV{'SCRIPT_NAME'} ) ? $ENV{'SCRIPT_NAME'} : "/cgi-
bin/wdbi.cgi";
$SECURE_WDBI = "/cgi-bin/wdbi.cgi";
$FORMDIR = "/usr/local/apache/cgi-bin/wdbi/fdf";
$USER = "web";
$PSWD = "nouser";
```

These changes reflect the file layout given earlier and the username and password I've used for the Info database.

Verify that the `wdbi.cgi` script is executable and that Apache's user can read all the files in both directory trees. WDBI is now installed, but before you can use it, you have to give it more information about your database tables, as shown in the next section.

4.7.4 Creating a definition file

While some systems generate interface forms on the fly, WDBI uses an FDF to describe each table and set which actions are allowed on the data. By customizing FDF files you can create very complete and usable interfaces for all of your tables.

The WDBI distribution's `bin` directory contains scripts for generating a basic FDF file for a given table. Choose the script that matches your database adapter (`mysqlfdf` in my case) and copy it to where you keep your executable scripts (such as `/usr/local/bin`). Verify that it is executable, then go to the FDF directory for your database (`/usr/local/apache/cgi-bin/wdbi/fdf/Info` for the example) and run it to create a file.

Here is how I created an FDF for the Addresses table:

```
mysqlfdf -d Info -t Addresses -u web -p nouser -o update,insert,delete
```

Most of the switches in the command line are self-explanatory. The options switch (`-o`) determines what actions can be performed on the table besides selecting rows. In this case, the user can insert, update and delete rows also.

The output of the command went to `Addresses.fdf`. You can use the file as-is, but I wanted to modify the field labels (which by default will be marked only by the field name) to match the previous example, so I edited the file and changed them:

```
FIELD  = Name
label  = Full name
column = Name
type   = char # 12;
length = 20

FIELD  = Address1
label  = Address
column = Address1
type   = char # 12;
length = 40
non_null

FIELD  = Address2
label  = .
column = Address2
type   = char # 12;
length = 40
non_null
```

You can see from these attributes how FDF describes fields. You can also change the labels on buttons and links if you wish, and add considerably more to the form. See WDBI's FDF documentation for more details.

4.7.5   Using WDBI

The FDF file is ready, so let's try it out in the browser. WDBI puts the database and table names into the URL of a request; the form created earlier has a URL of http://www.example.site/cgi-bin/wdbi.cgi/Info/Addresses/form. Note the path to the wdbi.cgi script is followed by the database name (not fdf) and then the table; form tells WDBI to display the main query form.

If you've set up the examples, change the URL in the example to match your site name and give it a try. You should see something like the screen shown in figure 4.1.

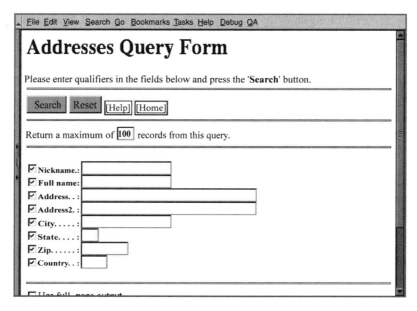

Figure 4.1   WDBI query screen

If you click Search you'll get a list of records in the Addresses table. Click More for a one-page display of a record's data; it doesn't look quite like our example, but it works just as well.

Returning to the main query form, try searching for records by entering data into one of the fields. WDBI's default search mode is to match the entered characters anywhere in the field, so putting Rd into the address field will bring up any record containing Rd. The search result is shown in figure 4.2.

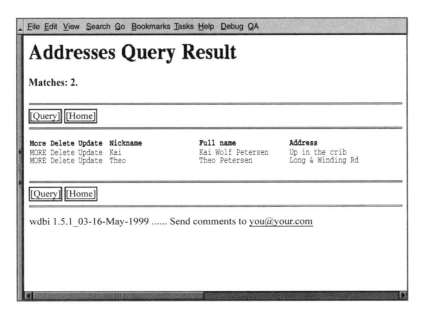

Figure 4.2 Search results

When searching, you can clear the form by clicking Reset. Check the Use Full Page Output box to have the search results displayed in a more readable format, as shown in figure 4.3.

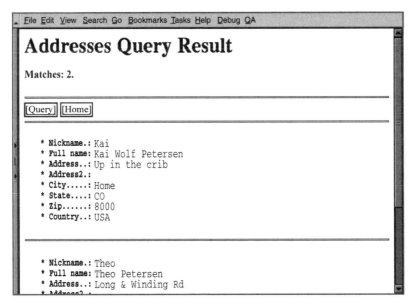

Figure 4.3 Full page output

After retrieving records with a search, WDBI offers links to Update and Delete along with each row. (This requires the concise output, not the full-page output just demonstrated.) Delete will remove the record from the table; Update takes you to a form shown in figure 4.4, where you can change values and send them back to the database:

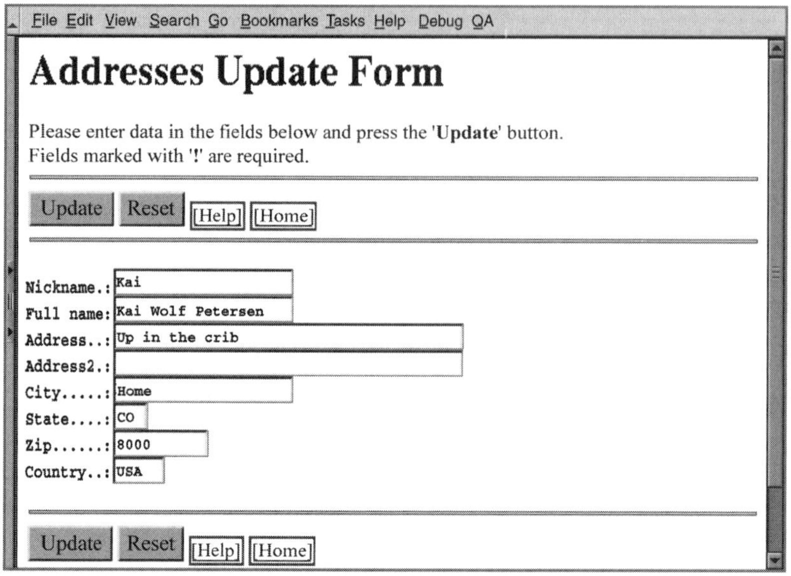

Figure 4.4   Update page

Inserting a record requires starting with a different URL: /cgi-bin/wdbi.cgi/Info /Addresses/insert_form. That brings up a form similar to the update page, with an Insert button to add the record to the database.

4.7.6   Enhancing forms

These examples show only the simplest of WDBI pages. FDF includes a large number of attributes for forms that allow each operation to be customized.

To be a suitable tool for general users, WDBI has to provide more than a simple form interface to SQL commands. For example, both individual fields and whole records must be validated before an insert or update, and other constraints apply to deleting records. While some databases allow administrators to specify these rules in the database itself, that won't help the hapless users whose form mysteriously doesn't do what he wants when he clicks a button.

FDF allows the form designer to include Perl code to perform these checks before writing or deleting data. You can also use Perl expressions to reformat a field (when retrieving or writing data, or both), compute a value, create menus, headers, and footers for your forms and take over almost any part of a query.

The FDF generation program creates single table forms, but WDBI also allows tables to be joined and sorted to create the query data. Some restrictions apply to updating joined tables. You can control the format of the table and page views of queries, set the maximum number of rows on a page and so on.

FDF also allows the designer to specify the user and password for a query, but doesn't allow them to be entered from a form. To provide secure interactions you'll need to create a separate password file and use it to authenticate users. See chapter 6 for more information.

If you are going to use WDBI for a large set of tables, you'll want to create administration menus for the various forms. A simple menu would consist of a list of FDF-enabled tables with links to the URLS for the query and insert forms. Fancier schemes might combine an authentication mechanism with a list of allowed actions permitted to the user.

Regular users of WDBI will want better performance than the CGI version gives. See the next chapter to find out how to make WDBI and other CGI scripts work faster using mod_perl.

CHAPTER 5

Better scripting

The scripts from chapter 4 provide glimpses of real-world web applications, but their usefulness stops at being examples. The scripts are slow, even with only one person using them. And that single user focus is another problem, limiting us to a personal web site application.

In this chapter we'll address the real-world issues that we put off in the beginning sections, and look at tools for better scripting.

5.1   *WHY CGI IS SLOW*

Let's look again at the workflow diagram (figure 5.1) of a CGI application:

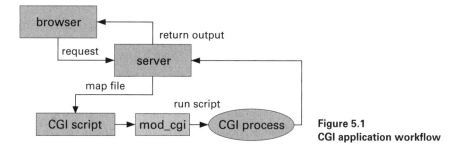

Figure 5.1
CGI application workflow

An interactive CGI application is a two- or three-step process. To start things off, the browser sends a URL request to the server, which is sitting around waiting for something to do. The server maps the URL onto a CGI script and runs it, shipping the output from the script back to the browser. The browser then displays it to the user, ending step one. We'll assume the script's output included form elements to get some kind of input from the user.

The user interacts with the form and clicks Submit, thus beginning step two. The browser sends another request to the server, using the URL given in the form's ACTION attribute. It either sends the input values along as part of the URL or posts them separately, depending on whether the action is a GET or POST. In any event, the server receives the request and the inputs and maps the URL onto a CGI application, either the same as in step one or a different script for handling inputs. It runs this application and passes the inputs along.

If the application doesn't give the user feedback, the process is complete. Commonly, however, an application will send some sort of confirmation back, which is step three: the output of the CGI is again sent to the browser and displayed to the user. Steps two and three are diagrammed in figure 5.2.

On a system with a bored web server and no other traffic, this scheme might work quite well. But consider the implications for a production system receiving, say, five queries or submissions per second: for each CGI interaction, the responding Apache

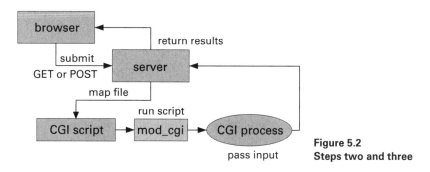

Figure 5.2
Steps two and three

child must (1) fork off a new process to execute the command shell, (2) compile the Perl script (or other interpreter action if the CGI app is in another language), (3) execute the scripts and clean up after itself.

Assuming the usual requirements of a business application make the picture even worse: each of those requests will connect to the database, compile queries, then disconnect. It's an amazing amount of overhead for a single client-to-server round of interaction.

The obvious method to reduce that overhead is to keep the CGI application alive between requests: start up the shell and Perl once, connect to the database once, and then keep talking to the browser until the user's business is finished. The actual solution is made more complicated by the stateless nature of the HTTP protocol.

5.1.1 Stateless protocol

Programmers who want to build better web applications quickly encounter an interesting challenge of web application programming: the HTTP protocol is *stateless*, meaning that no inherent information about previous interactions is maintained by a web server (or client for that matter).

This is a good thing if you are creating a web server for static content; Apache can use any number of child processes your system can handle and doesn't have to figure out which child should respond to a given request. Since the protocol is stateless, any Apache process listening at the given site and port can respond to any client.

Statelessness, however, adds to the challenge of speeding up CGI applications. If the Apache process can't predict who will talk to it next, it has to be ready to handle messages from any number of clients. A given client could be starting a new application, browsing through multiple pages of a list, or sending an update for the database.

One solution to both problems is to have the web server create "personalized" CGI processes for each client. When an initial request comes in, the web server spawns a new application process and redirects the browser to talk to it (by giving it a unique port number, say). The application process compiles and connects to the database just once, then acts as a miniserver for the browser, responding to each request until the user indicates that he is finished. At that point the application process can disconnect from the database and shut down.

While attractive at first, this approach has a number of drawbacks. For a busy site, the number of clients could be quite large, making for an equally large number of application processes on the server. Most of those processes will be idle, since the user has to interact with the form on his browser and then respond. The user could also make phone calls, read documentation, or forget to click the Finished button (this being a purely hypothetical example, of course), leaving the application process inactive for long periods. The programmer has to decide when to shut down an inactive process and how to respond if the user then tries to get back in touch.

Working around the statelessness of HTTP thus proves to open a can of worms that we'd prefer to leave closed. How can we stay within the protocol and solve the CGI performance problem?

5.1.2 Session-oriented persistent CGI

There are a number of products available for speeding up CGI, mostly built around the buzzword-laden model of *persistent* CGI applications with a *session-oriented* framework. Persistent means that the CGI application runs in a process that stays alive in between requests, allowing it to save on compile time and keep its database connections open. Session-oriented applications get around the statelessness of the protocol by storing data about the running application in some sort of session database. Each request is associated with a session, and the CGI application has some means of retrieving state information from the session and storing it again as the user works.[1]

Going back to the Apache workflow diagram (figure 5.3), let's see how this changes things:

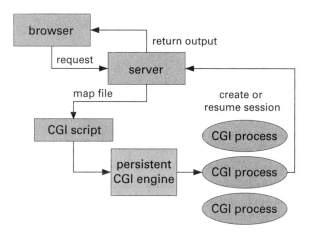

Figure 5.3
Workflow for persistent CGI

The user sends an initial request to the web server, which maps the request onto a CGI application and passes it to a persistent application process. It may have to start a new process if none are currently ready. The application process either creates a session or resumes an old one, depending on how the session framework is used in each case. The application sends a form back to the user's browser along with some means of identifying the session in the user's reply; it could use cookies, a hidden field, a specially coded URL, or combinations of these. The user interacts with the form and clicks Submit, which sends a request back to the server along with the inputs and the session identifier.

---

[1] Nonpersistent CGI applications also need some kind of session management if any of the data they serve is user-specific. I'm discussing them together because it seems common for a CGI application framework to offer both persistence and session management.

The web server picks up the request and hands it to a persistent application process as before. The request includes the session ID, which the application uses to retrieve the session data. It now knows everything it needs about the user and the work in progress, so it processes the user's inputs and sends back only results. By using sessions in this way, any ready application process can respond to any request.

After the exchange is over, the persistent application process goes into some form of wait state while the web server listens for requests. The next message to the CGI application could be from any user, so it can't maintain any user-related information. Neither can it expect to perform operations for different users in a given order. It's still stateless in that sense; all of the state information is kept in the sessions.

The persistent CGI applications must store any changes to the session data along with the ID each time the user sends a request to the server, and session data must be available to all of the CGI application processes equally. This makes the session framework a defining choice in how to implement faster CGI applications, along with the choice in how to make the application processes persistent. While it would be ideal if normal CGI scripts could be made persistent without change, developers should expect some trade-off of extra programming time for extra performance.

5.2   *FastCGI*

There are a number of CGI application products available in the commercial and Open Source spaces. FastCGI is one of the more popular entries, and happens to be in both categories: there is an Open Source FastCGI module for Apache and commercial versions of the product for other servers.

FastCGI is an interesting modification of the personalized application process notion I mentioned earlier. A FastCGI application starts out as a normal CGI application written in any language. To make it work as a persistent server, the developer wraps the application in a small procedure that performs FastCGI initializations and then enters a loop that waits for messages from the web server and processes them by running the application with appropriate CGI inputs. In many cases the application can be used as-is.

The Apache mod_fastcgi handles the web server portion of the FastCGI protocol. Its configuration tells Apache to map certain URLs onto FastCGI application wrappers. When Apache receives a request for a FastCGI application, mod_fastcgi intercepts it and sends the appropriate message to the application (which is waiting for messages in the FastCGI wrapper as described). If no application process is available, the module can start new ones up to configured limits.

That's the simple explanation, but FastCGI goes much further. Along with the request information and CGI inputs, FastCGI sends an execution environment to the application process. The CGI app can use environment variables and other system information reliably, even if the application and the web server are on different machines. That remote execution property allows FastCGI sites to balance their work load on multiple machines and isolate sensitive information behind firewalls.

FastCGI also has some goodies for developers: an application that has been modified for use in FastCGI can still run as a normal CGI application, allowing programmers to run new code in simplified environments and take advantage of CGI debugging aids.

FastCGI is a good choice for speeding up CGI applications, and it scales well to large, demanding sites. However, it does not provide anything further on the web server side. If your application calls for closer integration with Apache, you need to move on.

5.3 THE CASE FOR MOD_PERL

In selecting a web application platform, my own strong preference is for mod_perl, which integrates Perl into the Apache server and gives programmers complete control over their web applications.

Instead of making separate persistent CGI processes, mod_perl brings the application back into the web server. Each Apache process has the Perl interpreter built in, and can run Perl applications directly rather than spawning a child process to run the CGI application. Once the Perl code has been compiled it stays ready in the server process, along with any database connections made by the first pass, so the second and further runs of the same code will be very fast.

mod_perl's configuration directives allow the developer to specify modules and scripts to load at initialization time. When Apache forks off child processes, each child gets a copy of the parent's memory;[2] that includes the compiled Perl code and initialized modules, so these become shared by all of the server processes, making the whole setup even better for large applications.

It would be an injustice to compare mod_perl to other products only on the basis of its CGI performance features. mod_perl doesn't just embed Perl into Apache; it gives Perl scripts all of Apache's internal tools for translating and mapping requests onto resources. Perl programmers can write scripts that translate complex URLs onto applications (which can be mod_perl scripts or regular CGI) or files, or take over the whole request-mapping process for a site in other ways.

For example, suppose a site has a photo archive where images are stored in a relational database. The site wants to present the database as a simple directory, http://www.example.site/photos/, while keeping the images in the database instead of copying each to separate files. Using mod_perl, a developer could write Perl code which does these translations:

1 Intercept incoming requests to http://www.example.site/photos/ and return a page listing the images in the database as links. The page is created by querying the database for the current list of available images.

---

[2] Assuming you're using an OS that has fork, of course, and Apache is configured to use it. Thread-based Apache will be even more efficient when it's ready for production use.

2 For requests such as http://www.example.site/photos/cat.png, query the data-base and retrieve the image data, then send it back to the browser with appropriate MIME headers so that the user will see the image.

Remember, this all happens inside the same server process that received the request. If those suggestions got you thinking about DBI queries and building HTML, you'll want to learn more about mod_perl.

5.3.1 Buyer's guide

The questions from the buyer's guide mostly bring up mod_perl's strengths:

- *Stable version*—mod_perl releases are tied to stable versions of Apache, although there is often more than one release of mod_perl for a given Apache version as bugs get fixed. The mod_perl web site, http://perl.apache.org, always has a pointer to the stable version of mod_perl that goes with the production version of Apache.

- *Ongoing development and support*—mod_perl is developed primarily by Doug MacEachern, who is a member of the Apache Group. He is a very active member of the mod_perl mailing list, answering an amazing number of questions and supplying patches for many bug reports. The list members are also terrific about helping both new programmers and old hands who are trying out new things.

- *Documentation*—mod_perl has both printed and online documentation. When new converts send questions to the mailing list, replies often include pointers to relevant sections of the amazingly comprehensive online guide at http://perl.apache.org/guide/.

- *Leverage*—If you've committed to Perl for other business use, mod_perl is a terrific investment. Many add-on tools that I'll discuss later either require mod_perl or take advantage of it for better service.

- *Continuing costs*—mod_perl is not a trivial addition to Apache, but most of the cost in human terms is paid at the beginning. Once you've configured mod_perl and set up the applications, you'll find that it doesn't require any more on-going administration than does Apache itself.

What is the downside? The two issues that seem to come up most often on the mod_perl mailing list are resource usage and scalability.

As we've said, mod_perl brings all of Perl into the Apache web server. All of it. The resulting processes use far more memory and start more slowly than does a "straight" Apache process. Since Apache's default means of handling more traffic is to fork off more children, a busy mod_perl site can eat up memory at a frightening rate.

Being a glutton for system resources, mod_perl forces site administrators to face scalability issues before deploying applications. How can the traffic be divided among multiple machines? How do we get the best use of heavyweight mod_perl processes?

We'll discuss those issues later, but for now the short answer is that since mod_perl is in Apache, any scheme that would work for Apache can be employed to mod_perl's relief. Typical sites use a lightweight Apache or other server as a front-end that forwards traffic to the heavyweight application processes. More complex schemes use additional Apache modules to balance the work load.

While FastCGI has built-in tools for shipping work off to other machines, mod_perl has Apache. Apache's redirection and other capabilities provide the toolkit for handling these problems, but it is up to the site developers to use it.

5.4 INSTALLING MOD_PERL

While most Perl add-ons are easily installed using CPAN (as demonstrated in prior sections), mod_perl has a more complex configuration process that makes using CPAN difficult. You can download the module using CPAN, but then expect to continue the job by hand.

Apache modules can either be linked in statically or loaded at run-time from dynamic link libraries (as can Perl modules). Until recently however the dynamic method has been very buggy for mod_perl and some other Apache modules, and when it does work it is a bit slower and uses even more memory. So it's common to see mod_perl built directly into Apache. The installation instructions in the mod_perl distribution can guide you through either method, but in my examples I'll assume that mod_perl is statically linked.

In the static case, mod_perl requires an Apache source distribution, which is one reason I suggested earlier that most sites will want to install Apache from source. During the configuration and build process mod_perl compiles its library and stores other needed files inside the Apache source tree. It does not modify any actual Apache source files; the APACI configuration script finds the needed modules when you tell it to build Apache with mod_perl support. Pass along the location of your Apache source via the `APACHE_SRC=` option to `Makefile.PL` (the mod_perl configuration script).

mod_perl can be built dynamically without access to Apache sources using the newer APXS tools. If you have installed a binary distribution of Apache, make sure it came with APXS, and pass along its location to the mod_perl configuration via the `WITH_APXS=` option of `Makefile.PL`.

I mentioned that mod_perl's configuration is complicated, but it's actually very simple if you have already built Apache and you tell mod_perl to build in all of its features. That may sound as if it would make the already large mod_perl even larger, and I'm sure it does, but the difference between the minimum mod_perl server and the fully loaded version is not enough to trouble over; or put another way, once you've decided to link Perl into your web server, there's not much point in quibbling about details. Later, when you know what features you will be using you can strip down mod_perl to eliminate overhead and security risks.

5.4.1 Building and rebuilding

mod_perl is configured and built using the usual Perl process: run the Perl script `Makefile.PL`, then `make`, `make test`, and `make install`. It requires a few extra steps in between though to get Apache ready to run the tests.

`Makefile.PL` takes mod_perl configuration options as mentioned before. Here is an example configuration which will build mod_perl statically into Apache with all features enabled:

```
perl Makefile.PL APACHE_SRC=/usr/local/apache_1.3.12/src DO_HTTPD=1 \
    PREP_HTTPD=1 USE_APACI=1 EVERYTHING=1
make
```

Substitute the correct path to your Apache sources. If `Makefile.PL` ran without complaint, use make to build the Perl side of things. Then you can use make to build Apache.

```
cd /usr/local/apache_1.3.12
./configure --activate-module=src/modules/perl/libperl.a
make
```

If you previously built Apache with any other modules, add them to the `configure` line here also. Then build Apache with the requested modules before returning to mod_perl for testing.

```
cd /usr/local/mod_perl-1.24
make test && make install
```

If the tests went well, the Perl modules will be installed and ready for Apache to use. Go back to Apache's source directory one more time and install it also:

```
cd /usr/local/apache_1.3.12
make install
```

The installation documentation that ships with mod_perl will explain other ways of doing this, without so much jumping back and forth. I prefer the method above because it works from a clean set of sources as well as with an Apache I've built with other modules.

5.4.2 Apache run-time configuration

When we set up CGI scripts in Apache we needed to add lines to the `httpd.conf` configuration file telling the server what directory contained executable scripts. Similarly, we need to tell Apache when to use mod_perl to process a script.

It's a common Apache technique to use a directory for each type of script the server can run—CGI scripts go into `cgi-bin`, for instance. For simple CGI-style Perl scripts that run under mod_perl we'll create a `perl` directory at the same level, and tell Apache to send any requests to that directory through mod_perl:

```
Alias /perl/ "/usr/local/apache/perl/"
<Directory "/usr/local/apache/perl">
    SetHandler perl-script
```

```
    PerlHandler Apache::Registry
    Options ExecCGI
</Directory>
```

The directives in the example can be conveniently located next to the same set of directives that tell Apache how to handle the `cgi-bin` directory.

The first line creates a mapping from URLs that begin with `/perl/` onto the new directory. The `Directory` block which follows tells Apache three thing.:

1 `SetHandler perl-script` tells Apache that all of the scripts in this directory are mod_perl scripts. An Apache handler is a procedure that is invoked when a URL maps onto a file meeting certain conditions; the `AddHandler` directive applies handlers to files by type, while `SetHandler` applies them to files in a `Directory` or `Location` or `File` section. If we wanted to store mod_perl scripts among the static documents in Apache's `htdocs` directory we could use `AddHandler perl-script pl` to tell Apache which files were mod_perl's responsibility. Similarly, we could use the `cgi-script` handler to tell Apache to treat them as normal CGI scripts.

2 `PerlHandler Apache::Registry` in turn tells mod_perl how to handle the scripts. Think of it as the handler-within-a-handler that directs mod_perl to run the script via the Apache::Registry module. We'll discuss Apache::Registry in some depth shortly.

3 `Options ExecCGI` tells Apache that these files are executable. Without that option and appropriate file permissions, Apache would refuse to execute the scripts via mod_perl or any other means. Refresh your memory about the processing of `Options` directives to see how you could use this option to control the use of your scripts.

As a web site gets more complicated it becomes important to look at ways to keep the configuration manageable. In my server's `httpd.conf` file I have the three directives inside an `IfModule` section, along with settings for the usual command-line switches:

```
# mod_perl scripts
<IfModule mod_perl.c>
    PerlWarn On
    PerlTaintCheck On
    Alias /perl/ "/usr/local/apache/perl/"
    <Directory "/usr/local/apache/perl">
        SetHandler perl-script
        PerlHandler Apache::Registry
        Options ExecCGI
    </Directory>
</IfModule>
```

`IfModule` applies its directives only if the Apache server is built with, or has dynamically loaded, the corresponding module, which in this case is mod_perl. While wrapping those directives inside another section might seem like wasted overhead in this case, in principle it allows a site manager to create generic configuration files for multiple servers with sections that will apply only to those servers that are built with the appropriate code. To be more correct, the given section (and anything else which uses `Alias` or `ScriptAlias`) should be inside another `IfModule` block that checks for mod_alias.

The `PerlWarn` and `PerlTaintCheck` directives take the place of Perl's `-w` and `-T` command line switches respectively. We need to specify those values via the configuration file since Perl will be initialized by Apache, not a command line. If you are using Perl 5.6 or later you can replace `PerlWarn` with `use warnings` in your scripts and modules as you prefer, but there is no equivalent for taint checking—it is on for the whole interpreter or not.

Another way to keep the configuration manageable is to use the `Include` directive, which loads a specified configuration file similarly to the way the C language uses `#include`. If your site makes extensive use of mod_perl you'll probably have a correspondingly large amount of configuration instructions. By isolating all of these into their own file, say `mod_perl.conf`, you can edit the Perl and Apache configurations separately. In your `httpd.conf` file include the mod_perl configuration like so:

```
<IfModule mod_perl.c>
    Include conf/mod_perl.conf
</IfModule>
```

Note that the file path in the `Include` directive is relative to Apache's root directory, not to the current file.

Now you can build up your mod_perl configuration in its own file. This can be a tremendous boon if you maintain multiple sites with similar configurations. Remember to tell Apache to reload its configuration after making these changes.

Along a similar vein, the `IfDefine` directive applies its section if a corresponding `-D` switch was given on Apache's command line. While used mostly for development and debugging, it's possible for sites to turn on and off configuration settings for their servers via this mechanism. See the Apache documentation for more details if this sounds like something you can use.

5.5   SCRIPTING WITH MOD_PERL

Having Perl built into Apache opens up some amazing possibilities in the web application world. Many sites start using mod_perl to get a performance boost for CGI, which is where this book will start also. But to keep your mind open to greater schemes, consider that with mod_perl:

1 Anything you can do in Perl you can now do in Apache.

2 Anything you can do in Apache you can now do in Perl.

To begin at the beginning, let's see how to use mod_perl as a CGI booster.

5.5.1   Apache::Registry

The sample configuration given above used `PerlHandler Apache::Registry` to tell mod_perl how to handle scripts. Apache::Registry is mod_perl's CGI emulator, and so is commonly used at sites which are migrating from plain CGI. To explain how it works, let's follow a request through Apache to a sample script, `hello-mod_perl.pl`, illustrated in figure 5.4.

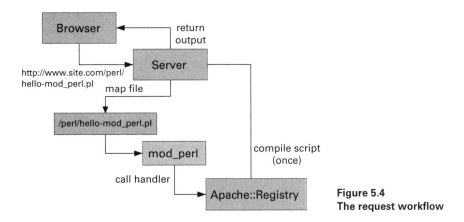

Figure 5.4
The request workflow

Using the sample configuration given earlier, Apache gets a request for http://www.example.site/perl/hello-mod_perl.pl. The `Alias` directive maps /perl/ onto `/usr/local/apache/perl`, where the `Directory` and `SetHandler` directives tell Apache that mod_perl will handle files.

The mod_perl code inside the Apache process has a `PerlHandler` directive which tells it to use Apache::Registry to process scripts. It loads the module if it hasn't already, then calls the `handler` function inside Apache::Registry to do the actual work.

Since Apache::Registry is emulating a CGI environment it follows the same rules about files as Apache does when spawning CGI processes. The file corresponding to the URL has to exist and be executable, and has to have an `ExecCGI` option applied somewhere in the configuration file. If those conditions are met, it proceeds.

Apache::Registry speeds up CGI scripts by loading and compiling them once, then re-executing the saved code. The next step then is to check whether this file has been loaded already, and if so whether the file on disk has changed. If the saved version is valid it jumps to the chase, but let's assume not.

To follow what happens next, first consider that the Perl interpreter understands only one program at a time; it can't load any number of programs and switch from one to another. A CGI script is written as a program, so we'll need some trick to load more than one of them into a Perl interpreter.

That trick is next: Apache::Registry loads the file and wraps Perl code around it to turn it into a function called a handler in a package that is unique to the file name.

It compiles that function and stores the modification time of the file so that it will know in later checks whether the compiled version is current.

Since the script is wrapped into a function, it cannot use __END__ or __DATA__. All other Perl code is valid, with this caveat: code which behaves well when run as a standalone program may break when run repeatedly as a function. Look for uses of global variables and other things which will retain their state between runs, and be prepared to clean up your scripts when moving them over to mod_perl. See the online guide for more common problems encountered by scripts that are making the transition.

Assuming the wrapped script compiled and all is well, Apache::Registry calls the handler function, which represents the original script. The script (now a function) can use CGI.pm or almost any other Perl tools that it used before. It processes its inputs and builds the HTML output which is sent back to the browser, hopefully more quickly than the CGI would.

Here is an example to demonstrate CGI migration, called hello-mod_perl.pl:

```perl
#!/usr/local/bin/perl -w

use strict;

# Use CGI.pm for inputs and output functions.
use CGI;
my $q = new CGI;

# Print the usual opening stuff.
print $q->header, $q->start_html($0 . ': mod_perl test');

# Put some text in an <H1> block.
print $q->h1('Hello, Web, it is', scalar(localtime));

# Check if we're running inside Apache or as a CGI.
if ($ENV{'MOD_PERL'}) {
    print "mod_perl environment detected";
}
else {
    print "running in CGI mode";
}

# Print the closing </BODY> and </HTML>.
print $q->end_html;
```

It's not much of a script, but it demonstrates how Perl code can detect whether it is running inside of mod_perl or not: the environment variable MOD_PERL is set to a true value.

Note one other interesting feature of the script: the global Perl variable $0 ordinarily contains the name of the program being run, but Apache::Registry modifies it to the name of the script it loaded before running the function it made from the script. Apache::Registry also turns on warnings if your script (would have) invoked Perl with the -w switch.

If you install this script in your regular CGI directory and run it, you'll see the "running in CGI mode" message. Then put it in a directory set up as per the example configuration and try it a few more times. If your test machine is slow enough, you should be able to see a speed difference on the second and later invocations of the mod_perl version; remember that Apache::Registry still has to load and compile the script on the first try.

5.5.2   Apache::DBI

When discussing the poor performance of regular CGI we mentioned that not only does a script get compiled for every request, it also has to connect to the database. Just handling the script with Apache::Registry doesn't fix that, but Apache::DBI does.

Apache::DBI is a module that takes over certain methods from DBI.pm. In particular, it catches `connect` and `disconnect` calls made from mod_perl scripts. When such a script calls `connect`, Apache::DBI checks a pool of open connections to see if it is already in touch with the requested database, using the same host, username, and password. If so, and the connection is still alive, it passes the cached connection back to the requesting script. When the script calls `disconnect`, Apache::DBI keeps the connection in the pool but returns a success status so that the caller is kept happy.

What's even better is that all of this happens without changing the Perl scripts. Instead, another configuration file change makes it work automatically. mod_perl's configuration file directive `PerlModule` tells each server process to load the named module before processing its first request. Thus we can have Apache::DBI invoked like so from `mod_perl.conf`:

```
# Load these modules on start-up.
PerlModule Apache::DBI
PerlModule Apache::Registry

# Apache::Registry scripts
Alias /perl/ "/usr/local/apache/perl/"
<Directory "/usr/local/apache/perl">
    SetHandler perl-script
    PerlHandler Apache::Registry
    Options ExecCGI
</Directory>
```

Note that I preload Apache::Registry in the same way; add any other modules to the list if all or most of your scripts require them. Large modules such as CGI.pm should also be in the list if any of your applications use them, since new server processes forked off by Apache will get a copy of the compiled code for those modules without compiling them individually.

Remember that a running Apache server needs to be informed when configuration details change. If you are preloading Perl modules then you should restart your servers instead of just signaling them to read the configuration files again; a running server won't ordinarily reload Perl code. If your traffic load is too heavy to permit reloads, look into using the `PerlFreshRestart` directive or other workarounds that reload modules as they change.

You can now move one of the DBI example scripts to mod_perl's script directory and see how Apache::DBI works. For single user tests the difference might not be noticeable unless the machine is slow to start with, but for more intense usage the change can be dramatic.

Is Apache::DBI always a good idea? That depends on how many Apache processes you run and how many distinct database users they employ. If you use a single user login to connect to the database for all applications, then Apache::DBI will open one connection per server process—ten servers means ten connections. However, if each user has a distinct login, then it's possible for each server to have a connection for each user who sends it a request. Twenty very active users could mean 200 connections in the same configuration.

No matter how you arrange your users and connections, occasionally monitor your database to verify that you are not overloading it with connects. Some databases have proxy schemes that allow multiple servers to pool connections to solve just this problem. Consider using the DBI::Proxy module or another solution.

5.5.3 When CGI attacks

As mentioned earlier, scripts run through Apache::Registry can exhibit odd behavior or bugs that don't happen when run as normal CGI. The longer and more complex the script, the more likely it is to have a problem. These problems usually stem from the fact that a CGI script is normally run once, while Apache::Registry invokes the same compiled code over and over, leaving global variables with whatever values they hold. The way that Apache::Registry wraps scripts inside of a function can also make the script's own functions into closures that retain lexical values.[3]

If you have a script that misbehaves when run in Apache::Registry, you have three options:

1 You can fix or rewrite it to get rid of the problem.

2 You can run it via Apache::PerlRun instead.

3 You can use FastCGI or another CGI tool to speed it up.

Assuming the first option is too time-consuming or otherwise expensive, give Apache::PerlRun a try. This module works similarly to Apache::Registry in that it runs Perl scripts inside of an Apache process and emulates the CGI environment. It compiles the requested script and runs it, but doesn't save it. Thus each time a script runs, it is compiled and initialized from scratch, more like a traditional CGI application.

---

[3] See the online mod_perl guide (http://perl.apache.org/) for a detailed explanation of the closure problem and how to deal with it.

This is faster than CGI, in that one process is used instead of two and the Perl interpreter is saved. It is still not foolproof, however, since a script can alter package variables or do other things to leave evidence of its presence even though the code is not saved.

If a script still doesn't work correctly using Apache::PerlRun, chances are it will have problems using other CGI accelerator tools as well. Either leave it as plain CGI or write a new application that behaves itself in public.

5.6   BEYOND CGI

Apache::Registry provides a good entry point for mod_perl, but it doesn't suggest how to go further. mod_perl can invoke a Perl function directly from an Apache request; indeed, that's what happens inside of Apache::Registry.

Recall that we configured Apache::Registry in `mod_perl.conf` like so:

```
Alias /perl/ "/usr/local/apache/perl/"
<Directory "/usr/local/apache/perl">
    SetHandler perl-script
    PerlHandler Apache::Registry
    Options ExecCGI
</Directory>
```

This string of directives tells Apache how to handle URLs beginning with `/perl`. Map the URL onto the directory given by the `Alias`, handle it via mod_perl, and further tell mod_perl to use the Apache::Registry handler. Apache::Registry's `handler` function does all the work to make CGI scripts run inside of Apache.

Now let's take a look at Perl code handling a request directly. Here is the short script we'll use as an example, `WebClock.pm`:

```perl
package Examples::WebClock;

use strict;
use Apache::Constants qw(:common);

# When our PerlHandler matches a URL, call this:
sub handler {
    # Get the request object, always the first argument:
    my $r = shift;

    # Print the standard HTML header.
    $r->send_http_header('text/html');

    # Print the current time in an <H1> block.
    print '<H1>The time is ' . localtime() . '</H1>';

    # Tell Apache that all is well.
    return OK;
}

# Modules return 1 to signal everything is set up.
1;
```

The first thing to note is that this isn't a script at all; it's a Perl module, as designated by the .pm extension on the file. Perl modules generally contain packages named the same as the file, where the '::' separator in a package name corresponds to a file path separator. Thus we'd expect to find Examples::WebClock defined by Web-Clock.pm in the Examples directory. Similarly, the CGI package resides in CGI.pm and Apache::Registry is in Apache/Registry.pm somewhere in one of Perl's library directories.

The next notable difference is the fact that the code is contained in the handler function. The PerlHandler directive specifies a package that handles certain requests; that package must contain a handler function to receive the requests. The first argument to the function is the request object, traditionally called $r; which contains everything the function needs to know about the request it is handling.

Finally there is the return value, OK. The function gets this value via the Apache::Constants package; OK indicates that the request has been handled properly. A handler can return DECLINED, NOT_FOUND, or FORBIDDEN to tell Apache to send back the usual error pages if the requester is not allowed or the request can't be handled for some reason. See the documentation on Apache::Constants for more information and status values.

To tell mod_perl to use this function, we need to decide what URL it handles. Rather than setting up an Alias for directories as with Apache::Registry, we can map requests directly to our handler in a Location directive. Here's a sample configuration for mod_perl.conf:

```
# Custom modules
PerlRequire "/home/theo/Examples/WebClock.pm"
<Location /time>
    SetHandler perl-script
    PerlHandler Examples::WebClock
</Location>
```

The first directive, PerlRequire, is similar to PerlModule in that both load Perl code into the servers at initialization. PerlRequire accepts a path to a file in the same vein as Perl's require function. This is convenient when developing a new module, but when the code is ready it should be installed under Apache's root directory and invoked via PerlModule. mod_perl looks for Perl modules in the usual Perl library directories plus the lib and lib/perl directories under the Apache root. So the module could be moved to /usr/local/apache/lib/perl/Examples/WebClock.pm when it's ready for prime time (assuming your Apache root is the same as mine), then loaded in mod_perl.conf like so:

```
PerlModule Examples::WebClock
```

The Location directive tells Apache how to handle requests to the URL http://www.example.site/time. The SetHandler directive tells Apache to pass the request to mod_perl, and `PerlHandler` in turn tells mod_perl to invoke the handler function of our Examples::WebClock module.

That's not much work for something as powerful as this; set up your configuration as shown or similarly and restart Apache. Check your error log to be sure that Examples::WebClock got loaded correctly; if so, invoke the URL and see the time on your web server.

Notice how different this is from a CGI script. For one thing, there is no `Alias` to map the URL onto a file; instead we tell Apache how to handle requests to this one URL directly. Also note that we didn't tell Apache that the code is executable, (although it needs to be readable by the web server processes).

At the start of our mod_perl discussion I gave an example of a Perl application which made a database of photographs appear to be a directory structure. Perhaps you can see now how that application would work: by associating a handler written in Perl with a given URL (such as /photos/*), we could have the application translate the URL into a database entry and return the appropriate image. If that prospect gets your imagination going then read through the mod_perl documentation and guide for more details on writing Perl handlers.

5.6.1 Beyond CGI.pm?

Note that the example didn't use CGI.pm to print its headers and HTML. It could have, although an extra initialization step is required: call `Apache->request` to save a pointer to the request object where CGI.pm expects to find it. Thus the code to create the usual opening sequence for a handler that uses CGI.pm is:

```
Apache->request($r);
$q = new CGI;
```

The rest of CGI.pm's input and helper functions should work as usual.

In many developers' minds the transition from Apache::Registry to direct handlers goes hand in hand with dropping CGI.pm, using mod_perl's helper functions for headers and cookies, and writing HTML output by hand. After all, CGI.pm is for CGI, and now we're doing handlers. There is also the performance issue: CGI.pm is a big module and leaving it out will save memory, shared or not.

One important consideration though is the fact that mod_perl won't automatically segregate applications that use CGI.pm from those that don't. If a server is configured to run Perl scripts (and possibly other handlers), and those scripts use CGI.pm, then you can assume that eventually your server will load CGI.pm. Thus if you want to get CGI.pm out of your servers, you have to take it out of all mod_perl scripts. Conversely, if you use it at all, use it anywhere you like (and preload it).

To illustrate life after CGI.pm, the rest of my examples will do without it. As always you should consult the readily available documentation in the Apache module to learn more; it has helper functions for sending headers as well as a full interface to all aspects of the request and server.

There are two other important modules for making the transition: Apache::Request analyzes a request object and parses out input parameters, and Apache::Cookie handles cookie data. Despite the confusing name, Apache::Request is not the request object ($r in the examples); it deals with the request data from the browser, via a `param` interface that is very similar to CGI.pm's function of the same name. Examples that use Apache::Request will invoke it like so:

```
use Apache::Request;
sub handler {
    my $r = shift;
    my $q = Apache::Request->new($r);

    # Check for parameters.
    my @params = $q->param;
```

Apache::Cookie provides the same functions as CGI::Cookie for setting cookies in outgoing HTML and retrieving them from the current request. To retrieve the cookies from a request into a hash, invoke it like so:

```
use Apache::Cookie;
sub handler {
    my $r = shift;
    my $cookies = Apache::Cookie->fetch;
```

The cookies will be loaded in the $cookies hash reference. Apache::Cookies will create a hash directly if asked, as in:

```
    my %cookies = Apache::Cookie->fetch;
```

The Apache::Session example below makes use of both of these mod_perl modules.

5.7 MOD_PERL GOODIES

The Apache Perl module ships with a number of useful tools besides mod_perl. If these brief comments spark your interest, check your documentation for more information.

Apache::Debug sends script errors to the browser instead of the error log. This is very useful in the early phase of debugging a script.

Apache::File adds extra file handling methods to the Apache class and provides a number of utility functions for applications. If your script needs to create uniquely named temporary files, look here.

Apache::Include integrates mod_perl and mod_include for better server-side includes. More tools for merging HTML and Perl are discussed in chapter 7.

Apache::Log provides an API for writing messages of different warning levels to the Apache log file. This allows a script to write debugging messages, for example, which will be kept in the log if the LogLevel directive is set to debug, and discard them otherwise.

Apache::SizeLimit and Apache::Resource set configurable resource limits for server processes. It provides a simple way to shut down processes that are using too much memory or CPU time (in case a script goes into an infinite loop, for example).

Apache::Table and Apache::Util provide Perl interfaces to various Apache internals.

Apache::URI has URL analysis functions that are faster than those in Perl's LWP library.

5.7.1   Apache::Status

While you might find a use for some or all of the goodies listed in the previous section, you'll almost certainly want to install it. Apache::Status provides a menu with classes of information about your mod_perl installation. You can see which version of Perl, Apache, and other modules it is running, which Perl modules have been compiled, the environment variables passed to a script, and so on.

Apache::Status can be extended by other modules to include more classes of information; you can build your own server command center using this feature. It is a short and clever module which would make a terrific example if only it had some internal documentation.

Enable Apache::Status in your `mod_perl.conf` file like so:

```
# Server status
<Location /perl-status>
   SetHandler perl-script
   PerlHandler Apache::Status
   order deny,allow
   deny from all
   allow from 192.168.
</Location>
```

Note the use of `deny` and `allow` directives to keep others from gathering information about your server. Change the IP address in the `allow` directive to match the network or machine you use to maintain your web server, and see the next chapter for ways to set password protection on this page.

5.8   MAINTAINING USER STATE

Web users have rapidly grown accustomed to sites that remember where they left off. E-commerce sites use shopping carts that hold users' selections. Some news sites keep track of what articles the user has read and bring unread material to the top of the list.

Cookies provide one way to keep track of the user. A cookie is a small piece of data stored on the user's system that is sent to the web server each time the user requests a page from the matching URL. Cookies are much maligned due to their abuse by banner ad sites and other agencies that try to turn web browsers into automatic marketing polls, but most users still run with cookies enabled and most sites that remember users do so with cookies.

Cookies normally contain several bytes, ranging upward to around 200. Applications, however, shouldn't trust browsers to store more than a short string, so cookies normally store a user ID of some sort on the client machine. When the user requests a URL that has an associated cookie, the data is sent along with the request and can be read similarly to a form input; the script then uses the data to retrieve the user's information. Both the Apache and CGI.pm modules have helper functions for retrieving cookie data from a request.

When using cookies, an application has to consider the cookie lifespan. The browser can be told to hold onto a given cookie until the user ends the program (known as a session cookie) or can be stored on the user's disk with an expiration date. The browser can delete cookies whenever it wishes, however, by accumulating more than a given number or total size, so applications can't count on them staying forever. Further, a given user could browse a site from different machines and thus not have the same set of cookies each time.

Unique URLs are another common means for keeping track of users. Each new user is assigned a URL as he registers; some form of user ID makes up the unique portion. By bookmarking this URL and returning to it the user tells the server who he is. The server extracts the unique portion of the URL and again looks up the user's data.

URL-based schemes fail when the user doesn't bookmark his location. Also, they open a security risk because one user could gain access to another user's data by guessing his URL.

Of course, the application could just ask the user to identify himself, and in practice most sites end up using that method in conjunction with cookies, URLs. or both. If the cookie or URL is lost, the user goes to a login screen and enters his ID (or a name and password pair, or whatever). The application can then send another cookie, create another URL, or proceed however it likes.

5.8.1   Apache::Session

By whatever road, an application associates a user with an ID that is stored in a database along with whatever information the application needs to keep about the user. The database code needed to store and retrieve the information is fairly simple, as is a table layout for the fields that comprise the user data.

If an application does extensive database work, adding a table of user IDs is easy enough. In many cases though, all the data used by the application would be stored in the user table. The developer in that case would certainly appreciate a tool which handled user information and let him concentrate on application business.

Apache::Session is such a tool. It keeps session data in a tied hash, such as described in chapter 4; each session has a unique ID generated by Apache::Session and whatever other data the script wishes to store in it, using hash keys and values as normal. The script has to provide the means of giving the session ID to the user and getting it back using cookies or URLs or what have you. Apache::Session takes care of the database work.

In fact, Apache:Session works with more than one kind of database. The version available at the time I'm writing works with MySQL, PostgreSQL, and Oracle databases, Berkeley DB hash files, and plain text files. It also provides locking options and other tools for more intensive applications.

Since Apache::Session makes the session data look like a Perl hash, your script can store anything it wants is a session such as strings, arrays, and more hashes, and does not need to know in advance what fields will be associated with a user. This is more convenient than database tables, where Perl data types are unlikely to be supported and adding new fields is a chore.

5.8.2 A to-do list

It's time for an example to illustrate Apache::Session as well as some of the other Apache modules described here. This script implements a simple to-do list (actually just a free form text box). It will run as a Perl module loaded by mod_perl and be invoked when a browser requests http://www.example.site/todo. The application uses a very simple form shown in figure 5.5.

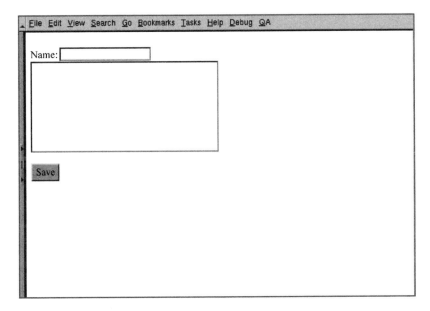

Figure 5.5   ToDo list form

I mentioned previously that the examples of earlier chapters had a single user focus. The to-do list is our first step away from that; this example will recognize new and returning users and keep them separate. The first pass will use unique URLs to identify users, and then we'll expand it to use cookies also.

Here is the application, `ToDo.url.pm`:

```
package Examples::ToDo;

use strict;
use Apache::Constants qw(:common);
use Apache::Request;
use Apache::Session::DB_File;
```

Remember that a Perl module has to identify itself using the `package` statement. The module uses Apache::Constants to get the return codes it needs and Apache::Request to parse inputs. We don't have to invoke Apache.pm directly since Apache::Constants and Apache::Request both do that.

I mentioned previously that Apache::Session could use various sorts of databases to hold session data. This module invokes Apache::Session::DB_File, which is a subclass that stores session data in a hash file. Apart from this line and the invocation below, the storage mechanism makes no difference to the Perl code.

The real application code is contained in the `handler` function:

```
sub handler {
    # Get the request object and parse it.
    my $r = shift;
    my $q = Apache::Request->new($r);
```

Note the use of Apache::Request to parse the inputs from the request object (`$r`) into the client request data object (`$q`).

The code then uses the `request` object to start the response by sending the standard header and opening HTML tags:

```
    # Print the standard HTML headers and start the document.
    $r->send_http_header('text/html');
    print '<!DOCTYPE HTML PUBLIC "-//IETF//DTD HTML//EN">',
          '<HTML><HEAD><TITLE>To do list</TITLE></HEAD><BODY>';
```

Now we check for a session ID in the URL. The request object knows what URI was used to invoke the application, so we get that information via the `uri` function:

```
    # Get the URI of the request, /todo/???
    my $sessionID = $1 if $r->uri =~ m{/todo/(\w+)};
```

This portion of code shows a typical Perl shortcut for initializing a variable. If the application was invoked as http://www.example.site/todo/id-string then the session ID is present; the regular expression match (`m{/todo/(\w+)}`) will not only find it but store it in the special variable `$1`. The boolean expression (the `if` clause) will be true and `$sessionID` will be initialized with `$1`. If the application was invoked as http://www.example.site/todo then there is no session ID and `$sessionID` will be undefined.

```
    # Load the session or create a new one.
    my %session;
    tie %session, 'Apache::Session::DB_File', $sessionID,
    {
      FileName => '/usr/local/apache/data/sessions',
      LockDirectory => '/usr/local/apache/locks',
    };
    $sessionID = $session{'_session_id'};
```

Apache::Session is invoked via the `tie` interface discussed in chapter 3. The arguments to `tie` are:

- The object to be tied, `%session`;
- The Perl module that has the tied functions, Apache::Session::DB_File;
- Arguments to that module's new function. In this case, `$sessionID` and the hash after it are the arguments.

Apache::Session examines the value in `$sessionID`; if not defined, Apache::Session creates a new, unique ID and initializes it in the session store. When `$sessionID` has a value, Apache::Session looks up that value in the hash and loads `%session` with the data stored there previously. This very helpful property saves the application from having separate pieces of code for creating a session or loading an old one.

Whether it's created a session or loaded an old one, the session ID is stored in the `_session_id` member of the hash, so the code reloads `$sessionID` with that value.

Now it's time to deal with user inputs:

```
# Store parameters in the session if received.
my $p;
$session{'name'} = $p if $p = $q->param('name');
$session{'todo'} = $p if $p = $q->param('todo');
```

Note that `$q->param` behaves very similarly to the CGI.pm examples of previous chapters, in spite of the fact that we're using only Apache modules now. This code uses more shortcuts to check for parameters and store their values in the session hash if they are present. In each case, `$p` is true only if the corresponding parameter was passed in from the browser, so the session hash is set only if the user has already loaded the form and sent in a request. The `name` parameter identifies the user, and `todo` contains the to-do list.

If this is the first request from the user then neither parameter will be set. However, if the user had a session and invoked the application with the right URL, then previous values for `name` and `todo` will be stored in the hash. The next section makes use of that.

```
# Put up the form for entering ToDo information.
print "<FORM METHOD=\"POST\" ACTION=/todo/$sessionID>";
if ($session{'name'}) {
    print "<H1>For $session{'name'}</H1>";
}
else {
    print 'Name: <INPUT TYPE="text" NAME="name"',
          'SIZE=20><br>'
}
print '<TEXTAREA NAME="todo" COLS=40 ROWS=8>',
```

```
                  $session{'todo'}, '</TEXTAREA><p>',
                  '<INPUT TYPE="submit" NAME="submit" VALUE="Save">',
                  '</FORM>';
```

The application starts a form with the <FORM> tag and sets the action to return to this session—note how the session ID is tacked on to the URL, so when the user submits the form the session ID will get passed back to the application. We could also have used a hidden field for this; using a unique URL lets the user bookmark his session and also separates session information from form data nicely.

If the session hash has a name stored in it, then that name is displayed over the to-do list text box. If not then we create a text input for the user to identify himself. Below that is the text box, created by the <TEXTAREA> tag. Unlike a text input, TEXTAREA creates a multiline text box that lets the user enter free-form text and in most browsers, provides simple editing functions.

The data between the opening <TEXTAREA> tag and the closing </TEXTAREA> is loaded into the box, including any white space and blank lines. This example loads the text box with $session{'todo'}, the data stored in the session hash.

Below that is a simple submit button that will be labeled Save in the user's browser. The following </FORM> tag ends the form.

Now you can see how the application works: when first invoked, the user sees any data stored in $session{'todo'} by previous visits to the application. If he adds or changes the text and clicks the submit button, the application will be invoked again with the text data, and possibly the user's name, as inputs. The application stores those values in the hash, then displays the same form again.

We still have more to do:

```
    # Time stamp the session.
    print "Last updated " . localtime($session{'time'})
      if $session{'time'};
    $session{'time'} = time();

    # End the document.
    print '</BODY></HTML>';

    # Tell Apache that all is well.
    return OK;
}

1;
```

Each time the application runs, the session is time stamped and, it if were set, the value of the previous time stamp is shown to the user. After that, the application prints closing tags and returns the OK code to tell Apache that the request has been handled. Don't forget the ending 1; which tells Perl that the module compiled normally.

The time stamp is important for two reasons. First, a more realistic application would need some way of getting rid of sessions, so the application marks each session with the time of its last use. Secondly, Apache::Session automatically updates sessions when the corresponding hash is untied (either deliberately by the code or by the end of the scope containing the hash). However, it will update the hash only if one of the key-value pairs of the hash has been changed.

In this example, all the data stored in the session is stored directly in key-value pairs—the name, the to-do list, the session ID, and the time all have their own keys. A more complex application could store arrays or hashes within the session, via references. If only referenced data changes, Apache::Session won't know that it needs to update the session data. Therefore it is always a good idea to time stamp your sessions whenever any session data changes.

To tell Apache to run this application we need to put the code into the library directory. In my server configuration it goes in /usr/local/apache/lib/perl/Examples/ToDo.pm. (Note the name change in the file.) We add it to mod_perl.conf like so:

```
PerlModule Examples::ToDo
<Location /todo>
    SetHandler perl-script
    PerlHandler Examples::ToDo
</Location>
```

After a restart, Apache will run the application whenever the matching URL is invoked. Note that the Location directive matches the beginning of the URL, so the application still runs correctly when a session ID is tacked on.

While this code isn't bad for an example, it's too brittle to use in a real application. The first problem that comes to mind (apart from the fact that it's not much of a to-do list) is that the URL-session ID mechanism won't work if the user doesn't bookmark the page. The application should warn the user of that of course, but there is no way to force the user to do so.

The second problem is that there is no check for a bad session ID. If the user types in an invalid URL, or bookmarks a session that later is somehow expired, Apache::Session will go looking for an ID that doesn't exist; it handles that situation by dying. That is, it calls Perl's die function which prints an error message and exits the program, which would be very bad indeed if we didn't trap it.

The next section will expand this example and deal with these problems (except for the one about this not being a very good to-do list).

5.8.3 Cookie sessions

As I mentioned, cookies are very commonly used to maintain user state in web applications. This example will show a combination of cookies and the unique URL method shown previously to give a user two ways to store his ID.

When a web browser handles cookies, it stores them in a database by URL (among other parameters). When the user requests a page, the browser checks its database for any cookies that match the URL and sends along all that match. The match can be by the site, some or all of the path, or both. (A cookie can also specify that it is sent only over secure connections. See chapter 6 for details.) The cookies are sent along in a format similar to CGI form data but in separate parts of the request.

Applications are more concerned with what a cookie holds than with how it is stored. From the application's standpoint, cookies are essentially key-value pairs; a cookie has a name and one or more values. It's not surprising then that Apache::Cookie and CGI::Cookie both implement a hash interface to cookie data.

Cookies also have a lifespan. If the application which sends the cookie doesn't specify an expiration date, the browser will keep the cookie in memory and thus lose it when the user closes the program. That's fine in cases where we want the user to log in via some other mechanism for each session, but in this example we'll use cookies that last longer.

This example expands on the previous section, and looks the same to the user; the code is in ToDo.pm. The initialization adds the cookie module:

```
package Examples::ToDo;

use strict;
use Apache::Constants qw(:common);
use Apache::Request;
use Apache::Session::DB_File;
use Apache::Cookie;
```

The beginning of the handler function is also similar, receiving the request object, parsing parameters, and storing the request's URI:

```
sub handler {
    # Get the request object and parse it.
    my $r = shift;
    my $q = Apache::Request->new($r);
    my (@ids, $sessionID);
```

As suggested by the existence of the @ids array, the application is going to try more than one ID. First it looks for one in a cookie:

```
    # Check for a cookie with the ID.
    if (my $cookies = Apache::Cookie->fetch) {
        $sessionID = $cookies->{'ID'}->value
            if $cookies->{'ID'};
        push @ids, $sessionID if $sessionID;
    }
```

An application which used more than one cookie could check them all inside the if block. Here we check only for a cookie called ID; note that the application has to verify that the cookie is in the hash before getting its value.

Each element of the cookies hash is a cookie object created by Apache::Cookie. Besides the value, the cookie objects have functions that return (or set) their expiration time, URL path, and other attributes.

Now the application checks for a session ID in the URL:

```
# The URI might have the ID also.
push @ids, $1 if $r->uri =~ m{/todo/(\w+)};
```

This is the same check that we had in the previous version, except that this time we're storing the value in an array if the URL matched the regex.

The application pushes an undefined value onto the array also, which will tell Apache::Session to create a new session if we get that far. It then loops over the values and tries each:

```
# Create a new session if all else fails.
push @ids, undef;

# Load the session or create a new one.
my %session;
foreach my $try (@ids) {
    eval {
        tie %session, 'Apache::Session::DB_File', $try,
        {
         FileName => '/usr/local/apache/data/sessions',
         LockDirectory => '/usr/local/apache/locks',
        };
    };
    last unless $@;
```

The eval block is Perl's technique for trapping errors signaled via die; if Apache::Session::DB_File errors out, the error message will be stored in the special variable $@. If no error occurs inside the eval block, $@ is false. Thus for each pass through the loop, the code will try to load or create a session, and if it works the loop exits via last.

```
    # If trying to create a new session failed,
    # we have a serious problem.
    unless ($try) {
        warn "Can't create session: $@\n";
        return SERVER_ERROR;
    }
}
$sessionID = $session{'_session_id'};
```

If the final value (which was undefined) failed, the application can't create sessions for some reason. In that case the script uses warn to write an error to the error log and returns SERVER_ERROR to the browser to inform the user that there is a problem on the server's end.

Assuming we came out of the loop, the script grabs the session ID as the previous example did. Now we want to send the ID back in a new cookie along with the HTML form. If the browser already had a cookie, this will serve to update its expiration date, so we send the cookie regardless:

```
# Send the ID back in a cookie.
my $cookie = Apache::Cookie->new($r,
```

```
            -name => 'ID',
            -value => $sessionID,
            -path => '/todo',
            -expires => '+1M',
        );
    $cookie->bake;
```

The new function creates the cookie object and sets its name, value, path, and expiration date. The path matches the application's URL. Since we don't specify the web site explicitly, Apache::Cookie will use the current site automatically. The expiration string '+1M' means that the cookie expires in one month.

The last function, humorously named bake, sends the cookie to the browser. Cookies are sent as part of the header string, and so they must preceed any HTML output. The browser parses the headers including the cookies and stores them (assuming it handles cookies at all), then displays the accompanying HTML.

The rest of the application code is identical to that in the previous version, so we don't need to display it here. To run it, copy ToDo.pm into the appropriate Apache directory as shown previously, then restart the server. Note that if you bookmarked the URL of the previous version, you can return to your bookmark and your to-do list is as you left it previously; this will also load a cookie with your previous session ID.

The main change is shown when you load the application as http://www.example.site/todo. Rather than starting afresh, this version will give you your previous to-do list, showing that the cookie with your session ID was sent to the server with the request.

5.8.4   Session management and user management

The previous examples used Apache::Session to store all of an application's data. That's fine for transient data that is not well-suited for a database. For example, a shopping cart's contents are associated with a particular user and need to be stored for hours or perhaps days, but not longer (although an e-commerce site might want to store a separate purchase history also).

If an application requires long-term information about a user, then an additional scheme is required. As we've mentioned, we can't trust the user's browser to store cookies indefinitely, and we also can't rely on the user to bookmark a URL. Besides that, either scheme would fail if the user loaded the application from a different machine, lost the bookmark file, or just changed browsers.

Apache::Session doesn't address the larger issue of user management. If the application is going to work with users for more than a day or so, we need to fall back on the familiar mechanism of user IDs and passwords to know who is who. We need user data as well as session data.

Consider a user running a CGI application with multiple pages. Each page has data; the application as a whole has more data, the sum of the pages, and any additional state information required. The application could also have user preferences or security information tied to the user name and password combination. Session data is the middle set—the data currently in the application, including state information—while user data is the longer term information which probably doesn't change much from one session to another.

Apache::Session is a terrific tool for handling session data. A multipage CGI application can store user inputs in a session hash, rather than building a large set of hidden inputs to pass information from page to page (as the examples in previous chapters did). Each time a request goes to the server, the application loads the session data via the session ID (stored in a cookie or unique URL) and thus has all the state information it needs to move the user along in the process.

The user creates a session by logging in, although we might let the user store his user ID and password in a cookie. The newly generated session ID is sent back in a cookie that expires in a reasonable time for the application—if the user is idle for an hour, say. Or, we could set no expiration and let the browser hold the ID until the program exits. As the user sends further requests to the server, the session data tells the application where he is and what he's been doing, creating the illusion of the application running as a continuous process.

In this style of application, some kind of session management is required—we don't want to build up old sessions endlessly in our session store. Apache::Session does not provide this directly, but it isn't difficult to work out, especially if the sessions are stored in a relational database; a small program can delete records from the table that are time stamped past an expiration time. If the application uses Apache::Session::DB_File or Apache::Session::File it will need to run through all the sessions and check the time stamps individually.

The application will also need user management—it may let users create their own user IDs or require a separate administrator action to do so, but in either case it requires password verification to validate the user's ID. That means the application is now sending sensitive data—information that could be valuable to a snooper—and should take precautions to hide that information from prying eyes.

Which leads us to the next chapter.

CHAPTER 6

Security and users

6.1 LISTENING IN ON THE WEB

It seems that every few months there are high-profile cases of credit card theft over the Internet; a popular site reports that its customer database was cracked, or a new exploit is discovered that lets a malicious application read information from browsers. As with the case in the physical realm, the bulk of crimes are low-profile and not reported to police. After a pleasant holiday season of shopping over the Web, strange charges turn up on a credit card, and the card holder calls their bank to have the charges removed and to get a new account number issued.

When these cases do make the news, consumers get vague warnings about using proper security when shopping over the Internet. We can hope that those who have been victimized learn their lesson and take precautions when giving out sensitive information.

Seldom, however, is there any comment on the fact that the Internet is not built for security. The most popular protocols for web browsing, email, and file transfer all send their contents without even trivial encryption. The closest physical-world analogy to normal email is to use postcards for all your letters; there isn't a whole lot stopping a snooper from invading your privacy.

Internet protocols send messages in the open primarily because it takes a determined effort to snoop on individual users. For instance, to read a romantic email message from Bob to Carol as it is transmitted, a snooper would need privileged access to Bob's machine, Carol's machine, or one of the machines along the route the message follows. The snooper needs either to listen all the time or to know just when to collect data. If one is really determined to read Bob's love letters, it is probably easier to break into his or Carol's files than to grab the messages on the fly.

On the other hand, if a cracker breaks into a busy Internet service provider (ISP), he can engage in a more opportunistic kind of snooping. By installing a "sniffer" program that reads various kind of Internet traffic, the cracker can look for messages that contain patterns of digits that look like credit card numbers, or phrases like "the password is …" Bob's passion for Carol might escape notice, but he could find his account number stolen the next time he orders something over the Web, only because he or the merchant used the cracked ISP.

Encrypting all Internet traffic sounds tempting at first, but would add expense and delay in the form of additional computation and extra bytes for each message. The most expedient solution is to encrypt traffic which contains sensitive data, and to leave the rest in the open.

This chapter starts with a discussion of Secure Sockets Layer (SSL), the protocol used for most encrypted Internet messages, and how to use it in your web applications. It goes on to cover user authentication schemes and basic user information management issues.

6.2 SECURE SOCKETS LAYER (SSL)

Consider the problem of creating secure Internet protocols. One might want to create new protocols for secure HTTP, FTP, or SMTP email, but that would break programs that worked with nonsecure versions.

HTTP and the other protocols are layered on top of TCP/IP, the basic communication layer of the Internet. Most applications that speak TCP/IP do so via *sockets*, which were originally part of BSD Unix but have since been ported to everything from handheld computers to mainframes. Network programmers talk about TCP/IP and sockets almost interchangeably. When a web browser downloads a page from a server, it first opens a socket to the server, which accepts or refuses the connection. Having established communication via TCP/IP, the two then proceed to speak HTTP over the socket connection.[1]

---

[1] Purists will point out that a socket doesn't have to use TCP/IP, and TCP/IP doesn't have to use sockets. The other common programming interface to TCP/IP is the Transport Layer Interface; interestingly the protocol that is set to supersede SSL is called Transport Layer Security.

By replacing the regular socket library with a secure TCP/IP communication scheme we can leave HTTP alone and still safely transmit sensitive information to and from web browsers. That's the role of the SSL; if the browser and the web server are built with SSL, they can create an encrypted channel and exchange data without fear of snoopers. HTTP rides on top of the layer without additional programming.

SSL is a terrific boon to network applications, but gets surprisingly little use outside of web traffic. Some mail servers and clients support it, but few require it, which is odd, considering that POP and IMAP mail protocols require a username and password to gain access to a server. Those passwords are all being sent in plain text across insecure channels, just as they are for FTP and TELNET sessions (which is why you are using ssh instead). Bob and Carol's true feelings may be known to more people than they realize.

SSL is itself a protocol description with both commercial and Open Source implementations, including SSLeay, a free implementation created by Eric A. Young and Tim J. Hudson, and OpenSSL, which followed on from SSLeay and has become the standard security library for Open Source network products. OpenSSL's developers include members of the Apache Group, so it's no surprise that I'm going to recommend it for use with their server.

6.2.1 Legal issues

You may be aware that there are both patent issues and import/export restrictions on software that uses encryption. In the United States and other countries, commonly used encryption algorithms are patented and require licenses from their patent holders for use. Export restrictions are changing as (some) governments realize that the main effect of legislation is to move encryption development to other countries.

Still, these issues were enough to prevent most US-based sites from distributing encryption software in the 1990s. Distribution web sites generally have guidelines on where to download those libraries, but before doing so you should thoroughly investigate the legalities of their use in your locality.

As the disclaimer goes, I Am Not A Lawyer, but here is my understanding of the legal situation in the United States: the patent holder of the RSA public key encryption algorithm placed the algorithm in the public domain in September 2000 (shortly before the patent was due to expire), so it is no longer necessary to buy a license from RSA or to use the RSAREF implementation. It is legal to use encryption on a US-hosted web site that communicates with the world at large; it may not be legal to let others download your encryption library however.

For hosting in other countries (or browsing, for that matter), see summaries of the legal situation posted at http://www.openssl.org/ for more information although they too will warn you that you need to investigate this on your own.

6.3   OPENSSL AND APACHE

So now that we know we want OpenSSL, how do we get Apache to use it?

I casually mentioned earlier that a server has to be built to use SSL instead of the usual sockets layer (as do browsers). This is not a trivial change, and can't be implemented solely through an add-on interface to Apache, such as mod_perl is. The guts of the server have to change to handle SSL.

There are commercial Apache SSL products that provide the necessary changes,[2] as well as a pair of Open Source solutions. The first on the scene was Apache-SSL, created by Ben Laurie; later Ralf Engelschall split off the Apache-SSL code to build mod_ssl on an expanded architecture. Both products use OpenSSL, actively track Apache versions (which is not surprising since the developers are part of the Apache Group), use the same license, and accomplish the same goal.

In terms of the buyer's guide, it is hard to tell the two products apart. Their mailing lists are active and helpful. The development pedigree of each product is impeccable and there is no reason to think that one is going to have more ongoing cost than the other. Both products are trivially easy to build and install. The few reports I've read comparing the two implementations comment as much on the developers as the code, so the choice seems to be a matter of personality for those who are active in the development community. I'll put forth a few technical issues and go on with my own choice, mod_ssl. If you choose Apache-SSL instead, the only changes you'll need to make to my examples are in the configuration files.

Both products assume that OpenSSL has been configured and built already. There is some convenience to having all of Apache, OpenSSL, mod_perl, and mod_ssl in one directory tree but it's not a requirement.

6.3.1   Apache-SSL

Apache-SSL provides a set of patches to a given Apache version, plus additional source files. Starting with a freshly unpacked Apache, unpack Apache-SSL into the same directory and apply the patches as instructed. Then configure and build Apache as you have previously, making sure you enable the apache_ssl module as well as mod_perl and any others you use. There isn't much more to it.

There also isn't much more to the documentation. Apache-SSL adds a page to the online manual explaining its directives, and has a configuration example, but doesn't go any further. That's fine for someone who knows about SSL and has a good grasp of Apache configuration, but personally I wanted more.

---

[2]   SSL products from RedHat, Raven, and Stronghold also provided licenses to the patented RSA algorithms for U.S. customers, but that restriction has expired.

6.3.2   mod_ssl

One could argue that the main thing mod_ssl adds to Apache-SSL is polish. The product has an extensive web site which looks better than that of most commercial products. The site has pages for downloading the source, reading the documentation or mailing list archives, getting news about mod_ssl, and checking the latest surveys to track the number of installed servers.

The documentation is quite good, and explains the workings of SSL's suite of cryptographic tools and how a web browser and server decide what to use. The installation instructions that ship with the source are better than the shortened online version, and include instructions on how to build OpenSSL, Apache, mod_ssl, and mod_perl all together. The process isn't that hard to figure out, but having the commands laid out in one file will help the first time web builder.

Those Apache developers who don't like mod_ssl complain that it adds too much to the server. mod_ssl patches Apache to include an extended API, then implements SSL through that API. It also optionally uses the developer's shared memory library to speed up some operations between servers. The result, though, is that mod_ssl acts in many ways like a standard Apache module, and I like the architecture almost as much as I like the generous documentation.

6.3.3   Installing mod_ssl

mod_ssl versions are tied to Apache versions, so if you are downloading newer software, make sure you get the distribution that matches your Apache source.

As mentioned, mod_ssl assumes the current release of OpenSSL is already in place. If you are going to use the MM shared memory library you'll need to set that up as well. This example builds the server using OpenSSL 0.9.5a, Apache 1.3.12, mod_ss 2.6.4, mod_perl 1.24, and MM 1.1.2, all unpacked in /usr/local, following the build process as described in the OpenSSL and mod_ssl installation documentation.

```
$ cd /usr/local/openssl-0.9.5a
$ sh config
$ make
$ make test
```

OpenSSL is built with all the defaults, which is fine for the U.S. I moved on to MM, the shared memory module:

```
$ cd ../mm-1.1.2
$ ./configure --disable-shared
$ make
```

The --disable-shared directive here disables shared libraries, not shared memory. Since Apache is the only application we're likely to build with MM, there isn't any benefit to having the MM code in a shared library.

Then we'll go to mod_ssl, telling it where to find OpenSSL and MM:

```
$ cd ../mod_ssl-2.6.4-1.3.12
$ ./configure --with-apache=../apache_1.3.12 \
```

```
                    --with-ssl=../openssl-0.9.5a \
                    --with-mm=../mm-1.1.2
```

And on to mod_perl. Here we skip testing mod_perl before going on, but if you've built mod_perl previously that's fine.

```
$ cd ../mod_perl-1.24
$ perl Makefile.PL EVERYTHING=1 APACHE_SRC=../apache_1.3.12/src \
        USE_APACI=1 PREP_HTTPD=1 DO_HTTPD=1
$ make
$ make install
```

Finally, we build Apache. Note the configuration directives for mod_ssl and mod_perl:

```
$ cd ../apache_1.3.12
$ SSL_BASE=../openssl-0.9.5a ./configure --enable-module=ssl \
        --activate-module=src/modules/perl/libperl.a \
        --enable-module=perl
$ make
$ make certificate
$ make install
```

Note the step to create the server's certificate, which we discuss in the next section.

If you have already installed Apache, I recommend shutting down your current server and moving its installation aside, letting `make install` start fresh. Among other things, it will put in a new blank configuration file which has examples of all the SSL directives and an `IfModule` section where you can put SSL-specifics. Compare the newly created `httpd.conf` to your previous one and reinstate your changes (port numbers, aliases, mod_perl configuration, etc.).

6.3.4   Certificates

Before your server can engage in secure sessions it needs a valid certificate which identifies it to browsers. The certificate contains identifying information for your server, a *public key* used to encrypt messages to you, identification of your certifying authority, and a *digital signature* from the certifying authority that the browser can use to prevent malicious servers from forging certificates.

As part of the mod_ssl installation you can create a temporary certificate to be used for testing your server. That will get you through the rest of this book, but before you open your site to the public you will need a proper certificate from a well-known certifying authority (CA).

To explain why this is, we need to delve for a moment into how SSL encrypts Internet messages.[3] When the SSL client contacts an SSL server, the server sends its certificate back along with acknowledgment of the connection. This communication takes

---

[3] Or at least, how SSL version 2 does so using the RSA algorithm. Version 3 is able to negotiate and use other options for the first secret exchange and the session encryption method.

place in the clear—no secrets have been exchanged yet. Figure 6.1 shows the exchanges in this section.

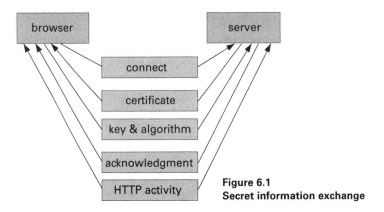

Figure 6.1
Secret information exchange

To establish an encrypted channel, the two parties need to exchange secret information. In particular, they need to decide on a *session key* which will be used to encrypt the data, and the encryption method which applies to it. Obviously if the session key is sent in clear text it won't necessarily stay a secret. To exchange information before establishing the session key, the two parties use *asymmetric* or *public key* encryption.

Public key cryptography, most strongly associated with the RSA algorithm, uses a pair of large numbers called the public and private keys to encrypt and decrypt messages. A message encrypted with the public key can be decrypted with the private key, and a message encrypted with the private key can similarly be decrypted with the public key. The crucial aspect of the algorithm is that a party with only one key can not both encrypt and decrypt a message, thus the term asymmetric encryption. Suppose I give everyone my public key (which is why we call it that) and keep my private key a secret. To send a secure message I encrypt it with my private key, and anyone who has my public key can both decrypt it and also be certain that it came from me, since only I can create a message that can be decrypted with the public key. Anyone who has my public key can send me a secure message also, by encrypting it with that key. Assuming that only I have the secret key, only I will be able to decrypt the result.

Public key cryptography is an amazing example of pure mathematics turned useful. It is also computationally expensive, far too much so to be used for large amounts of web traffic. That's why SSL (and other security protocols) use public key cryptography to exchange an initial message between parties that include a session key for *symmetric* encryption, the more traditional kind of encoding where both parties use a single key to encrypt and decrypt messages. The assumption is that if the session key is used only briefly and is never reused, it is very unlikely that a snooper will figure out the encryption before it is changed again.

Back to our SSL example: the client verifies the certificate (more on this shortly) and uses the server's public key to encrypt a message containing a session key and a choice of algorithm that both parties can use to quickly encrypt and decrypt further messages. The server decrypts the message using its private key, then sends an acknowledgment back that has been encrypted using the session key and a symmetric algorithm.

The role of the certificate, then, is to package up the server's public key along with identifying information used to verify the certificate. This verification is important; it prevents a malicious server from creating a certificate that identifies itself as another party. Part of the certificate is the identity of a CA, which is basically a company that sells trust.

As stated earlier, a certificate contains not only the server's public key and identity but also the CA's identity and digital signature of the public key. That signature is created using the CA's private key to encrypt the server's identification and public key; thus if you have the CA's public key you can decrypt the signature and verify that the server's identification matches their key. Since only the CA's private key can be used to create a valid signature, the browser can trust the certificate—if it trusts the CA, that is.

That sounds like a chicken-and-egg problem, but SSL-enabled web browsers are typically shipped with the identification and public keys of a number of well-known CAs. When a browser gets a certificate signed by an unknown CA it should display a dialog explaining what has happened and warn the user of possible problems; the user can then accept or reject the certificate. Chances are good that you've never seen this warning since sites that use SSL are almost always registered with one of a few popular CAs.

And that leads us to the point of this section: your site must go through the certification process with one of those CAs before you can expect to handle SSL traffic with the Internet at large. Both the Apache-SSL and mod_ssl web sites have lists of CAs which can create certificates for you. The security configuration of your browser will also tell you which CAs your browser will recognize without a warning, so check that list against the list of candidate CAs and then shop around for a good deal with a reputable firm.

As mentioned before, the `make certificate` step will offer to create a temporary certificate for your testing purposes. Go ahead and use that for now; if nothing else it will show you what the warning about an unknown certificate looks like.

6.3.5 Configure and test

If you let `make install` create an `httpd.conf` file, open it and restore your changes to the original for mod_perl and CGI. mod_ssl also will add a new port number section such as:

```
<IfDefine SSL>
    Listen 80
```

```
    Listen 443
</IfDefine>
```

The `Listen` directive tells Apache to open additional ports for requests. Port 443 is the standard port for HTTPS (secure HTTP), just as port 80 is the standard for regular HTTP traffic. If your server is listening on some other port for HTTPS, you'll need to specify the port number as part of the URL.

There should also be a new section in the virtual host configuration that looks something like this:

```
<VirtualHost _default_:443>
    #  General setup for the virtual host
    DocumentRoot "/usr/local/apache/htdocs"
    ServerName secure.example.site
    ServerAdmin theo@example.site
    ErrorLog /usr/local/apache/logs/error_log
    TransferLog /usr/local/apache/logs/access_log

    #   Enable/Disable SSL for this virtual host.
    SSLEngine on
</VirtualHost>
```

Apache's `VirtualHost` sections create a sort of server within a server; the parameters to the directive tell Apache when incoming requests are intended for the virtual host. This is typically done by IP address, but can be managed by host name or by port number as shown here. mod_ssl uses a virtual host section to contain directives that apply only to secure HTTP.

A virtual host can have its own document root and log files, and directives placed in this section will apply only to requests for that host. Thus in this case requests that are sent to port 443 will share the usual log files with those sent to port 80, but any error messages will identify the server as secure.example.site. Most importantly, the directive `SSLEngine` turns on SSL communications for port 443.

You can use this section to configure rules that apply only to secure requests. This is a good way to set up applications that require SSL, or to direct users to different applications depending on how they connect. Later we'll use this trick to have one URL display two different pages depending on whether the user makes a secure connection.

After checking and changing your configuration, you are ready to restart Apache. First bring it up in nonsecure mode:

```
/usr/local/apache/bin/apachectl start
```

You should be able to browse the default Apache splash page with your browser. If you have reconfigured your mod_perl and CGI scripts they should work as they did before.

Now shut down Apache and restart it with SSL enabled:

```
/usr/local/apache/bin/apachectl startssl
```

If you encrypted your temporary certificate during the installation, apachectl will prompt you for your pass phrase when you start the server. That's great for security but not practical for a server that needs to be started from a script at boot time. To decrypt your certificate, use the openssl utility that was built as part of OpenSSL:

```
cd /usr/local/apache/conf/ssl.key
cp server.key server.key.crypt
/usr/local/openssl-0.9.5a/apps/openssl rsa -in server.key.crypt -out
server.key
```

Apache will now start without asking for the pass phrase. Make sure that `server.key` is owned by root and that only root can read it.

When Apache starts correctly with SSL enabled you have a secure server. Tell your browser to open https://www.example.site/ to see the default page. Note that URLs beginning with https are directed to port 443 automatically; if you have Apache listening on a different port, you'll need to include the port number in the URL.

The rest of your applications should work fine. Your code can check the HTTPS environment variable to determine if it is running in a secure session:

```
if ($ENV{'HTTPS'}) {
    print 'SSL session';
}
else {
    print 'Not secure';
}
```

But we're getting ahead of ourselves. We want a secure channel so we can handle sensitive information, which nearly always means we want to handle user data (as defined in the last chapter). We'll start by identifying the users.

6.4   USER AUTHENTICATION

Novice web programmers are sometimes surprised that web servers have no real idea whom they are talking to when serving up files and running scripts. Programmers who learned their skills on Unix and other user-oriented operating systems are accustomed to having a function that returns a user ID. Mailing lists for most any web development product get questions like "Where do I get the user's name?"

The web server knows the IP address of the requesting browser and an identifying string that should indicate its make and model,[4] but not much more. Most ISPs recycle IP addresses for dial-up users, and even if the address is static there is no guarantee that a particular user will always use the same machine, so this information isn't useful as a user ID.

---

[4] Applications which use advanced HTML or client-side scripting rely on the HTTP_USER_AGENT environment variable to identify the browser, so they can decide on which set of incompatible features to use.

There are two basic approaches to user authentication in a web application: use the authentication protocol built into HTTP or do it yourself.

6.4.1 Using HTTP authentication

Chances are you've already encountered the HTTP authentication protocol already: you request a URL from your browser, and before a new page appears the browser pops up a window or displays a prompt asking for your username and password. That's the authentication protocol in progress.

What's actually going on is more complex than it appears. The protocol works this way:

1 The browser sends the usual request to the web server for a URL.

2 The web server's configuration indicates that authentication is required for that URL. It sends back a 401 response to the browser along with a *realm* for authentication; the realm is a human-readable name used by the server to identify a group of secured documents or applications.

3 If the browser implements authentication caching, it checks its cache for the given realm and server ID. If it already has a username and password for the realm, it uses it to skip the next step.

4 If the browser doesn't have a cache, or the realm isn't there, it displays a dialog box or prompts the user for his username and password for the given realm. The realm should be displayed here so that the user knows which user and password to send.

5 The browser sends the URL request to the server again, including the username and password in the request headers.

6 The server checks the URL, sees that it requires validation (again—remember that this is a stateless protocol), and sees that it has validation headers. It looks up the given username and password in some form of database.

7 If the information is valid, the web server applies the authentication rules for the URL and verifies that the user is authorized to read the associated document or run the application. Everything proceeds as normal if so; if not, it sends back an error page.

8 If the username and password didn't validate, the server sends another 401 response back to the browser, and the cycle continues.

The main advantages of using HTTP authentication is that it already works; Apache has excellent support for it and comes with a few simple user database modules. mod_perl extends Apache with a module that provides authentication against any DBI database, making it trivial to keep your user IDs and other user data together (see the Apache::DBI module's documentation for more information). Many databases (including MySQL and PostgreSQL) have Apache authentication modules as well, so slimmed-down Apache servers can share an authentication database with mod_perl or other applications.

The primary disadvantage of the HTTP authentication mechanism is that it is unfriendly to new users. GUI browsers display a small dialog box prompting for the username and password without much in the way of helpful information. One way to work around this problem is to send a helpful page of information when user authentication fails, instructing the user on how to get an account or what to do at the prompts; this also lets experienced users log in without hand-holding.

HTTP authentication is good for protecting static pages, download directories, or other data for which you would not otherwise write a custom application. It's also fine for administrative functions or private applications when the users will know what to do.

The next section will discuss other reasons to handle authentication yourself. In the meantime, let's look at an example using Apache's simple text file user database.

Suppose we want to protect a page of server status information—the Apache::Status example from the previous chapter. Recall that it was configured in mod_perl.conf like so:

```
# Server status
<Location /perl-status>
   SetHandler perl-script
   PerlHandler Apache::Status
   order deny,allow
   deny from all
   allow from 192.168.
</Location>
```

The deny and allow directives restrict access to a protected network. For purposes of remote administration it would be more helpful to set password protection on the /perl-status URL. The new configuration to handle that is:

```
# Server status
<Location /perl-status>
   SetHandler perl-script
   PerlHandler Apache::Status
   AuthUserFile data/admin_users
   AuthName "Administrator functions"
   AuthType basic
   require valid-user
</Location>
```

Optionally we could keep the deny and allow directives to further restrict access.

The AuthUserFile directive gives the path to a password file to be used in authenticating requests. Remember that all relative file paths begin with Apache's root directory. AuthName gives the realm name for authentication, and AuthType basic tells Apache that it shouldn't expect the browser to encrypt the information— more on that later in the chapter. The require valid-user directive tells Apache that any user with a valid password may retrieve the URL.

Now we need a password file. Apache comes with a utility for creating and managing passwords: htpasswd. Run it with the -c switch to create a password file and add a user:

```
/usr/local/apache/bin/htpasswd -c /usr/local/apache/data/admin_users theo
```

The name of the password file matches the path given in `AuthUserFile` earlier (if you add Apache's root directory to the front). The program will prompt for a password, or you can supply one on the command line after the username.

After performing these steps, restart Apache and try the /perl-status URL. If all is well you will be prompted for the user you just created, and then will see the status information page. That's all there is to adding password protection to important pages.

There are more options than shown in this example. For instance, `require` can list a subset of valid users, or specify groups instead of usernames. See the online Apache manual for more information.

The password file created by htpasswd contains user names and encrypted passwords. Make sure that the file is readable by Apache's user. If your applications add users automatically or let them change passwords, then the application's effective user will need write access also.

The text file system is fine for pages that aren't accessed too often and only by a small number of users. To validate the user, Apache has to scan through the file sequentially until it matches the username, so this mechanism will be too slow for a larger user base. Apache comes with hash file authentication modules that are more efficient, but if you have a large user base you probably also have a relational database somewhere. See the examples in the next section for ways to have Apache use your database for authentication.

6.4.2 Doing your own authentication

As you probably know, many web sites have their own login pages, rather than using the mechanism shown in the previous section. Why is that preferable? There are a number of reasons to choose to do your own logins:

- Having your own login page means not relying on browsers to behave correctly. Some browsers had bugs in the caching code for realm information which would cause the browser to send an invalid user and password pair to the server over and over (as the server kept sending back invalid authentication responses). It also allows the application to bypass the cache if the developer wants to force the user to log in.

- I mentioned previously that the standard mechanism is unfriendly to new users. By using your own page, you can control what your users see, provide clear instructions, and tell them what authenticating information you want. You might also use a cookie to store the username and prompt only for the password. I've seen sites that have a custom login page which offers an option to store both username and password in a cookie, allowing the user to choose less security and more convenience.

- Most browsers indicate when SSL is in use by displaying a lock icon. Letting the user log in from a special page gives a visual reassurance that they are sending their password securely. Alternatively, if you offer the page over both HTTP and HTTPS you can warn users when they are using an insecure connection.

- A login page is one more chance to display announcements, important links, and advertising.

The most obvious disadvantage of writing your own login page is that you have to do the coding yourself, but that's not terribly difficult. The CGI input set includes the password input, which behaves like a regular text input but doesn't echo back the user's characters; and on most OSs Perl includes a `crypt` function which performs quick one-way encryption. (You could store passwords in your database without encrypting them, but then anyone with unrestricted access to the database could steal user passwords, resulting in one of those high-profile cases mentioned at the start of the chapter.)

Here is a very simple login procedure, from `Login.pm`:

```
sub handler {
    # Receive and parse the request.
    my $r = shift;
    my $q = Apache::Request->new($r);
    my $username = $q->param('username') || '';
    my $password = $q->param('password');
```

This is the usual opening code; parse the request, get the expected parameters. The application needs to display a login form, but it needs to display it in more than one case, so the form is built in a variable using Perl's here-doc syntax:

```
    # The login form.
    my $loginForm = <<ENDHTML;
<FORM METHOD="POST">
 <TABLE>
  <TR>
   <TD>Username:</TD>
   <TD><INPUT TYPE="text" NAME="username"
              VALUE="$username" SIZE=10></TD>
  </TR>
  <TR>
   <TD>Password:</TD>
   <TD><INPUT TYPE="password" NAME="password" SIZE=20></TD>
  </TR>
 </TABLE>
 <INPUT TYPE="submit" VALUE="Log in">
</FORM>
ENDHTML
```

The syntax looks odd but it works well once you are used to it. Everything from the line after the label (marked by <<) to the next line beginning with the label is stored in the variable $loginForm (or passed to the print function in later examples). In this case, the label is ENDHTML and the variable contains all those lines of HTML. This syntax works anywhere that a quoted string would work. In fact, it behaves just as double quotes, so that variables in the here-doc are interpolated as they are in a double quoted string. We use that property to put the current value of $username into the form. If the application is invoked more than once, the username will be preserved (but the password will not). That's also why $username is initialized if the parameter wasn't passed in, to avoid errors about use of uninitialized values.

The here-doc syntax can be used with other forms of quoting; see Perl's perldata documentation for more information. Since web applications often print large blocks of HTML, it is common to see this syntax in Perl CGI or mod_perl scripts. It's not uncommon to use an HTML editor to create the HTML blocks and then cut and paste them into the body of the script. In the next chapter we'll look at other ways to merge Perl and HTML.

Meanwhile, back to the example. Note that the login form uses a password input type (also named password). As you'll see if you run the example, the browser echoes asterisks (or nothing) as the user types there. Also note that the form specifies METHOD="POST". The default method is GET, which would pass the username and password as part of the URL (and thus probably display them on the browser's URL line and log them in the server's access log).

Having stored the form, the application can now print it:

```
    # If no username then just display the form.
    unless ($username) {
        my $title = $ENV{'HTTPS'} ?
        'Secure login form' : 'Insecure login form';
        $r->send_http_header('text/html');
        print <<ENDHTML;
<!DOCTYPE HTML PUBLIC>
<HTML>
 <HEAD><TITLE>$title</TITLE></HEAD>
 <BODY>
  <H1>Enter your username and password</H1>
  $loginForm
  To create an account, go <A HREF="/create">here</A>.
 </BODY>
</HTML>
ENDHTML
        return OK;
    }
```

If the username isn't passed in, the application assumes that the user hasn't yet seen the login form. It prints it, then returns OK to Apache.

Note that the title of the page depends on whether or not the user is logging in over a secure connection. Of course, a more security-minded application might want to redirect users logging in without SSL to another page, or offer a stronger warning. The title is interpolated into the string via the here-doc syntax again, as is the entire login form. The application also offers a link to the page for creating an account (which we'll get to later in the chapter).

If we did get parameters, we check for the user and password in the database:

```
    # Check the username and password.
    if (defined($username) && defined($password)) {
        my $dbh = DBI->connect('DBI:mysql:Info:localhost',
                               'web','nouser');
        return error($r, "Can't connect to Info") unless $dbh;
        my ($try) = $dbh->selectrow_array
          ('SELECT password FROM Users WHERE username = ?',
             undef, $username);
        if ($try && $try eq crypt($password,$try)) {
          $r->send_http_header('text/html');
            print <<ENDHTML;
<!DOCTYPE HTML PUBLIC>
<HTML>
 <HEAD><TITLE>Hello $username</TITLE></HEAD>
 <BODY>
   Login successful.  Please proceed.
 </BODY>
</HTML>
ENDHTML
        return OK;
}
    }
```

After getting the parameters and checking that we got some kind of value for each, the code connects to the database as it did in the examples from chapter 4. If DBI->connect doesn't return a value, the handler calls error to display an error page; the code is left out for brevity here.

Assuming we're talking to the database, the code next retrieves the given user's record from the Users table. $try is set to the password retrieved from the table. If $try is not set, that means there is no such user in the table, and the handler will drop out to the next section.

The handler then calls crypt on the password and the value stored in the table. (The need for passing in the already-encrypted value from the database is explained later in this section.) If the given password encrypts to the same value stored in the database, the user is valid and the application can go on to whatever it is going to do.

If not, or if any of the other tests given previously failed, the handler goes on to the next section:

```
    # Invalid user or password.
    $r->send_http_header('text/html');
```

```
    print <<ENDHTML;
<!DOCTYPE HTML PUBLIC>
<HTML>
 <HEAD><TITLE>Invalid login</TITLE></HEAD>
 <BODY>
   <H2>The username and/or password you entered is not valid.
   Please try again.</H2>
   $loginForm
  To create an account, go <A HREF="/create">here</A>.
 </BODY>
</HTML>
ENDHTML
    return OK;
}
```

This section simply displays a page indicating that the user can't log in with the given password. It offers the login form again right here, instead of just telling him to go back. The username will be defaulted into the field already but he will have to type his password again. This makes use of the default ACTION attribute for the form— the Submit button invokes the same URL again with the current parameters.

The handler needs to be added to mod_perl's configuration:

```
PerlModule Examples::Login
<Location /login>
    SetHandler perl-script
    PerlHandler Examples::Login
</Location>
```

Before trying it, we need to create the Users table. Here is a sample command:

```
CREATE TABLE Users (
      username CHAR(12) NOT NULL,
      password CHAR(13) NOT NULL,
      name CHAR(30),
      email CHAR(24),
      PRIMARY KEY (username)
      );
```

Don't worry about the name and email fields for now. They'll be used by a later example.

We need to add a user to the table, along with an encrypted password. Suppose we want the user to be named 'fred' with password 'tuesday'. We need the encrypted string before we can add Fred.

MySQL has an encryption function, so if that's our database of choice (as shown in the examples) we could use that. But I previously mentioned that Perl makes the crypt function available if the operating system provides it, so let's look at a more generic example:

The arguments for crypt are the string to encrypt and a two character *salt* value, used by the algorithm in a way similar to the seed of a random number generator.

crypt returns a 13 character encrypted string whose first two characters are the salt value. That's why the last block of code retrieved the encrypted password value from the database first before validating the unencrypted test string. The encrypted value was passed along with the test string to crypt which looks only at the first two characters of the salt. Without the correct password and salt string it is mathematically unlikely that crypt will generate a matching value.[5]

To create a valid user entry then we need to first create a salt value and encrypt the password with it. We could use any two characters for the salt (as long as they are letters, numbers, or '.' or '/'), but it would be best to generate a random value for each user. Here is a short Perl procedure from the Examples::CreateUser module that generates the salt and returns a string encrypted with it:

```
sub createPassword {
    my $password = shift;
    my @salts = ('a'..'z', 'A'..'Z', 0..9, '.', '/');
    my $salt = join("", map {$salts[rand(scalar(@salts))]} (1,2));
    return crypt($password, $salt);
}
```

We need to call this function with fred's password. Fortunately, Perl lets us concoct scripts on the command line. By invoking the Examples::CreateUser via the -M switch we can call it like so:

```
perl -MExamples::CreateUser -e \
    'print Examples::Createuser::createPassword("tuesday"), "\n"'
PQTpxFNiroTcU
```

Note that you need to either tell Perl where to find Examples::CreateUser via the -I switch or run the command from the directory which holds Examples, such as /usr/local/apache/lib/perl in my example configuration.

Add user fred with the encrypted password to the database:

```
INSERT INTO Users VALUES ('fred', 'PQTpxFNiroTcU');
```

Now you should be able to log in as fred. Remember that the database user (web) and password given in the example code have to be valid for the database, and the web user must have access to the Users table.

The following examples will make use of createPassword in building a user manager.

---

[5] While it is important to keep the original password a secret, the salt string is less important. There are 4,096 possible salt values (64 choices for each of two characters), and while a human wouldn't want to type them all in, a trivial program could find the right salt given the correct password.

6.4.3 Do I need SSL for this?

Whether you use HTTP authentication or write your own, you face the choice of encrypting the login transaction or not. There are plenty of sites that don't, depending on the situation and what is at risk:

- If the application and its users are protected behind a firewall, encryption is probably not necessary. Conversely, business data which needs to be hidden from employees' casual curiosity should not be on a web site.

- Encryption may be too expensive for high-traffic systems, especially if the user data doesn't contain sensitive information. If you track only user preferences, for example, you (and your users) probably aren't concerned about password theft.

- The HTTP authentication protocol includes another `AuthType`, digest, which does not send passwords in clear text. If your users run browsers that implement digest authentication, then you don't need to add the overhead of SSL. Unfortunately, digest authentication isn't implemented dependably in browsers.

Obviously any e-commerce site which accepts credit cards, Social Security numbers, or other important identifications should use SSL. If your site would be liable to a suit were a user's data stolen, you must encrypt the channel or warn the user of the risk. The simplest practical test is: what could happen to a user whose information is stolen from this site? If your users could be harassed in some way, or your data would help a criminal in committing a crime against them, you are obligated to protect their information.

6.5 USER MANAGEMENT

If a site has user data, it probably needs user management: functions for creating new user accounts and modifying their information.

A site can offer public registration, which allows anyone to create an account and access the site, or have private registration where the potential user fills in a form or sends a mail message to an administrator who then creates an account. Sites that use private registration might still have a web application to create accounts, although the application and other administrative functions would be protected from public use.

To fill out the login handler started earlier, we'll add a page for filling in user information and creating an account. This will also extend the Users table into something more useful and add goodies such as telling the user when the account was last used.

The code samples here are from `CreateUser.pm`:

```
sub handler {
    # Receive and parse the request.
    my $r = shift;
    my $q = Apache::Request->new($r);
    my $username = $q->param('username') || '';
    my $password = $q->param('password');
    my $name = $q->param('name') || '';
```

```
    my $email = $q->param('email') || '';
```

This is the standard beginning, checking for and initializing parameters. It also builds the entry form in a variable, using the parameter values:

```
    # The entry form.
    my $form = <<ENDHTML;
<FORM METHOD="POST">
 <TABLE>
  <TR>
   <TD>Desired username:</TD>
   <TD><INPUT TYPE="text" NAME="username"
             VALUE="$username" SIZE=10></TD>
  </TR>
  <TR>
   <TD>Password:</TD>
   <TD><INPUT TYPE="password" NAME="password" SIZE=20></TD>
  </TR>
  <TR>
   <TD>Your real name:</TD>
   <TD><INPUT TYPE="text" NAME="name"
             VALUE="$name" SIZE=30></TD>
  </TR>
  <TR>
   <TD>Your e-mail address:</TD>
   <TD><INPUT TYPE="text" NAME="email"
             VALUE="$email" SIZE=24></TD>
  </TR>
 </TABLE>
 <INPUT TYPE="submit" VALUE="Log in">
</FORM>
ENDHTML
```

The code carries forward the previous values (if any) of the username, name, and email fields, blanking the password (which isn't echoed anyway). You might recall from the examples in chapter 3 that CGI.pm held onto parameter values automatically (it calls them "sticky parameters"). Coding your own HTML means having to take care of this yourself or it means not having to work around CGI.pm features, depending on whom you ask.

If your password creation form doesn't echo password inputs, you should probably require the user to type the password twice and verify that both inputs are the same before creating the account. Some registration systems create a random password for the user and email it to a requested address. In that case, ask for the address twice to help avoid typos.

```
    # Get all the required inputs
    unless ($username && $password) {
        my $title = $ENV{'HTTPS'} ?
          'Secure login form' : 'Insecure login form';
        $r->send_http_header('text/html');
```

```
        print <<ENDHTML;
<!DOCTYPE HTML PUBLIC>
<HTML>
 <HEAD><TITLE>$title</TITLE></HEAD>
 <BODY>
  <H2>Please fill in the following information:</H2>
  $form
 </BODY>
</HTML>
ENDHTML
        return OK;
    }
```

This section prints the form if the required fields, username and password in this case, haven't been filled in. A more complex application should give the user a clear indication of what is required.

Note that when we created the Users table we allowed nulls in the name and email fields. We also don't require them to be input here. In general, a field which is required on a form shouldn't allow nulls in a database and vice-versa.

The next section verifies that the username is unique:

```
    # Check for a unique username.
    my $dbh = DBI->connect('DBI:mysql:Info:localhost',
                            'web','nouser');
    return error($r, "Can't connect to Info") unless $dbh;
    my ($try) = $dbh->selectrow_array
      ('SELECT password FROM Users WHERE username = ?',
        undef, $username);
    if ($try) {
        $r->send_http_header('text/html');
        print <<ENDHTML;
<!DOCTYPE HTML PUBLIC>
<HTML>
 <HEAD><TITLE>Already exists</TITLE></HEAD>
 <BODY>
  <H2>User $username already exists.</H2>
  $form
 </BODY>
</HTML>
ENDHTML
        return OK;
    }
```

The retrieval code is the same as that of the previous example, but in this case a successful SELECT means that the requested username is taken. It doesn't really matter what we select from the table, so long as we'll know if the record exists. If not, we can go on to add the record:

```
    # Encrypt the password.
    $password = createPassword($password);
```

```
    # Write the user record.
    $dbh->do('INSERT INTO Users VALUES (?,?,?,?)',
             undef, $username, $password, $name, $email)
      || return error($r, $dbh->errstr);
```

This uses the `createPassword` function shown earlier to encrypt the password and then store it in the database. DBI's convenient `do` function prepares and executes the given statement. Recall that the first argument after the statement is for attributes, and the rest are placeholder values. There's nothing left to do but confirm things with the user.

```
    # Tell the user that they're one of us now.
    $r->send_http_header('text/html');
    print <<ENDHTML;
<!DOCTYPE HTML PUBLIC>
<HTML>
 <HEAD><TITLE>Account created</TITLE></HEAD>
 <BODY>
  <H2>Account created.</H2>
  Welcome to our site.
 </BODY>
</HTML>
ENDHTML
    return OK;
}
```

Add this handler to your configuration file and restart Apache as usual:

```
PerlModule Examples::CreateUser
<Location /create>
    SetHandler perl-script
    PerlHandler Examples::CreateUser
</Location>
```

Note that the handler is assigned to /create, the URL which was given in the previous login example.

Although the creation example is meant to tie in to the login example, it could also be used by sites with HTTP authentication. The Apache::DBI module includes an authentication hook that validates users in a database using DBI. The creation form could be used to create the necessary record, and regular HTTP authentication takes over from there.

Application designers should bear in mind that users come to a site for content, not user management. If a user requests protected pages without logging in, give them the login page, then go directly to the requested content after the user is validated. HTTP authentication appears to do this automatically (though actually it is the browser's authentication cache that quietly identifies the user for each page); techniques for doing it yourself follow in the next section.

6.6   LOGIN SESSIONS

Users expect web applications to behave as desktop programs: they log in once, and that validation is good until they exit the system. Unfortunately, the nature of web browsing doesn't mesh well with this, particularly in that "exit the system" part.

The typical web approximation is to keep a *login session*: the user is asked for validation the first time he makes a request, and that validation is good as long as the user remains active. If the user doesn't send a request for a certain time period—say, one hour—the session expires and the user is "logged out" (even though in reality he was never logged in).

This kind of validation checking should be unobtrusive, as described at the end of the previous section. We won't require the user to start at a particular page, but will detect when the user needs to log in; having done so, we'll serve up the requested content.

The following example, `Directory.pm`, offers web access to a regular file directory. While this is a very poor way to serve static content, it does demonstrate login sessions and also how a mod_perl application can simulate a file directory (as described in the previous chapter). The program is divided into two functions: `handler` receives the requests and either calls `serveDocument` or displays the login form.

First let's look at `handler`:

```
sub handler {
    # Get the request object and parse it.
    my $r = shift;
    my (%session, @ids, $username);

    # Connect to the database.
    my $dbh = DBI->connect('DBI:mysql:Info:localhost',
                           'web','nouser');
    return error ($r, "Can't connect to database")
      unless $dbh;
```

This is typical opening code. Most paths through the function will use the database, so we open it here for simplicity. Remember that Apache::DBI will be secretly caching database connections, so in most cases this code will simply return a waiting database handle.

Next we check for a session ID:

```
    # Check for a cookie with the ID.
    if (my $cookies = Apache::Cookie->fetch) {
        my $cookieID = $cookies->{'ID'}->value
            if $cookies->{'ID'};
        push @ids, $cookieID if $cookieID;
    }
```

This is the same sort of test we saw in other session examples. As in the previous chapter, we'll check for the session ID both in a cookie and in the URL to support browsers that don't manage cookies for us. The URL is checked for the session ID when we look for the document name:

```
# Examine the URI; it may have a session id,
# and also probably has the requested file.
my $path = $r->uri;
if ($path =~ m{/protected/sessions/(\w+)(/.*)?}) {
    # Session ID is in the URL.
    push @ids, $1;
    $path = $2;
}
elsif ($path =~ m{/protected/(.+)}) {
    # Session ID (if any) will be in a cookie.
    $path = $1;
}
else {
    # Display the directory.
    $path = '';
}
```

If there was a session ID in either, we check that it is a valid session and hasn't expired. Note that this example uses Apache::Session::MySQL to store session info; see the documentation on that module for how to create the required table in your database.

```
# Did we get a session ID somewhere?
if (@ids) {
    my $inSession;
    foreach my $try (@ids) {
        eval {
            tie %session, 'Apache::Session::MySQL', $try,
                {Handle => $dbh, LockHandle => $dbh};
        };
        next if $@;
```

If eval noted an error then the session ID isn't valid. Some periodic task should run through the Sessions table and remove data that is too old to be useful. The following shows how this example uses expired sessions:

```
# Check the expiration.
if (time() - $session{'time'} < 3600) {
    # Less than one hour, so we're good.
    $inSession++;
    last;
}
else {
    # Get the username, then delete it.
    $username = $session{'username'};
    tied(%session)->delete;
    undef(%session);
}
}
```

If less than an hour has passed, the session is still good (and as you'll see later, we reset the timer for another hour). If the session is too old, we extract the username from the session so that we can supply it as a default on the login form. Thus we shouldn't delete old sessions from the database too aggressively, since the information is valuable at least in providing this default.

```
    # If we have a session ID, go on to the document.
    if ($inSession) {
        # Display the document.
        return serveDocument($r, $path, \%session);
    }
}
```

If a valid, unexpired session is waiting, the application calls the function that serves up the requested content. The serveDocument function is discussed later in this section.

A more complex application might have a dispatch section here, where the appropriate function is called for the URL or other parameters.

The rest of the handler takes care of the login process:

```
# If we don't have a session ID (or it expired), the
# user must log in.  Check for parameters.
my $q = Apache::Request->new($r);
$username = $q->param('username') || $username || '';
my $password = $q->param('password');
if ($username && $password) {
```

If the handler receives CGI input parameters, then it has already been invoked from the login form; validate those values and proceed.

The initialization of $username may look a bit odd here. If it was passed in as a parameter, we want to use that value—that's what the user typed in. If, however, $q->param('username') doesn't return a value, then use the value extracted from an expired session (discussed earlier in this section) if there was one, otherwise just set it to an empty string to avoid the "unitialized value" error message when we print $username.

The next section validates the username and password as previous examples did:

```
    # Validate the parameters.
    my ($try) = $dbh->selectrow_array
        ('SELECT password FROM Users WHERE username = ?',
          undef, $username);
    if ($try && $try eq crypt($password,$try)) {
        # Everything is valid, so create a session
        # (and set the cookie too).
        eval {
            tie %session, 'Apache::Session::MySQL', undef,
                {Handle => $dbh, LockHandle => $dbh};
        };

        # Log errors if trying to create a new session failed.
```

```
            if ($@) {
                return error($r, $@);
            }
```

This example creates sessions explicitly by passing `undef` to the `tie` call. It reuses the opened database handle (as the section that validated an open session did) for writing the session data to the database.

The final step is to add the username to the session data before displaying the requested content:

```
            # Store the username.
            $session{'username'} = $username;

            # Serve the document.
            return serveDocument($r, $path, \%session);
        }
    }
```

If we get this far, the user hasn't seen the login form yet, or has supplied invalid information. This section displays the form as shown before:

```
    # No username or invalid username/password.
    $r->send_http_header('text/html');
    print '<!DOCTYPE HTML PUBLIC "-//IETF//DTD HTML//EN">',
          '<HTML><HEAD><TITLE>Please log in</TITLE></HEAD><BODY>';
    if ($password) {
        print '<H2>The password you have entered is invalid.',
              'Please verify your username and continue</H2>.';
    }
    else {
        print '<H2>Please log in.</H2>';
    }

    # Print the form.
    print <<ENDHTML;
<FORM METHOD="POST">
 <TABLE>
  <TR>
   <TD>Username:</TD>
   <TD><INPUT TYPE="text" NAME="username"
              VALUE="$username" SIZE=10></TD>
  </TR>
  <TR>
   <TD>Password:</TD>
   <TD><INPUT TYPE="password" NAME="password" SIZE=20></TD>
  </TR>
 </TABLE>
 <INPUT TYPE="submit" VALUE="Log in">
</FORM>
ENDHTML

    # That's it.
    return OK;
}
```

Note that the handler will use the previous value for the username as a default, but will clear the password each time.

The default action is to request the current URL again when the user clicks the Submit button. We take advantage of that fact here. If the user requests a file but isn't logged in, or his session has expired, he will see this form. After submitting a valid username and password, the maintained URL will be used to look up the requested file.

Note that our session data here is pretty trivial; we could store this much data in a cookie. However, we keep the time stamp data in the session database, where the user can't fake it. Also by expiring sessions quickly we limit the possibility of a snooper stealing an open session. After the session expires, the most a malicious user can learn from an old session ID is the username which created it.

Now let's take a look at the second function, `serveDocument`:

```
sub serveDocument {
    my ($r, $path, $session) = @_;
```

The function receives the request object (`$r`), the document name (`$path`), and the session data as arguments. Note that the caller passed a reference to the session hash: `\%session` in the caller turns into `$session` here.

The function starts by sending a cookie to the browser with a revised expiration:

```
# Set or refresh the session ID cookie.
my $cookie = Apache::Cookie->new($r,
                    -name => 'ID',
                    -value => $session->{'_session_id'},
                    -path => '/protected',
                    -expires => '+1h',
                    );
$cookie->bake;
```

Here the cookie's expiration time is the same as the session expiration time used in the handler function. That makes sense, but it would actually be better to set a longer expiration on the cookie—days or months. There is no sensitive data in the cookie itself; the session ID is carried along to set the default username in the login form.

Alternatively, the application could use two cookies: one for the session ID, set to expire in the right amount of time, and one for the username, with a long lifespan, thus supplying the desired default information.

Depending on the path, the function takes one of two paths:

```
# Send other headers and start the document.
$r->send_http_header('text/html');
print '<!DOCTYPE HTML PUBLIC "-//IETF//DTD HTML//EN">';
if ($path) {
    print "<HTML><HEAD><TITLE>$path</TITLE></HEAD><BODY>";
    if (open(DOC, '<', "$docRoot/$path")) {
        print <DOC>;
        close DOC;
    }
```

```
else {
    print "No such document: $path";
}
}
```

If the document root directory (stored in a global variable, $docRoot, which is initialized outside these functions) and path together form a valid file name, the function opens the file and prints its contents. If not, it displays an error message. That's mostly to catch cases where a user types in a bad URL; the next section shows that the user can get a list of valid files if they don't supply a path:

```
else {
    # Show the directory.
    print '<HTML><HEAD><TITLE>Directory</TITLE></HEAD>',
          '<BODY><H2>Documents:</H2>';
    opendir DIR, $docRoot;
    while (my $entry = readdir DIR) {
        next unless -f "$docRoot/$entry";
        print '<A HREF="/protected/sessions/',
        $session->{'_session_id'}, "/$entry",
        '">', $entry, '><br>';
    }
    closedir DIR;
}
```

This section shows the list of documents (all regular files in the document root directory). Note the way the function constructs links to the document, each of the form:

```
<A HREF="/protected/sessions/sessionID/filename>
```

where *sessionID* is the value also sent in the cookie and *filename* is the actual file name. This supports users whose browsers don't handle cookies, and preserves the file name in the URL. The code in the handler which analyzes the URL will pick up both values and pass them back to this function.

The function refreshes the time stamp in the session and exits:

```
# Refresh the session timeout.
$session->{'time'} = time();

# End the document.
print '</BODY></HTML>';
return OK;
}
```

This example didn't require SSL. If the data being served is sensitive data, it would be simple to modify the handler to check the HTTPS environment variable and refuse to serve users on unsecured channels. It could also set the security attribute of the session ID cookie to send the ID only when the user connects with SSL.

To run this example, configure the handler in mod_perl.conf, then modify the code for an appropriate document root. Don't forget to add the session table to your database if you are going to use Apache::Session::MySQL, which also documents the required table layout. Here is the configuration section:

```
PerlModule Examples::Directory
<Location /protected>
    SetHandler perl-script
    PerlHandler Examples::Directory
</Location>
```

That takes care of security and user administration. The next chapter deals with ways to merge Perl and HTML more cleanly than shown by the long clumsy `print` statements in these examples.

CHAPTER 7

Combining Perl and HTML

7.1 HTML DESIGN

Chapter 3 focused briefly on using Perl to generate HTML. The intervening chapters have shown more complex scripts that created ever more HTML, sometimes printing long lists of strings or here-docs. If you think about this trend while contemplating a large web application, you can see that we are headed for trouble: large sections of the Perl code would actually be HTML, clumsily handled within the text of the scripts.

And where do those HTML sections come from? If you create complex HTML layouts (or work with a designer), chances are your HTML editor is different from your Perl editor. While HTML can be composed with any text editor, many web page designers prefer a specialized HTML editor that helps create error-free layouts more effectively.[1] Similarly, Perl programmers want an editor that helps with Perl coding. Although there are people with both skills, it is far more common for a development group to include programmers and page designers on the same team.

You may be thinking, "ah, but Perl is very clever about file handling; I can have my Perl script load an HTML file and print sections as needed!" That's a terrific idea, but program-centric. HTML is display-oriented, and there are advantages to laying out the HTML first and having it refer to Perl code (or any of the many other web programming languages). A web page designer can lay out a page and mentally fill in the blanks where a program will add the dynamic content.

This leads naturally to the next clever idea: "since Perl is even more clever about text handling, I can write a script that reads an HTML file, finds special tags, and replaces them with program output." This very clever idea has sparked several commercial products and a surprising number of Perl implementations, not to mention whole new languages like PHP. Before you start on your own embedded Perl system please take a look at the rest of this chapter; the tool you need may be waiting for you on CPAN.

7.2 SERVER-SIDE INCLUDES

Since the early days of web publishing, designers have been frustrated by the "flat" nature of HTML. It seems very natural to have an HTML file refer to other files to display common elements of sites. For example, a web site could have a header, navigation bar, and footer that each of its pages use to maintain consistency and preserve a common look and feel.

It's not surprising that one of the first extensions to HTML provided this mechanism, called SSI. The web server performs the necessary file merging, then sends a single document to the requesting browser.[2] In Apache, SSIs are performed by mod_include, which is normally configured as a handler for files ending in `.shtml`.

When triggered by a request, mod_include scans through the requested document looking for comments of this form:

```
<!--#element attribute=value ... -->
```

The comment is replaced by the value of the element, depending on the type. The range of elements handled by mod_include goes far beyond file merging. The elements can also reference variables or the output of a command, depending on the element, as well as `if`, `else`, and `elif` elements for conditional document sections. A

---

[1] I tend to use Emacs for both, but then, I'm the sort of person who tends to use Emacs.

[2] Client-side includes would presumably involve the browser fetching multiple documents and displaying them together. This is how frames work, and graphics are handled via separate fetches, but I can't think of anything which does this with merged HTML inside the browser (apart from doing so via JavaScript).

web page for a business that takes orders over the phone could use conditional elements to display different text during business hours and off-times.

Here is a simple example of Apache's SSI used to display a clock, in `clock.shtml`:

```
<!DOCTYPE HTML PUBLIC "-//IETF//DTD HTML//EN">
<HTML>
  <HEAD><TITLE>Another clock</TITLE></HEAD>
  <BODY>
    <H2>Current time on <!--#exec cmd="hostname" --></H2>
    <H1><!--#echo var="DATE_LOCAL" --></H1>
    <H6><!--#echo var="DOCUMENT_NAME" --> last modified
      on <!--#echo var="LAST_MODIFIED" --></H6>
  </BODY>
</HTML>
```

The example uses two different include elements. The `exec` element runs a command:

```
<!--#exec cmd="hostname" -->
```

Here it runs the `hostname` command to find out the name of the web server. Any shell command should work here, with its output substituted back into the original document. The `exec` element can also be used to run CGI scripts and include their HTML output, via the `cgi=` attribute, but the preferred way to do this is via the `include` element, which will be described shortly.

The `echo` element displays the value of a variable. mod_include predefines a handful of variables (most of which are shown in the example), and the document can create more via the `set` element. The example uses `echo` to show the current time, the name of the file, and the date and time the file was last modified.

To run the example, place `clock.shtml` in your server's document directory (`/usr/local/apache/htdocs` in my configuration), then check to be certain that `httpd.conf` allows includes. You can do that by adding a handler for the chosen file type (usually `.shtml`) or by using the `XBitHack` directive and making the files executable. Here's the first method:

```
    AddType text/html .shtml
    AddHandler server-parsed .shtml
```

The second method sets `XBitHack` for the directory:

```
    XBitHack On
```

Then mark the files that should be parsed for includes as executable:

```
$ chmod a+x *.shtml
```

`XBitHack` can also be set to `Full`, which tells Apache to set a Last-Modified header in the parsed results before sending them to the client. This enables client caching of dynamic pages—of course, you may not want the client to do that if the content changes from moment to moment.

Further, the directory containing the example has to enable includes in its options; that is, `Options Includes` must be in effect for the `Directory` or `Location` that controls the file.

Of course, the primary reason for using SSI is to merge HTML files via `include`. This element can pull in a file directly via the `file=` attribute or fetch a document by its URL with the `virtual=` attribute. The latter is preferred for all usage, and works for any document or application on the same server. Virtual includes allow a document to use the output of a CGI script or any other program that the web server itself can handle.

Here is `hello.shtml`, another small example using actual includes:

```
<!DOCTYPE HTML PUBLIC "-//IETF//DTD HTML//EN">
<HTML>
  <HEAD><TITLE>Hello</TITLE></HEAD>
  <BODY>
    <H2>The output from hello-web.pl is:</H2>
    <!--#include virtual="/cgi-bin/hello-web.pl" -->
    <H2>The to-do list:</H2>
    <PRE><!--#include file="todo.txt" --></PRE>
  </BODY>
</HTML>
```

This document merges the output from one of our first examples with the contents of a simple text file. Note that a virtual include accepts an absolute or relative URL, but not a site specifier; the server must handle the document itself. The URL can map to a document, application, or even another file handled by SSI, resulting in nested includes.

The second include in the example loads a text file inside of `<PRE>` tags to preserve its line breaks and white space. You can include regular HTML files also, or anything else for that matter. The `file=` attribute is limited to relative file paths, and the including document is responsible for surrounding the file content with appropriate tags to format it correctly.

7.2.1   SSI with mod_perl and Apache::Include

One of mod_perl's strengths is the way it integrates Perl with other Apache modules. When built with support for mod_include it provides a new element type, `perl`, which runs Perl handlers directly. Here is an example, from `faster.shtml`:

```
<!DOCTYPE HTML PUBLIC "-//IETF//DTD HTML//EN">
<HTML>
  <HEAD><TITLE>Hello</TITLE></HEAD>
  <BODY>
    <H2>The output from hello-mod_perl.pl is:</H2>
    <!--#perl sub="Apache::Include" arg="/perl/hello-mod_perl.pl" -->
  </BODY>
</HTML>
```

The `sub=` attribute specifies the handler, and the `arg=` attribute passes information the handler needs. In this case the handler is Apache::Include, which runs the Apache::Registry script specified by the `arg=` attribute.

Without Apache::Include we could have included the same application this way:

```
<!--#include virtual="/perl/hello-mod_perl.pl" -->
```

When the `virtual=` attribute refers to a URL handled by mod_perl, Apache invokes it via the appropriate handler (Apache::Registry or the handler specified by `PerlHandler`) and returns the results. While this works fine, it involves some extra server overhead.

The `perl` element's `sub=` attribute can refer to any Perl function or module, including the ones created as examples in previous chapters. For instance, to display the login form from chapter 6 in any SSI document, use this tag:

```
<!--#perl sub="Examples::Login" -->
```

When `sub=` is given a module name, it automatically calls the `handler` function in that module. If you want to call a function defined inside one of your custom modules, give the full name of the function, i.e., Examples::Login::password.

Any arguments given in the `arg=` attribute are passed after the request object. Here is an example that chooses randomly from one of its arguments and prints it:

```
<!--#perl sub="sub {shift; print $_[int(rand(scalar(@_)))]}"
          arg="One" arg="Two" arg="Three" -->
```

For even more enhancements to mod_include, look for the Apache::SSI module, which lets you create your own new element types.

Server-side includes give page designers a good tool for consistent layout and simple access to scripts and Perl functions. They don't really merge scripting with HTML, however. For more complex pages we want the HTML and Perl code to work together as a unit. For that we need more tools, as described in the following section.

7.3   SCRIPTING IN HTML

To go beyond SSI we need a tool which allows HTML and scripting to flow naturally together, in the same way that an HTML document or a Perl procedure have a natural flow. It should allow conditions, loops, and other simple program blocks. It should make it easy to interpolate variables and function results into normal HTML. In-line scripts and called functions should be allowed to generate arbitrary HTML, and integration with other Apache and CGI modules is a big plus.

Merging Perl with HTML is not a new idea. A quick search through CPAN shows several modules with names that suggest this capability (HTML::Template, HTML::EmbPerl), and a closer look will turn up several more. Since the task plays to Perl's strengths of text handling, pattern recognition and dynamic code generation, a number of talented programmers have written modules to do this. Untold similar modules run specialized variants on many web sites.

Though each of these many modules is distinct, they more or less break down into two approaches. Some allow Perl code to be embedded directly in HTML and interpreted as the enclosing document is requested, and others define templates with their own minilanguages that use data supplied by an accompanying script. All of them to some degree add new HTML tags or other mark-up language to denote the scripting sections.

Both approaches have their merits, and both have strong entries. The following sections show examples of each approach using an assortment of modules. This area is changing rapidly, so as always you should look around and see which modules have features and style that match your application best.

7.3.1 Perl and HTML

The approach that appeals most strongly to Perl coders is to have Perl and HTML intermixed. This can be as simple as having specially tagged Perl statements that are interpreted in order, or can involve more complex schemes that mix Perl and HTML sections in a document. These modules include an interpreter that reads the document and processes the Perl sections, merging their output with the static text and printing the result. Example modules include Apache::ASP, HTML::EmbPerl and HTML::Mason.

Apache::ASP began as a port of Microsoft's Active Server Pages (ASP) to Apache and Perl. The HTML tag syntax will be familiar to those who have developed ASP pages, with <% %> marking Perl code sections and <%=%> marking variable interpolation.

Suppose we have a hash called %members which stores a list of organization members and their email addresses. To simplify the example we'll assume some other part of the document loads the hash. Using Apache::ASP, we might display the list as follows:

```
<H2>Our members and their addresses:</H2>
<TABLE>
  <% foreach (sort keys %members) { %>
    <TR>
      <TD><%=$_%></TD><TD><%=$members{$_}%></TD>
    </TR>
  <% } %>
</TABLE>
```

Here we have Perl code embedded in a table. For each element of the %members hash, the code generates a table row with one cell for the name and one for the email address. Note how the key and hash value for each row are interpolated into the cells.

The same task in straight Perl code would look something like:

```
print '<H2>Our members and their addresses:</H2><TABLE>';
foreach (sort keys %members) {
    print "<TR><TD>$_</TD><TD>$members{$_}</TD></TR>";
}
print '<TABLE>';
```

The code could be tighter, and CGI.pm's helper functions could also be used to simplify things, but you get the idea.

The Perl code for looping through the %members hash and printing the key and value is the same in both approaches. The difference is that the Apache::ASP example could easily have been created by an HTML designer and then filled in by a programmer. Tell the designer to create a one-line table with some sample data, for example, and then edit the Perl code into the result. The designer could also modify the layout after the code has been added—many HTML editors are aware of the ASP tag syntax and will leave it alone, making it safe for designers to work in their editor of choice.

This is a trivial example of course; the advantages of using embedded scripts increase for more complex pages, where a specialized editor helps to keep the HTML standard and correct.

HTML::EmbPerl is even more editor-friendly. It is specifically designed to allow Perl and HTML to be written from an HTML editor. Perl sections are tagged with a variety of brackets: [- -] for Perl code, [+ +] for interpolation, and so on. EmbPerl accounts for the kinds of translations an HTML editor will inflict on Perl code, removing <BR> from the ends of lines and changing < back to < in code sections before sending it to the Perl interpreter.

EmbPerl also crosses over into the minilanguage school by adding its own form of common Perl constructs such as loop control, bracketed by [$ $]. The example appears slightly different in EmbPerl:

```
<H2>Our members and their addresses:</H2>
<TABLE>
  [$ foreach (sort keys %members) $]
    <TR>
      <TD>[+ $_ +]</TD><TD>[+ $members{$_} +]</TD>
    </TR>
  [$ endforeach $]
</TABLE>
```

HTML::Mason takes a building-block approach to creating pages that stresses creating reusable pieces. It provides the same kind of tools for mixing Perl into HTML: <% %> tags Perl expressions for interpolation, and any lines beginning with % are interpreted as Perl. Longer sections of Perl code can be blocked off with the <%perl> and </%perl> tags, which execute code and discard its output.

Here's the example again using Mason's tags:

```
<H2>Our members and their addresses:</H2>
<TABLE>
% foreach (sort keys %members) {
   <TR>
     <TD><% $_ %></TD><TD><% $members{$_} %></TD>
     </TR>
% }
</TABLE>
```

Just from this example and discussion, it is hard to tell these modules apart. All of them work well in Apache as mod_perl handlers or can be configured to run as CGI scripts. If your site needs only some simple Perl code mixed into HTML, any of them will serve you well; I'd recommend EmbPerl for its editor-friendly nature. I prefer Mason's architecture for more complex applications, which I'll discuss in detail after a quick tour of template modules.

7.3.2 Templates

While mixing Perl and HTML appeals to programmers, templates seem to appeal more to architects and designers. The idea behind templates is simple: a template document contains text and directives. A template processor reads the document and runs an associated script (or the processor is run by the script). The script then supplies data to the directives. The processor prints text from the template until it encounters a directive; then it takes data from the script and substitutes it for the directive in the output, continuing on until the end of the template.

Template modules separate code clearly from documents. The document designer and programmer create independent files that work together to produce the final output. Template systems are in many ways the natural follow-on to SSIs.

Template modules are also known as minilanguage modules when their directives start to take on elements of programming. This speaks to the fact that creating a complex document requires more than simple one-for-one substitution; they need loops, conditionals, and nested elements. As these minilanguages build in more features, they get closer to the embedded scripting school (and their creators lose more arguments about the need to separate documents and code).

There are a number of template modules to choose from with varying styles. Some, such as Text::Template allow Perl variables in directives, while others like HTML::Template, and the Template Toolkit keep the Perl code at arm's length, using named parameters to mark data that is supplied by the corresponding script.

The templates processed by Text::Template look a lot like embedded scripts. I classify it as a template module mostly because it requires a separate program. Here is an example that once again displays the member list, after a header showing the date:

```
<H2>Members as of {$date}</H2>
<TABLE>
{ foreach (sort keys %members) {
    $OUT .= "<TR><TD>$_</TD><TD>$members{$_}</TD></TR>\n";
  }
}
</TABLE>
```

The loop looks remarkably like the pure Perl example from the previous section. Note how the header interpolates the date: Text::Template interprets any section marked off by {} as Perl code, and substitutes its results into the output. The loop itself has no output, but uses the special variable $OUT to accumulate the rows of the table.

To use this template, we need a Perl script to supply values for `$date` and `%members`, and then call Text::Template. A minimal version might look like this:

```perl
#!/usr/local/bin/perl -w

use strict;
use Text::Template;

my %params = (
    'date' => scalar(localtime),
    'members' => {
      'Theo Petersen' => 'theopetersen@yahoo.com',
      'Ima User' => 'user@example.site',
    },
    );
my $template = Text::Template->new(
    TYPE => 'FILE',
    SOURCE => 'members.tmpl',
    );
print "Content-type: text/html\n\n";
print $template->fill_in(
    HASH => \%params,
    );
```

Text::Template allows the script to pass the data to the template in a number of ways, including local variables. This example builds all of the template's data into a hash, `%params`, which has elements for each variable named in the template. Note that the `members` element is itself a hash.

After building the hash it loads the template from the file `members.tmpl` into a processor object, `$template`. It then runs the template via the `fill_in` method, passing in the `%params` hash. The output of `fill_in` is the completed template:

```
<H2>Members as of Wed Jun 28 14:47:23 2000</H2>
<TABLE>
<TR><TD>Ima User</TD><TD>user@example.site</TD></TR>
<TR><TD>Theo Petersen</TD><TD>theopetersen@yahoo.com</TD></TR>

</TABLE>
```

Text::Template is not at all puritanical about separating documents and code, as you can see; it uses Perl code for directives in nearly all cases. The script that uses the template generally does whatever database work is needed to load the data, then calls Text::Template to run the logic embedded in the document.

By comparison, HTML::Template enforces the separation quite strongly—the template and code communicate only through named parameters. A template for our example would be:

```
<H2>Members as of <TMPL_VAR NAME=DATE></H2>
<TABLE>
  <TMPL_LOOP NAME=MEMBER_LIST>
    <TR><TD><TMPL_VAR NAME=NAME></TD>
```

```
    <TD><TMPL_VAR NAME=EMAIL></TD></TR>
  </TMPL_LOOP>
</TABLE>
```

The new tag <TMPL_VAR> tells HTML::Template to substitute the named variable into the document. The <TMPL_LOOP> </TMPL_LOOP> block provides looping as the name suggests. The template processor expects an array of the given name, whose rows contain the variables to be substituted within the enclosed block. Any literal text in the block is repeated for each row in the array.

Here is the corresponding script:

```
#!/usr/local/bin/perl -w

use strict;
use HTML::Template;

my $template = HTML::Template->new
  (filename => 'members.htmp');
$template->param(
    'DATE' => scalar(localtime),
    'MEMBER_LIST' => [
      {'NAME' => 'Theo Petersen',
       'EMAIL' => 'theopetersen@yahoo.com'},
      {'NAME' => 'Ima User',
       'EMAIL' => 'user@example.site'},
    ],
  );
print "Content-type: text/html\n\n";
print $template->output;
```

The script loads the template document into a processor object, then feeds it data via the param method. Note that DATE and MEMBER_LIST correspond to the names given in the first <TMPL_VAR> tag and the <TMPL_LOOP> tag. Each row of MEMBER_LIST is a hash containing more variables—rather as if each were another call to param, just for that row.

HTML::Template is also editor-friendly, in that all of the tags can be written in a comment style:

```
<!-- TMPL_VAR NAME=DATE -->
```

In real-world usage, most of the logic of an HTML::Template script is involved in building up the arguments to param. Since the arguments to param form a hash, the order of the elements isn't important, so the logic of the script doesn't have to match the flow of the document. If there were several tables involved, the script would need to build a corresponding number of arrays, each loaded with hash values. The order of rows in arrays is important of course, since the document will display the data in the same order for that array. After doing all that, invoking the template and getting its output are trivial.

The document can also contain some logic—there are `<TMPL_IF>` and `<TMPL_ELSE>` tags—but in general the code and template are completely separate. One can imagine having a script supply data for multiple templates, either in different languages or displaying different sets of data. Documents (and further templates) can be pulled in via `<TMPL_INCLUDE>`, though a common method among developers is to process a template and pass its output to another template via `<TMPL_VAR>`.

The Template Toolkit has perhaps the most impressive pedigree of any of the modules discussed in this chapter. It had previous incarnations as Text::MetaText and other tools, and sports a long list of contributors and add-on modules. Version 2 was a major overhaul to improve performance, which made this module the target to beat in speed comparisons with the other tools I've mentioned. One of the major success stories of the Toolkit is Slashdot (http://slashdot.org/), the popular news site. The Slash engine is Open Source also, and many community site builders are learning about Template Toolkit as they learn Slash. See chapter 8 for more information on Slash and community sites.

The Toolkit is also the ultimate minilanguage module, defining so many directives that one questions the mini part. Besides the usual tags for interpolating variables, it has two styles of loops, four conditionals, function calls, includes, macros, filters, directives for loading its own plug-ins, and even an optional directive to embed Perl code. This leaves the Text::Template fans asking "why not just use Perl," but the Toolkit's power is worth a closer look.

As always, here is the member list template:

```
<H2>Members as of [% date %]</H2>
<TABLE>
  [% FOREACH member = member_list %]
    <TR><TD>[% member.name %]</TD>
      <TD>[% member.email %]</TD></TR>
  [% END %]
</TABLE>
```

And the corresponding script:

```
#!/usr/local/bin/perl -w

use strict;
use Template;

my $template = Template->new();
my %params = (
    'date' => scalar(localtime),
    'member_list' => [
      {'name' => 'Theo Petersen',
       'email' => 'theopetersen@yahoo.com'},
      {'name' => 'Ima User',
       'email' => 'user@example.site'},
    ],
    );
```

```
print "Content-type: text/html\n\n";
print $template->process('members.t2k', \%params)
  || die $template->error;
```

Variable interpolation is handled by putting the name of a parameter into a [% %] tag, as shown in printing the date. More interesting is the FOREACH directive; this takes a list parameter and iterates the enclosed block for each row in the list. In this case, the list contains hashes, and the Toolkit has a distinctive syntax for getting the hash members—they are interpolated as [% member.name %] and [% member.email %] respectively.

Apart from those differences, it is hard to tell the Toolkit from HTML::Template just by this example. The real power comes in the use of its plug-ins, such as its DBI interface. To see more of what the Template Toolkit can do, look at its extended example in the section titled the *Template Toolkit*.

7.4   *HTML::MASON*

Having taken a quick tour of available modules, let's settle on one and look more closely.

My personal choice among the tools I've mentioned is HTML::Mason (or just Mason to its fans). I like the component-based architecture and the depth of its tools. It also comes with adequate documentation, a statement which I can rarely make.

I'd like to offer a point-by-point proof why my own choice is better than the rest, but I don't think there is a simple answer. After reviewing the other modules again, trying out examples and asking other developers for their recommendations, I can say for sure only that they're all good. Like many choices in software, I prefer Mason because I like the way it works, and others will pick different modules for the same good reason.

Now that I've gotten that off my chest, I'll show you why I like Mason. You'll also see more of it in chapter 10, which has an extended e-commerce example built from components.

7.4.1   The case for Mason

Like most embedded Perl tools, Mason started out life as a site's private Perl module. It has been in active development as a CPAN module for over two years, and has a wide user base, including a number of large commercial sites. Mason has its own web site (http://www.masonhq.com) which features example components sent in by users, and separate mailing lists for users and developers.

Mason scores well on most buyer's guide points. I've mentioned its extensive documentation; the users' mailing list is very active and supportive, especially the product's chief programmers (Jonathan Swartz and Dave Rolsky). The list often features examples and pointers to new working sites. Mason integrates well with other Apache and CGI tools, so prior development isn't lost, and it doesn't introduce any ongoing support costs.

One of the things that I like about Mason is its learning curve: I was able to create working documents very quickly when I first tried it, and whenever I probe deeper I learn more about what it can do. I feel the same way about Perl itself, that it is kind to beginners and rewards those who spend time learning its intricacies.

Since reaching its 1.0 release milestone in 2001, both Mason's popularity and development pace seem to have increased. New features are coming out regularly, so take a look at the web site for the latest information.

7.4.2   Installation

Mason can be installed via CPAN (remember that the module is called HTML::Mason), but requires some manual steps to run.

1 After unpacking the distribution (or installing it via CPAN), look for `Config.pm` under Mason's directory. This module defines some global configuration information which tells Mason how to store cache information. The default is to use GDBM_File, but if your system doesn't have that module or you prefer otherwise you can switch it to DB_File or another hash file database.

2 You will need to choose a *component root* and a *data root*, explained in more detail in this chapter. The component root is the top-level directory for Mason files, much like Apache's document root. The data root is for Mason's temporary files and cache data. I put my Mason components under Apache's root in `/usr/local/apache/mason`, and set the data root to the same directory I use for other application files, `/usr/local/apache/data`. Remember to set permissions on the directories so that Apache's user can read and write files.

3 For a simple Mason configuration you can set up everything you need in your mod_perl configuration, but for most applications you will probably want a custom handler script for Mason requests. The distribution ships with examples such as `handler.pl` which do the minimal work needed. I use an enhanced version of `session_handler.pl` which sets up sessions the way my other examples do. Copy your handler of choice to another directory (I put mine in `/usr/local/apache/lib/perl/mason_handler.pl`) and edit it to pass Mason the component and data roots, or set those values in the configuration file as shown in step 4.

4 Add Mason to your mod_perl configuration. If you aren't using a custom handler, then set the values for the component and data roots:

```
PerlSetVar MasonCompRoot /usr/local/apache/mason
PerlSetVar MasonDataDir /usr/local/apache/data
PerlModule HTML::Mason::ApacheHandler
```

If you are using a custom handler, then load it via `PerlRequire`:

```
PerlRequire /usr/local/apache/lib/perl/mason_handler.pl
```

Note the use of `PerlRequire` rather than `PerlModule` to load mason_handler.pl. The handler script is actually part of HTML::Mason, but lives outside of it for ease of modification. By either method, you'll also need to tell Apache which files are Mason components:

```
Alias /mason/ "/usr/local/apache/mason/"
<Location /mason>
    SetHandler perl-script
    PerlHandler HTML::Mason
    DefaultType text/html
</Location>
```

The Alias directive maps Mason's component root onto URLs beginning with /mason. The DefaultType shouldn't be necessary if your Mason files end in .html, but I prefer distinctive file types as you'll see in my examples.

You should be ready to try out the examples in the distribution. If you want to run my examples without change, you'll probably need my handler script (which you'll find on the book's web site along with the examples).

7.4.3   Making pages from components

While Mason can be used to simply embed Perl into HTML, its real usefulness is for creating more complex documents. Mason builds documents out of pieces called *components*.

A component contains HTML (probably interspersed with Mason tags) and Perl sections. The component that corresponds to a requested URL is called the *top-level component*; it also controls the general page layout. A component can contain all of the content for a page, or can refer to other components for pieces. These *subcomponents* can refer to additional components and so on.

Suppose our company's web site offers various reports that exist as text files. Our Mason example is a page that offers a list of reports and lets the user display selected reports on his browser. The top-level component is `reports.mhtml`:[3]

```
<& /header.mcmp, title => 'Reports' &>
  <H2>Reports for
    <% $session{'username'} || 'Anonymous' %> </H2>
    <TABLE>
    <TR><TH>Name</TH><TH>Size</TH><TH>Date</TH></TR>
%    if (my @files = $m->comp('reportList.mcmp')) {
%      foreach my $file (@files) {
          <& reportEntry.mcmp, file => $file &>
%      }
%    }
%    else {
```

---

[3] In my examples, top-level components end in `.mhtml` and subcomponents end in `.mcmp`. This choice is arbitrary, and Mason is perfectly happy with any names, although it is best to use some convention that allows your handler to prevent users from accessing subcomponents by URL.

```
          No reports available.
%    }
   </TABLE>
<& /footer.mcmp &>
```

This example is very different from the earlier Mason demonstration of embedded Perl. There is relatively little HTML; most of the content is contained in < & &> tags, so let's start there.

In Mason, the < & &> tag is used to invoke a component. The tag contains the component path followed by arguments specified as key-value pairs (as with hash elements). A component path can be absolute or relative, like a URL. /header.mcmp is an absolute reference, so the corresponding file should be under the component root. The component receives a title argument whose value is 'Reports'.

Here is header.mcmp:

```
<!DOCTYPE HTML PUBLIC "-//IETF//DTD HTML//EN">
<HTML>
 <HEAD><TITLE><% $title %></TITLE></HEAD>
 <BODY BGCOLOR="#FFFFCC">
  <H3>Welcome to NotYourActualSite.com!</H3>

<%args>
 $title => 'www.example.site'
</%args>
```

This component contains considerably more HTML. It has the usual document opening, a <HEAD> block and the opening <BODY> tag. Inside the <TITLE> is an example of Perl variable interpolation, which we saw in the previous example: <% $title %> is replaced with the value of the $title variable. This variable is in turn passed as an argument from the calling component.

Arguments are specified inside the <%args> tag block. Each line specifies one argument, giving the name followed by a default value if any. If an argument doesn't have a default value, the component's caller must supply a value or Mason will indicate an error.

The header.mcmp component was invoked by the top-level component like so:

```
<& /header.mcmp, title => 'Reports' &>
```

Thus inside of header.mcmp we expect <% $title %> to be translated to 'Reports'. The component also includes the standard HTML header tags and sets a background color for the document, then displays a simple banner. The color and banner line could have been arguments as well.

Looking back at the top-level component, let's skip down to the end to look at footer.mcmp:

```
  <p><H6>Copyright 2001 by example.site</H6>
  </BODY>
</HTML>
```

This component contains the matching </BODY> and </HTML> tags for the blocks that were opened in the header component. It also puts a copyright notice in fine print at the bottom of the page. It doesn't have any Perl code or arguments—components can be simple text.

By using components for document headers and footers, Mason makes it easy to standardize a site. Other common elements such as navigation bars or notices can be incorporated into all of your pages without having to change each page when a link or the text of a message changes.

Back to the top-level component—after the header, it displays a title that includes an interpolated Perl expression:

```
<% $session{'username'} || 'Anonymous' %>
```

For the moment, let's not worry about where %session comes from—you'll see it initialized later in the discussion of the session handler. Note that we can have any simple Perl expression in a <% %> tag, including function calls or computed values. In this case, if the username is set in the session, then that value is displayed; if not, it displays 'Anonymous'.

The top-level component then sets up a table and prints the column headers. The rows of the table are displayed by a foreach loop:

```
%    if (my @files = $m->comp('reportList.mcmp')) {
%      foreach my $file (@files) {
          <& reportEntry.mcmp, file => $file &>
%      }
%    }
%    else {
       No reports available.
%    }
```

The list of reports and the rows of the table are both supplied by yet more components. Lines beginning with % are straight Perl, used here to more easily intersperse code, HTML, and component tags. Code can invoke components too as seen here: $m->comp('reportList.mcmp') calls the named component as if it were in <& &> tags, even allowing us to pass arguments if desired. $m is the Mason request object; it is passed to all components, as is the Apache request in $r. The comp method is used to invoke a component and pass its output (if any) to the calling Perl code.

Here is reportList.mcmp:

```
<%perl>
  if (opendir REPORTDIR, $reportDir) {
    my @reports = grep /\.txt$/, readdir REPORTDIR;
    closedir REPORTDIR;
    return @reports if @reports;
  }
  return ();
</%perl>
```

```
<%args>
 $reportDir => '/home/reports'
</%args>
```

This component makes the list of reports, and consists entirely of Perl code. Rather than marking each line with `%`, it uses the `<%perl>` tag to set off the section that looks for report files. It receives one argument, `$reportDir`, which is defaulted to `/home/reports` if the caller doesn't supply a value. It scans through the directory looking for files that end in `.txt`, and returns a list of them. In a component, `return` works the same as it does in a Perl function, ending further execution.

There is reason for debate over the value of a component that contains just Perl code. On the one hand, keeping all the code together in components is convenient for developers, and has the advantages of automatic recompilation when code changes. On the other hand, a regular function in a module makes more sense for anything beyond the scope of short scripts of the kind seen here.

The return value in this example is supplied to the caller's `foreach` loop. Inside that loop, each file name is passed to `reportEntry.mcmp`:

```
<TR>
 <TD><A HREF="reports/<% $file %>"><% $link %></A></TD>
 <TD><% $size %></TD>
 <TD><% scalar(localtime($date)) %></TD>
</TR>

<%args>
 $reportDir => '/home/reports'
 $file
</%args>

<%init>
 my $link = $file;
 my ($size,$date) = (stat("$reportDir/$file"))[7,9];
 $file .= '.html';
</%init>
```

This component demonstrates good structure for a nontrivial Mason component: the output HTML is all at the top, followed by argument processing and then code in the `<%init>` section. The HTML section makes use of values passed in directly or set by the Perl code section. Having things in this order makes for a clean break between display and code, and doesn't bother Mason's interpreter in the least: it handles the `<%args>` section first, then the `<%init>` section, then executes the rest of the Perl code in order of appearance.[4] Use of `<%init>` for readability is strongly encouraged among Mason developers.

---

[4] The `<%cleanup>` and `<%once>` tags also have special execution times, and there are other tags that set up variables or create components. See the HTML::Mason documentation for details.

Note how each line of the report contains a relative URL. Each file becomes a link under /mason/reports, although that's not where the files are. We'll look at Mason's tool for handling missing files in the section on dhandlers.

7.4.4   How Mason interprets components

Now that we have a substantive example, let's see what Mason does when a user requests reports.mhtml.

First the browser sends Apache a request for:

http://www.example.site/mason/reports.mhtml.

That URL matches the pattern we assigned to Mason in `mod_perl.conf`, so Apache passes the request along to the handler you created (`mason_handler.pl` in my example setup). The handler does any setup work you've given it,[5] then passes the request to Mason via the call to:

`HTML::Mason::ApacheHandler::handle_request.`

Mason finds the requested component (or not—see the next section on what happens when a component is missing) and compiles it into Perl function. If there is a `<%args>` section, each line is changed into a my variable (and initialized if there is a default value). Literal text in the component is replaced with calls to Mason's output routine, passing the text as an argument. The compiler converts `<& &>` tags into calls to `$m->comp`; these will in turn load and compile their respective components. `<% %>` tags and other Perl sections are added to the function more or less as-is (though the `<%init>` section is moved to the beginning of the function). If anything goes wrong during this phase it logs the errors and sends an error page back to the requester.

Assuming everything is compiled, Mason then calls `$m->comp` for the top-level component. If the original request to Apache included parameters (either in the URL or via the `POST` method) Mason turns them into arguments for the top-level component. That means a top-level component can have a `<%args>` section and receive named arguments just as a subcomponent can.

The component's function runs, generates output, and sends the results (via Mason, and via Apache in turn) back to the browser. If the URL and the components don't contain any clues, the browser will have no way of knowing that the document was generated on the fly.

On subsequent requests for the same top-level component, Mason skips the compilation step after checking its cache and verifying that its code is up to date. After you set up some components, take a look in the directory you gave Mason as the data root.

---

[5] Your customized handler is a good place to do any added security checking. A session-oriented handler loads or creates a user session in this phase also.

There will be a subdirectory of files named the same as your components, containing the Perl code that Mason generated.

To see Mason's cache checking in action, make a visible change to one of your components and then request it again. You may need to tell your browser to ignore its own cache and really send the request to the server. The change is reflected immediately. Behind the scenes, Mason checked the modification times of the component files against the times stored in its cache, noticed the change and recompiled anything that is new.

Checking every component file for every request can add up to a lot of work on a busy system. See the *Mason resources* section later in this chapter and look in Mason's administration documentation for ways to make Mason's cache checking more efficient.

7.4.5 Faking missing components with dhandlers

In the report list example, report files are represented by URLs such as http://www.example.site/mason/reports/file.txt.html. I mentioned previously that we would not create components for each file; instead we'll use another Mason technique.

Since the URL matches the pattern assigned to Mason, Apache passes the request along to Mason's handler. Mason looks in the reports directory of its component root (which you'll remember is not the directory where the files are actually located) but doesn't find the file. Before returning an error, Mason checks the directory for a *dhandler*.

A dhandler is a piece of catch-all code that can take the place of a missing component. If you have installed my Mason examples on your system, you'll find this dhandler in /usr/local/apache/mason/reports/dhandler:

```
<& /header.mcmp, title => $file &>
  <H2><% $file %> as of <% $date %></H2>
  <PRE><% $body %></PRE>
<& /footer.mcmp &>

<%init>
 my $file = $m->dhandler_arg;
 $file =~ s/\.html$//;
 $file = "/home/reports/$file";
 my ($date, $body);
 $date = -M $file;
 if ($date) {
   $date = localtime($date);
   if (open(REPORT, '<', $file)) {
     local ($/) = undef;
     $body = <REPORT>;
     close(REPORT);
   }
   else {
     $body = 'Cannot open file';
   }
 }
```

```
  else {
     return NOT_FOUND;
  }
</%init>
```

As you can see, a dhandler looks more or less like a regular Mason component. The main difference is that it uses a special function, $m->dhandler_arg, to find out the path of the component that it was called to replace. In this example the name of the report file is part of the path, so the dhandler takes off the .html extension and uses the remainder to look for the text file in the real reports directory. The <%init> section gets the modification date of the file and loads the text into $body, both of which are then interpolated in the text of the component. A <PRE> block is used around the text to preserve the file's formatting.

Notice that the dhandler component reuses the header and footer components we saw previously. It invokes them via absolute paths, since this component lives in a subdirectory of the component root.

dhandlers could be used in any circumstance in which you want to create the illusion of a directory or can generate a component based on path information. For example, an image database could use dhandlers to serve up both images and thumbnails. One dhandler would retrieve the image and send it as-is, while another could use a Perl module to reduce the image size and send the result.

When Mason goes looking for a dhandler, it starts in the directory where it expected to find the missing component, then looks at each parent directory in turn until it finds a dhandler. In general, only one dhandler is called for a component, but Mason's documentation explains how and why you can have a dhandler defer processing.

Mason has another kind of handler, the autohandler, which is called before processing a top-level component. That technique is used in the next section.

7.4.6   Autohandlers

Let's tie this chapter's examples into the previous discussion of security and protected pages.

Suppose our report server has documents that are not meant for the general public. Web sites commonly gather usage statistics[6] and make them available to administrators. We could protect such reports via HTTP authentication, but in this case we'll use more features of Mason to do the job.

We'll set aside a subdirectory of Mason files which will contain protected documents and applications, and call it protected as we did in previous examples. When a user requests a URL under http://www.example.site/mason/protected we want to

---

[6] There are a number of free tools that will analyze Apache's access log and generate statistics on usage of your site. Many of these tools are written in Perl; there is even one written in Mason, available from the component archive.

automatically present him with a login form if he isn't already authenticated. We'll track authentication via the session mechanism.

In order to check every request to the protected directory for authentication we'll use an *autohandler,* a component which runs before the top-level component. Autohandlers are like dhandlers in that they apply to a directory and its children. However, autohandlers apply only to components that exist, while dhandlers take the place of components that don't exist. Also, if a component's parent directories contain autohandlers, all of them are run from the top down. The autohandler is then responsible for running the requested component.

The simplest kind of autohandler is one which enforces document standards such as headers and footers. For example, we could have an autohandler in our component root which looks like this:

```
<& /header.mcmp &>
% $m->call_next;
<& /footer.mcmp &>
```

Remember that the autohandler will be called for each top-level component in its directory or a child directory, so if this code were in the component root (in a file called `autohandler`) it would be invoked for every Mason request. It invokes the header and footer components that we've seen before; in between it calls `$m->call_next`, a function that is peculiar to autohandlers. `call_next` invokes the requested top-level component along with its arguments, or the next autohandler in the chain of execution.

While the example autohandler is convenient for enforcing standards, we should note that we've lost the capability for each top-level component to pass a title to `header.mcmp`. Mason's developer documentation explains how to use component attributes and methods to work around this. The autohandler could request the title and other attributes from the component.

An autohandler isn't restricted to just invoking the requested component. It can present a different page entirely, as this example does in `/usr/local/apache/mason/protected/autohandler`:

```
<& /header.mcmp, title => 'Protected pages' &>
 <%perl>
  if ($session{'authenticated'}) {
     $m->call_next;
  }
  else {
     $m->comp('login.mhtml',
              'goto' => $m->fetch_next->path,
        @{$m->caller_args(-1)}
              );
  }
 </%perl>
<& /footer.mcmp &>
```

This autohandler is mostly a Perl section, although it also enforces the header and footer components as the previous example did. (Of course, if the previous example were in the component root, then this autohandler wouldn't need to enforce the standards—the higher level autohandler would already have run.) It checks for an authentication flag in the session hash. If present, it invokes the requested component via `call_next`.

If the authentication flag is not set, the autohandler instead uses `$m->comp` to display a login component. It passes the requested component's path via `$m->fetch_next`, along with any arguments for the top-level. `fetch_next` and `caller_args` are more Mason helper functions that are meant specifically for autohandler use (although other components can use `caller_args` too).

Let's take a look at the login component, `protected/login.mhtml`:

```
% if ($session{'authenticated'}) {
  <& $goto &>
% } else {
%   if ($password) {
      <H2>Username or password is invalid.</H2><P>
%   }
  <H2>Please enter your username and password</H2>
  <FORM METHOD="POST">
   <TABLE>
    <TR>
     <TD>Username:</TD>
     <TD><INPUT TYPE="text" NAME="username"
             VALUE="<% $username %>" SIZE=10></TD>
    </TR>
    <TR>
     <TD>Password:</TD>
     <TD><INPUT TYPE="password" NAME="password" SIZE=20></TD>
    </TR>
   </TABLE>
   <INPUT TYPE="submit" VALUE="Log in">
  </FORM>
% }

<%args>
  $username => $session{'username'} || ''
  $password => ''
  $goto => ''
</%args>

<%init>
  if ($username && $password) {
    my ($try) = $dbh->selectrow_array
      ('SELECT password FROM Users WHERE username = ?',
             undef, $username);
    if ($try && $try eq crypt($password,$try)) {
        $session{'authenticated'}++;
        $session{'username'} = $username;
```

```
    }
  }
</%init>
```

This is the biggest component we've seen yet, so let's break it down in order of execution.

The `<%args>` section shows that the login component is expecting a username, a password, and the component to go to after successful authentication. None of the arguments are required, since the username and password won't be present when the form is first displayed and the user may have requested the login form directly.

The `<%init>` section does the authentication check, using code that we've seen in our previous examples. Don't worry about where $dbh came from. It is initialized in the same place as the session hash, as will be shown in the next section. If the given username and password are valid, the section also sets the authenticated flag in the session hash and stores the username there too. You may recall that previous example components displayed the username in a banner if it was set—that value comes from here.

Now for the actual page contents. If the authenticated flag is set, the component simply evaluates to `<& $goto &>` which invokes the component whose path is in $goto. That component is the one that originally triggered the autohandler. We'll come back to this in a moment.

If the authenticated flag isn't set, the component displays a form and defaults in the username if one was passed in or was set in the session. This is a convenience for anyone who is logging in again after a timeout or had a typo in his password. Since the form doesn't set an ACTION attribute, the default action will be to return to this same URL (and thus this component) when the user clicks the Submit button.

The order of actions for authentication is:

1 The user requests a URL under /mason/protected, thus triggering the autohandler.

2 The autohandler sees that the user is not authenticated, and so calls `login.mhtml` instead, passing the requested component as an argument.

3 `login.mhtml` doesn't see a valid username and password, so it displays the form.

4 The user fills in the form (correctly, let's say) and clicks Submit, which sends a request for the same URL he'd requested in step 1.

5 The autohandler once again invokes `login.mhtml`, and again passes the requested component.

6 `login.mhtml` checks the username and password, and sets the authenticated flag. It then displays the requested component.

Here is an example component, `secureReports.mhtml`, that can reside in the `protected` directory:

```
<H2>Secure reports for <% $session{'username'} %> </H2>
 <TABLE>
 <TR><TH>Name</TH><TH>Size</TH><TH>Date</TH></TR>
```

```
% foreach my $file ($m->comp('/reportList.mcmp',
%                      'reportDir' => '/home/secure')) {
    <& /reportEntry.mcmp, file => $file,
        reportDir => '/home/secure' &>
% }
 </TABLE>
```

This version closely resembles reports.mhtml, except that it passes a different directory to the reportList and reportEntry components, and its banner assumes the username is set in the session hash (and it will be before this component is shown). The header and footer are also absent—the autohandler took care of them for us.

Now that we have secured pages, let's see where that session hash comes from.

7.4.7 Session management

Mason includes an example of a session managing handler, session_handler.pl. I used it as the basis for my own, changing the session store to MySQL and adding in the initialization of a global database handle. This makes the Mason examples compatible with the scripts and handlers from the previous chapters.

This is the short version of my modified session_handler.pl; the longer version integrates URL-based sessions, but that adds considerable complexity, since the URL has to be remapped onto components after the session ID is removed.

```
package HTML::Mason;

use strict;

use HTML::Mason::ApacheHandler (
    'args_method' => 'mod_perl',
    );
use HTML::Mason;
use Apache::Session::MySQL;
use Apache::Cookie;
use Apache::Constants qw(:common);
```

Note (as I mentioned previously) that the handler puts itself in the HTML::Mason package. If you'll recall the Apache configuration section for Mason you'll realize why this is—HTML::Mason is registered as the PerlHandler, so naturally the handler function needs to be in that package.

The extra arguments passed to HTML::Mason::ApacheHandler tell that module to use Apache::Request to parse CGI input arguments. It also upgrades the request object ($r in each component) to an Apache::Request instance. The default is to parse inputs with CGI.pm.

```
{ package HTML::Mason::Commands;
  # Modules and variables that components will use.
  # Include Constants again here to give components
  # its exported values.
```

```
use vars qw($dbh %session);
use Apache::Constants qw(:common);
```
}

The `package` command at the beginning of this section places the variables and use statements in HTML::Mason::Commands, the package where components run. Thus anything we put here will be available to components, which is why they didn't have to declare the session hash or database handle. Note the use of `use vars`, which makes the indicated variables available anywhere in the HTML::Mason::Commands package.

Components that need particular modules can also invoke them via use statements, in their `<%init>` sections, a `<%perl>` block, or wherever it is logical and convenient.

```
# Set up Mason interpreter and Apache handler.
my $interp = HTML::Mason::Interp->new
  ('parser' => HTML::Mason::Parser->new,
   'comp_root' => '/usr/local/apache/mason',
   'data_dir' => '/usr/local/apache/data',
  );
my $ah = HTML::Mason::ApacheHandler->new
  ('interp' => $interp,
   'top_level_predicate' => sub {$_[0] =~ /\.mhtml$/},
  );
```

This section initializes the required Mason objects. Notice the component and data root directories—Mason gets those values here, not from the configuration module. Multiple handler instances can have different roots.

The Apache handler object ($ah) takes an incoming Apache request and turns it into a call to the interpreter. As a convenience it allows us to specify which components are allowed to be invoked by users—that's what the `top_level_predicate` attribute does. When I introduced top-level and subcomponents I suggested that all have distinctive file names. If you can tell one from the other via a simple pattern match as shown here then you can have Mason refuse to serve anything which doesn't look like a top-level component.

```
# Make Apache's user the owner of files Mason creates.
chown(
      [getpwnam('nobody')]->[2],
      [getgrnam('nobody')]->[2],
      $interp->files_written
     );
```

This section resets the ownership of Mason's temporary files. Pass chown the user and group that you configured in `httpd.conf`. If Apache isn't running as root, this section will silently fail, but that's okay—if Apache is running as the target user then the file ownership will be correct anyway.

The handler function finally gets under way:

```
# Get session info and dispatch the request.
sub handler {
    my ($r) = @_;

    # Connect to the session database.
    unless ($HTML::Mason::Commands::dbh) {
        $HTML::Mason::Commands::dbh =
            DBI->connect('DBI:mysql:Info:localhost','web','nouser')
                or return SERVER_ERROR;
    }
```

The database handle is initialized once in each server child process, then reused by each request. Then we look for a session ID as other examples have:

```
# Look for a session ID in a cookie.
my @ids;
my $cookies = Apache::Cookie->fetch;
push @ids, $cookies->{'ID'}->value if $cookies->{'ID'};
push @ids, undef;
```

The code uses the ID array technique from previous examples, making it easier to add URL-based session IDs. As with previous examples, it loops through the possible IDs although in this case there is only the ID from the cookie, if any, and undef:

```
# Load or create the session.
foreach my $try (@ids) {
    eval {
        tie %HTML::Mason::Commands::session,
        'Apache::Session::MySQL', $try,
        {'Handle' => $HTML::Mason::Commands::dbh,
         'LockHandle' => $HTML::Mason::Commands::dbh};
    };
    last unless $@;
}
unless ($HTML::Mason::Commands::session{'_session_id'}) {
    warn "Unable to create or load a session: $@";
    return SERVER_ERROR;
}
```

Note that Mason's handler can return Apache error codes while processing a request, if there is a problem in Apache::Session as there is in this case. Also note the fully qualified variable name for the session hash and database handle—the handler function and those variables are in different packages.

Assuming things went well, send back a cookie with a reasonable lifespan:

```
# Send back (or refresh) a cookie.
my $cookie = Apache::Cookie->new
    ($r,
     -name => 'ID',
     -value => $HTML::Mason::Commands::session{'_session_id'},
     -expires => '+1h',
     -path => '/mason',
```

```
                                      );
            $cookie->bake;
```

This handler doesn't automatically expire sessions since they are used for secure and
public pages. If tighter security is an issue, the autohandler for the protected pages
could handle expiration of the authenticated flag separately from the session.

The final section finally hands the request off to Mason, then cleans up:

```
        # Pass the real work off to HTML::Mason::ApacheHandler.
        my $status = $ah->handle_request($r);

        # Clean up.
        untie %HTML::Mason::Commands::session;
        return $status;
}
```

ApacheHandler's `handle_request` function handles the mapping of Apache
request (`$r`) to the corresponding Mason component, and calls the interpreter. It also
handles input parameters, turning them into arguments for the top-level component,
and provides ways of controlling output, error messages, debugging, and other
options. See the Mason documentation for more details.

That wraps up the Mason examples. Let's look briefly at other tools Mason offers
to site managers.

7.4.8   Mason resources

One of the things I like about Mason is its active community. Examples, problem
solutions, and neat tricks are often posted to the mailing list, and the developers
respond quickly to suggestions.

An example of the community nature of Mason users is the component archive
on the Mason headquarters web site, http://www.masonhq.com/. While the archive
isn't huge, you may find something you need there, or at least a few good examples
to follow.

Components on the archive range widely in size from date menu widgets to a complete frequently asked questions manager. There is also a log analyzer for creating statistics from Apache's access log and a CGI-to-email bridge.

The headquarters site also has links to other sites developed with Mason. If you
see something you like and ask nicely, you can probably get tips from those developers as well.

The most extensive Mason tool available on the site is not in the archive. The
Mason Content Manager (CM) is a suite of site management tools controlled through
CGI. It includes site browsing, file search, uploads via FTP, and editing of pages in-
place. CM optionally includes version control support via RCS and staging of a com-
plete site revision from development to production. See chapter 11 for examples of
CM in action.

CM's editor includes some nice features for component developers. You can set up
a boilerplate document to be used as a starting point for new components, and CM's

spelling checker can validate component text while ignoring HTML and Mason tags. Saving or transferring a component automatically triggers compilation, so errors are discovered early.

Earlier, when discussing how Mason's cache worked, I mentioned that there was a way to make the cache checking more efficient. CM has built-in support for Mason's *reload file* feature, explained in Mason's administration documentation. The reload file takes the place of the individual component file tests. Only the modification time of the reload file is checked, and when Mason notices a change it recompiles components indicated in the file.

As with any web tool, Mason and its tools and modules are always changing, so take a look around the headquarters to see what's new.

7.5 THE TEMPLATE TOOLKIT

Having taken a close look at an embedded Perl module, let's also give templates a longer look. I'll use a shorter example here than in the Mason section, since the basic application techniques of embedded Perl apply here also; we'll focus just on what is different.

The Template Toolkit is my favorite module of this camp, for its rich set of tools and add-ons that provide for very smart templates. Besides the basics of variable interpolation, loops and conditionals, Template Toolkit implements real *display logic* in the template side, making the template and associated script equal partners in building pages. The script's job is to supply the needed data and environment. The template builds the page based on that environment, but is free to request more than the script provides via its own tools.

Some of its critics say that Template Toolkit goes too far, preferring the strictness of HTML::Template in limiting the template to very simple logic and interpolation. Having worked with both, I can see their point when the templates are written by designers with a very strong HTML focus and not much database or programming experience; the script handles all those details and the templates aren't much more complicated than normal web documents.

The problem I found with the HTML::Template approach was that the programmers had to supply every nit-picking detail required by the templates, when it made more sense to me for the templates to be able to do simple formatting and other data manipulation on their own. Using Template Toolkit, the template can, for example, set the case of text information, the format of numbers and dates and other basic kinds of display rules.

Also, my own work group includes web designers with programming and database experience, who readily took up Template Toolkit's minilanguage to build very smart templates. The result of both the display rule advantages and the wider set of logical elements made for a better division of labor in that group.

Once again, the choice of modules depends mostly on finding a tool that works the way you want to, so your experience with the same situation may lead to the opposite choice. But give Template Toolkit a close look—there is a lot to like here.

Those who prefer embedded Perl tools will find that they haven't lost anything in going to the Template Toolkit; it optionally allows full Perl code sections right in the template code. You can use these to aid your migration (and in fact you can move Mason components or other embedded Perl pages rather easily to Template Toolkit, showing how cross-pollinated this whole suite is), but don't make it a long-term plan. You will do far better in the long run by dividing the labor as the Toolkit intends, with scripting and display cooperating in their separate roles.

Installing Template Toolkit is a simple matter of telling CPAN that you want it (the name of the module is just Template for installation purposes), and it doesn't require the kind of configuration that Mason does so I won't bother with the details here. The Toolkit provides similar compilation and caching of templates, and is an excellent overall performer for modules of this type.

I'll build yet another document manager as an example here, since that will contrast nicely with the previous work. We'll start with an application for uploading documents into the system, then go on to a display page that shows some of Template Toolkit's add-on modules.

7.5.1 Template environment

A template-based application consists of a calling script and a template file (which may include more template files). It's reasonable to start with the script then, and see how it sets up the environment that our templates will use.

Recall that in the Mason world, a request went to a handler first, which called the Mason interpreter. The equivalent in template-based applications is to have a common script which receives all requests and chooses a template based on a parameter or other information. This common script sets up global variables, initializes the template engine, connects to the database, and does anything else that the actual application logic needs to do its job. We could also set up a script for each page (or top-level template, to borrow again from Mason terms) and call a common initialization module, but the script approach seems typical.

Moving to the mod_perl world, the script naturally becomes a handler. We can assign the handler to a location that is designated for templates (or the document root, if we're doing everything with one package as a logical site would[7]) and let every URL under that location correspond to a top-level template. The handler can then dispatch to a function for each of those top-levels, or group them in whatever way suits the logic of the site.

Here is `template_handler.pm`, my template dispatcher:

---

[7] I had a professor in a programming class who responded to criticism of his code by saying that he wrote good examples, not good programs. I hope my example sites and code work in the same way.

```perl
package TemplateApp;

use strict;
use Template;
use Apache;
use Apache::Constants qw(OK NOT_FOUND SERVER_ERROR);
use Apache::Request;

my %handlers = (
                 'docmgr' => \&doc_manager,
                );

sub handler {
    my ($r) = @_;
    my $file = '/usr/local/apache' . $r->uri . '.tmpl';
    return NOT_FOUND unless -s $file;
    $file =~ s{^.*/tt2/}{};

    # Each directory/top template has its own handler.
    my ($handler) = $file =~ m/^(\w+)/;
    return NOT_FOUND unless $handler &&
        ($handler = $handlers{$handler});

    # Global template handling code.
    my %globals = (
                    user => $r->user,
                    );
    my $template = Template->new({
        INCLUDE_PATH => '/usr/local/apache/tt2',
        VARIABLES => \%globals,
        PROCESS => 'standard.tmpl',
    });

    # Call the handler for this template/path.
    eval { &$handler($template, $file, $r); };
    if ($@) {
        warn $@;
        return SERVER_ERROR;
    }
    return OK;
}
```

The handler starts by loading the modules it will need; by requiring this module in
mod_perl.conf, we don't need to load those modules via separate PerlModule directives:

```
PerlRequire /usr/local/apache/tt2/template_handler.pm
Alias /tt2/ "/usr/local/apache/tt2/"
<Location /tt2>
    SetHandler perl-script
    PerlHandler TemplateApp::handler
    DefaultType text/html
    AuthUserFile data/docmgr_users
    AuthName "Document manager"
```

```
    AuthType basic
    require valid-user
</Location>
```

The need for authentication will be apparent shortly—we don't want just anyone uploading documents to or deleting documents from the server.

Before the handler code, I load a hash of functions that correspond to the legal URLs; anything else is rejected. That's fine for a small number of pages, where the functions will all be in this one module. A more complex and robust site might map the URL onto a module and function, and verify the legality of the URL by checking that the function exists. There will be only one top-level URL in this example, but we'll see later how the corresponding code handles multiple pages.

The handler verifies that the URL it was given maps to a template (standardizing on the use of .tmpl for Template Toolkit files here, but any extension you prefer will work) and also that there is a handler function for the first part of the URL. This is akin to Mason's problem where we needed some way of ensuring that a URL mapped to a top-level component. In this case, the existence of a function in the `%handlers` hash means that it is legal to proceed.

The next task is to set up any global data given to all templates and initialize the template processor. The example loads only one value into the `%globals` hash, the authorized user as given by `$r->user`. This function would return `null` if we were on pages that weren't under HTTP Authentication control (which would happen if, for instance, this handler controlled both public and private pages).

The template processor is next, with these options passed to the Template object:

```
my $template = Template->new({
    INCLUDE_PATH => '/usr/local/apache/tt2',
    VARIABLES => \%globals,
    PROCESS => 'standard.tmpl',
});
```

The `INCLUDE_PATH` option tells Template where to look for both the top-level template files and any component templates they include. Relative paths to template files will be considered relative to this path. By default, Template Toolkit doesn't allow absolute paths (a good security precaution), but you can override that by specifying `ABSOLUTE => 1` in the options.

`VARIABLES` specifies data given to every template, the `%globals` hash in this case. If we were processing multiple templates with one processor, this would be useful for common data items. In our case, it sets up the data given to any of the templates processed by the subhandler functions.

`PROCESS` provides the name of a template to process instead of the one given to the actual `process` function in the subhandler. That sounds odd until you look more closely at the documentation. The template specified by the `PROCESS` option receives the name of the template that `process` was told to handle, and thus serves as a wrapper for the "real" page. We'll see how shortly.

The Template object is quite complex and can take a large number of configuration options; see the documentation for details. If you want your templates to be able to process Perl code directly, you'll need to set the EVAL_PERL option to true. There are also options for determining what Template does with the white space before and after a directive; you can have it trim the leading space, trailing space, or both. White space isn't normally important in HTML, but trimming it is convenient inside of text area inputs, preformatted blocks, and other places where blank lines and spaces are displayed.

Having set up the environment, the handler now calls the appropriate subhandler function, inside of an eval block. If something goes wrong inside the subhandler, eval traps the error and lets the handler do something with it. In this case, the error is displayed to the browser, which is fine for development and not very helpful in a production program.

Now let's look at that wrapper template, which works similarly to an autohandler in Mason. Here is standard.tmpl:

```
<!DOCTYPE HTML PUBLIC "-//IETF//DTD HTML//EN">
<HTML>
 <HEAD><TITLE>[% $title %]</TITLE></HEAD>
 <BODY BGCOLOR="white">
  [% PROCESS $template %]
 </BODY>
</HTML>
```

This is pretty standard stuff for wrapping around the guts of a web page. The pieces of interest are the interpolation of the title ([% $title %]) and the handling of the requested template ([% PROCESS $template %]). The title is interesting mostly because the wrapper template received only global data; we'll see how $title is set when we look at the upload template page.

Handling the requested template is a little more interesting. As explained in the documentation, the wrapper receives the target template as a file name in $template. The PROCESS directive then tells Template Toolkit to handle the template in place, with all current data. Thus the target template will receive the %global hash and the data passed to the process function; if the wrapper defined any data of its own the target would receive that too. PROCESS is a little more efficient than INCLUDE, which would also pass along all data to the requested template, but in localized environment that would encompass the target and leave the wrapper's data unchanged.

Now let's look at one of the target pages and see how it works with the wrapper.

7.5.2 Uploading a document

None of the previous document manager examples had an upload page, so we'll start with one here to make things more interesting. The template is upload.tmpl, under the docmgr directory. Remember how the URL has to both match a template and an entry in the %handlers hash. The URL to run this template is http://www.site.com/tt2/docmgr/upload.

```
[% META
   title = 'Upload files'
%]

<H2>Welcome, [% user %]! Upload files here.</H2><P>
<FORM METHOD="POST" ENCTYPE="multipart/form-data"
      ACTION="/tt2/docmgr/upload">
  Local file: <INPUT TYPE="file" NAME="incoming"><BR>
  Public  <INPUT TYPE="radio" NAME="filedest" VALUE="public"
                 [% IF filedest == 'public'  %]CHECKED[% END %]>
  Private <INPUT TYPE="radio" NAME="filedest" VALUE="private"
                 [% IF filedest == 'private' %]CHECKED[% END %]>
  <BR>Document name:
  <INPUT TYPE="text" NAME="filename" VALUE="[% filename %]">
  <P><INPUT TYPE="submit" VALUE="Upload">
</FORM>

[% IF upload_error %]
   <P><H3>Error uploading [% file %]</H3>
[% END %]
<P>[% message %]
```

This template starts off with a block enclosed by the META directive. This allows a template to specify some data about itself; Template doesn't define or require any particular metadata. The interesting thing is that data in a META block is defined and available at an early point in the compilation of a template, so the wrapper template can use values set in the target. This is how the title defined in the META block here winds up inside the wrapper's title tags.

Other uses for the META block include version control information and file-level switches. For example, you could define a testing variable in this block and use it to turn debugging features on and off, or provide some test data for the template before the script is fully developed.

The template doesn't need HTML header or body tags since the wrapper is providing those. It jumps right to the meat of the matter. The welcome line shows a typical variable interpolation—[% user %] is transformed into the user name set in the %globals hash, the user name provided via HTTP authentication. Then the template builds a form that includes a file input—this is the upload widget, which the browser will use to invoke a file dialog that lets the users find and send the file they want to upload.

The radio button set allows the user to specify that this is a public or private document. Note the use of conditionals to check one value or the other:

```
[% IF filedest == 'public'  %]CHECKED[% END %]>
```

This will check the radio button which contains the current value of the filedest parameter, which we'll see in the template's handler code. Template won't implement sticky parameter values for you as CGI.pm does, but it is easy enough to work them out yourself.

The form also has an input for the document's name on the receiving server, and a submit button. After that it checks to see if the handler caught an error in uploading, and if it does, it displays an error and the contents of the file parameter. It also prints message, which could be more error text, a success message, or anything else the code wants to be displayed to the user.

Now for the code, in doc_manager (also in template_handler.pm):

```
sub doc_manager {
    my ($template, $file, $r) = @_;
    my $apr = Apache::Request->new($r);
    my %data = ('docdir' => '/home/reports');
    $data{'private'} = $data{'docdir'} . '/private';
    $data{'public'}  = $data{'docdir'} . '/public';
```

The first section receives parameters from the main handler, then gets an Apache::Request object for parsing parameters from the request. $template is the Template processor object, and $file is the template file that matches the requested URL. The %data hash will be passed to the template, and the code sets up some file paths for that purpose.

Then we get to the section that handles the upload page:

```
if ($file =~ /upload/) {
    my $upload = $apr->param('incoming') ? $apr->upload : 0;
```

This code checks for the presence of the upload parameter; if it exists it gets an Apache::Upload object that has the uploaded file's name and other attributes, as well as an open file handler.

Then we work out a path for the incoming file based on the radio button settings for public or private, and untaint the filename if it doesn't contain any dangerous characters:

```
        $data{'filedest'} = $apr->param('filedest') || 'public';
        $data{'filename'} = $apr->param('filename');
        if ($data{'filename'} =~ /^(\w+)$/) {
            $data{'filename'} = $1;
        }
        elsif ($upload) {
            $data{'message'} = "Illegal document name " .
                delete $data{'filename'};
        }
```

If a file was uploaded and a legal name was given, then it will save the file:

```
        if ($upload && $data{'filename'}) {
            my $size = $upload->size;
            if ($size < 1024 * 1024) {
                my $fh = $upload->fh;
                my @file = <$fh>;
```

```
      $data{'message'} =
          "Incoming $data{'filedest'} file is $size bytes, " .
              scalar(@file) . " lines.";
      my $path = join('/', $data{'docdir'},
                          $data{'filedest'},
                          $data{'filename'} . ".txt"
                          );
      if (open OUT, ">$path") {
          print OUT @file;
          close OUT;
      }
      else {
          $data{'message'} = "Error writing to $path";
      }
  }
  else {
      $data{'upload_error'} = 1;
      $data{'message'} = "File is too large";
  }
}
```

If one of those conditions wasn't true, it will tell the user what's missing via the message parameter:

```
  elsif ($upload) {
      $data{'message'} ||= "Enter the destination name";
  }
  elsif ($data{'filename'}) {
      $data{'message'} ||=
          "Please choose a file from your system for uploading";
  }
  else {
      $data{'message'} ||= "Ready for uploads";
  }
}
```

The next section of the code deals with the display page. We'll skip past that and get
to the end of the function, where the Template processor is called at last:

```
$r->send_http_header('text/html');
$template->process($file, \%data, $r) or die $template->error;
}
```

This code prints the standard header specifying the content type, then calls the process method which will do the actual work of interpreting the template. Ordinarily,
process would spew the resulting output to standard out, but we can tell it to print
via the Apache object instead by passing that as the third parameter.

The first parameter is the template to process (although the wrapper will be handled first, remember) and the second is the data hash the template will use, plus the
%global values. The template can't tell the global and data values apart—for all it
knows, we merged the two hashes and called it with the results.

The upload page is simple and to the point. It has the nice feature of remembering previous inputs between runs, and welcomes the user (a good application is a friendly application). The page is shown in figure 7.1.

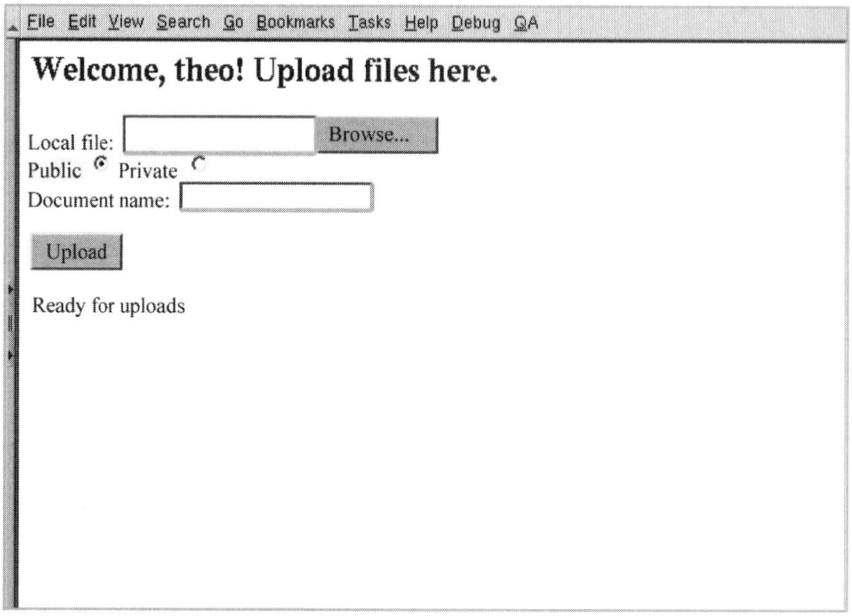

Figure 7.1   The upload page

Now let's go on to the more complex template used to manage uploaded documents.

7.5.3   Viewing the upload directories

In the directory page, we want to see what documents are in the public and private areas, and also let the user delete files from either. I've shown other examples of directory listings, showing the file name, modification date, and size. In this version, we'll take advantage of Template Toolkit's plug-in modules to make things simpler.

The plug-in library is Template's equivalent of Mason's component archive, except that most of the available plug-ins are shipped with Template Toolkit's distribution. The library is broad and useful, providing filters for data formatting and conversion, HTML construction kits (for those who like CGI.pm's helper functions for making correct tags and attributes), and more complex tasks such as database and file system queries.

I particularly like the DBI plug-in which lets a template do its own database lookups (or even updates, if you are so inclined). I alluded to that capability in the introduction of this section when I said the template wasn't constrained by the calling script when gathering data. For example, if a script passes a template a list of customer IDs to display, the template can do its own queries to get customer contact information and sales history from the database. The programmer writing the script doesn't need to know (or more importantly, provide) all the data used by the script, leading to better scripting and more modular design.

The simplified example I'll show here uses Template's File and Directory plug-ins to get information from the file system. I've shown other examples of how to do this in Perl, but with Template we can let the libraries do the work.

The directory page will display the files in given directories and let the user delete them. To get the contents of a directory we use the Directory plug-in, and for each file, the File plug-in provides detailed information. We can combine the two like this to show all the public documents:

```
[% USE pubdir = Directory('/home/reports/docs/public') %]
[% FOREACH file = pubdir.files %]
  [% file.name %]: [% file.size %] [% file.mtime %] [% file.path %]<BR>
[% END %]
```

The USE directive loads the named plug-in and passes it parameters. In this case, the Directory plug-in receives the directory path of interest. The plug-in interface is created as `pubdir`, and is treated by the Template minilanguage in a fashion similar to a Perl object, particularly when we use the `files` method to retrieve a set of directory entries.

The set of files is returned as a Template Iterator object, which the FOREACH directive uses to control a loop. Each file is displayed with its name, size, modification date, and full path; those are all attributes of the File plug-in object. Compare that approach to calling `stat` or the Perl file test operators in a hand-coded loop.

Of course, we want to do this on multiple directories, so the code above should go into a component template that is called by the directory page. And we want to let the user delete documents too, so there should be a form for each file. Here is the actual directory template from my example, `directory.tmpl`:

```
[% META
   title = 'Manage files'
%]

<H2>Public documents</H2><P>
[% INCLUDE 'includes/showdir.tmpl' showdir=public %]

<H2>Private documents</H2><P>
[% INCLUDE 'includes/showdir.tmpl' showdir=private %]

<HR>
[% message %]
<FORM METHOD="POST" ACTION="/tt2/docmgr/directory">
  <INPUT TYPE="submit" VALUE="Refresh">
</FORM>
```

Note the same sort of META block as in the previous section to set the title and anything else the wrapper needs to know. Then the template uses the INCLUDE directive to load `includes/showdir.tmpl`, calling it once for each path of interest and passing that path via the `showdir` parameter. (Yes, I could have made a loop of paths. It's a good example but not a good template.)

After displaying the directory contents, the template provides space for a message from the script, such as notification of a successful deletion or an error and a form to refresh the page. That's all simple enough, so let's take a look at `showdir.tmpl` to see how the plug-ins are used:

```
[% USE dir = Directory(showdir) %]
[% USE date %]
<TABLE>
  <TR>
     <TD><B>Name</B></TD>
     <TD><B>Size</B></TD>
     <TD><B>Date</B></TD>
  </TR>
  [% FOREACH file = dir.files %]
    <TR>
     <TD>[% file.name %]</TD>
     <TD>[% file.size %]</TD>
     <TD>[% date.format(file.mtime) %]</TD>
     <TD>
       <FORM METHOD="GET" ACTION="/tt2/docmgr/directory">
         <INPUT TYPE="hidden" NAME="path"
                VALUE="[% file.path %]">
         <INPUT TYPE="submit" VALUE="Delete">
       </FORM>
     </TD>
    </TR>
  [% END %]
</TABLE>
```

The Directory plug-in is loaded first, along with the Date plug-in which will let us print a more readable form of the file modification time. The template creates a table with headers for the file name, size, and date, then uses the same kind of loop we saw before, iterating over the files in the directory.

When the template displays the file date, note that it passes it through the Date plug-in to format the value. The plug-in uses Date::Calc in turn to transform the `stat` value into a calendar date and time.

The template also creates a form for each line, containing the value of the file path in a hidden field. This will get passed back to the handler if the user clicks a Delete button, telling the code which file to delete. It's not generally a good idea to trust hidden fields this way—a malicious user could alter the value in a form and tell the script to delete more valuable files—but since this application is on a protected page, we'll trust it for purposes of an example.

Here is the subhandler code for this page (figure 7.2), which you'll recall is part of the `doc_manager` function:

```
    elsif ($file =~ /directory/) {
        if (my $path = $apr->param('path')) {
            if ($path =~ m{^($data{'docdir'}/(public|private)/\w+\.\w+)$}) {
                $path = $1;
                if (unlink $path) {
                    $data{'message'} = "Deleted $path";
                }
                else {
                    $data{'message'} = "Error deleting $path: $!";
                }
            }
            else {
                $data{'message'} = "Illegal path $path";
            }
        }
    }
```

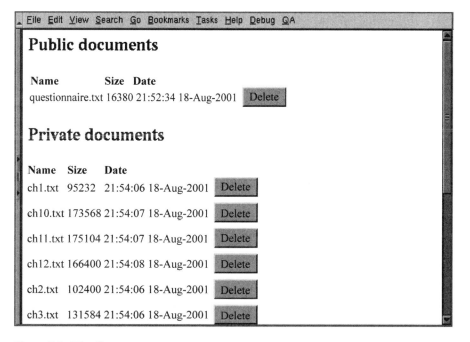

Figure 7.2 The directory page

This section is considerably shorter than the upload handler, since it doesn't have many conditions to check. It looks for an incoming `path` parameter, and if the path matches the document directory configured into the function it attempts to delete the file via Perl's built-in `unlink`. Checking the path not only provides better security, it also gives us a chance to untaint the value, which would have caused `unlink` to complain otherwise.

The code stores messages to the user based on the various results, and then proceeds to the `process` call discussed in the previous section.

7.5.4 Template Toolkit resources

I hope this brief example has given you a glimpse of how much a template can do. Documenting the Toolkit properly would be a book-sized project on its own, so I'll direct you to better resources instead.

The Toolkit's home page is http://www.tt2.org/, where you will find the current code, documentation, and pointers to mailing lists for developers, users, and enthusiasts of all kinds. It also describes a number of tools built with the Toolkit, such as a pair of programs for transforming static files into HTML, Postscript, and other formats. If you maintain paper documentation as well as web pages, these tools will build greatly on your investment in learning the Toolkit.

The Splash plug-in library is also described there, along with examples of the documentation filtered through it. Splash provides stylishly themed form elements and other HTML building blocks that fill gaps in the basic CGI widget set. For instance, it provides a tab box for notebook-like pages that switch content sections while maintaining headers or other information.

If you are considering a project with Template Toolkit or just wondering what others are doing with it, join their mailing lists and tune in. You'll find a helpful crowd of people who are building some amazing pages.

7.6 XML ALTERNATIVES

If you are evaluating web tools, it's very likely that you've encountered XML, another child of the same language family as HTML. The Extended Markup Language offers much that appeals to web developers, most importantly a cleaner separation of data, processing, and presentation.

Many articles on XML describe a future in which XML will be sent directly to browsers, along with style sheets and other display processing information, so that web servers will get out of the presentation business and concentrate on applications and data handling. That's an exciting future indeed, but I can't help wondering why those articles' authors think that XML browser developers will do a better job of adhering to standards than their HTML ancestors have.

XML on the server side is a different issue entirely, and there are already a number of good tools for working with XML data and style sheets in Perl, which shouldn't be a surprise given Perl's web-friendly nature.

Merging Perl and XML is in some ways easier than with HTML; an XML document with properly tagged Perl code is still a valid XML document, while all of the HTML modules discussed in this chapter used nonstandard tags. Developers who want to embed Perl in XML have almost as many choices for tools as those working in straight HTML. The modules discussed in this chapter can be used with XML, either directly (in the case of the template modules) or with some modification to handler scripts. There are also new modules that have followed on from embedded Perl tools, such as XML::EP.

One module that covers a range of XML tools is AxKit, which offers style sheet processing, translation to HTML and other formats, and component-based documents. The developer has taken a very pragmatic look at web applications, and uses the tools to emphasize that servers have to offer browsers what browsers can view, rather than depending on any particular language standard. AxKit feels the same way about style sheet tools, apparently, since the developer has a choice of Perl and C modules, and this same flexibility is exhibited through the rest of the module.

Since XML is viewed as the wave of the future, this area will undoubtedly develop rapidly, but more information at this stage is beyond the scope of this book.

That brings us to the end of Part II. Your web site now has an excellent suite of tools for building your applications. The next part will show examples of sites and how these tools and other modules bring them to your browser.

Example sites

The server is ready and the tools are in place; it's time to build the web site. The following three chapters will show and discuss sample site designs:

- Chapter 8 talks about sites for news, message forums, chats, and other services to a community of interested users.
- Chapter 9 is about intranet sites which provide applications and other services to a fast, protected network.
- Chapter 10 covers e-commerce sites, reviewing security precautions and exploring tools available for download.

CHAPTER 8

Virtual communities

One of the most fascinating aspects of the Internet is the way in which an impersonal, digital medium brings people together. A quick search can locate Web sites, news groups, chat channels, and mailing lists for most any hobby, sport, profession, or passion. Virtual communities form on the Web in ways that are impossible in the physical realm, seemingly out of nothing.

This chapter discusses community sites—desirable features, tools that provide them, what you'll need to build, and how to build it. The online resources section also has a few tips for getting your site listed in the above-mentioned searches.

8.1 SERVING THE COMMUNITY

Chances are you are already a member of a virtual community—you joined by subscribing to a mailing list or frequenting a web site devoted to your favorite band, TV show, or team. Since this is such a diverse area, it is hard to pin down exactly what a community site is, but we can list some common characteristics:

- The community is defined by a common interest, goal, or job—maybe even a physical location.
- The site offers a mix of "official" postings and user-contributed messages. They commonly consist of a main news page connected to forums that let users post messages and chat rooms that allow real-time communication.
- Membership is not required. Community sites generally offer public pages. Some sites require a user to join before posting messages, others remain completely open.
- Membership is open. Users might be able to register themselves or may be required to go through an administrator, but generally speaking, the public at large can join.
- The site offers links to related sites in the same or similar communities—they are friends, not competitors.

Community sites do not have a commercial focus. Of course, hosting a site involves initial and ongoing costs, so no one should begrudge a community site selling merchandise or reasonable levels of advertising, but that should not be the main point of the site.

Community sites are interactive. Virtual communities need meeting places and communication. A site which offers information but doesn't allow the readers to comment and discuss that information does not build a community (though in the act of publishing it can offer a valuable service). A successful community site takes on a life of its own, helped and perhaps guided by its administrators but not tightly controlled by them.

Depending on the size of the community, these sites might run on a single workstation connected via modem or on several servers with huge bandwidth. In order to pay their bills, high-traffic sites are naturally more commercial. One can envision a kind of site evolution chart that shows the progression from a page on a free web host to a local ISP to a major service provider, along with the addition of advertising and the increasing probability of the site being bought outright.

8.1.1 Community site examples

Now, we'll discuss a few sites that show the features of a good community builder. The sites listed here are all definitely high end and commercially funded, but they also provide good success stories for the tools I've described in this book.

slashdot.org

"News for Nerds. Stuff that Matters." Slashdot provides Open Source enthusiasts, Linux hackers, and other technophiles with links to interesting news gathered from sites around the world, plus editorials, reviews, and the occasional feature story. Although the site is run by an editorial staff, most of the links are supplied by eager community members, as is the commentary accompanying each link.

Each story posted on Slashdot is accompanied by a message forum where registered users and "Anonymous Cowards" discuss the content and each others' opinions. Slashdot innovated a score system for user posts in which moderators give posts a plus or a minus; comments with more points become more visible. Even more innovative is their method for choosing moderators on the basis of the ratings their own posts have received, and in rotating the moderator pool through transient access. Moderators are in turn metamoderated by registered users on a volunteer, random basis, so that good moderators are more likely to get access in the future (and bad ones get banned).

Slashdot also offers configurable *channels*, small summaries of other sites. When registered users request the main page, they see the current news links plus their chosen channels. By consolidating many user interests on one page they make it more likely that users will start their browsing sessions at Slashdot, thus increasing the value of their advertising.

For users who want real-time interaction, Slashdot spawned off slashNET, a set of chat channels which has since taken on a life of its own.

Slashdot runs on Apache, MySQL, and mod_perl. Its developers publish the code used to generate their pages and also their hardware specifications and usage statistics, making this an attractive site for those looking to publish information on how popular portals work.

It is normal for popular sites to be cloned by others when setting up their own services. (The owner of some sites being copied without permission may use stronger terminology.) Slashdot, however, openly encourages this by publishing its code and hosting a community site just for its users, http://slashcode.com/. This has created a common look and feel among the sites based on Slash, forming a metacommunity helped by the fact that the sites often link back to Slashdot and Slashcode, and sometimes to one another.

We'll discuss Slash in more detail in section 8.4.

imdb.com

The evolution of the Internet Movie Database is a microcosm of the changes in virtual community growth over the last dozen years. It began life in the rec.arts.movies newsgroup, where frequent posters developed a database of movie facts—release date, director, cast, writer, and other credits, along with plot synopses and trivia. The rapid growth of the database met nicely with the rise of the Web, allowing it to move to replicated servers in different countries. It is one of the most frequently cited examples when people talk about large database search problems and Internet information publishing.

The IMDb grew (and survives) on the contributions of users, initially to the database of information on past films, then into reviews of current films and TV shows as it became more focused on modern releases. The database contains hundreds of thousands of titles, each of which has its own message board (although only a small fraction of those are utilized) and fact sheets. Users can expand or correct information about a film and provide links to related sites, and vote on the many polls for favorite this and that.

IMDb features message forums for movie genres, industry news, and film techniques, as well as favorite actors and directors. In that way it has gone back to its newsgroup roots, serving its community of film buffs with the trivia and gossip they love. It supplies its own editorially controlled news pages also, along with pages for games and contests. Readers in the U.S. can also see what is currently playing and even find show times for nearby theaters.

Registration is not required to view the site or search the database, but is necessary to post information or messages. Users can configure the display of movie fact sheets and message boards, and can build a list of "My Movies" for which IMDb will send notification of TV show times and video releases.

As IMDb's popularity grew it became a natural target for acquisition, and (at the time of my writing) is owned by Amazon.com, with movie pages linked to Amazon's video store so that the curious searcher can order finds directly from the information pages. After getting past the current offers on the main page, this presence isn't overly intrusive, keeping the site focused on its users.

IMDb's site is built with Apache and mod_perl, using the Berkeley DB package. Messages boards use a commercial package, WWWThreads, which will be mentioned again later. They do not publish details about their code or search mechanisms, but they do offer the database itself in various forms for noncommercial use.

investorama.com

Investorama started out as an Internet publishing site and developed into a community. The original site featured investor news, links, and stock reviews. In 1999 it expanded greatly and offered message boards and other community-building services.

Investorama often straddles the line between community and commercial Internet service, mostly in good ways. The site features question-and-answer forums with noted financial advisers alongside member forums and chats. Members get a free email account on the site (which must be accessed through the site, of course), a personalized start page, and configurable content displays. There is an optional newsletter and other mail-out services for those who don't want to check the site daily. Users can choose to be available for instant messaging with other members, giving the site a real-time feel that appeals to those who like to discuss breaking news or just see who's up for a chat.

Investorama gets into the portal business by maintaining a database of links suggested by members and offering searches and directories. They also offer a shopping directory for consumer e-commerce sites.

In some ways, Investorama serves as an example of why a commercial service needs to become a community to survive. The site needs a powerful draw to compete with pages blessed by big-name investment firms and widely published advisors and it gets it through its members. Investors love information, and the site builds on their desire to ask questions and offer answers.

Investorama runs on Apache, mod_perl, and MySQL. Dynamic pages are generated by HTML::Mason, and feature a hierarchical navigation bar for quick jumps back to previously viewed sections. The site does not publish its code or details about its hardware.

8.2   IMPLEMENTING FEATURES

Now that we've seen example sites that implement desirable features, let's consider how to build them.

There is always the option to code everything yourself, but this is seldom necessary or even desirable. Many freely available packages on the Web will serve the needs of a community site perfectly. Some (like Slash) make a complete site while others serve as components for developers to plug in as they see fit.

If you are planning a site that requires user registration for some or all features, it is natural to think that you need to decide on user administration first. Instead, delay any thoughts about the user model until after you have chosen packages for your site. You may discover that the package you need has its own ideas about users, or if using packages that didn't grow up together you might have to do some work to get different user models to cooperate.

8.2.1   News

A community site's front page generally shows community news—announcements, hosted stories, links to news on other sites, or all three. This is what your regular users want to see first when they return to your site.

This may seem like a simple matter of editing a static page now and then to add new announcements and links. While that certainly works, it isn't the best choice for a busy site—mistakes happen when editing text manually, and your browser might handle a broken tag differently than your users' browsers, causing mysterious results. It would be better to let static pages be static.

A news page is a natural choice for one of the dynamic content tools we've discussed previously. The report page example using Mason from the previous chapter could easily be adapted to a news page that offers all the stories available in a directory.

If each news story had its own component, Mason's object methods could be used to extract a title and category from the component and offer a link to the full text page.

Newslog

If your news items will be only a sentence or paragraph (possibly containing a link to a full story), consider using Newslog, a script by R. Steven Rainwater posted at http://www.ncc.com/freeware/.

This simple utility doesn't require a database; it uses one HTML file to hold the current stories, and moves additional stories off to archive pages which are also HTML. It works well with an existing front page; the news section can be included into a column or frame as desired. News items are posted via a CGI script which inserts the new entry at the top of the list and scrolls older items into the archive automatically. (It can run under mod_perl via Apache::Registry if you prefer, but unless you post news moment by moment I don't see a need for it.) Configuring it took a bit of hacking, but I had a working example page in about 15 minutes.

Newslog provides news entries that look like:

> **2000 Jul 8 (Sat), 15:26** New version of SAMBA loaded.
> Samba has been upgraded to version 2.06. This should take care of anything that ever went wrong. Nothing will break again, we're certain.
>
> **2000 Jul 8 (Sat), 14:14** The NT server will go down at 16:00 for no apparent reason.
> If this is inconvenient, please try our <u>Linux Cluster</u>.

The date is in bold face and the first line of text continues from the same line. Newslog doesn't add any HTML to the posted entries, so line breaks and paragraphs must be entered manually by the person adding the story.

Newslog keeps the current set of news items in a file which is meant to be inserted into your front page via SSI or the tool of your choice. Here is a simple example page, `news.shtml`, that uses mod_include:

```
<!DOCTYPE HTML PUBLIC "-//IETF//DTD HTML//EN">
<HTML>
  <HEAD>
    <TITLE>Here is the news</TITLE>
  </HEAD>
  <BODY>
    <!--#config timefmt="%A, %B %d, %Y" -->
    <H2>The news as of
      <!--#flastmod virtual="/newslog/todays.news" --></H2>
    <!--#include virtual="/newslog/todays.news" -->
    <H3>Older news is in the
      <A HREF="/newslog/oldnews">archive</A></H3>
  </BODY>
</HTML>
```

Since I was running the page through mod_include anyway, I dressed this up a little to display the date of the last news item added via the `flastmod` element. Note the inclusion of `todays.news`, the file generated by Newslog, and the link to `/news-log/oldnews` where Newslog maintains an archive of stories.

Newslog's code consists of a configuration file (`newslog-cfg.pl`) and the news posting script (`newslog.cgi`). Configuration is done through setting Perl variables directly; the comments in the file will tell you what you need to change for your site (although I've removed them from the following example for purposes of brevity). The values I used were:

```
$scriptURL = 'http://www.example.site/cgi-bin/newslog.cgi';
$newsFile = '/usr/local/apache/htdocs/newslog/todays.news';
$archivePath = '/usr/local/apache/htdocs/newslog/oldnews';
$arcURL = 'http://www.example.site/newslog/oldnews/';
$arcSuffix = '-news.html';
$redirect = '/news.shtml';
$tmpDir = '/tmp';
$MaxItems = 4;
```

Under Apache's document root I created the `newslog` and `newslog/oldnews` directories (as shown in `$newsFile` and `$archivePath` in this example) and put `news.shtml` in the document root directly. The URL for the archive (`$archURL`) corresponds to the archive directory, where Newslog will create an `index.html` file that offers the archive pages. The URL in `$redirect` should refer back to your front page, and `$MaxItems` is the number of news items to display.

After editing `newslog-cfg.pl`, copy both scripts to the `cgi-bin` directory or the directory handled by Apache::Registry if you want to run Newslog via mod_perl. In that case, be sure to remove any `__END__` tokens from both files. Make sure Apache's user can create the current news file and can write new files to the archive directory. Then have your browser request the posting script. Figure 8.1 shows the news posting page.

Enter the text of the item into the box. Add any HTML tags you need for line breaks, emphasis, or links; Newslog won't add any for you. After you have the item ready, click the Preview News Item button to submit it. Newslog will show you how the item will look on the page, giving you a chance to fix the text or tags as necessary. When the item is ready, click Post item to add it to the current news.

Newslog isn't very fancy, but it's not very complicated either. The script is less than 300 lines, much of it blocks of HTML, and is easily customized for taste. For example, to modify the time stamp printed with stories, just edit the `sprintf` call that loads `$main::date` at the beginning of the script.

If you choose to put Newslog into production, you'll want to add some security to keep unwelcome parties from adding news. The simplest way to do this is to add

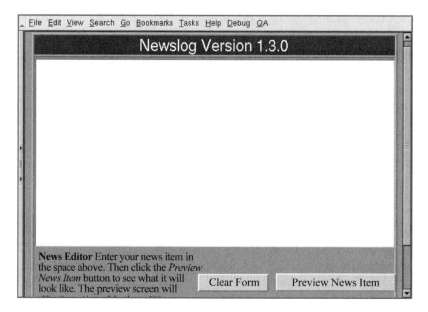

Figure 8.1 The news posting page

HTTP authentication to `newslog.cgi`, and keep a password file for those who are allowed to add stories. Here is a quick addition to `httpd.conf`:

```
<Location "/cgi-bin/newslog.cgi">
    AuthUserFile data/newslog_post_users
    AuthName "Newslog story posters"
    AuthType basic
    require valid-user
</Location>
```

Then create the password file:

```
cd /usr/local/apache
bin/htpasswd -c data/newslog_post_users a-user-name
```

Add additional users as required (just drop the `-c` switch) and you're securely off and running.

8.2.2 Forums

A community site builds community through member interaction. The usual mechanism is the message board or forum where users can start topics of interest, add message postings, reply to one another, rant and flame, or exchange whatever other sorts of communication they desire. This is where virtual communities began, on UUCP-based networks and pre-Web Internets. As a result, forums are well-established in the minds of mature users, who will recognize and possibly even appreciate a feature-rich message system.

Forums are more dynamic than news pages, and generally call for user registration and a database of some sort to store and search for messages. As such, rolling your own is a much larger project and shouldn't be undertaken lightly. Fortunately there are plenty of free alternatives to consider. Here are a few:

WWWThreads

This product is well-established in the web board field, and includes impressive customers such as the IMDb. The product is commercial, and to get the current version you must purchase a license. However there is a free limited version for download from http://www.wwwthreads.com/. If you need the most features and options for your forums, try the free version and determine if you can afford the license.

WWWThreads works with mod_perl and both MySQL and PostgreSQL, with support for other databases in the works at this writing. It has the advantages and features list of a product with a long development history: moderation, multiple languages, themes, user and group registration with permission management, and even support for turning message posts into a news page like the previous section's example. This is the product which sets the standard for comparison, at least in Perl-based boards.

BAZAAR

BAZAAR started out life in an earlier version of WWWThreads, but remains Open Source and noncommercial (although its claim to be the only GPLed forum product for Perl and MySQL is incorrect). It shares much of the richness of the earlier product, and adds even more theme support, more filters, and a restructured code base that promises better extendibility. The polling system is a nice add-on that users seem to expect more and more often. BAZAAR crosses over into the news and chat lines, providing a Java-based IRC client and a link library manager.

BAZAAR attempts to help out the new site builder with a script that installs all the required modules via CPAN. It isn't tough to do this by hand though, and the product isn't as complicated as it initially looks. Learning how to make effective use of it is a challenge still.

BAZAAR is at an early adopter's stage, but is worth checking out if you are looking for forums with loads of features. Look for it at http://nl.linux.org/bazaar/, or via http://sourceforge.net/ or http://freshmeat.net/.

mwForum

After two feature-rich offerings, mwForum comes across as a lightweight entry, but don't be put off. This comparatively small product works with mod_perl and MySQL and provides threaded message boards, multiple boards per site, score moderation, file attachments, limited HTML mark-up in messages, and more. Boards can be public, private to a group of users, or read-only (thus providing a news page). Users can be given administrative access to some boards and not others; and accounts can be banned temporarily or permanently by any administrator. Users can read boards from the Web or by email (if the site chooses to permit it) and the search interface is adequate.

mwForum stays lean in browser requirements also, shying away from anything that requires more than a lowest common denominator of HTML, but site builders can dress up their forums if they desire. The threaded message display gives good visual cues about how messages relate, and the designers can choose fonts and colors as they like.

mwForum is also lean on documentation, but I found it easy enough to set up. The product's page at http://www.mawic.de/mwforum/ has a pointer to a demonstration forum that also serves as a support board, and many common installation difficulties are discussed there.

mwForum requires MySQL as mentioned. It also requires outgoing mail service of some sort, although this doesn't have to be on your web server itself—any open SMTP mail server will do. In order to register, a user must supply a valid email address, which will be used to mail the new user's password and send notices and email subscriptions.

CGI setup works fine for a board with low activity, and is a good way to test the product to see if you like it. mod_perl installation cures mwForum's CGI sluggishness and requires only a few more steps.

To set up the CGI version, create three directories under Apache's root: `htdocs/mwf` for graphics, `htdocs/mwf/attach` for file attachments (if you'll allow attachments to messages), and `cgi-bin/mwf` for the code itself. Then unload mwForum's distribution and copy everything in the `img` subdirectory to `htdocs/mwf`. These graphics supply navigation buttons for mwForum's screens and also a logo (which you will probably want to replace for your site).

Now for the code: copy the files from mwForum's `cgi` subdirectory to `cgi-bin/mwf`. This will include the Perl modules used by mwForum. If you haven't altered Perl's default setup then the scripts will find their modules in that directory. Next, customize `MwfConfig.pm` (which you just copied to `cgi-bin/mwf`) to set things up the way you want. Here are the settings I used (with comments and unchanged defaults left out for brevity):

```
$cfg{'dbUser'} = "web";
$cfg{'dbPassword'} = "nouser";
$cfg{'adminEmail'} = "root\@localhost";
$cfg{'url'} = "http://localhost/cgi-bin/mwf/forum.pl";
$cfg{'attachments'} = 1;
$cfg{'timeFormat'} = "%m/%d/%y %H:%M";
```

Most of the defaults are fine; I changed the database user to be the same as the other examples, altered the default fake domain name and enabled file attachments, then changed the time format to the one I'm used to.

Make all the scripts executable, and set Apache's user to own the new directories and files under the document root. Then it is time to create the database.

mwForum comes with scripts to configure its database, waiting in the distribution's `sql` directory. Edit `grant-access.sql` to use the username and password you selected earlier, and if you aren't going to call the forum database mwforum then edit `create-tables.sql` also to supply the correct name. Then just run the commands:

```
mysqladmin -p create mwforum
mysql -p < ~/mwf/sql/grant-access.sql
mysql -p < ~/mwf/sql/create-tables.sql
```

If you run the commands from an account other than root, specify the designated mwForum database user with MySQL's `-u` switch.

If all the commands have worked and the scripts are all executable, you should be ready to create the chief administrator account. Have your browser connect to mwForum at the URL given earlier, and you should see the first screen. Figure 8.2 shows the successful installation of mwForum.

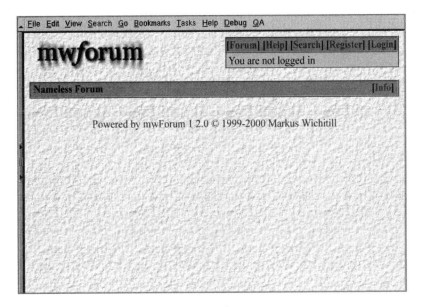

Figure 8.2   Successful installation of mwForum

Since the database is empty, the only option that will do anything useful is `'Register'`, which allows you to create a user account. The first account created is automatically made the master administrator, so enter the username you want to use for administration and your local email address, then click the Submit button. mwForum will generate a password for you, and send the browser to the login screen where you can try it out. Passwords are also stored in the database in clear text, so if for some reason the mailing didn't work you can go to MySQL and retrieve your password there.

Having successfully logged in, you can now create categories and message boards. Categories organize boards, and boards contain messages. The options are reasonably self-explanatory, and if you find you've set up something that you don't like, you can easily change things or just delete the board and start again.

mwForum's administration tools become more interesting when you have multiple users and boards. You might want to create a handful of each and try out the different options for posting, setting administration access, and moderating messages.

If you find that mwForum meets your needs, you'll want to get mod_perl involved for significantly better performance. Just move `cgi-bin/mwf` to `perl/mwf` under Apache's root (assuming that is the directory managed by Apache::Registry), then move the Perl modules (`*.pm`) in `perl/mwf` to `lib/perl`. Change the configuration module to reflect the change in URL (change `cgi-bin` to `perl` if you've used the same setup I've shown) and you should be set to go—the database and static files should work as before.

When I tested mwForum under Apache::Registry, it didn't work; Apache kept sending the wrong MIME type, Perl script instead of text/html. The aforementioned support forum already had a topic about the problem, but no resolution. I added more information about my setup, and the developer (Markus Wichitill) posted his own mod_perl configuration, which made clear that I needed to tell mod_perl to handle headers for mwForum scripts—my other Apache::Registry scripts had all taken care of this manually. So I added this to `mod_perl.conf`:

```
<Directory "/usr/local/apache/perl/mwf">
    PerlSendHeader On
</Directory>
```

That got mwForum working perfectly (and much faster) under mod_perl as advertised. If you experience anything similar with the latest version of mwForum, try that configuration change.

While it was disappointing that the product didn't make the change transparently, the incident reminded me of what I like best about the Open Source world, namely responsive developers. The whole exchange took place over an afternoon; Markus replied quickly with the information I needed.

As a result, I can recommend mwForum in spite of the light documentation, since I'm confident that the developer or another user can help out with anything that goes wrong.

8.2.3   Chats

While the virtual community was born in mailing lists and message boards, it gained a great deal of life in real-time forums. These grew from early programs like Unix's talk into Internet Relay Chat (IRC) and text-based games. One could argue that the commercial online services of the '80s made most of their money from chat rooms; certainly real-time talking absorbs a good deal of Internet bandwidth today.

While I've been a fan of real-time chats for years (I met my wife on one), I haven't been as thrilled with web-based chat clients, which have tended to use Java and other browser technologies to try to make up for the basic mismatch of static HTML display and real-time conversation, resulting in typical browser wars incompatibilities and semisuccesses. If your site will have an associated IRC channel, I suggest you provide users with IRC clients. There are a number of good ones, even some written in Perl.

Short of a full-time channel, many sites want to host occasional gatherings—meetings with the staff, interviews with a luminary of the field, and so on. For short conversations and group discussion, an HTML-based chat may suffice. These are simple chats that take input from a Java- or CGI-based interface and write it to an HTML file, then use the autorefresh feature of supporting browsers to load the file and display new text. They have the added advantage that the HTML automatically becomes a log and archive of the meeting.

Like a news page, an HTML-based chat isn't hard to write, but why not start with one that is already written? Here is information on some freely available HTML chats.

EveryChat and derivatives

This amazingly small script is made freely available by EverySoft (http://www.every-soft.com) and has since been cloned into new versions by others. It consists of a CGI script (`everycht.cgi`) and a few HTML files. `chatframes.html` provides a frame-based interface with autorefresh, and `chatform.html` makes a simpler interface with manual refreshing and without frames. `chattop.html` is displayed at the top of the frame version, so customize this as you desire for your site.

Installation is quite simple: drop the script in your `cgi-bin` directory, then create a subdirectory of Apache's document root for chat files, such as `htdocs/chats`. Put the HTML files mentioned earlier and the starter chat file, `messages.html`, into this directory. Then open the interface files and the script in your favorite editor and fix the URLs to match the paths you've created.

My changes from the defaults were:

- `chatframes.html`—I changed the path to the chat file from `messages/messages.html` to `messages.html` to keep everything in one directory, and changed the URL for the chat script. You'll also want to change the login message (look for "Hi everybody!").

- `chatform.html`—Change the path to the chat script and the login message as earlier.

- `everycht.cgi`—I changed the path to the chat directory to my example setup:

```
$filepath='/usr/local/apache/htdocs/chats/';
```

Give the installation a try by having your browser load either the form or frame page (not the script itself). You should get a login screen—EveryChat doesn't reserve or register names, so you can call yourself anything you like. Figure 8.3 shows the Every-Chat start page.

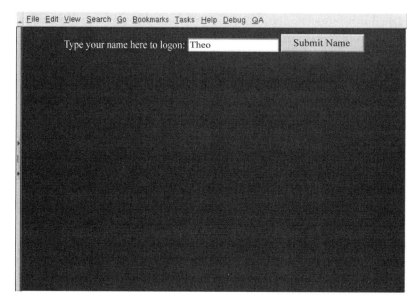

Figure 8.3   The EveryChat start page

If you'd rather run EveryChat under mod_perl, move the script over to your Apache::Registry directory. The version I tested also required `PerlSetHeader On` as mwForum had, but otherwise ran without problem.

Apart from autorefresh, EveryChat avoids any modern browser features. The script has an option to push messages down from the top rather than add them to the bottom for browsers that reposition the page on a refresh. By default it removes HTML tags from input, but you can disable this feature if you like with a few quick strokes of your text editor.

EveryChat provides for multiple chat rooms by duplicating the interface and message files. To create a room, copy the interface files, create a new message file, fix the URLs to refer to the changed paths, and have your browser load the new form or frame page. While this isn't terribly efficient, the files are not large. If the duplication bothers you, turn the files into Mason components.

The thing I like best about EveryChat is the size, not just because it makes the script quick, but because it makes it easy to read and understand the code and to use it for other projects. Apparently I'm not the only one, since EverySoft's page for Every-Chat includes pointers to other chat systems that started from this code base, ranging from those that provide prettier interfaces using JavaScript to specialized chess- and checkers-playing systems. Also there are several add-on modules contributed by users that extend EveryChat to provide user pictures, text filtering, link tags, and more.

Chat servers in Perl

Site developers that want more in a Perl-based chat system should take a look at two interesting projects which take Apache out of the loop.

EveryChat's Server Edition takes the basic chat script and turns it into a persistent server which can have its own site, port, or both. Start the server and have your browser connect to the site and port number, and the server will send back the current page of the chat. After that, it uses the same auto- or manual refresh to keep the browser up to date, but since the requests are going to the EveryChat server instead of Apache, response is even faster than running under mod_perl. The script is still tiny, and running several chats on one machine would be no problem.

At the time I'm writing, the Server Edition is in beta and is not clearly released with an Open Source license, but that may have changed.

Another server which is in an early stage is Entropy Chat, produced by John N. Koston and Virtual Development Inc. This script is about five times the size of Every-Chat, but adds considerable features: multiple rooms, a listing of active users, private messages, image posting, limited HTML posts, and more. The server setup is as trivial as EveryChat's—just give it a port and run the script, and it will stay in the background listening for connections and messages.

Entropy Chat uses JavaScript for a much nicer interface, and has many features that will be familiar to IRC users. The script isn't too large to learn and customize, making it a good choice for the intrepid developer. Look for it via a search service such as freshmeat.net to see how it has matured since my brief look.

Any of these products can be added to your site to provide real-time interaction for your community, bringing your users closer and building a sense of commonality that gives the Web life.

8.2.4   Search engines

It's no surprise that search engines are a common and expected feature of web sites. If your site has a large amount of static content, it needs a search engine. No matter how cleverly you lay out the subject matter of your site, users who know what they are looking for will want to go straight to the material they need.

Searching also plays to Perl's strengths, so it's no wonder that there are many examples of search engines written for Perl and CGI. Modest sites can use direct search methods, applying a Perl regular expression to the text of files and building URLs for those that match.

Sites with more content need a faster approach. The usual method is to create a keyword index, where every word in every file is entered into a database with a list of pointers back to the files where it was found. Once this database is built, it is very simple to display a list of files matching a keyword; if multiple words are specified, the engine can show either the union or intersection of the file lists for each word. More advanced features such as phrase and pattern matching can be implemented on top of a keyword index by applying complex searches to candidate files found from word matching.

Keyword indexes are a natural fit for hash file databases. The word is the index, and the associated record has a list of short unique strings that identify matching files. Another hash file turns the identifier string back into a file path or URL. To display more information with search results, add more data to the file hash (or just use more hash files)—document title, description, and so on.

Before you start to code your own search script, take a look around the Perl archives—I have examples following this approach that date back to the first articles and books I read on CGI. If your site content is in static HTML or text files you should be able to use the engine demonstrated next without change. If you store articles in a database or some other format that doesn't map files to URLs directly then you're probably going to have to write the indexing script yourself, but you can still use a working example.

PerlfectSearch

PerlfectSearch from http://www.perlfect.com/ is a good Open Source package that is actively maintained and adds some nice features to the basic search. The code is compact and the search script runs quickly as a CGI, and even more quickly via Apache::PerlRun (see the next example). It even comes with a setup script that will take care of the few configuration details for you.

Like most search packages, PerlfectSearch is split into two parts, the indexer and the searcher. The indexer examines static content and builds the database. It must be run every time content is added, perhaps via a cron job or some other automatic mechanism. The searcher reads the database and builds an HTML page that displays matches.

PerlfectSearch's index scans a configured list of directories for indexable files (matching the types you tell it to seek), and drops any that match names or patterns given in the exclusion list you provide. It then checks to see if the file contains HTML title and description tags, and if so it records those in individual databases. Then it removes common words from the file (also using a configured list), adds the remaining words to another database keyed by a unique ID for each word, and records the file and word ID pairings in a fourth hash file. The script has some nice optimizations to speed up the process, such as building a single regular expression to match all the excluded common words, and compressing repeated character strings.

The search script takes a given list of keywords and locates the matching files, then generates a list of matches. When given multiple keywords it ranks the files matching all words first, then the files matching any words. It also implements forced matches (+keyword) and exclusions (-keyword).

The results page is built from a template which you can configure to match the look of your site. Each matching file displays a title (linked to the URL), description (if any), and the full URL. If there are more matches than the configured limit, the first set of matches is displayed along with links to URLs that will generate the succeeding pages. Like most search engines, PerlfectSearch gives the illusion of maintaining state via these links but actually generates the matches each time it runs.

Installing PerlfectSearch is simple; unpack the distribution, then run the setup script which handles the basic tasks of copying files and receiving some configuration information from the user. Select the running mode by choosing to install in either `cgi-bin` or `perl`. In the latter case some additional directives will be required.

After copying the files, the installation script will prompt you for directories and file types to search. I included Mason (.mhtml) files out of curiosity, although that would index only keywords found in top-level components directly because dynamic content is not generated by the indexing process. You can run the indexer directly from the installation script if you wish, or manually afterwards.

PerlfectSearch can run via mod_perl, but not via Apache::Registry; the script uses global values in ways that mess up subsequent searches. Instead I ran it via Apache::PerlRun, which executes a CGI script in the context of the Apache process but doesn't save the compilation or global values. This is faster than CGI, since the Perl interpreter is already running and the process isn't forked. Here is the addition to `mod_perl.conf`:

```
<Directory "/usr/local/apache/perl/perlfect/search">
    PerlHandler Apache::PerlRun
</Directory>
```

Note that this `Directory` block inherits some settings from `/usr/local/apache/perl`, since PerlfectSearch's installation directory (`perl/perlfect/search`) is a subdirectory. I didn't have to tell Apache to let mod_perl handle the requests or that the directory contains executable scripts. I only reassigned the `PerlHandler` to Apache::PerlRun.

After you've completed the installation you'll want to try some searches. Go to your main or search page and add the following small form (changing the action path to match your URL if you haven't installed things according to my example):

```
<FORM ACTION="/perl/perlfect/search/search.pl">
  <INPUT TYPE="text" NAME="q">
  <INPUT TYPE="submit" VALUE="Search">
</FORM>
```

Then give it a try. Figure 8.4 shows my search page with a sample result:

My test installation indexed the online documentation for Apache, mod_ssl, mod_perl, and a few other products, totaling 175 files and about 15,000 indexable words. The indexer handled this load in less than a minute, making me confident that I could use PerlfectSearch on a larger site without a problem. If you upload files to your site via some automatic process, the indexer could be incorporated at the end or run via a nightly cron job. Users can continue to search the site while the indexer is

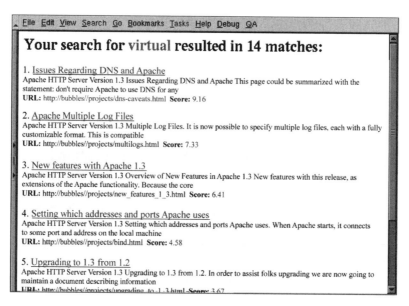

Figure 8.4 A simple results page

running, as it builds new indexes in temporary files and then moves them over to the main data location.

8.3 BUILDING A SITE

We now have all the tools needed to build a working community site. Assuming you have the machine ready and a worthy Internet connection, all you need are time, patience, and of course, content.

As an example, let's build a sample site, http://www.ourcommunity.org/, using the tools listed in the previous section. If you are experiencing "blank page" syndrome in designing your own site then following through these steps may help you get started in putting things together.

The first step is to decide what content our site will host. In this example we'll have:

- Articles of community interest stored in HTML files, with topic pages that group the articles

- A news page that has site announcements and links to new articles on this site and related sites

- A search engine for the articles and news

- A message board for discussing the content

- A web chat service for community meetings

Next we need to decide on tools for handling the content, and to determine how much traffic our site will handle.

If this is a low- to medium-traffic site, handling a peak load of as much as one request per second, then a decent modern computer running most any OS that supports Apache and Perl will do. If the average load is more than one request per second, or the peak is much higher, the hardware and OS will have to be chosen more carefully, and will probably involve multiple high-end servers. In that case the choice has likely been made already. Since discussion of current hardware is beyond the scope of this book, readers looking for recommendations should check platform evaluations on sites dedicated to their desired OS.

Let's assume for our example that the site will run on a single server running a Unix variant, and the hardware is adequate for the peak load (meaning that we don't have to do a great deal of tuning). We could choose to serve the static content with a small dedicated web server such as thttpd, but to start with we'll run everything from one Apache installation, with Perl scripts and mod_perl to handle dynamic content. We'll create the topic pages for the content files and link in the content manually, and products discussed in the previous section will provide the other features. Since we won't capture sensitive user data, we won't need encrypted channels, so mod_ssl and OpenSSL are optional. The message forums will store their messages in a MySQL database.

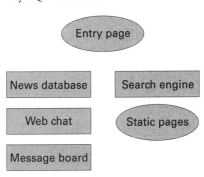

Figure 8.5   General site functions

A high level site design document will serve as a road map in laying out the elements. If you are an experienced HTML designer you may prefer to do this by creating the site's front page and a few sample feature pages; those with database or system design backgrounds might like some kind of entity-relationship diagram instead, or a simple work flow.[1] Figure 8.5 shows a diagram that is sufficiently vague to get anyone started.

That's enough information to get to work—let's build the site. You can work through the next section yourself, or download the site configuration and sample pages from the book's web site. You'll still need to install the required products and databases, however.

8.3.1   Installation

There's quite a bit of code to get in place even for a small site, so plan on plenty of downloading and setup time. Doing everything listed here can take half a day or several, depending on your familiarity with your system and your ability to deal with oddities as they occur.

---

[1] My own background is in programming and system administration, so my first move would be to install things and write scripts, but that doesn't set a very good example.

Apache, Perl, and the feature products will be set up according to my previous examples. This site doesn't call for any special Apache modules that aren't linked in by default, other than mod_perl. We could get fancy with the builds and slim down Apache and mod_perl to the minimum features necessary, but that can be done after the site is working—first we want to get the basics in place.

1 Create the user that Apache will use, such as 'web'.

2 If Perl is not installed, download it from http://www.perl.com/ and install it.

Download the current Apache distribution from http://www.apache.org/, and mod_perl from http://perl.apache.org/, then install them both as shown in chapter 5.

1 Apache is now installed in `/usr/local/apache`, which we'll refer to as Apache's root directory as before. Manually create the `perl`, `lib`, `lib/perl`, and `data` subdirectories from the root.

2 Edit `httpd.conf` as shown in the next section, then start Apache and test it locally. If you have your own static content ready, you can install it in the `htdocs` subdirectory now; if not, use Apache's manual as a sample. Make sure Apache's user can read the files.

3 Copy an example script into the `cgi-bin` subdirectory and test it. Make sure Apache's user can read and execute the script.

4 Edit `mod_perl.conf`, then restart Apache. Put an example script in the `perl` subdirectory and test it to ensure that mod_perl is working correctly.

5 Create the front page (or copy the example page from the book's web site) with links to the search engine, forums, and chat. Put an empty file in `htdocs/newslog/todays.news` so that the `include` directive will work, then test the front page.

6 Install Newslog, and secure the posting script, then post a news item and test your front page again.

7 Install MySQL as per chapter 4. The next step will test it, but you can use the examples as a confirmation test also.

8 Install mwForum, then test the front page link. Create the chief administration user.

9 Install EveryChat and test the front page link again.

10 Install PerlfectSearch, index whatever content you have, and then test the search box on the front page.

Sounds easy enough, doesn't it? Now for the details.

8.3.2 httpd.conf

Apache's main configuration file will serve largely as-is. Rather than include the whole file, I'll list my changed sections here.

If the Apache installation set a `Port` or `Listen` on a port other than 80, change them to the defaults. Comment out any `Port` or `Listen` directives referring to port 443, since this installation won't use SSL.

```
Port 80
Listen 80
#Listen 443
```

Set the `ServerAdmin` and `ServerName` to refer to the site. The traditional mailing address of 'webmaster' should be aliased to your administrator's account.

```
ServerAdmin webmaster@ourcommunity.org
ServerName www.ourcommunity.org
```

In the `Directory` block for `/usr/local/apache/htdocs` (the document root), enable `Includes`, but turn off the other features. Enable `FollowSymLinks` if you will be controlling the contents of the directory and want to use symbolic links. Disable the use of `.htaccess` files via `AllowOverride`.

```
<Directory "/usr/local/apache/htdocs">
    Options Includes FollowSymLinks
    AllowOverride None
    Order allow,deny
    Allow from all
    DirectoryIndex index.html index.shtml
</Directory>
```

The last directive in this section, `DirectoryIndex`, is new to our discussion. It tells Apache what files to look for when a user requests a directory, that is, a URL that doesn't end in a file name. The most obvious example of a directory request is the site's front page, which we want to display when a user requests http://www.ourcommunity.org/.

In our example we want to use an SSI in the front page, but in subdirectories we will use plain HTML. Rather than setting each one individually, we set a list of files for Apache to look for here.

Configure Newslog now (or make all the changes at once, if you prefer):

```
<Location "/cgi-bin/newslog.cgi">
    AuthUserFile data/newslog_post_users
    AuthName "Newslog story posters"
    AuthType basic
    require valid-user
</Location>
```

Also for Newslog, uncomment the directives that enable SSI:

```
AddType text/html .shtml
AddHandler server-parsed .shtml
```

Finally, include the mod_perl configuration file:

```
<IfModule mod_perl.c>
```

```
      Include conf/mod_perl.conf
</IfModule>
```

Then create an empty `mod_perl.conf` before restarting Apache. You should now be able to view any static content you have loaded on your web site. If you don't get the files you expect, check file permissions and the errors in `logs/error_log`.

8.3.3   mod_perl.conf

The mod_perl configuration file for this server assigns the `perl` subdirectory to Apache::Registry and Apache::PerlRun. If we were using any of the example handlers from other chapters, they'd go here too.

```
# Load these modules on start-up.
PerlModule Apache::DBI
PerlModule Apache::Registry
PerlModule Apache::PerlRun

# Scripts run via mod_perl instead of CGI
Alias /perl/ "/usr/local/apache/perl/"
<Directory "/usr/local/apache/perl">
    SetHandler perl-script
    PerlHandler Apache::Registry
    Options ExecCGI
    PerlSendHeader On
</Directory>
<Directory "/usr/local/apache/perl/perlfect/search">
    PerlHandler Apache::PerlRun
</Directory>
```

We load Apache::DBI so that database connections will be cached, which will help speed up mwForum. Then we load the two modules for running CGI scripts. Anything in the `perl` directory or its children will run via Apache::Registry with `PerlSendHeader On`. The scripts in `perl/perlfect/search` run via Apache::PerlRun.

After setting up this file, restart Apache and verify that it loads the new configuration without complaint. Don't worry about the fact that the scripts mentioned earlier aren't in place yet. We need only to test that mod_perl reads its configuration correctly. If Apache says that `PerlModule` is an unknown directive, then mod_perl is not built into Apache correctly; review the installation steps.

8.3.4   The front page

The first page of the site has a few tasks to accomplish in a short space:

- It identifies the community as concisely as possible
- It has news of interest to returning users, and categories for the static content
- Links with brief descriptions lead to the features of the site, all within view of the page as it loads
- It should balance attractiveness with quick loading time

The typical way to accomplish this is with a newspaper-like layout consisting of a banner identifying the site over columns of information. In my example, the left column has links for static content, the middle column contains news and the right column links in the other dynamic features.

Since the file will include the news items via SSI, it needs to be a `.shtml` file. I called it `index.shtml` but you can use any name you wish, and change the `DirectoryIndex` directive either to look for it or link it into place:

```
<!DOCTYPE HTML PUBLIC "-//IETF//DTD HTML//EN">
<HTML>
 <HEAD><TITLE>OurCommunity News and Information</TITLE></HEAD>
 <BODY BGCOLOR="#FFCC66">
  <CENTER><H1>OurCommunity News and Information</H1></CENTER>
  <TABLE CELLSPACING="20" COLS="2">
   <TR VALIGN="TOP">
    <TD>
     OurCommunity has served the members of this community since
     the beginning of the millennium.
    </TD>
    <TD>
     <I>People who like this sort of thing will find herein the
     sort of thing they like.</I><BR>-Abraham Lincoln
    </TD>
   </TR>
  </TABLE><P>
  <TABLE CELLSPACING="6" COLS="3">
   <TR>
    <TD ALIGN="LEFT" WIDTH="20%">
     <H3>Articles of interest to OurCommunity</H3>
    </TD>
    <TD ALIGN="CENTER" WIDTH="60%">
     <H2>Community News</H2>
    </TD>
    <TD ALIGN="LEFT" WIDTH="20%">
     <H3>Member Services</H3>
    </TD>
   </TR>
   <TR VALIGN="TOP">
    <TD>
     <A HREF="goal.html">Our goals</A><BR>
     <A HREF="projects">Ongoing projects</A><BR>
     <A HREF="proposals">Proposals for the future</A><P>
     <FORM ACTION="/perl/perlfect/search/search.pl">
      <B>Search the articles:</B><BR>
      <INPUT TYPE="text" NAME="q"><BR>
      <INPUT TYPE="submit" VALUE="Search">
     </FORM>
    </TD>
    <TD VALIGN="TOP">
     <!--#include virtual="/newslog/todays.news" --><P>
     <H3>Old news</H3> For previous items see the
     <A HREF="/newslog/oldnews">archive</A>.
```

```
      </TD>
      <TD VALIGN="TOP">
       <H3>Forums</H3>
       Discuss community news and interests on our
       <A HREF="/perl/mwf/forum.pl">Message Boards</A><P>
       <H3>Chats:</H3>
       Join in scheduled discussions or just meet other
       members on-line, either
       <A HREF="/chats/chatframes.html">with frames</A>
       or <A HREF="/chats/chatform.html">without frames</A>.
      </TD>
     </TR>
    </TABLE>
    <HR>
    <H5>
     Copyright 2001 by OurCommunity.Org Inc.<BR>
     Please send comments and bug reports about this site to
     <A HREF="mailto:webmaster@ourcommunity.org">Theo Petersen</A>
    </H5>
   </BODY>
  </HTML>
```

Like my other HTML examples, this one stresses brevity over beauty. Elements of the page are organized by space, but might get run together on browsers that don't support the CELLSPACING attribute. In that case, using BORDER might be more appropriate.

The page will look a bit odd if you view it as-is, due to the empty News column. Here it is after adding a few items from the next section. Figure 8.6 shows the front page with some news items.

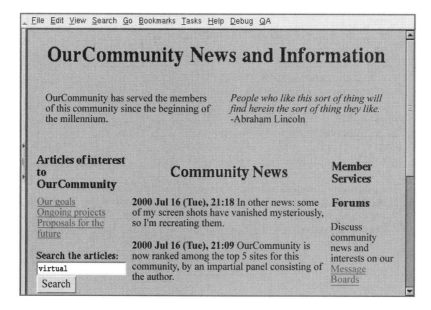

Figure 8.6   The front page

The main idea of the design is to draw new users into the community description (the block of text under the banner and to the left) and returning visitors to the news and member sections. A user who has seen the site before will skip the static elements and drop down into the center section, but that section shouldn't be so large that a new viewer is distracted from reading the overall page.

The static content section on the left has links to a document (`goal.html`) and two directories which correspond to article categories. Those directories will need their own `index.html` or `index.shtml` pages to organize the content they carry. Test the links by copying some sample documents into place.

The middle section is mostly a placeholder for `newslog/todays.news`, which will be generated automatically by Newslog. After displaying the current stories it offers a link to the archive; the index.html file in `newslog/oldnews` is also created by Newslog.

The right section has member features, the forum, and chat links. Those will be made operational in later sections.

8.3.5   News

Now we can liven up the site with current information. Install Newslog as described earlier in this chapter, with these values in `newslog-cfg.pl`:

```
$scriptURL = 'http://www.ourcommunity.org/cgi-bin/newslog.cgi';
$newsFile = '/usr/local/apache/htdocs/newslog/todays.news';
$archivePath = '/usr/local/apache/htdocs/newslog/oldnews';
$arcURL = 'http://www.ourcommunity.org/newslog/oldnews/';
$arcSuffix = '-news.html';
$redirect = 'http://www.ourcommunity.org/';
$tmpDir = '/tmp';
$MaxItems = 4;
```

Create `htdocs/newslog/oldnews`, then make Apache's user the owner of everything from `htdocs/newslog` on down—remember that it must create and modify the files in these directories.

Copy `newslog.cgi` and the modified `newslog-cfg.pl` to `cgi-bin`, then test a posting. If things are configured correctly you should be able to enter a news item via http://www.ourcommunity.org/cgi-bin/newslog.cgi. Note that there is no link on the main page to this URL; the news administrator can bookmark it separately. After entering and previewing the item, post it and verify that your browser displays the main page again.

If you haven't secured Newslog yet, do that now by adding the authentication directives to `httpd.conf`:

```
<Location "/cgi-bin/newslog.cgi">
    AuthUserFile data/newslog_post_users
    AuthName "Newslog story posters"
    AuthType basic
    require valid-user
</Location>
```

Then create the password file, using htpasswd:

```
/usr/local/apache/bin/htpasswd -c data/newslog_post_users newsgod
```

Restart Apache after making these changes and test a posting again. If Apache can't authenticate you, verify that the password file and directory are readable and that the paths are correct.

8.3.6   Forums

Installing mwForum is similarly easy. Create `htdocs/mwf` and `htdocs/mwf/attach` directories, resetting ownership to Apache's user, then create `perl/mwf`. Copy everything from mwForum's `img` directory to `htdocs/mwf`, then everything from cgi into `perl/mwf`. Customize `MwfConfig.pm` with these settings:

```
$cfg{'dbUser'}          = "web";
$cfg{'dbPassword'}      = "nouser";
$cfg{'smtpServer'}      = "localhost";
$cfg{'adminEmail'}      = "webmaster\@ourcommunity.org";
$cfg{'forumEmail'}      = "forum\@ourcommunity.org";
$cfg{'cgiPath'}         = "/perl/mwf";
$cfg{'url'}             = "http://www.ourcommunity.org/mwf/forum.pl";
$cfg{'attachments'}     = 1;
$cfg{'forumName'}       = "Our Community Forum";
```

The default database username and password are fine if you won't be running any of the other example scripts on this site. If you change them as shown here, also change the `grant-access.sql` script in mwForum's `sql` directory.

The mail settings will need to be customized for your site in order to make the example work. If you use mail services on a different server, put its address in place of localhost. Also, 'webmaster' and 'forum' should be aliases to a real account.

Now create the database:

```
mysqladmin -p create mwforum
mysql -p < sql/create-tables.sql
mysql -p < sql/grant-access.sql
```

This is enough to test the forum. Remember that the first user who registers will be made chief administrator, so do that now.

For a real site we would want to customize the images in `htdocs/mwf` and set the colors in `MwfConfig.pm` to match the site scheme.

8.3.7   Chat

Install EveryChat as shown previously in the chapter. Create `htdocs/chat` and put all of EveryChat's HTML files there, change ownership, then copy `everycht.cgi` to `perl`. Customize the following files:

- `chatframes.html`—Change `messages/messages.html` to `messages.html` and the URL for the chat script to `/perl/everycht.cgi`. Change the login message to something you prefer.
- `chatform.html`—Change the path to the chat script and the login message as in the example, then match the background color to the site.
- `chattop.html`—Set the color scheme to match the site.
- `everycht.cgi`—Change the path to the chat directory:

```
$filepath='/usr/local/apache/htdocs/chats/';
```

Verify that Apache can run `everycht.cgi` and can modify the message file, then test it out.

8.3.8   Searching

We'll use the PerlfectSearch engine to provide searches of static content; the forums have their own search system. The two can be merged with some effort, but I'll leave that as an exercise for the reader.

Installation follows the procedure given earlier in the chapter: run the setup procedure and tell it to install the scripts in the `perl` directory, then let it run the indexer on whatever sample content you are using. By directing it to Apache's document root, PerlfectSearch's indexer will index the articles and the news archive.

After the setup procedure is finished, go to `perl/perlfect/search/templates` and customize `search.html` to match the site's color scheme. Add a link back to the main page, and to the content index if you have one.

PerlfectSearch's configuration additions to `mod_perl.conf` were given earlier. Add them now if you haven't already, and restart Apache. Then you're ready to test the searches on your sample files.

Congratulations, your site is ready!

8.3.9   Improvements

While this site design will work fine for a small amount of static content, problems are bound to arise as the number of articles increases. The list of categories on the main page has to be kept up-to-date, as do the index pages for each category. The articles have to be edited to match the site's colors and fonts, and navigational links must be correct for each.

Mason would be a good solution for this problem. A component on the main page would look through the article subdirectories and create an entry for each category, and the category indexes could similarly be generated automatically from the list of files. An autohandler could provide standard colors, fonts, and navigation links.

Making search engines work with Mason (or any dynamic content tool) is a challenge. We do not want to generate dynamic pages for indexing, and we don't want to fix up the search database afterward.

One solution is to make each indexable document a top-level component, using an autohandler to wrap the component in standard header and style elements, and use subcomponents for navigational elements. The search engine's links will point to top-level components, so all URLs will be correct, and as each file is requested it will be generated in a standard way.

Another missing element is a section of links to related sites. These might be chosen by the site editors, or via a suggestion system such as used by Investorama. Get your users to discuss their surfing habits in your forums, and build your community and your links at the same time.

8.4   SLASH, THE SLASHDOT CODE

Having now built a site of our own, let's revisit an option briefly mentioned before.

In a nice example of the ways in which Open Source benefits those who give away their code, the developers of Slashdot have packaged the scripts and database schema that power their site and made them into a separate product. Users of Slash can take advantage of the forum on http://slashcode.org/ to discuss installation problems as well as tips and strategies for deploying a site. The developers in turn get informed feedback, performance improvements, and the occasional bug fix for their code.

Slash has an amazing array of features of interest to a community site. It can publish news, original content, and member forums with a search engine that covers them all. Its user registration and management package is very complete, and ties in to the score moderation system innovated by Slashdot. It also offers Slashdot's channel mechanism for packaging its own content and news from other sites into user-configurable slash-boxes that allow each user to build a custom portal.

Slash is not just a collection of scripts, it is a packaged product—and as such it expects to run your whole site. That's not a problem if you are building a fresh site and you like Slash's features. If you have an existing site that you want to integrate with Slash, I suggest that you rebuild the site using Slash first, then hook your scripts and content back in after you have Slash working.

Slash is very good quality code with very light documentation. Unless the developers have had considerable time to invest in manuals between my writing and your reading, expect to spend time reading slashcode.org and asking questions before you get everything right. But if you do pursue it, you will be rewarded with an excellent set of tools and a feature-rich site.

The requirements for Slash read almost as a Who's Who of Open Source: Apache, mod_perl, MySQL or PostgreSQL, and the Template Toolkit for building pages from templates. The required Perl modules are in a CPAN bundle (Bundle::Slash), so you can try installing that first to fill in any major pieces.

After installing all the components, download and install the Slash code. This will include building the Slash server (slashd) and its various utilities. It will even create startup scripts for slashd and put them in the appropriate system directory. The installation procedure builds an Apache configuration file (slash.conf) which you can include in your main `httpd.conf`.

One of the great advantages of Slash for large sites is its scalability. The Slash server, database server, and web server (or servers) can reside on separate machines as desired. See the documentation at the Slash site for how to build a web farm for your community.

8.5 ONLINE RESOURCES

After your site is ready, you will need to take steps to promote it to your community. Here are a few ways to bring the users to your pages.

First, get other related sites in your community to link to yours (and return the favor). If there is a community web directory or news page, try to have them review your site before you go public—get your positive press lined up and link to any commentary about your debut.

Similarly, join any web rings that pertain to your site. If you aren't certain, try the directories at http://webring.org/ and look for ring links on the sites you asked for pointers. Web rings are one of those nice ideas that haven't worked out so well, due to the high turnover rate of web sites, but they do serve as community directories.

Mailing lists, news groups, and other forums provide a transient way to let people know your site is open. It is best to subscribe to and read a forum for some time before posting an invitation, even a well-meant one. If the posting goes against the forum's charter, members may view such announcements as spam advertising.

8.5.1 Search engine submission

I regularly receive email from companies that claim they can get my sites listed on thousands of search engines for a small fee. Getting your site listed on major search engines is an important step, but it is easier than some people would have you believe.

The major public search engines all have submission forms where you can directly enter your site. Choose the search engines you use yourself—chances are your users like them also. Search sites generally post their requirements for getting a listing, such as META tags for keywords and description. Make sure your site is in compliance before submitting it, and then be patient. Robot-based sites should add your entry soon after you meet their requirements, but search engines that employ human editors can take months to add a listing.

If you want to get broader entry, go to one of many sites that offers free submission to multiple engines. http://www.submitit.org/ is one example, presenting a form for entering information on your site and sending it on to the search engines. Another is http://www.scrubtheweb.com/, which also offers analysis of META tags and offers feedback on whether your site is likely to be accepted.

Be aware that such utilities don't guarantee that your site will meet the listing requirements of the particular search engines, or will be accepted even if they do. If your listing doesn't appear in a reasonable time, go to the search engine's submission form and try adding your site directly.

Before your site gets busy, you'll want to establish good maintenance and performance management procedures. The last two chapters of the book offer guidelines on coping with popularity and recovering from disasters. Start managing your success early—when your site is swamped, it is already too late.

C H A P T E R 9

Intranet applications

When the Internet boom of the '90s struck, businesses suddenly needed public sites for product information, sales contacts, feedback, and so on. An equally important though less noticeable change happened inside companies, bringing with it a new buzzword for the business lexicon: *intranet applications*, those which run on an internal company network.

While it is simple to set up an internal web server, the real challenge is to build a set of internal applications that uses an intranet's advantages, combining the speed and locality of an internal network with Perl and Apache tools. This chapter will discuss a number of common scenarios and tools that will help out both users and administrators of local area networks (LANs).

9.1 DOCUMENTATION AND FILE SERVER

Many internal web servers start out as quiet, unassuming documentation libraries and file servers. This is a natural outgrowth of the fact that many free and commercial products ship documentation as HTML files (or as PDF files, which are also easily managed by a web server). Gathering it all into one place gives developers and users one-stop shopping for information. Once a group has a repository for one kind of file, it naturally extends it to others.

9.1.1 Documentation directory tree

The simplest kind of documentation server is just a tree of directories under Apache's document root. You don't even need to create a page for your documentation directory. Apache's index feature will create a simple but effective index page if `Options Indexes` is enabled.

Automatic index generation requires the mod_autoindex module be built into Apache, as it is by default. The `IndexOptions` directive gives you several options for controlling how the page is generated:

- `FancyIndexes` can be used to enable a view somewhat like the typical GUI file manager, showing the file name, icon, size, modification date, and an optional description.

- To extract the titles of HTML files into the description field for the index page, use the `ScanHTMLTitles` option.[1] You'll probably also want to expand the description field by setting `DescriptionWidth` to a reasonable value, 80 characters or so. For non-HTML files, the `AddDescription` directive lets you specify the description field.

- `FoldersFirst` will make subdirectories appear at the top of the list, as they do in many GUI file managers.

You can further customize the appearance of the page by including a header and readme file, which are displayed at the top and bottom of the index page respectively. By default these are called `HEADER.html` and `README.html`, although `HEADER` and `README` will also work, and in a pinch you can use the `HeaderName` and `ReadmeName` directives to point to other files.

Product documentation likely comes with an `index.html` file that will be displayed automatically when a browser requests the directory. If not, you can either continue the index generation scheme into the directory or tell Apache which file you want displayed by default, using the `DirectoryIndex` directive. For a large documentation tree, you may find it more manageable to localize the configuration using

---

[1] Note that ScanHTMLTitles requires Apache to look through all the HTML files in a directory and extract their title tags; this is fine for occasional use on a machine without other duties, but is not efficient for large, frequently accessed directories.

.htaccess files instead of one monolithic httpd.conf. Remember to set AllowOverride appropriately on the directory to enable their use.

Of course, if you spend a lot of effort on a header and readme, adding descriptions and tinkering with the index format, you might be better off just creating an index page in the first place. Generated indexes are best for pages whose content changes regularly, such as file download pages. Documentation is less likely to fluctuate.

On the other hand, autoindexing is great for general file servers, as we'll see next.

9.1.2   File server

Most organizations have other kinds of files to share between workstations: updates, nonweb documents, graphics, work-in-progress, or completed projects. These may be lumped together on a system which shares with directories client machines via NFS or SMB file services;[2] a web server can act as a generic file server as well, providing cross-platform services available for any browser. Some browsers even allow drag-and-drop from web pages to the local file manager.

Once again, the simplest way is to gather all the needed files into a directory or directories under Apache's document root. Using the mod_autoindex directives described in the previous section, Apache can create a simple page that guides the user to what they need. Group files together into directories and use headers and readmes to instruct the users.

In addition to those directives, make the page more visually interesting with appropriate file icons. Apache ships with a wide selection of icon graphics in its /icons directory, and you can add more as needed. mod_autoindex allows you to assign icons by file extension (AddIcon) or by MIME encoding (AddIconByEncoding) or type (AddIconByType). The Apache online documentation recommends using AddIconByType for any file with a defined MIME type, but violates its own recommendation in the sample configuration file. In practice, if you have to add a MIME type to identify a file, you'll also need to add an icon directive for it one way or another, so use whichever approach makes sense to you. Here are some sample directives from the default httpd.conf:

```
AddIcon /icons/binary.gif .bin .exe
AddIconByEncoding (CMP,/icons/compressed.gif) x-compress x-gzip
AddIconByType (TXT,/icons/text.gif) text/*
```

The directive options follow one of two formats. The first is to provide a path to the icon graphic, relative to Apache's home directory (not the document root as you might expect for a graphic). The other is a pair of options enclosed in parenthesis, giving the ALT text followed by the icon path. The ALT text will be displayed by

---

[2]   While a web server which is exposed to the Internet should not have either of these services, an intranet server is assumed to be on a protected network. There's nothing wrong, apart from the administrative hassle, with having an internal web server also share files via other services.

browsers that don't display graphics, as per the ALT attribute of an IMG tag. You can also specify text tags for icons using the AddAlt, AddAltByEncoding, and AddAltByType directives.

One more important consideration for file servers is what not to serve. By default, if a file in an autoindexed directory is readable to Apache, it is readable to users. The IndexIgnore directive lists file extensions, names, or patterns to be left out of generated pages. For instance, to keep your header and readme files out of the list, use this directive:

```
IndexIgnore HEADER.html README.html
```

Without an IndexIgnore directive to the contrary, Apache will show the full contents of a directory, including files that Unix systems consider "hidden" (beginning with a .) and backups (ending with a ~). This notably includes .htaccess and the Unix directory entries for the current (.) and parent (..) directories, so a more complete IndexIgnore should remove those files from the list:

```
IndexIgnore HEADER* README* .* *~
```

This will also catch other variations of the header and readme file names. You will also need to tell Apache not to serve such files if the user types in the file name after the directory URL. The default httpd.conf handles this for .htaccess:

```
<Files ~ "^\.ht">
    Order allow,deny
    Deny from all
</Files>
```

9.1.3 Generating index pages

You may want to take over the index generation process completely. For example, if you are serving files that have description information Apache doesn't know how to extract, you can write a Perl script to examine the files and send back a properly built index. A more complex script might cache a generated page, see if anything has changed, and send the cached text back if not.

The DirectoryIndex directive allows scripts as well as static files to serve as a directory index. The script still has to follow the usual rules for executables: it has to reside in a directory marked by ScriptAlias or have a type Apache knows to be CGI. This directive would tell Apache to run index.pl for the text/reports subdirectory of Apache's documentation root:

```
<Location /text/reports/>
    DirectoryIndex /cgi-bin/index.pl
</Location>
```

Here's a trivial example in which index.pl creates the page:

```
#!/usr/local/bin/perl -w

use strict;
```

```
use CGI;
my $q = new CGI;

# Print the opening HTML.
print $q->header,
  $q->start_html('Text reports'),
  $q->h1('Text reports:');

# Open the directory and make a list of contents.
my $dir = '/usr/local/apache/htdocs/text/reports';
opendir REPORTS, $dir or die "Can't open report directory $dir.";
my @files = grep /^[^.].*[^~]$/, readdir REPORTS;
closedir REPORTS;
foreach my $file (@files) {
    print $q->p($q->a({href => $file}, $file));
}

# Close and exit.
print $q->end_html;
```

Note that the file list is built using grep to remove the same files mentioned earlier—hidden files and backup copies. It also requires files to have names at least two characters long. The script then builds a very simple page with a link for each file. If the files all matched a format that Perl could understand, the script could open the files and extract summary information or other useful text to display on the page along with the links.

Using a generated index doesn't work around the fact that Apache will serve up any files it can read, barring configuration directives to the contrary. Since a directory with a generated index has to be under the document root to be browsed at all, any file in that directory is still available to a user who knows its name, regardless of whether or not it appears in the index page. To work around this problem, you must either keep sensitive files out of the document root or apply an HTTP authentication scheme to the directory.

9.1.4   mod_perl for indexing

Even though this script is set up as a simple CGI, there's no reason mod_perl couldn't be involved. The URL given in DirectoryIndex is resolved via the normal rules, so all we need to do is to specify a script or location that is handled by mod_perl. Of course, at that level of complexity, there isn't much difference between using DirectoryIndex to specify an index page generator and just configuring a location in httpd.conf to run a mod_perl application, as was shown in the report page example of chapter 7.

There is an intermediate step between letting Apache do all the work and taking on the entire matter. The Apache::AutoIndex module (on CPAN as usual) provides a Perl handler which implements the functions of mod_directory and mod_autoindex. As a direct replacement, it reads and honors directives intended to describe index pages as shown previously. It also adds some nice features of its own, such as generating thumbnail graphics for image directories via Image::Magick.

If you have a strong need to code your own index handling, Apache::AutoIndex also serves as a valuable starting point by showing how to read and implement standard directives and also add your own (as the module does with thumbnail descriptions). The documentation provides examples of installing a Perl handler for directory requests.

9.1.5   Searching

Once you have your documentation organized, you'll want tools to make it easier to use. Chapter 8 has a section on search engines that are freely available, so start there if you haven't looked already.

Since documentation can be in many formats besides HTML, you may need tools that handle other file types. SWISH-E has filter modules that work with PDF and other formats. It is available at http://sunsite.berkeley.edu/SWISH-E. The SWISH-E indexing and search engines are written in C, but interaction is through front-end scripts written in Perl and other languages. The related SWISH++ is a rewrite of SWISH-E into C++.

The Harvest project (available on SourceForge) includes tools for indexing both local files and other web sites, or even FTP sites and news groups. Harvest-NG is a Perl implementation of the indexing tools. It supports various document formats using a filter module architecture familiar to Perl developers, and stores results in a database that is easily accessible to other scripts. It comes with its own minidatabase engine which can be replaced with a DBI interface for those who want to use SQL. Mailing lists and archives are advertised on the Harvest web pages.

Namazu (http://www.namazu.org/) is another Perl/C hybrid, although in this case the indexing is done by Perl and the search engine is written in C. Besides supporting a wide variety of file formats (including TeX), it uses Perl and GNU library tools for internationalization and Japanese character sets.

9.2   OFFICE APPLICATIONS

Having spent the time to set up an internal web server, it is natural to want more from your efforts. Going beyond documentation and file services, a quick search will discover a large number of office applications available free: email, calendars, scheduling, and other typical business tools.

Because desktop applications in this genre have been around for years, we might take a moment to ask: why move them to the Web? Commercial intranet application vendors have been selling the idea of browser-as-desktop since the beginning of the Internet boom. Each application run via a browser instead of a program installed on the client workstation reduces administration overhead and per-seat expense (by the cost of disk space and workstation maintenance, if not licensing).

That said, the payoff doesn't really happen until all or nearly all applications have moved off the workstation and onto the browser, requiring a reversal of the trend toward more local computing. And it conflicts with desktop economics: a computer that is capable of running one of today's hefty browsers is also capable of running hefty desktop applications, while stripped-down versions have only marginal success in the business market.

Some applications migrate more easily than others; if the service in question requires some form of central monitor or database to be useful, it is a natural fit for a web application. Groupware, mail, and personal scheduling applications all have incarnations that run in a browser, some in Perl, others in PHP and other popular languages. I'll mention some Perl examples here, but if you are serious about running a web-based office, don't be afraid to consider the alternatives.

9.2.1   Email

Before the Web claimed headlines, email and news were the killer applications of the Internet, and the number of available email clients reflects the history and popularity of text messages. Users take their choice of mail reader almost as personally as their messages, and getting entrenched users to change clients can be difficult. There are advantages for administrators and users in moving to a one-client, web-based mail system, but if the users won't change, a mixed solution is still feasible.

Before considering a web mail reader, we first have to look at the protocols used for reading mail. The early Unix mail systems wrote incoming mail to a spool directory,[3] and the mail client read (and deleted) it directly from there. More feature-rich clients such as Pine and Elm pick up spooled messages and maintain multiple mail folders housed under the user's own directory. All messages were read directly from disk, so the client had to be on the same machine as the mail server.

The POP protocol, and later IMAP, relieved the locality restriction by connecting client programs to like-minded servers; the client sends a query to the server asking what messages are available and the server sends a synopsis, which can then be used to request actual messages. The client may again store messages in local folder directories (typical of POP systems) or may keep messages and folders on the server (IMAP's focus).

The POP protocol gained popularity with home Internet accounts, allowing users to read their mail via a graphical client with a point-and-click interface. POP's major deficiency for business users is tied to its folder management, which requires keeping a local copy of messages and deleting them from the server; while POP clients can leave messages on the server, they can't organize them there, and the local message folders

---

[3] Another leftover piece of terminology: spooling is a generic term for writing files to a temporary directory so that they can be picked up and processed by another program. In practice, most mail clients leave the spooled mail in place, making the temporary storage permanent.

are available only to the local client. This results in either a cluttered collection of old messages on the server or isolated messages on one or more client machines.

IMAP addresses this by providing server-based folder management as part of its protocol. Users can create and delete folders and move messages among them. Any IMAP client for a given user on any system sees the same folder hierarchy. Of course, this requires the client to be connected to the server in order to read stored messages; IMAP clients can copy messages to local files also, but this results in the same scattering and redundancy as in POP clients.

Web-based clients can use either or both of these protocols. The browser displays folders and messages, but the real client in this case is the application running on the web server; it will talk to the POP or IMAP server or read the local mail folders, and send the contents back to the browser as HTML.

At first I thought that web-based email was a strange idea, since there are so many good, free email clients. A CGI application would almost have to be less friendly and easy, so why would anyone use it? Besides, the popular browsers have email clients built in, so another client seemed redundant. But reading email via a web application does have some distinct advantages for both users and administrators:

- If all mail is read through the browser (i.e., there are no other email clients), administrators can shut off POP and IMAP services. On a protected server this is a convenience. If a company provides access to internal mail over the Internet, removing open services and their inevitable security holes is of much greater importance.

- Users (or their admin helpers) have one less thing to configure when setting up a desktop machine. Those who read mail from more than one location will see a consistent interface.

- If security is paramount, web-based mail can be run through SSL, protecting passwords and contents of messages. While many POP and IMAP clients and servers allow secure messaging, in practice the security features are seldom used.

In order to do away with POP and IMAP services, the web server must also be the mail server. Incoming mail has to be stored in the mail spool directory for the web application to read. If that's not convenient, or the other client protocols are still required, then mixed services are still possible.

One other significant point for administrators to consider is that installing any web mail system is a chore. Those that use POP or IMAP require a great many Perl modules to run. Those that don't have to be integrated into your mail system. Examining each of the example systems described next took considerable effort, so plan on spending a day or so installing and configuring your system of choice.

NeoMail

This is a strong entry in the stand-alone category. NeoMail is a very configurable, full-featured web mail client, easily customized to a company's graphic standards. It supports multiple languages, user-defined folders, importing address books from other clients and many other desirable features. See the project's page on SourceForge (http://neomail.sourceforge.net/) for a more detailed list.

NeoMail comes with a setup script that tries to make installation easier, creating the software's installation directories and editing paths into scripts. My own system required considerable tinkering before I was able to logon and read mail. On the positive side, nearly every problem I encountered had already appeared and been addressed in NeoMail's mail archive.

NeoMail reads mail directly from the mail spools, so it needs to be able to get at files that are normally protected from web server CGI applications. On Unix systems it uses `suidperl`, a program which is optionally built when Perl is configured and installed. As the name implies, `suidperl` allows a Perl script to honor the `suid` and `sgid` bits in a file's mode, which in turn let the script run as the user or group which owns the file, instead of the user or group of the process. Thus we can make NeoMail's scripts owned by `root` or `mail` and give them access to files that Apache couldn't (and shouldn't) normally touch.

NeoMail's installation documentation explains the needed settings, but doesn't provide any information on `suidperl` itself. Since I'd never needed it before, I had to go back to my Perl distribution, run the configuration script again to enable setuid scripts, and build and install `suidperl`. Then I modified each of NeoMail's scripts with the path to `suidperl` instead of the usual Perl interpreter.

NeoMail also requires access to the password file to verify user identities. Since it is reading the password file directly (`/etc/shadow` in my case, or `/etc/passwd` if you don't use shadow passwords), I had to modify the group ownership of the file to permit NeoMail's scripts. A better solution would be to create a user for NeoMail and add it to both the `mail` group and a group permitted to read the password file.

After all that was done, NeoMail still didn't run due to a number of permission problems, even on directories its setup script had created. If you have the same troubles, go through each new directory and verify that NeoMail can read and write in appropriate places. Figure 9.1 shows the NeoMail configuration screen.

While all of that was frustrating, I was pleased with the result. NeoMail ran without further difficulties and had no trouble reading and sending messages. I tried out some of the styles that shipped with the software and had no trouble adding my own background graphics.

While NeoMail is a good fit for an organization's mail interface, there's no reason it can't be used for home systems too. One intriguing possibility is to use fetchmail to gather messages from remote mail servers and store them locally, then use NeoMail as the client. fetchmail cleverly fixes up headers in downloaded messages to route

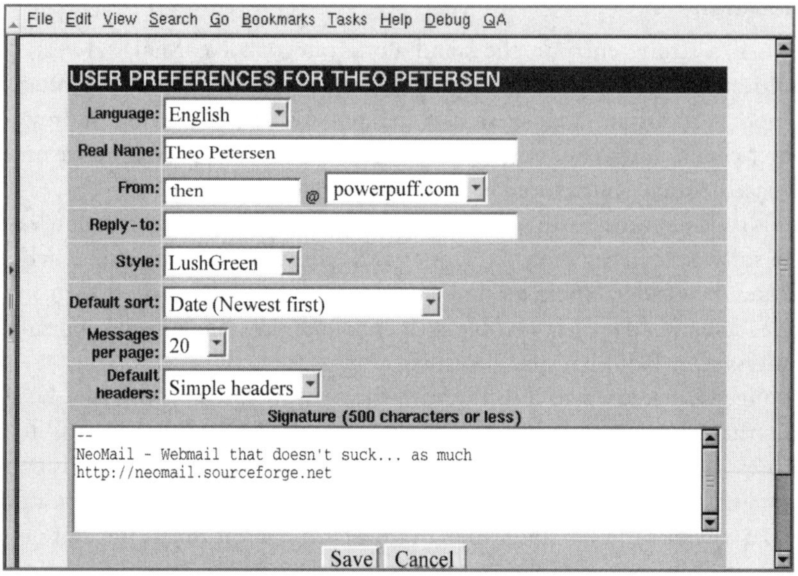

Figure 9.1 NeoMail configuration screen

replies correctly, and works with most email client protocols. (It doesn't work with web-based mail services such as Yahoo! and Excite mail, yet.)

NeoMail is a sizable script and uses CGI.pm for various helper functions, so it can be slow on an older or busy system. Unfortunately the use of `set-uid` scripts precludes running NeoMail in mod_perl. We can't change the Perl interpreter's user ID without changing the Apache process, which would be a security risk. We might think to configure Apache to run as root, which would give it all the necessary privileges, but Apache objects to this unless compiled with a special switch, `BIG_SECURITY_HOLE`, which more or less tells you what the Apache Group thinks of the idea.

If you like NeoMail but need better performance, consider running the script via FastCGI, which has no trouble with `set-uid` programs. The script will get compiled once and stay resident in its own process, saving considerable resources.

Other stand-alone mail packages

As more sites grow concerned with Internet security, some of the network's venerable packages are being replaced with variants that are built with those concerns in mind. One such is qmail, which handles SMTP traffic usually delegated to sendmail, and which advertised a $1,000 prize to anyone who could find flaws in its security.

qmail replaces sendmail completely, so utilities that relied on sendmail's quirks often don't work with it. oMail (also available via SourceForge) provides a web interface to qmail. The developer started with NeoMail and modified it to provide support for qmail and other administration packages.

SqWebMail is a mail client written in C and Perl that is part of the Courier mail package (http://courier.sourceforge.net/). Courier provides a variety of mail protocols including stand-alone mail, POP, and IMAP.

POP and IMAP

If your organization needs to support other clients in addition to web mail, there are a number of good applications that can help. The simply titled Perl Webmail at http://opensource.jaos.org/ and Spmail (on SourceForge) both work with POP servers. I've mentioned the limitations of POP though, and since most IMAP servers also provide POP services, there are good reasons to consider IMAP instead.

WING (available on CPAN) and acmemail (http://www.astray.com/acmemail) are the most discussed IMAP-web mail gateways available in Perl. Installing either is a big job, involving a large number of Perl modules and considerable configuration work. Both get their IMAP connectivity via the Mail::Cclient module, which in turn requires the c-client library from Pine (a popular text-based email client) or the University of Washington's IMAP server. WING requires PostgreSQL, while acmemail makes database support optional and provides sample scripts to use MySQL or PostgreSQL. WING runs only via mod_perl, while it is optional (but recommended) with acmemail.

acmemail has a very attractive interface and excellent MIME support, including HTML mail and inline image display. Oddly enough though, when a discussion of the merits of acmemail versus WING ran through the mod_perl mailing list, acmemail's developer recommended WING. The latter is heavily tested at its home at Oxford University and has been proven to handle huge numbers of users. Meanwhile, acmemail is facing reincarnation as Project Sparkle at the hands of a new developer, promising a more modular architecture for easier installation as well as support for a number of address books and imports.

Perl modules

If you aren't satisfied with any of the available implementations, or just have to have things your way, CPAN provides the tools for building your own web mail gateway. Browse through CPAN to find the large number of Mail:: and Net:: modules that offer message retrieval, formatting, and connections to the server of your choice.

9.2.2   Calendar

Personal calendar applications for PDAs and desktops are terrific for people organized enough to use them. Shared calendars are even better for groups that have project deadlines, meetings, and other important dates to track among members. Hosting group calendars on an intranet web site is a natural fit. Like internal email, it may also be worth providing access outside the protected network.

Calendar applications require a place to store dates and events, so look for the database requirements of your application of interest when shopping around. Good candidates provide levels of user access with appropriate password protections, so that you can specify who can see a given calendar and who can add events (and those should be separate privileges).

The Perl community has produced two notable web calendars, with other projects in beginning stages.

The mod_perl calendar system

This application (http://www.gallanttech.com/) provides a very complete system built on (you guessed it) mod_perl, MySQL (but the author claims it migrates well to other DBI drivers), and the cal program found on most flavors of Unix. It has a strong feature set: customizable appearance (based on a mix of style sheet and database entries), user privileges as described above, and filtered HTML in event descriptions to prevent the event writers from taking over the calendar pages. Calendars can refer to one another, so that administrators can build a hierarchical set of calendars (with different privileges) and display them all on one master page.

The developer has kept a large number of calendar usage and security issues in mind, as you can see from reading through the configuration and management documentation. The application does its own session management for loggedin users (based partly on the mod_unique_id Apache module, which is not built in by default). Sessions are expired via a script which must be run separately via cron or a similar mechanism. Each calendar occupies a set of tables in the database, plus one more table that identifies the calendars. The table layouts are provided without documentation, but it wouldn't be hard to integrate the data into another application if desired.

Each calendar may also have its own set of HTML templates used to generate the pages. There are template tokens for all of the elements of a calendar page, allowing the interested designer to rearrange things as he desires. The developer has his own system for converting these templates into HTML.

While rich in features, the system is very light on documentation. It comes with a short installation and configuration page and another page of information on the template tokens and some database layouts. Setting all of this up is a good bit of work. The product's page doesn't mention any free support forums, but does offer commercial support via the developer.

WebCal

Michael Arndt offers this application (http://bulldog.tzo.org/webcal/webcal.html). It is also rich in features, including tools to sync a WebCal calendar to a Palm computer via the pilot-link package (link software and PDA not included). The distribution supplies modules to store event data in flat file, MySQL, or PostgreSQL databases. The flat file version worked fine for my testing, but I recommend one of the others for anything more serious. The supplied db_merge script allows administrators to combine databases, so there is no harm in experimenting with one and switching later.

WebCal doesn't go much further than the mod_perl Calendar System referred to earlier in this chapter, but does include an installation script that does most of the work. To my surprise it ran perfectly on my Mandrake Linux system (although none of the defaults applied). The only manual step was to add the configuration directives to `httpd.conf`:

```
<Directory /usr/local/apache/cgi-bin/webcal>
    AllowOverride AuthConfig
    Options ExecCGI
</Directory>
```

To run WebCal via Apache::Registry, add a few more lines inside the `Directory` block:

```
SetHandler perl-script
PerlHandler Apache::Registry
PerlSendHeader On
```

After restarting Apache I was able to log in as the admin user (which has a default password set by the installation script—remember to modify it immediately) and bring up the site settings page, shown in figure 9.2.

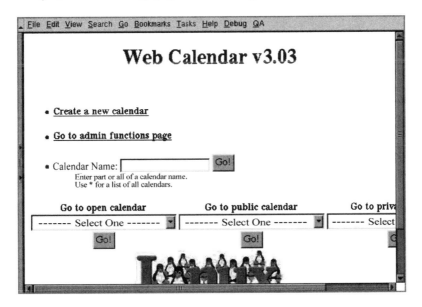

Figure 9.2 WebCal options

WebCal's privilege system is not quite so obvious (to my way of thinking) as that of the mod_perl Calendar System. Each calendar is either private, public, or open. Private calendars require a password to write events, and have a list of users who are permitted to read them (so a user must log in before reading). Public calendars also require a password to write events but allow anyone to read, and open calendars need no passwords at all. This requires sharing passwords among all those privileged to add events to a calendar.

Preferences are set by calendar, not user. From a given calendar's preferences page you can "subscribe" to other calendars to display their events, allowing a rich hierarchy. WebCal's distribution includes a U.S. holidays calendar which I added to my own. The preferences page also lets the owner set colors, background images, time zone, date formats, and other basic options. Modifying the actual layout of a page would require altering code, but I couldn't see anything I would actually want changed.

WebCal offers year, month, week, and day views, and navigation between them is obvious and painless. Adding events or displaying their details requires JavaScript to be enabled, so take client-side security into account.

WebCal can send out event notifications via email or pager services (although the latter isn't explained anywhere in the scant documentation). Email notification requires a cron job, which the installation script will add for you if you like.

The few administrative tasks are handled from a small set of pages. Administrators can set sitewide preferences, delete calendars, and add or delete users. The sitewide options determine if users can create their own calendars and what options they can set.

Free support is offered via mailing lists and the product's web site. I haven't found an archive of the lists themselves, but other mailing list archives have plenty of references to WebCal, speaking well of its user base. I'm confident that the application can be used by a larger group than my own with no trouble.

Other calendars

eXtropia.com offers a calendar package as part of its Open Source script library, also called WebCal (http://www.extropia.com/scripts/calendar.html). eXtropia.com lists an impressive installed base, and offers message forum support at its site to registered users. It has a unique license for its products, but don't be frightened—it is a merger of two other respectable licenses.

9.2.3   Project management

Scheduling, tracking, and charging resources are common needs for groups of software developers and other creative people. Involving the trackees in this process makes life much easier for the trackers, so project management applications are another natural fit.

While there are a number of good Open Source project management packages available, the pickings from the Perl camp are rather limited. Web Projects by Emmanuel Pierre (http://www.e-nef.com/perl/) offers a strong feature list, but the project is in French, needs more documentation, and the developer is hoping to find a new maintainer. There are other projects in a beginning stage on SourceForge.

If you mostly need to account for how time is spent, onShore offers a very complete time sheet application (http://www.onshore-timesheet.org/) that has impressive reporting capabilities and can be configured to email alerts to project managers. The application is built on PostgreSQL, and can be run as regular CGI or via Apache::Registry.

If a desktop application fits your needs as well as a web app, there are a number of time-tracking and project management tools available for the GNOME and KDE desktops. If a web application is required, consider some of the alternatives available from PHP developers (such as Achievo at http://www.achievo.com/), or (if you are working on an Open Source project) move your project to SourceForge and take advantage of its groupware tools.

9.3   INTERFACES TO NONWEB APPLICATIONS

No matter how quickly office applications move to the Web, we'll still have command-line utilities for some things. Common user maintenance tasks such as changing passwords and managing files already have web wrappers, as we'll see. For other needs, Perl provides tools for putting a web face on shell commands.

Perl executes simple commands via one of three interfaces: exec, system, or the backtick operator. The first of these may be familiar to Unix programmers who have worked with "fork and exec" servers, which respond to a request by creating a child process (forking) and then use the exec system call to start another program in the child. On Unix systems (as well as on Windows systems with Perl 5.6 and above), Perl's exec and fork work the same way, allowing you to write this sort of server in Perl if you wish. exec replaces the running Perl interpreter with the requested command. Your script never returns from an exec. To use it in a web interface, your script needs to output required headers and any initial page contents before calling exec. The command's output will complete the page.

Here is a quick example (showservers.pl) of a CGI script that calls exec to show what httpd processes are running.

```
#!/usr/local/bin/perl -w

use strict;

print "Content-Type: text/htmls\n\n";
print "</head><body><h1>Server processes:</h1><p><pre>";
exec('ps -C httpd -l');
print "</pre></body></head>";
```

If you drop this script in your cgi-bin directory and run it, you can confirm the behavior of exec: the final line to print closing tags isn't called. Most browsers are quite forgiving about this, however; the page will still be displayed.

To call a command from your script and then return for further processing, use either system or the backtick operator. system internally does a fork and exec, just as described earlier, packaging them in an easy-to-use function. The result returned by `system` is the exit status of the called command. This often confuses first-time programmers who more often want the command's output.

You would expect Perl to make that easy, and you'd be right. The backtick operator treats the string surrounded by backticks as a command, and yields the command's output. Here is the same script using this mechanism:

```
#!/usr/local/bin/perl -w

use strict;

print "Content-Type: text/html\n\n";
print "</head><body><h1>Server processes:</h1><p><pre>\n";
print `ps -C httpd -l`, "</pre></body></head>\n";
```

In this version, the command output is merged into the stream sent back to the browser, including the closing tags. If you try the example, you may need to use your browser's source viewing function to see the difference (or alter the example to print something else after the backticks).

9.3.1 Other Perl interface tools

`exec` and its relatives are fine for simple command-line programs, but what if the interface is more complicated?

Don Libes' Expect has been very popular with system administrators for years. It enables a script to run a program that has a scrolling prompt or curses-based interface (the curses side is always more challenging), by providing a set of expected outputs (thus the name) and programmed responses.

Expect uses Tcl for scripting the interactions with target programs. Perl programmers long admired Expect's utility, but of course wanted to stay in their own language. There have been various Perl-based implementations of Expect, but the most current and easy to use variant is Expect.pm, available from your CPAN repository.

A typical Expect (or Expect.pm) script works like this: the script starts a command (by forking a child process as usual) and waits for it to produce a given string. When the script spots the string it sends its first input to the command, and waits for another output. Both utilities have tools for matching outputs based on regular expressions or waiting for one of a series of patterns to match and branching through logic based on the response.

As an example, let's consider GNU Privacy Guard, (gpg). This encryption suite manages public and private keys and uses them to encode or decode files, mail messages, or what have you. It is a free implementation that started as an emulation of Pretty Good Privacy (pgp) and has since expanded its scope.

To generate a new public and secret key pair, run gpg with its `--gen-key` option. gpg won't ordinarily do this from the command line, however. To create key pairs from a script, we need to use another tool, preferably the Crypt::GPG module, available from CPAN, which has a function for creating key pairs.

Here is an example script, `genkey.pl`, that runs gpg to create keys (the example is contrived to show Expect.pm):

```perl
#!/usr/local/bin/perl -w

use strict;
use Expect;

my $user = 'theo';
my $password = 'notmypassword';
my $realname = 'Theo Petersen';
my $email = 'theopetersen@yahoo.com';
my $comment = 'Apache Wrangler';
my $passphrase = 'this is not very secure';

my $exp;
$exp = Expect->spawn('telnet localhost') or die "Couldn't telnet";
$exp->expect(30,'login:') or die "Didn't get login prompt";
print $exp "$user\n";
$exp->expect(30,'Password') or die "Didn't get password prompt";
print $exp "$password\n";
$exp->expect(30,'$ ') or die "Didn't get shell prompt";
print $exp "gpg --gen-key\n";
$exp->expect(30,'selection?') or die "Didn't get selection";
print $exp "\n";
$exp->expect(30,'want?') or die "Didn't get keysize";
print $exp "\n";
$exp->expect(30,'for?') or die "Didn't get expiration";
print $exp "\n";
$exp->expect(30,'?') or die "Didn't get confirmation";
print $exp "y\n";
$exp->expect(30,'name:') or die "Didn't get name prompt";
print $exp "$realname\n";
$exp->expect(30,'address:') or die "Didn't get address prompt";
print $exp "$email\n";
$exp->expect(30,'Comment:') or die "Didn't get comment prompt";
print $exp "$comment\n";
$exp->expect(30,'?') or die "Didn't get confirmation";
print $exp "O\n";
$exp->expect(30,'passphrase:') or die "Didn't get passphrase prompt";
print $exp "$passphrase\n";
$exp->expect(30,'passphrase:') or die "Didn't get passphrase prompt";
print $exp "$passphrase\n";
$exp->expect(360,'created and signed') or die "Didn't generate keys";
exit(0);
```

This script has all of its inputs hard-coded and doesn't show any Expect logic other than matching one given response, but it shows a few good points. It connects to the target machine via telnet, which requires passing a valid username and password through the script, thus ensuring that the user should be allowed to override the keys. After getting a prompt back from the shell, it runs gpg, taking the defaults for all key generation options, and then passes the hard-coded inputs in for the user information. After verifying that gpg sent back the expected success message, it exits normally.

The Expect object is created via the `spawn` method, as shown here:

```
$exp = Expect->spawn('telnet localhost') or die "Couldn't telnet";
```

Expect either returns an object handle or a false result, in which case the script dies with the given message. The spawned command runs in its own process. We tell Expect to wait for it to produce output via the `expect` method:

```
$exp->expect(30,'login:') or die "Didn't get login prompt";
```

The Expect object can be used as a file handle for printing, and this is, in fact, how user input is sent to the spawned command, as shown:

```
print $exp "$user\n";
```

The script moves along through pairs of these statements, waiting for an expected output and responding with the next input.

To make this script into a web front-end for gpg, we would need to turn the hard-coded values into CGI inputs. We'd also need to take into account the behavior of gpg the first time a user runs it, which is to create required subdirectories and then exit with a warning. Of course it should be run via an SSL session to protect the sensitive information.

Net::Telnet and Net::FTP

Most Expect example programs involve using rsh, ssh, telnet, or an FTP client to connect to another machine and then do the command of interest. Perl has modules that make those tasks easier without resorting to Expect.pm. Net::Telnet handles the login exchange as a simple function, and includes a `waitfor` method that has most of the Expect functionality. Net::FTP implements a standard FTP client and has methods for all of the usual commands. And for many common tasks, a quick search on CPAN may turn up a module that does what you want already.

9.3.2   Passwords

If your goal is to have a server with user facilities but no shell access (or none required, at least), you'll have to find some way to deal with basic user management issues. The most common of these is password maintenance.

On Unix systems, a user can change his own password, and the superuser can change it for any account. That's as it should be for desktop applications which run with the user's ID and permissions, but makes a web application more challenging, as was the case with email products mentioned in the Email section. The obvious solution is to have a web application front-end another application that runs as `root` via a set uid mechanism.

BRINK is a ready-made password application built to use `suidperl` as NeoMail did. It is named for its author (Andrew Brink), but also claims that its name stands for Bad Risky Insanely Noodleriffic Kludge, which somewhat exaggerates the risk factors associated with `suidperl` scripts. It is available at http://www.brink.cx/.

BRINK can work with regular or shadow password file systems, even though the code implies that it works only with a shadow file. Edit the script to change `/etc/shadow` to `/etc/passwd` if you don't use a shadow file. BRINK edits the file directly, which must have been pretty exciting during development. It does make a backup copy before changing things in case the script bombs.

The installation instructions that come with BRINK are easy to follow. There are no provisions for customizing the script other than editing it directly, but there's not that much code and it is easy to read as well. If it fits your needs and you already have `suidperl` in place you can have BRINK in operation quickly.

If you need more than simple password file maintenance, look into WebPass, available at links you can find via Freshmeat. At this writing it is at an early stage, but it looks promising. It can handle POP3 and IMAP user authentication among other features, and uses `pw` or `usermod` to make changes instead of editing important files directly.

For sites that use LDAP-based services, another Freshmeat search will lead to `changepass.cgi`, an application which uses the Net::LDAP module to maintain user information. It is also at an early stage, but is in active development with an informative site (http://www.cloudmaster.com/~sauer/projects/fom-files/cache/90.html).

9.3.3   File management

If your intranet server is also a file server, chances are you already have NFS, SMB, or other distributed file services in place for their use. Adding a web interface to such gives your users another way to view their files, with direct browsing of HTML and graphics.

It's possible also that the server is available only through the Web and FTP or ssh, in which case a web front end for basic file management is needed. If the server is only for web use, then a content management system may be more appropriate than a general file manager. See chapter 11 for suggestions on WebDAV and other systems for managing web site files and directories.

Simple file managers are not hard to write, and a number of them are available on the Web. The PHP community offers a few that look promising, while most of the Perl entries are either too new or suspiciously inactive. One explanation for the lack of more robust file managers might be that writing one is a first step toward building a complete content management system, or going on to a system management suite, or both.

One of the Perl offerings is WebRFM, an offshoot of WebRSH. It doesn't seem to be actively developed, but the version available via Freshmeat seems to work fine for an internal site. It requires a set `uid` mechanism to run with target users' permissions, as you would expect. Once configured, WebRFM offers a reasonable interface for basic file tasks. It can also handle publishing requests from HTML editors that send files directly to the target server.

Another approach to file management is to use a web-based FTP client; after all, FTP allows files to be renamed and deleted as well as uploaded or downloaded. Web-FTP is available at its home page (http://www.web-ftp.org/). It offers a reasonable interface and can also be used as a gateway client to FTP sites on the other side of a firewall. In general, however, it still looks like FTP.

While WebRFM does a reasonable job, chances are you'll want more than just file management for your server. Look into the content management applications in chapter 11 for better user tools. In the next section I'll discuss some system management tools that also offer file handling.

9.4 SYSTEM ADMINISTRATION

Perl has long been a favorite tool of system administrators, and earned its nickname of "Swiss Army chainsaw" for its integration into (or outright replacement of) various utilities. Given its similar popularity with web developers (and the fact that many web programmers are their own system administrators or vice-versa) it's not surprising to see system administration tools migrating to the Web via Perl or other means.

Many administrative information tools have web interfaces built in—routers, network monitors, and so-on built in. SAMBA has a web-based configuration manager, and there are a number of such tools for managing Apache and other web servers as well as mail and news services.

If your particular need doesn't already have a web interface, take a look on CPAN to see if there is a Perl module that will make it easy to write your own. When I wanted a network status script, I found Net::DNS and Net::Ping modules waiting, and tossed one together quickly from the examples in their documentation:

```perl
#!/usr/bin/perl -w

use Net::DNS;
use Net::Ping;

my $res = new Net::DNS::Resolver;
my $check = Net::Ping->new('icmp');

for (my $i = 1; $i < 255; $i++) {
    my $address = "192.168.1.$i";
    if (my $query = $res->query($address)) {
        my ($ptr) = $query->answer;
        my $name = $ptr->ptrdname;
        if ($check->ping($address)) {
            print "$name ($address) is alive\n";
        }
        else {
            print "No answer from $name ($address)\n";
        }
    }
}
```

This script spins through the addresses I use on my internal LAN and pings each one that resolves to a real host. While it doesn't do anything that can't be accomplished with a ping to a broadcast address, the output is easy to read (especially by, say, someone trying to help a remote administrator over the phone).

Note that if we wanted to add a web interface to this script, we need to do a little more than just output the appropriate headers. Like most administrative tools, this needs to be run as `root`, so `suidperl` is required.

9.4.1   WebMIN

Speaking of Swiss Army cutlery, there is already a package of interfaces that has many common problems solved. WebMIN started out as an openly developed product intended to go commercial one day, but along the way the development company was acquired by Caldera. Now it is offered under a BSD-like license at http://www.webmin.com/webmin/.

WebMIN runs as its own server, listening to a designated port (usually 10000). When a browser connects it presents an authentication screen, requiring each permitted account to logon. After entering a correct username and password the browser receives a menu screen showing the user's configured modules.

Most anything that can have a web front end could be a WebMIN module. The server ships with dozens of standard modules that cover everything from Apache configuration to MySQL, PostgreSQL, various mail and FTP servers, and WebMIN itself. The module architecture makes it comparatively easy for a developer to add capabilities to the server, and in fact WebMIN's site has pointers to many add-ons.

Each module presents a CGI-based interface and shares certain core elements, including the ID and permissions of the user. The look and feel of most modules is intentionally bland to avoid browser issues, although some (such as the file manager) employ Java for a more interactive interface.

Figures 9.3 and 9.4 show a few example screens showing how WebMIN can make the tasks shown in this book easier:

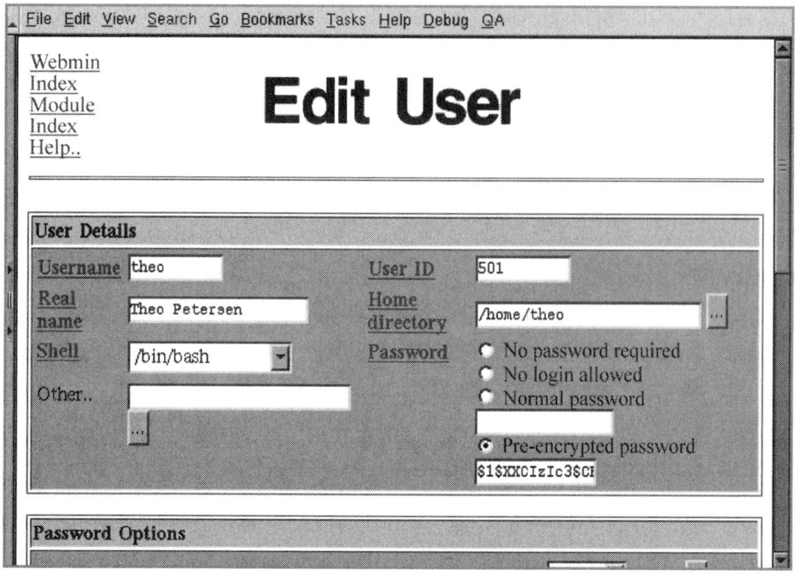

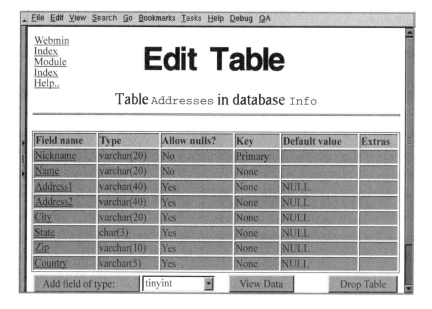

Figure 9.3   WebMIN's user administration

Figure 9.4   MySQL administration

One interesting feature of the product is that different users can be configured with access to different modules, and since the underlying processes run with the user's ID and permissions, the result is reasonably secure. This opens the possibility of using

WebMIN's file manager for general user access. The module uses Java to create a typical GUI file manager in a browser. The file manager is shown in figure 9.5.

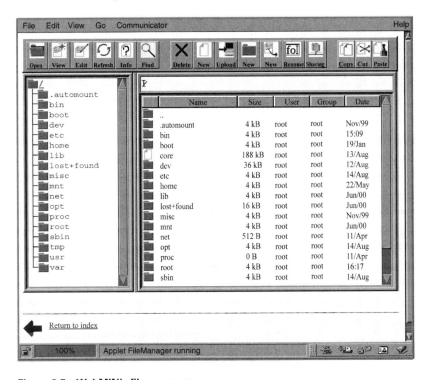

Figure 9.5   WebMIN's file manager

For light duty, this interface will serve your users fine. I find it too slow and clumsy to use more than that (but then, I hate graphical file managers).

A few buyer's guide points for WebMIN: it is actively developed and is supported by mailing lists with archives on their site. The site also includes documentation from the developers and a new manual created and maintained by Caldera.

9.5   BUILD YOUR OWN PORTAL

You have your office applications, documentation, and other services running on an internal network. Chances are this has involved multiple servers, either because all the necessary applications didn't run comfortably on one machine or the required services were spread over different systems. Even if you built it all on one box to start with, you'll probably spread to additional machines as you add applications or users, or try new things on test systems.

This being the Web, all these things can be joined naturally via links—create a main page on your intranet web server with links to the applications and pages on their various systems. As users become familiar with the applications, however, they will tend to bypass your link page and go directly to the applications and services they use, either through bookmarks or through links of their own. This is the natural tendency of the web-savvy, much to the annoyance of portal developers everywhere.

That wouldn't be an issue if things on the Web (intranet or Internet) stayed put, but over time you may need to relocate applications and pages, or servers may come and go. This will break user bookmarks and links, leading to frustration all around, especially for the person who has correctly maintained the unused portal page.

Fortunately, the tools to solve this problem are readily at hand. Apache's alias and rewrite modules give web administrators plenty of ways to redirect traffic.

9.5.1   Maintaining links

Suppose you have a documentation server as described at the beginning of the chapter. After adding enough documents you rearrange things into a logical structure, but then you get user complaints about broken bookmarks.

One solution is to maintain both structures through soft links in the file system. You can keep the actual documents in their new directories but let Apache find them in old locations too, on request. By displaying only the new structure on your index page you enforce the new arrangement. However, this scheme doesn't work well for generated indexes, which will show all the entries.

Another way of managing this kind of change is through the `Alias` directive, which allows us to tell Apache how to map URLs onto the file system. `Alias` takes two arguments: a URL fragment and its corresponding directory (which doesn't have to be under the document root—very convenient for managing documents across file systems). `Alias` directives are read by mod_alias, which is built into Apache by default.

Suppose that we had a directory of product documentation, and each product has its own subdirectory. After a time the directory becomes cluttered and we decide to divide products into categories. In the old scheme, there were directories for Emacs and vi like so:

```
/usr/local/apache/htdocs/products/emacs
/usr/local/apache/htdocs/products/vi
```

In the new scheme we want those files to reside in a subdirectory for editors, but we don't want to break bookmarks. The new directories will be:

```
/usr/local/apache/htdocs/products/editors/emacs
/usr/local/apache/htdocs/products/editors/vi
```

These `Alias` directives will map the old URLs onto the new locations:

```
Alias /products/emacs /usr/local/apache/htdocs/products/editors/emacs/
Alias /products/vi    /usr/local/apache/htdocs/products/editors/vi/
```

Notice that the first argument of the `Alias` directive matches a URL path, while the second matches a full directory specification. The directory is not relative to the document root, which is why we can use `Alias` to map in directories outside of Apache's normal view.

The related `AliasMatch` uses a regular expression to match a URL and a substitution to map it to a new location, which allows us to change directory or file names in simple ways. For example, suppose we have converted all the GIF files on our site to PNG. Rather than going back through all the documents and changing all their image tags, we can use `AliasMatch` to make the switch:

```
AliasMatch ^(.*)\.gif$ /usr/local/apache/htdocs/$1.png
```

`AliasMatch` is also convenient when we've moved some files from a directory but not others, as long as we can use a regular expression to spot the moved files. For example, suppose we've moved all the .shtml files in the document root to a new `SSI` subdirectory. This `AliasMatch` takes care of any requests for the old locations:

```
AliasMatch ^/(.*)\.shtml$ /usr/local/apache/htdocs/ssi/$1.shtml
```

The `Alias` family works very quickly, so even a large set of directives won't slow Apache noticeably. They work only for straightforward changes in file arrangements, however. If we move files to another server, we need to use `Redirect` to maintain the links.

`Redirect` is also part of mod_alias, but its operation is quite different. The second argument to the directive is a URL instead of a file path. When an incoming request matches a `Redirect`, Apache sends the browser a redirect status code and the new URL. The browser will then try the new URL (which could get another redirection, but we hope not).

Suppose we've accumulated so much documentation on Perl modules that we need a whole server just for that. On our old documentation site, /perl-modules contained the files, so we want to redirect any requests for that path to the new server, called perldoc; it has all the files in its `modules` directory. Here's a `Redirect` that accomplishes that:

```
Redirect /perl-modules http://perldoc/modules
```

Any incoming URL that begins with /perl-modules will be sent to the new server.

Similarly, `RedirectMatch` uses a regular expression and substitution to transform the URL on the fly.

Redirection is obviously slower than aliasing. The browser sends a request to one server, gets a message back, then sends a changed URL to a different server which has the requested document. On an internal network that shouldn't be too slow, but the processing delay can still be noticeable. While this may be the effect you want if you are trying to get users to change their bookmarks, you can help speed the process by telling their browsers whether or not the change is permanent.

By default, `Redirect` directives send browsers a *temporary* redirection, indicating that the browser should check the original URL again if the user requests it. By changing the status to *permanent*, a clever browser can avoid delays when requesting the same URL later on. It caches the redirection and uses the new location directly. The status argument is optional and comes before the URL path, so a permanent version of our above server switch would be:

```
Redirect permanent /perl-modules http://perldoc/modules
```

If your site changes in ways that are beyond the scope of simple aliases and redirection, you can still maintain links and bookmarks through the much richer capabilities of Apache's rewrite engine. mod_rewrite provides a powerful toolkit for transforming URLs, but it has a certain reputation for incomprehensible complexity which is only somewhat deserved. My own experience in getting things to work with mod_rewrite is similar to the way in which I learned Perl, by finding an example that was similar to what I wanted and poking at it until it fit.

Apache ships with two sets of documentation for mod_rewrite: the modules page has an explanation of how the engine works, and the URL Rewriting Guide has a number of examples and fixes for common problems.

And of course, we can use mod_perl to intercept requests and translate links as well. The next section shows mod_rewrite, and the section after that has equivalent mod_perl examples.

9.5.2 UserDir, Redirect, and mod_rewrite for user maintenance

In chapter 2 we briefly discussed ways of arranging user directories, from simple uses of the UserDir directive to suggestions of larger schemes. A typical UserDir scheme is:

```
UserDir public_html
<Directory /home/*/public_html>
    AllowOverride All
    Options Indexes SymLinksIfOwnerMatch
</Directory>
```

This UserDir directive tells Apache to map URLs beginning with a tilde (~) onto the home directory of the user, followed by public_html; that is, http://www.example.site/~theo maps to /home/theo/public_html. (You can have any number of other arrangements, as mentioned in chapter 2 and in the UserDir documentation.) The Directory block afterward sets open permissions for those user directories. In particular, AllowOverride All lets users set any directives they want in local .htaccess files, even if they override the options given here. The options in this block will still serve as defaults, however.

Suppose that after setting up the internal portal, users begin migrating private pages and applications to other machines—a development system or their own workstations. If all users move to one machine, it is easy to map them using UserDir again. Suppose we've moved all the users from www.example.site to users.example.site:

```
UserDir http://users.example.site/*/public_html
```

If `UserDir`'s argument is a URL instead of a directory, Apache sends a redirect to the browser to the new site. This use of `UserDir` is equivalent to:

```
RedirectMatch ^/~(.*)$ http://users.example.site/~$1
```

If you are happier working with regular expressions directly, this may suit you better.

If users are migrating individually, you can handle them with individual redirects. Suppose Fred has moved his pages to his own workstation, fred.example.site. This redirect will take care of things:

```
Redirect /~fred http://fred.example.site/
```

If you have a large number of users, maintaining the redirect lists could get onerous. mod_rewrite, however, has a solution: given a URL that matches an expression it will look for a user in a database and redirect the request, or send it to a default server if the user wasn't found. `RewriteMap` supports text file databases, DBM files, and even external programs that do the lookups elsewhere.

For example, suppose some of our web developers have moved their pages but most of the users are still on users.example.site. Set up a list of the exceptions in a file that Apache can read; my example uses `/usr/local/apache/webbies.map`:

```
bob      bobsbox.example.site
carole   carole.example.site
ted      frodo.example.site
```

Now tell Apache to check user requests against that database using `RewriteMap`:

```
<IfModule mod_rewrite.c>
    RewriteEngine on
    RewriteLog /usr/local/apache/logs/rewrite
    RewriteLogLevel 0
    RewriteMap webbies txt:/usr/local/apache/webbies.map
    RewriteRule ^/~([^/]+)/?(.*)$ http://${webbies:$1|users.example.site}/
~$1/$2
</IfModule>
```

These directives first configure mod_rewrite by turning it on and telling it where to log rewrite debugging information. By setting `RewriteLogLevel` to 0 we aren't actually writing any debugging output, but if you do much work with mod_rewrite you'll want its help eventually.

The `RewriteMap` directive tells mod_rewrite about the text database, giving it a map name and the path to the file. The map name can then be used in the following `RewriteRule` directive (or anywhere else in the file, for that matter).

Let's take a closer look at the regular expression used here. It matches username URLs of the familiar form ~user/path (or just ~user); the parts of the expression in parentheses turn into variables $1 and $2. Thus a request for http://www.example.site/~bob/page.html matches with $1 set to bob and $2 set to page.html. If no path is given after the username, then $2 is empty.

The substitution portion of the rule makes reference to ${webbies :$1|users.example.site}. This uses the map database in much the same way as a Perl hash, where webbies identifies the map and $1 is the key to look for in the table. If found, the corresponding value is substituted; if not, the default value users.example.site will be used. Thus the example above will be translated to http://bobsbox.example.site/~bob/page.html, while a request for http://www.example.site/~alice will still go to http://users.example.site/~alice as desired.

Some Perl developers complain about the "voodoo" nature of mod_rewrite; having learned one language with a bad rep, why learn another? Never fear, with mod_perl we can take on all URL translation and redirection tasks using familiar Perl tools.

9.5.3 mod_perl for translation and redirection

Previous mod_perl examples have been application-oriented, in that the Perl code was taking the place of an HTML page or a script (or both). As I've mentioned previously, however, mod_perl can get involved in any step of Apache's process for translating a request to response and content. This is one of the best reasons for learning mod_perl, as you gain advantages far beyond speedy CGI applications.

As an example, let's toss out mod_rewrite and implement the user translation shown earlier as a Perl module. It will run as a handler (as all our previous mod_perl examples have) invoked when Apache receives a request for a user directory, and will look up the user in a simple database. The code is in FindUser.pm:

```perl
package Examples::FindUser;

use strict;
use Apache::Constants qw(:response);

my %ownHosts = (
                bob => 'bobsbox.example.site',
                carole => 'carole.example.site',
                ted => 'frodo.example.site',
              );

sub handler {
    my $r = shift;
    my $uri = $r->uri;

    # Check for ~user (though a LocationMatch should handle that).
    if ($uri =~ m(~([^/]+)/?(.*))) {
        if (my $host = $ownHosts{$1}) {
            # This user has his own server.
            $uri = "http://$host/~$1/$2";
        }
        else {
            # Normal user.  Redirect to users.example.site.
            $uri = "http://users.example.site/~$1/$2";
        }

        # Send the redirect to the browser.
        $r->header_out(Location => $uri);
```

```
        return REDIRECT;
    }
    return OK;
}

1;
```

We'd hope that such a simple task can be performed in a short bit of perl code, and it is. Most are declarations, including the database of users from the previous section. While for simplicity's sake this code has the database in a regular hash, in practice it could be stored in a hash file, a relational database, or anything else which makes sense.[4]

Some new things to note in this code: it imports a larger set of constants from Apache::Constant than other examples. The response set includes the REDIRECT status, which we use to tell the browser to look elsewhere. After loading the constants it has the typical opening for a handler, and verifies that the request it is handling is in fact for a user directory. The regular expression match which checks that also puts the user name in $1 and the rest of the request in $2.

The user name is checked in our database of users who have their own hosts. If found, the URL is rebuilt with the new host in place, and if not, the default users.example.site is used as we had in the previous section.

When sending a redirection to a browser, Apache has to send both the redirection status and the new location for the requested document. The code handles this by setting the Location header to the new URL, then returning REDIRECT, the status value that Apache will pass along to the requester.

As always, we need to tell Apache to load this code and when to invoke it. Add the following to mod_perl.conf (or where ever you keep your mod_perl directives):

```
PerlModule Examples::FindUser
<LocationMatch "^/~">
    SetHandler perl-script
    PerlHandler Examples::FindUser
</LocationMatch>
```

This example uses LocationMatch instead of the usual Location, because we want to match a regular expression instead of a partial URL path. As with previous examples, SetHandler tells Apache to pass the requests through mod_perl, and PerlHandler in turn tells mod_perl which module to use. It's worth mentioning that we've told Apache that we're handling all user directory requests. This handler redirects all such requests to other sites, but if we also have to serve local users on this machine, we'd have to take a different approach.

---

[4] The code to read the map file used in the previous section and load it into a hash is left as an exercise for the reader. It should be no longer than a handful of lines and should make use of map and split. For extra credit, add a check to reload the hash when the modification time of the map file changes.

If you like the do-it-yourself approach to translating URLs, why not replace all of the redirections and aliases used in the prior section with Perl code? mod_perl allows this as promised, but via a different mechanism than we've seen previously.

In this case, we don't want to take over serving up HTML entirely just so that we can fix URLs. Instead we want our code to intervene in the mapping process while allowing Apache to do the bulk of the work. To that end, we'll register a *translation handler*.

When Apache is translating URLs and mapping them to files, it calls one or more translation handlers. Each handler receives the request in its current state and can modify the URI, set the file name, send back a redirection, or take other actions. When a translation handler makes a final decision about what file corresponds to the requested URL it returns OK to tell Apache that this phase of the request is over.

By registering our own translation handler, we can get first crack at incoming requests, and apply our own rules to them. Here is a sample handler (from `Fixup-URL.pm`) that performs all the manipulations discussed in the first part of this section:

```
package Examples::FixupURL;

use strict;
use Apache::Constants qw(:response);

sub handler {
    my $r = shift;
    my $uri = $r->uri;
    my $status = OK;
    my $file;

    # Look for products that have migrated.  Equivalent to:
    #Alias /products/emacs docroot/products/editors/emacs/
    #Alias /products/vi    docroot/products/editors/vi/
    if ($uri =~ m{^/products/(emacs|vi)}) {
        # remap the filename to the new directories.
        $uri =~ s{/products/}{/products/editors/};
        $r->internal_redirect($uri);
    }
    elsif ($uri =~ m{\.gif$}) {
        # Translate gif file requests to PNGs.  Equivalent to:
        # AliasMatch ^(.*)\.gif$ docroot/$1.png
        $uri =~ s/\.gif$/.png/;
        $file = $r->document_root . $uri;
    }
    elsif ($uri =~ m{/([^/]+)\.shtml$} ) {
        # Moved .shtml files to docroot/ssi.  Equivalent to:
        # AliasMatch ^/(.*)\.shtml$ docroot/ssi/$1.shtml
        $file = "/usr/local/htdocs/ssi/$1.shtml";
    }
    elsif ($uri =~ m{^/perl-modules(.*)}) {
        # Send any requests for /perl-modules to a new server:
        # Redirect /perl-modules http://perldoc/modules
        $uri = "http://perldoc/modules/$1";
        $r->header_out(Location => $uri);
```

```
            $status = REDIRECT;
    }
    else {
        # Pass the buck to another handler.
        $status = DECLINED;
    }
    $r->filename($file) if $file;
    return $status;
}

1;
```

The code replaces each `Alias`, `AliasMatch`, or `Redirect` directive with appropriate chunks of Perl. The first one handles the migration of the `/product/emacs` and `/product/vi` directories to `/product/editors`:

```
if ($uri =~ m{^/products/(emacs|vi)}) {
    # remap the filename to the new directories.
    $uri =~ s{/products/}{/products/editors/};
    $r->internal_redirect($uri);
}
```

It alters the URI to insert the new directory, then calls `$r->internal_redirect` to tell Apache to start the process over again. The altered request will go through the translation process, even calling this handler again. That seems inefficient, but it keeps things simple. On the next pass other translations can occur, such as the GIF to PNG step shown next. We could structure the code to take care of that, of course, but for a complex handler that may add unnecessary difficulty.

The next steps perform straightforward fixes:

```
elsif ($uri =~ m{\.gif$}) {
    # Translate gif file requests to PNGs.  Equivalent to:
    # AliasMatch ^(.*)\.gif$ docroot/$1.png
    $uri =~ s/\.gif$/.png/;
    $file = $r->document_root . $uri;
}
elsif ($uri =~ m{/([^/]+)\.shtml$} ) {
    # Moved .shtml files to docroot/ssi.  Equivalent to:
    # AliasMatch ^/(.*)\.shtml$ docroot/ssi/$1.shtml
    $file = "/usr/local/htdocs/ssi/$1.shtml";
}
```

In the first case, we want just to map one file type to another. A simple substitution of GIF to PNG takes care of that, then the code appends the fixed URI to the document root to form the file name. In the second case, we've moved all files ending in .shtml to another directory, so the code fixes the file name directly.

Skipping over the other cases for a moment, the section in the earlier example will drop down to this code:

```
$r->filename($file) if $file;
return $status;
```

Since we set `$file` in both of these sections, the code will call `$r->filename` to set the file name in the request. Returning `OK` for the status tells Apache that translation is finished. (But look ahead a few sections to see the limitations of this approach.)

Handling `Redirect` directives in Perl code is similarly straightforward:

```
elsif ($uri =~ m{^/perl-modules(.*)}) {
    # Send any requests for /perl-modules to a new server:
    # Redirect /perl-modules http://perldoc/modules
    $uri = "http://perldoc/modules/$1";
    $r->header_out(Location => $uri);
    $status = REDIRECT;
}
```

In this case we're sending requests for /perl-modules to another server. We set the new URL in the `Location` header and return the `REDIRECT` status so that Apache will send the new location back to the browser.

I'll explain the default case (that sets the `DECLINED` status) in a moment. To install our handler we need to add the configuration to `mod_perl.conf` (or where you keep your mod_perl directives):

```
PerlModule Examples::FixupURL
PerlTransHandler Examples::FixupURL
```

Note the use of `PerlTransHandler` instead of `PerlHandler` in this case.

Try out the example and you should see Perl handling the URL translations quite handily. Now what is that `DECLINED` status about?

As an experiment, change the `else` case in the handler like so:

```
else {
    # Map the file.
    $file = $r->document_root . $uri;
}
```

That's the normal mapping for Apache, appending the URL path to the document root to form a file name, so it seems perfectly reasonable. The handler will set the resulting file name and return `OK`, telling Apache that translation is done. Restart Apache and it will serve up normal files and graphics with no trouble.

If you test the server more heavily, though, you might get a surprise—no `Alias` or `ScriptAlias` directives in `httpd.conf` work! That includes CGI scripts (requiring `ScriptAlias` to tell Apache how to handle cgi-bin), icons, and anything else involving mod_alias.

The reason is that the changed handler returns the `OK` status to Apache, telling it that the translation phase is over. That means Apache won't call any other translation handlers. In particular, it won't call the code in mod_alias that handles other important directives.

We could work around this by adding code to handle everything mod_alias does, fixing up CGI requests and all. It's not terribly difficult, following the examples for each case. However there isn't a great need for that when instead we can just play by the rules of chained handlers.

The `PerlTransHandler` directive installs our code at the top of the list of handlers Apache will call for this phase, keeping its list of other handlers—most importantly the handler used by mod_alias. To call the next handler in the chain, our code should return `DECLINED` instead of `OK`. While that sounds odd, it tells Apache that the phase is not over and the file name hasn't been set. Restore the `else` clause as given in the example and restart the server, and the `DECLINED` status will allow mod_alias to do its job.

A handler can also take another approach: instead of calling `$r->filename` to set the file, the code can change the URI via `$r->uri`. The next handler in the chain is going to look at the URI (just as our code does) and apply its rules to map the request to a file, and any current value in the file name will likely be ignored. Thus we could apply our translations like so:

```
elsif ($uri =~ m{\.gif$}) {
    # Translate gif file requests to PNGs.  Equivalent to:
    # AliasMatch ^(.*)\.gif$ docroot/$1.png
    $uri =~ s/\.gif$/.png/;
    $r->uri($uri);
}
```

In this case we can apply translations via Perl code and mod_alias directives to the same URL. By restricting itself to URI manipulations and returning the right status, the code can do its job while letting mod_alias to the rest of the work.

9.6   JOINING MULTIPLE INTRANETS

At the beginning of this chapter, I listed a number of advantages that intranet applications have, chiefly the speed and security of a local network. If you've built a successful intranet site, you may find others asking for admission to it from outside—users who telecommute and need access to mail and calendar info, or perhaps another office that hosts its own network and wants to share applications.

With the advent of broadband access for both home and business users, it is possible to provide external users with speed comparable to that which they enjoy at the office. We wouldn't want to do this without giving them equal security, however.

One solution is to build all web applications with the security tools discussed in chapter 6. This adds complexity and development time, however, and voids the whole advantage of being inside a secured network. We might also have to discard an otherwise good product if it doesn't work with secure channels.

The better choice is to apply security to the link between the internal and external networks. In network industry buzzwords, we want a virtual private network (VPN).

9.6.1   VPNs

With the rise of networked computers, many large corporations built private networks to link their various offices into an electronic community.[5] These wide area networks (WANs) consisted of leased phone lines or more exotic connections and were the products of considerable investments. When such networks joined the Internet, they did so first through gateway systems that converted internal mail and other messages into their TCP/IP-based counterparts. Messaging within the enterprise stayed within the private network.

As more users began to take advantage of the Internet, corporate gateway systems became overloaded, and each LAN got its own connection. Soon, WAN managers started to wonder if the company couldn't do without the private network and instead use the Internet for business transactions. (These days you hardly hear people talk about WANs any more. Perhaps all those network managers got jobs in the rapidly growing broadband and firewall industries.)

At the same time, new businesses were starting up without the assumption of having private networks at all. What both groups wanted was to use the Internet for the same secure, internal traffic they would have from building their own private community. That's where the V in VPN comes from: using public Internet connections to build a virtual private network.

The principle behind a VPN is simple: intercept LAN packets that are headed out to a VPN member network, and use hardware or software to encrypt them. At the receiving member site, decrypt the packets and deliver them as if nothing had happened in between. Commercial VPN hardware usually takes the place of (or adds to) network routers in the member sites.

By encrypting traffic between member sites, VPNs provide the security of a private network, but without the cost of leased lines, et cetera. Administration is simplified since the managers of the member sites can assume that internal traffic stays private, and can focus on screening the outside world from internal news.

With the advent of telecommuting, VPNs are even more important, since more users want to connect their home and office systems. This leaves many companies looking for cheap ways to implement secure private connections. And of course I wouldn't be leading the discussion this way if there weren't an Open Source solution. Actually there are a few choices here—IP Sec and CIPE both offer ways of sending secure IP traffic through the Internet, and both have Open Source implementations. If you are integrating with a Microsoft PPTP network you can find Linux implementations of that protocol as well. The solution I discuss in the next sections has the advantage of using simple and well-established tools available on most OSs.

---

[5] When I worked for Digital Equipment Corporation in the 1980s, the company's "e-net" network of news and mail services was considered a major job benefit for those who enjoyed virtual community. DEC's gateway to Usenet gave me my first exposure to the Internet at large.

9.6.2 PPP

As TCP/IP networking became dominant, users with dial-in connections became familiar with tools for connecting networks over regular phone lines. Most probably encountered SLIP (Serial Line IP) first for connecting individual machines to a host network, but PPP (Point-to-Point Protocol) rapidly came to be the tool of choice for its routing capabilities and other reasons. To connect two networks via a phone line all we need is a computer with a modem and PPP on each side. One machine initiates a call to the other, and then each tells its PPP service to use the resulting serial connection. The PPP services then shake hands with each other and route appropriately-addressed network traffic through the phone line to the other side.

An important feature of modern implementations of PPP is ARP proxying. ARP on Unix systems is the Address Resolution Protocol, which is used to map the addresses used by Ethernet networking onto TCP/IP addresses. PPP uses ARP proxying to make the partners in the serial connections appear to be local machines on each others' networks, which makes it possible to route traffic through them.

After establishing PPP connections, the systems on either side publish routes to their network that tell how to route traffic through the bridge. TCP/IP routing does the rest, without requiring any special knowledge of the PPP gateway itself.

9.6.3 SSH

SSH is already familiar to you as the tool for encrypting a shell session or performing simple file copies and remote command invocations between known hosts. SSH does more than it appears at a casual glance—for instance, it can be configured to create encrypted X-windows sessions and handle other transports as well. In this discussion it is SSH's simple capability to create an encrypted channel that is of interest.

The first implementation I encountered of this style of VPN used SSH from the local machine to invoke PPP on the remote target and send PPP traffic back through the SSH encrypted channel. The more current implementation is different, however, in that SSH is used in conjunction with pty-redir to create an encrypted serial device; it then tells PPP to use that device to connect to the remote side. The mechanism is quite elegant and is described in detail for Linux systems in the VPN_HOWTO written by Matthew D. Wilson (and available on any number of Linux documentation sites as well). The same tools can be used on other operating systems, although you'll have to work out far more of the details yourself.

9.6.4 Put it all together, it spells...

Once you have the pieces in place (as described by Wilson's document), you create the VPN by first creating the encrypted channel device using SSH and pty-redir. This takes place over the network connection you have between the local and remote networks, which may in fact be a serial line running another layer of PPP. After both sides have established the channel and the device is ready, invoke PPP on the local machine with the device, and give it the IP addresses to use on either side of the bridge.

Assuming PPP connected to the remote machine, you now have an encrypted channel sending TCP/IP traffic between the two systems. Publish routes to each network telling it to route traffic through the connected machines, and your VPN is complete.

While this implementation is far from trivial, it makes use of free software and hardware components you are likely to have already. The two ends of the VPN bridge can be older Intel Pentium machines that wouldn't make it as modern desktop systems (the HOWTO author recommends Pentium 90s), and can also take on firewall and DNS tasks in the bargain, making a very economical package.

CHAPTER   10

The web storefront

The big story of the Internet boom is of course e-commerce, e-business, and the rise and fall of the dot-coms. The eager spending of venture capitalists led to lavish site-opening parties and Superbowl ads, then to panic as profits failed to materialize. While I've been writing this, a second wave of investment has begun and new web stores are opening.

If you are lucky enough to be starting a web business, or you are keeping an existing Internet storefront running, then you are surely looking for tools to help with your job. But before we dive in to catalogs and payments, we'll need to review the requirements for a well-run e-commerce site. This chapter will then work through an example of a partial e-commerce site, using tools we've discussed previously to build a catalog, shopping cart, and checkout system. After that we'll discuss ways to make your site more interactive, building in features from the chapter on community sites. Site-building tools and credit card processing wrap up the chapter.

10.1 E-COMMERCE REQUIREMENTS

In chapter 2 we discussed the hardware and environmental requirements for a few sample scenarios. An e-commerce site calls for high quality hardware and bandwidth if it is to have enough traffic to pay for itself. Patrons of a volunteer-run community site may put up with slow machines, but paying customers expect responsive applications and quick feedback.

This site is the least likely to be running on leftover hardware, and in fact if you are building such a site for a serious business, chances are good the hardware decisions (and probably many software choices) have already been made. Once again, that's not necessarily a problem, as the tools discussed in this book run practically anywhere one can expect to find a web site, but if someone else is making (or has made) the hardware decisions, review them as soon as you can for anything that will pose a problem.

Bandwidth is of crucial importance here also. Far too many developers are caught off guard when they encounter the load placed on their network by the number of users required to make a business site succeed. If the bandwidth is sufficient, you may find yourself in a memory crunch or running out of other resources as Apache generates processes to meet demand. Chapter 12 discusses these and related problems.

Performance is not just about starting with good hardware, and when business survival is at stake, it is even more important to make every decision with an eye toward delivering. The web server should have a machine to itself, possibly even hosting databases and order processing applications on separate hardware. Any change which involves running new processes on critical machines should be evaluated by all responsible parties.

As this implies, an e-commerce site is very likely to be a cluster of machines, also known as a web farm. Chapter 12 also discusses how to build such a configuration with Apache and other Open Source tools.

10.1.1 Security and privacy

In most other contexts, securing a site means preventing break-ins and other cracker activities. A business site must do far more. Customers expect that their financial transactions will be made over secured channels (even if they don't ask for them) and that the private data required will be kept private.

Industry news channels seem to thrive on stories of credit card databases being cracked, Social Security numbers and financial history information being exposed, and other foibles of web businesses. I certainly don't need to warn a future e-business to guard its data. In the last few years other privacy concerns have started to make almost as many headlines, as various consumer groups began to call for web businesses to publish their policies for use of customer information. Sites that keep data on their users are now expected to have a clearly displayed link to their privacy policy, and legislation is in progress in many countries that will further limit what businesses may do with databases.

When building an e-commerce site, it is of great importance to start with security in mind. Resist the temptation to begin with a development system and a plan to secure the site later. Create the minimum accounts necessary and use randomly generated passwords for them. Disable all services that won't be used when the site is opened to the public. Make sure the site has all security precautions in place before it is connected to the public network.

Security and performance both tend to slip after a site is opened. The daily and emergency needs of running the site make it easy to take shortcuts or put off needed fixes. That makes it even more crucial for security maintenance to be part of the regular administration activities for the site. Review what accounts are open and what services are available, manually and with a network-scanning tool. Keep up with security patches for your OS, web server, and other software. Evaluate performance regularly, and if something is amiss, plan and implement improvements before the problem becomes critical.

10.1.2   Stress testing

One much-touted advantage of e-commerce is how it lets businesses meet the global market and 24 hour business days. In fact, however, most business web sites still have comparatively local markets (constrained to a nation or continent), and thus have peak traffic hours. This certainly isn't just a problem for e-business; the advent of home broadband access in the United States created the Internet Rush Hour effect, when numbers of users who'd just gotten off work tried to get to their favorite music sites. Regardless of the service you provide, your site is likely to be busier some time of the day than others.

With a business site, however, peak traffic hours can reveal weaknesses in site design that aren't as critical to others. If the network bandwidth for the site handles the peak, the high number of incoming requests will also cause Apache to spawn its maximum number of servers. Some of those servers will be making simultaneous connections to your database, and if you use tools such as Apache::DBI to cache connections, all of the application servers will holding database resources.

The result can surprise developers and database administrators who haven't planned and tested for maximum load. Applications that don't handle connection failures will die mysteriously; naïve locking schemes will cause hangs and crashes. Database servers that never crashed during development may suddenly dump cores or worse, slow to a crawl without triggering restart mechanisms. Any of the above results in frustrated and bewildered customers and loss of business.

The first step to preventing these cases is to use a database that can handle the highest load expected of your site. Database vendors (Open Source or otherwise) use such information to market their products, but of course a real-world test is best. Early on in your design phase, try some kind of load test on your database of choice, even if you have only the vaguest notion of what your final designs will look like. If a database has been chosen for you, this gives you a chance to either make a case for another product or find out what problems you'll need to work around. If the choice is yours, evaluate more than one product, even if you're prejudiced. Having done a comparison, you'll have ammunition at hand should someone question your choice later.

Having chosen a product that can handle the load, you need to make a habit of testing it again as development progresses. When you have a working server and an application of some sort, put it under stress right away. This gives you another early warning of difficulties to follow. An amazing number of applications fail when loaded beyond the single developer working with a system of his own.

Tools for monitoring the database's load and resource usage are just as important as the ones you used to develop your system in the first place. When mysterious failures begin, you want both the tools for finding out what's wrong and familiarity with how to handle problems. While your stress tests are running, get up to speed with your database's analysis tools and with other monitoring and debugging aids.

Even with the best products and planning, mysteries will likely occur. This is where the support mechanism of your chosen database will become crucial to your long-term success. Can you go to someone and describe the problem? Is there a mailing list or forum for administrators where you can post your symptoms or search for similar cases? Good support is as important to your survival as good tools.

Developers of surprisingly few sites test their support during development. Before it becomes critical, become familiar with the resources available to you and try out reporting a problem or asking a question, based on some mystery of configuration or early programming. At the very least you'll learn what to expect, and you may make valuable contacts in the process.

As discussed at length in the next chapter, mission-critical systems require comprehensive and proven backup plans and recovery procedures for both hardware and software. While you should make regular backups of your applications and system files, many relational databases have special requirements for backing up data in a consistent state. Become familiar with the needs of your database early in the site's life and establish appropriate backups, then give your recovery plan a test once you have some applications working. By verifying that you can repair the system when it's broken, you'll address important business concerns and give yourself confidence and assurance when a real emergency comes.

10.2 COMPONENTS OF AN E-COMMERCE SITE

Business web sites have common elements, just as different sorts of businesses do. While you'll strive to give your site a unique appeal, you'll want to do so in a way that gives your customers a familiar sense of what they are doing.

The first e-commerce web sites were essentially online catalogs. Some allowed orders to be filled in from the browser and emailed to a service representative, but a good number directed the customers to phone in or fax their orders after making a decision. These days customers expect credit card processing as a matter of course, although web-savvy users may also use and prefer other online payment methods.

While we've made great strides in order processing, many e-commerce sites are still "brochure-ware," catalog sites with nothing interactive other than the taking of orders. Various high-profile sites have attempted to create something called an "online shopping experience," which seems mostly to involve burdening pages with so many graphics that nonbroadband users return to offline alternatives. In later sections we'll discuss better ways to make your site more than a catalog, but the core components of a site will still be there: a catalog of products, a database of customer information, a shopping cart that joins the two, and customer services applications that manage orders and shipments.

Rather than staying with abstract ideas, let's consider those components in context by building an example site: a T-shirt store called QuipShirts, which sells shirts with various quippy slogans. The (so far) mythical example site is http://www.quip-shirts.com/, and is built to handle a few dozen shirt designs with alternatives for color, style and size.

10.2.1 Catalog

An online catalog is very similar to its paper predecessor, presenting the basic products you sell, their add-ons and variations, and as much sales literature as you can reasonably expect the reader to read. Small sites that sell only a few products may build their catalogs entirely in static pages, but larger operations quickly turn to dynamic content built from a product database. Even those storefronts that use handmade pages may have a file or table of product codes and prices.

For QuipShirts, the product is shirts that have these characteristics:

- Quip, which is the text displayed on the shirt, or some sort of distinguishing title.

- Graphic, the actual layout of the shirt including text and picture(s).

- Styles, which may include T-shirt, polo, tank top, and others.

- Colors (not necessarily available in all styles).

- Sizes (again, possibly an incomplete selection for colors and styles).

- Price in U.S. dollars.

In most cases a catalog represents a full product line, including current stock and planned production. To reduce the number of tables in the example the QuipShirts catalog represents only the store's inventory.[1] The catalog pages are generated from records in the Inventory table:

---

[1] We'll assume for the moment that QuipShirts is making T-shirts in bulk and selling what they have, rather than taking orders and printing them on demand. Of course, an online shop that mastered print-to-order T-shirt making would be far more revolutionary than what we're going to show here, especially if it made a profit.

```
CREATE TABLE Inventory (
    Bin VARCHAR(10) NOT NULL,
    Quip VARCHAR(80),
    Graphic VARCHAR(20),
    Style VARCHAR(10),
    Color VARCHAR(10),
    Size VARCHAR(5),
    Quantity INTEGER,
    Price REAL,
    PRIMARY KEY (Bin)
    );
```

This inventory layout merges what might be two or three tables in a more full-featured application. The first column, Bin, tells us where to find the physical stock in the warehouse. We'll assume that bins have some kind of labeling mechanism that makes sense to the stock workers, and that the labels don't exceed ten characters. The next group of columns describes the contents of a bin: the quip, graphic, style, color, and size of the shirt. The Quip column contains either the whole slogan or a brief version that is suitable for the catalog, while the Graphic column contains the name of a JPEG file which shows the printed shirt.[2] Style, Color, and Size are all in text that will appear on the catalog as-is and make sense to a casual reader, such as "polo, green, XXL."

Now that we have the first table, we'll create web pages that will show the current inventory to customers and allow them to see more details on shirts of interest. I'll use Mason in these examples to simplify the mix of HTML and Perl code; the QuipShirts site is configured the same as the Mason report example in chapter 7. Code and sample data for the site are available on this book's web page.

Here is stockshirts.mhtml, a front page component that shows what shirts are currently in stock:

```
<& qphead.mcmp, title => 'Inventory' &>
<H2>QuipShirts Current Inventory</H2>
% if ($session{'realname'}) {
  <H3>Welcome back, <% $session{'realname'} %></H3>
% }
<TABLE>
  <TR><TH>Shirt</TH><TH>Size</TH><TH>Style</TH><TH>Color</TH></TR>
% foreach my $bin (@$bins) {
    <& shirtrow.mcmp, bin => $bin &>
% }
</TABLE>
<P>
<A HREF="cart/checkout.mhtml">View your shopping cart</A><br>
<A HREF="orders/status.mhtml">Check order status</A>
<& qpfoot.mcmp &>
```

---

[2] Storing the image in the database itself would be far cooler of course, and is left as an exercise for the reader.

```
<%init>
  my $dbh = DBI->connect('DBI:mysql:QuipShirts:localhost',
                         'web','nouser')
    or return SERVER_ERROR;
  my $sth = $dbh->prepare_cached
        ("select Bin from Inventory where Quantity > 0 ".
         "order by Quip, Style, Color, Size")
    or return SERVER_ERROR;
  my $bins = $dbh->selectcol_arrayref($sth) || [];
</%init>
```

I won't go into the header or footer components here, since they are more or less the same as the examples in chapter 7 with a few name and color changes. As usual with Mason, most of the code happens in the `<%init>` section. The component connects with the database,[3] selects all the shirts from bins with a positive quantity, then makes an array of bins sorted by the shirt title and characteristics. The error handling is very simple (return an error page if anything goes wrong) to keep the example short.

If the database interaction is puzzling you, review chapter 4 for information on the DBI module. Since my mod_perl configuration loads Apache::DBI, the component will connect to the database only if it is the first application to request a connection. Apache::DBI overrides the `connect` method to cache connections and return a free handle if one is available, speeding up things considerably. The `prepare_cached` method further saves prepared statement handles (caching them in the reused database handle), and passes the handle to `selectcol_arrayref` to receive an array holding the column values of interest—the bins with shirts.

The top part of the component has the Mason code, mixing HTML and components to build the page. Note that the session hash is used as described in chapter 7—we'll see how the value of `$session{'realname'}` gets loaded in the next section. The component creates a table, then invokes a subcomponent (`shirtrow.mcmp`) for each bin. If we accepted CGI parameters on this page we could refine the display to matching strings or other characteristics, but again this example is meant to be simple.

Here is the table row component:

```
<TR>
 <TD><A HREF="shirts/<% $bin %>"><% $quip %></A></TD>
 <TD><% $size %></TD><TD><% $style %></TD><TD><% $color %></TD>
</TR>

<%args>
 $bin
</%args>

<%init>
```

---

[3] Since QuipShirts has its own database, the components need their own database connection, rather than using the one opened by `mason_handler.pl`. The handler's database connection is still used for session data. A real site could get by with one connection if desired.

```perl
my $dbh = DBI->connect('DBI:mysql:QuipShirts:localhost',
  'web','nouser');
my $sth = $dbh->prepare_cached
("select Quip, Size, Style, Color from Inventory " .
 "where Bin = ?");
my ($quip, $size, $style, $color)
 = $dbh->selectrow_array($sth, undef, $bin);
my $maxlen = 30;
if (length($quip) > $maxlen) {
  my $at = rindex($quip, ' ', $maxlen) || $maxlen;
  $quip = substr($quip, 0, $at) . '...';
}
</%init>
```

This component is laid out in the same structure, apart from the fact that it does accept an argument: the bin whose shirt is to be displayed in the table. It retrieves the row from the database, extracts the title, size, style, and color fields, then makes a table row out of them. The title is shortened to a displayable size if necessary.

A more ambitious version of this page could contain thumbnails (Perl's Image::Magick module is terrific for this) of the shirt graphics and limit the number of lines in the table so as to display quickly in the customer's browser. Figure 10.1 shows the output, after the addition of sample data.

Clicking a shirt title takes us to the product detail page for that shirt. The row component creates a URL for the shirt based on the unique bin value. We use Mason's dhandler feature to convert that into a page, as shown in `QuipShirts/shirts/dhandler`:

Figure 10.1   The inventory page

CHAPTER 10   THE WEB STOREFRONT

```
<& ../qphead.mcmp, title => $quiptitle &>
<H2><% $quip %></H2>
<TABLE>
 <TR><TD>
% if ($path) {
  <IMAGE src="<% $path %>">
% } else {
  No image available.
% }
 </TD><TD>
  <TABLE BORDER="2" CELLPADDING="5">
    <TR><TD>Style</TD><TD><% $style %></TD></TR>
    <TR><TD>Color</TD><TD><% $color %></TD></TR>
    <TR><TD>Size</TD> <TD><% $size  %></TD></TR>
    <TR><TD>Price</TD><TD><% $price %></TD></TR>
  </TABLE>
 </TD></TR>
</TABLE>
<H3><A HREF="../cart/<% $bin %>">Add this shirt</A>
  to your shopping cart.</H3>
<& ../qpfoot.mcmp &>

<%init>
  my $bin = (split('/',$m->dhandler_arg))[-1];
  my $dbh = DBI->connect('DBI:mysql:QuipShirts:localhost',
         'web','nouser')
    or return SERVER_ERROR;
  my $sth = $dbh->prepare_cached
  ("select Quip, Graphic, Size, Style, Color, Price " .
    "from Inventory where Bin = ?")
    or return SERVER_ERROR;
  my ($quip, $graphic, $size, $style, $color, $price)
   = $dbh->selectrow_array($sth, undef, $bin);
  return NOT_FOUND unless $quip;
  my $quiptitle = $quip;
  my $maxlen = 40;
  if (length($quip) > $maxlen) {
    my $at = rindex($quip, ' ', $maxlen) || $maxlen;
    $quiptitle = substr($quip, 0, $at) . '...';
  }
  my $path = "/images/$graphic";
  $path = '' unless -s "/usr/local/apache/production/htdocs$path";
  $price = sprintf('$%1.2f', $price);
</%init>
```

Recall that a Mason dhandler is called when Mason is asked to process a top-level component that doesn't exist. The dhandler is invoked with the full URL. Since in this case the URL contains the bin of interest, we extract that information via the dhandler_arg method. It then goes on to connect to the database (although it almost certainly is using a cached handle instead), prepare a query (cached likewise), and retrieve the shirt data. If the query fails, it returns a "404 Not Found" status to the browser—the user could contrive a URL with a bad bin.

After getting the values from the row, the component checks to see if the graphic exists, using Perl's -s function which returns a file's size. If the file is there (stashed under the static document root) the component makes an <IMAGE> tag to display it on the page, and prints an apology if not. The rest of the shirt's attributes go to another table, and the component makes a link to the shopping cart page at the end. Figure 10.2 shows the result.

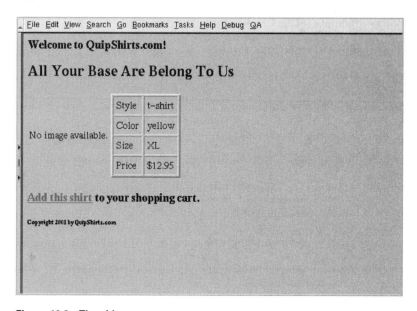

Figure 10.2 The shirt page

So now that we have a catalog, we need user data. We'll recycle some more examples to get that, and then place orders.

10.2.2 Account data

The controversy of data gathered by web sites about users has provoked several well-deserved reviews about the intersection of privacy and e-commerce. QuipShirts wants to gather just enough data about customers to facilitate repeat business, by filling in address information automatically when a returning user places an order.

Here is a simple Accounts table:

```
CREATE TABLE Accounts (
    Username VARCHAR(10) NOT NULL,
    Password VARCHAR(20) NOT NULL,
    RealName VARCHAR(20),
    Addr1 VARCHAR(50),
    Addr2 VARCHAR(50),
```

```
City VARCHAR(30),
State VARCHAR(10),
Postal VARCHAR(10),
Country VARCHAR(15),
PRIMARY KEY (Username)
);
```

The primary key is the username, but the customer isn't required to enter one—we'll see why shortly. The rest of the data is self-explanatory. We could add columns for a phone number or email address to notify the customer about shipments and so on.

To make customer data unobtrusive, we don't require the customer to enter any information until time to place an order. We'll handle that trick via a dhandler in the next section. When account information is required, the customer will come to account.mhtml. It's a complex piece, so we'll look at it in chunks:

```
<& qphead.mcmp, title => 'Shipping information' &>
% if ($password && !$session{'authenticated'}) {
  <H2>Account name or password is invalid.</H2><P>
% } else {
  <H2>Customer information</H2>
% }
```

The opening section prints the usual header, then checks to see if the user has authenticated himself. The invalid message is displayed if the user entered a password which didn't match the database.

```
<FORM METHOD="POST">
 <TABLE>
  <TR>
   <TD COLSPAN="8">
      Please enter your shipping information here.<br>If you
      have given us this data before, skip to the account
      name below.</TD>
  </TR>
  <TR>
   <TD>Name:</TD>
   <TD><INPUT TYPE="text" NAME="realname"
           VALUE="<% $realname %>" SIZE=30></TD>
  </TR>
```

This opening snippet shows the HTML form and how we use variables defined later to load default values into the entry boxes. Note that the action of the form is left out, so the default will be to return to this page.

I'll skip the bulk of the form definition for the sake of brevity. Here is where the component receives the form values as arguments:

```
<%args>
  $username => $session{'username'} || ''
  $password => ''
  $goto => 'stockshirts.mhtml'
  $realname => ''
```

```
    $addr1 => ''
    $addr2 => ''
    $city => ''
    $state => ''
    $postal => ''
    $country => 'USA'
</%args>
```

Since all of the arguments have default values, Mason won't object if any are left out. The username defaults to the value in the session hash if any, and the goto argument defaults to the front page of the site. We'll see how those are used in the following Perl code.

```
<%init>
  my $dbh = DBI->connect('DBI:mysql:QuipShirts:localhost',
                         'web','nouser')
    or return SERVER_ERROR;
  my ($accountExists);
  if ($username && $password) {
    my $sth = $dbh->prepare_cached
        ('select Password,RealName,Addr1,Addr2,City,State,' .
         'Postal,Country from Accounts where Username = ?')
      or return SERVER_ERROR;
    my @try = $dbh->selectrow_array($sth, undef, $username);
    $accountExists = @try;
    if ($accountExists &&
        $try[0] eq crypt($password,$try[0])) {
      $session{'authenticated'}++;
      $session{'username'} = $username;
      $realname  ||= $try[1];
      $addr1     ||= $try[2];
      $addr2     ||= $try[3];
      $city      ||= $try[4];
      $state     ||= $try[5];
      $postal    ||= $try[6];
      $country   ||= $try[6];
    }
    else {
      delete $session{'authenticated'};
    }
  }
```

This section connects to the database (probably cached by Apache::DBI) and validates the user if he entered an account name and password. It retrieves the account record from the database, then encrypts the password to see if it matches the stored value. If so, the rest of the address variables are loaded from the record.

Next we check to see if we have a complete address:

```
if ($realname && $addr1 && $city && $state && $postal
    && $country ) {
  $session{'realname'} = $realname;
```

```
      $session{'address'} = [$addr1, $addr2, $city, $state,
                             $postal, $country];
    if ($accountExists) {
      my $sth = $dbh->prepare_cached
        ('update Accounts set RealName = ?, Addr1 = ?, ' .
         'Addr2 = ?, City = ?, State = ?, Postal = ?, ' .
         'Country = ? where Username = ?')
        or return SERVER_ERROR;
      $sth->execute($realname, @{$session{'address'}},
                    $username) or return SERVER_ERROR;
    }
    elsif ($username && $password) {
      my $sth = $dbh->prepare_cached
        ('insert into Accounts (RealName,Addr1,Addr2,City,' .
         'State,Postal,Country,Username,Password) ' .
         'values (?,?,?,?,?,?,?,?,?)')
        or return SERVER_ERROR;
      $password = crypt($password,$realname);
      $sth->execute($realname, @{$session{'address'}},
                    $username, $password)
        or return SERVER_ERROR;
      $session{'authenticated'}++;
      $session{'username'} = $username;
    }
```

If all the address fields have been filled in (note that the optional second address line isn't checked) then we store the name and address in the session hash and also update the database. This makes it easy for users to update their information without going to some sort of edit account page. A real site would probably check to see if the user actually changed something before updating the database.

If the account information hasn't been entered before, the component adds a new record automatically. This again avoids a second page, but might be presumptuous for real-world use—offer the users a button to explicitly add their accounts instead.

When we have all the address information we need we want to go directly to the page of interest without requiring more user action. This code takes care of the redirection:

```
    # Re-direct to the requested component.
    $m->clear_buffer;
    $r->method('GET');
    $r->headers_in->unset('Content-length');
    $r->content_type('text/html');
    $r->header_out('Location' => "/mason/QuipShirts/$goto");
    return REDIRECT;
  }
</%init>
```

Thanks to Denis Shaposhnikov and the Mason FAQ for having the trick on hand when I needed it. Recall that redirection is handled via sending a special header to the browser, so we don't want to send any regular HTML at all. The call to $m->

`clear_buffer` resets the buffer where Mason builds its response, making way for the header. `$r->method('GET')` clears the POST data from the Apache request. Then we set the location to go to in the redirection header, and return the response code that we want.[4]

If you invoke this component directly and fill in the form, it will take you back to the main QuipShirts inventory page. What we really want is to have the form appear automatically when needed as the user places an order. We'll see how in the next section.

10.2.3   Shopping cart

The user has viewed the catalog and a product detail page. Now he wants to add the product to his shopping cart.

A shopping cart is simply an order that is in progress. As the customer clicks on products they are added to the cart, building up a list. The customer (we hope) eventually clicks the link to check out and place the order.

To handle this list building we need another table:

```
CREATE TABLE Carts (
    Username VARCHAR(10) NOT NULL,
    Bin VARCHAR(10) NOT NULL,
    Quantity INTEGER,
    PRIMARY KEY (Username, Bin)
    );
```

This table simply serves to associate the user with a product and a quantity. We'll add an entry to it when the customer clicks the Add to cart link in a product detail page.

I mentioned previously that we would handle orders via a dhandler, similarly to the way the detail pages are done. That component lives in `QuipShirts/cart/dhandler`. As with the previous large component, we'll examine it in chunks, starting with the HTML portion:

```
<& ../qphead.mcmp, title => 'Your shopping cart' &>
<H2>Order for <% $session{'realname'} %></H2>
<FORM METHOD="POST">
  <TABLE>
    <TR><TH>Shirt</TH><TH>Size</TH><TH>Style</TH>
      <TH>Color</TH><TH>Price</TH><TH>Quantity</TH></TR>
% foreach my $shirt (@shirts) {
    <& orderline.mcmp, %$shirt &>
% }
  </TABLE>
  <INPUT TYPE="submit" VALUE="Make changes">
</FORM>
```

---

[4]   REDIRECT is a constant defined by Apache::Constants, but you have to request it explicitly in the Mason handler script:

`use Apache::Constants qw(:response);`

```
<A HREF="../stockshirts.mhtml">Keep shopping</A><p>
<A HREF="checkout.mhtml">Proceed to checkout</A>
<& ../qpfoot.mcmp &>
```

This simple page displays the order in progress. It uses an array of entries (created later in this section) to build a table. Each line is built by a subcomponent, order-line.mcmp, which displays the details about the shirt and allows the user to change the quantity ordered.

The Perl section of the component starts by checking to see if the user has filled in his address information, and if not, redirects him to do so:

```
<%init>
  my $bin = (split('/',$m->dhandler_arg))[-1];
  unless ($session{'realname'} && $session{'address'}) {
    $m->clear_buffer;
    $r->method('GET');
    $r->headers_in->unset('Content-length');
    $r->content_type('text/html');
    $r->header_out('Location' =>
        "/mason/QuipShirts/account.mhtml?goto=cart/$bin");
    return REDIRECT;
  }
```

The URL includes a value for account.mhtml's goto parameter that will take the customer back to this page when he has entered his information. Remember that we don't require the user to login and create an account, but the Carts table has user-name as a component. If the user isn't authenticated we will add a temporary entry to the Accounts table, using the session ID for the name:

```
  my $dbh = DBI->connect('DBI:mysql:QuipShirts:localhost',
                         'web','nouser')
    or return SERVER_ERROR;
  my $username = $session{'username'};
  unless ($username) {
    $username = substr($session{'_session_id'}, 0, 10);
    my $sth = $dbh->prepare_cached
        ('select Password from Accounts where Username = ?')
      or return SERVER_ERROR;
    my @try = $dbh->selectrow_array($sth, undef, $username);
    unless (@try && $try[0] eq 'temp') {
      $sth = $dbh->prepare_cached
        ('insert into Accounts (RealName,Addr1,Addr2,City,' .
         'State,Postal,Country,Username,Password) ' .
         'values (?,?,?,?,?,?,?,?,?)')
      or return SERVER_ERROR;
      $sth->execute($session{'realname'},
                    @{$session{'address'}},
                    $username, 'temp')
        or return SERVER_ERROR;
    }
  }
```

Ten characters of the session ID aren't really enough to provide a unique value, but collisions aren't likely in the expected lifespan of the session data. The code tries to select an Accounts record by that name, and if not found, adds one with the current address information. By setting the password field to 'temp' we can easily remove these temporary entries from the table later. The rest of the components in the application will use the ten character ID abbreviation if the user isn't authenticated.

Now we verify that the customer is adding a valid item by fetching the price from the Inventory table. This is always a good thing to check, since the user could fake a URL by adding any string to the dhandler path:

```perl
my $sth = $dbh->prepare_cached
    ("select Price from Inventory where Bin = ?")
  or return SERVER_ERROR;
my ($price) = $dbh->selectrow_array($sth, undef, $bin);
return NOT_FOUND unless defined($price);
```

We'll display the contents of the cart by retrieving any records added thus far and then appending a record for the new shirt. Along the way we'll check to see if the user has changed any quantities, and update those records if so:

```perl
my (@shirts, $found);
$sth = $dbh->prepare_cached
  ('select c.Bin, c.Quantity, i.Price from Carts c, ' .
   ' Inventory i where Username = ? and c.Bin = i.Bin')
    or return SERVER_ERROR;
$sth->execute($username) or return SERVER_ERROR;
while (my ($inbin, $quantity, $inprice)
            = $sth->fetchrow_array) {
  if ($inbin eq $bin) {
    $found++;
    $ARGS{$inbin} ||= 1 if $quantity < 1;
  }
  if (exists($ARGS{$inbin})
      && $ARGS{$inbin} != $quantity
      && $ARGS{$inbin} >= 0
    ) {
    my $u = $dbh->prepare_cached
      ('update Carts set Quantity = ? '.
       'where Username = ? and Bin = ?')
      or return SERVER_ERROR;
    $u->execute($ARGS{$inbin}, $username, $bin)
      or return SERVER_ERROR;
    $quantity = $ARGS{$inbin};
  }
  push @shirts, {bin => $inbin,
    quantity => $quantity,
    price => $inprice} if $quantity;
}
```

This code takes advantage of Mason's %ARGS hash, which contains the component's arguments as name/value pairs. We use this method instead of the usual <%args> section because the code doesn't know in advance what the arguments will be. The form inputs are created by orderline.mcmp with an entry field for each shirt where the user can change the order quantity. As Mason parses the form inputs it converts them into the %ARGS hash, using the input name for the key and storing its value there (the shirt quantity, in our case). We check for the user's changes by matching up bins with arguments.

The user got to this dhandler component by clicking on a shirt in the inventory. If that shirt wasn't in the cart before, we add it to the list now:

```
unless ($found) {
  $sth = $dbh->prepare_cached
      ('insert into Carts (Username, Bin, Quantity) ' .
       'values (?,?,1)')
      or return SERVER_ERROR;
  $sth->execute($username, $bin)
      or return SERVER_ERROR;
  push @shirts, {bin => $bin,
                 quantity => 1,
                 price => $price};

}
</%init>
```

Note that the @shirts array contains a hash for each shirt in the cart. When the dhandler invokes orderline.mcmp it uses the hash as the argument list:

```
% foreach my $shirt (@shirts) {
    <& orderline.mcmp, %$shirt &>
% }
```

That's the same as invoking the subcomponent with explicit arguments like these:

```
% foreach my $shirt (@shirts) {
    <& orderline.mcmp, bin => $shirt->{bin},
                       quantity => $shirt->{quantity},
                       price => $shirt->{price} &>
% }
```

But the short form is far more convenient, and requires fewer changes if we change the arguments for the subcomponent.

Speaking of which, here is orderline.mcmp:

```
<TR>
 <TD><A HREF="../shirts/<% $bin %>"><% $quip %></A></TD>
 <TD><% $size %></TD><TD><% $style %></TD><TD><% $color %></TD>
 <TD><% $price %></TD>
 <TD>
% if ($fixed) {
   <% $quantity %>
% } else {
```

```
   <INPUT TYPE="text" NAME="<% $bin %>"
    VALUE="<% $quantity %>" SIZE=3>
% }
 </TD>
</TR>
```

The component is very similar to the inventory line component, but notice the use of a conditional section depending on the $fixed parameter; if set, the price is displayed as text, but if not, a form input is created with the current price as its value. This allows us to use the same component in the shopping cart form and the order confirmation page, as we'll see later.

The Perl section fills in the variables from the database as usual. Note the default setting for $fixed:

```
<%args>
 $bin
 $quantity
 $price
 $fixed => 0
</%args>

<%init>
  my $dbh = DBI->connect('DBI:mysql:QuipShirts:localhost',
                         'web','nouser');
  my $sth = $dbh->prepare_cached
        ("select Quip, Size, Style, Color from Inventory " .
         "where Bin = ?");
  my ($quip, $size, $style, $color)
        = $dbh->selectrow_array($sth, undef, $bin);
  my $maxlen = 30;
  if (length($quip) > $maxlen) {
    my $at = rindex($quip, ' ', $maxlen) || $maxlen;
    $quip = substr($quip, 0, $at) . '...';
  }
  $price = sprintf('$%1.2f', $price);
</%init>
```

After ordering a few shirts we build up a shopping cart that looks like figure 10.3.

The links at the bottom let the users return to the catalog or place their order, which leads us to the next task in building the application.

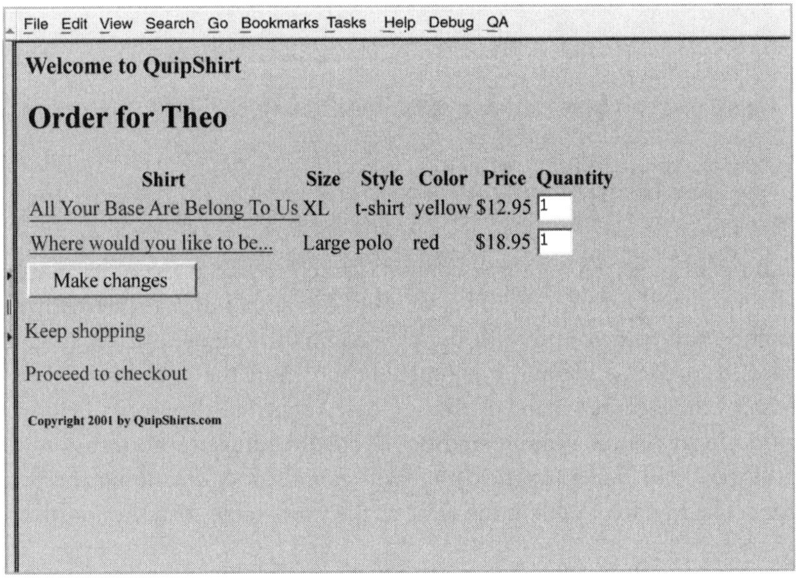

Figure 10.3   The shopping cart

10.2.4   Taking the order

Turning a shopping cart into an order involves a few steps:

1 Accept and verify a credit card number or other payment method received from the customer.

2 Move the entries from the shopping cart to another table to track orders.

3 Process the order.

So far there has been no mention of credit cards or other payment options. We don't bother customers with such details until they decide they want to buy their items. When the user clicks the link to check out, we start the next process.

As usual this requires more tables in the database. First we need a table to contain the credit card number, expiration, and other information needed to process the order. We'll also need a table for the items in the cart—we're going to clear the cart as soon as the order is accepted, so that the customer can start another order immediately.

Here are the two tables for this task:

```
CREATE TABLE Orders (
    OrderN INTEGER NOT NULL,
    Username VARCHAR(10) NOT NULL,
    Card VARCHAR(20) NOT NULL,
    Expiration VARCHAR(10) NOT NULL,
    Notify VARCHAR(50),
    Status VARCHAR(80),
    PRIMARY KEY (OrderN, Username)
```

```
    );
CREATE TABLE LineItem (
    OrderN INTEGER NOT NULL,
    Username VARCHAR(10) NOT NULL,
    Bin VARCHAR(10) NOT NULL,
    Quantity INTEGER,
    PRIMARY KEY (OrderN, Username, Bin)
    );
```

Both tables are keyed on a new column, OrderN. This is the order number, a unique value to identify the order.[5] This simplified example uses a timestamp for the order number, and combines it with the user name for uniqueness. We might receive two orders in the same second, but probably not from the same user. The Orders table contains the credit card and expiration date, as well as the Notify field where the user can optionally enter a phone number or email address for notification that the order is shipped, and the Status field that will contain text describing the progress of the order. The LineItem table is the same as the Carts table with the addition of the order number field.

When the customers click the link to check out, they go to `checkout.mhtml`. We'll skip most of the HTML portion of the component for brevity. It displays the shipping address, the ordered shirts, and the totals including shipping. Here is the form section that has new inputs:

```
<H3>Billing:</H3>
<FORM METHOD="POST" ACTION="confirm.mhtml">
  <TABLE>
    <TR>
     <TD>Credit card:</TD>
     <TD><INPUT TYPE="text" NAME="creditcard"
            VALUE="<% $creditcard %>" SIZE=20></TD>
     <TD>Expiration:</TD>
     <TD><INPUT TYPE="text" NAME="expiration"
            VALUE="<% $expiration %>" SIZE=10></TD>
    </TR>
  </TABLE>
  If you would like notification when your order is
  processed, please enter an e-mail address or phone
  number below.  This information will be removed
  from our database when your order is complete.<BR>
  <INPUT TYPE="text" NAME="notify"
        VALUE="<% $notify %>" SIZE=50>
  <P>
  <INPUT TYPE="submit" VALUE="Process order">
</FORM>
<& ../qpfoot.mcmp &>
```

---

[5] We can't call the column "order" because that is a reserved word in SQL syntax.

When the customer clicks the Submit button he'll go to the component that writes the order, `confirm.mhtml`. That component will send the customer back here if there are any problems in confirmation, so we see all the inputs in the `<%args>` section also:

```
<%args>
  $creditcard => ''
  $expiration => ''
  $notify     => ''
</%args>
```

The `<%args>` values provide defaults for the inputs in the case where an order is rejected.

The Perl section is mostly code we've discussed before. This section builds the order display portion and calculates the totals:

```
  my (@shirts);
  my $sth = $dbh->prepare_cached
    ('select c.Bin, c.Quantity, i.Price from Carts c, ' .
     'Inventory i where Username = ? and c.Bin = i.Bin '.
     'and c.Quantity > 0') or return SERVER_ERROR;
  $sth->execute($username) or return SERVER_ERROR;
  my $items = 0;
  my $shipping = 0;
  while (my ($bin, $quantity, $price)
            = $sth->fetchrow_array) {
    push @shirts, {bin => $bin,
                   quantity => $quantity,
                   price => $price,
                   fixed => 1};
    $items += $price * $quantity;
    $shipping += $quantity * 0.5;
  }
  my $total = sprintf('$%1.2f', $items + $shipping);
  $items = sprintf('$%1.2f', $items);
  $shipping = sprintf('$%1.2f', $shipping);
  my ($addr1, $addr2, $city, $state, $postal, $country)
     = @{$session{'address'}};
</%init>
```

Note that it uses the same technique of building an array of hashes, so that the HTML section can pass them as arguments to `orderline.mcmp`:

```
% foreach my $shirt (@shirts) {
    <& orderline.mcmp, %$shirt &>
% }
```

In this case the hashes include `fixed => 1` so that the resulting table contains text, not inputs.

Shipping is handled as a simple multiplier of the number of items; each adds $0.50 shipping cost. The totals are formatted and displayed in the order section.

The resulting page looks like figure 10.4.

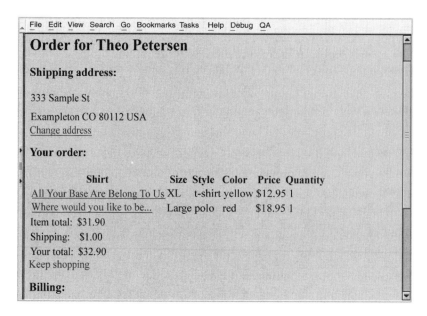

Figure 10.4 Checkout page

When the user clicks the "Process order" button he goes to confirm.mhtml. This is where a real application would verify the credit card and billing information, double-check inventory, and so on. Our simple example has a stub for that logic but ignores it:

```
<& ../qphead.mcmp, title => 'Order confirmation' &>
% if ($confirmed) {
  <H2>Order confirmed for <% $session{'realname'} %></H2>
  Your order <% $order . '-' . $username %> was received.<P>
  <A HREF="../stockshirts.mhtml">Shop some more</A><P>
  <A HREF="../orders/status.mhtml">View status</A><P>
% } else {
  <H2>There was a problem processing your order.</H2>
  <% $error %>
  <FORM METHOD="POST" ACTION="checkout.mhtml">
    <INPUT TYPE="hidden" NAME="creditcard"
           VALUE="<% $creditcard %>" SIZE=20>
    <INPUT TYPE="hidden" NAME="expiration"
           VALUE="<% $expiration %>" SIZE=10>
    <INPUT TYPE="hidden" NAME="notify"
           VALUE="<% $notify %>" SIZE=50>
    <INPUT TYPE="submit" VALUE="Back to checkout">
  </FORM>
%}
<& ../qpfoot.mcmp &>
```

If $confirmed is true, the page displays a confirmation message and offers links to the order status page and the catalog. If not, it expects $error to contain a message explaining what is wrong. The hidden inputs on the form contain the values <%args>, which will get packaged and sent along when the user clicks the Submit button to return to the checkout page.

The Perl section performs the task of moving the order from the shopping cart to the Orders table. We'll skip to that part:

```
if ($confirmed) {
  $order = time();
  $username = $session{'username'} ||
              substr($session{'_session_id'}, 0, 10);
  my $dbh = DBI->connect('DBI:mysql:QuipShirts:localhost',
                         'web','nouser')
    or return SERVER_ERROR;
  my $sth = $dbh->prepare_cached
    ('insert into Orders (OrderN, Username, Card, ' .
     'Expiration, Notify, Status) values (?,?,?,?,?,?)')
      or return SERVER_ERROR;
  $sth->execute($order, $username, $creditcard, $expiration,
     $notify, 'Unprocessed') or return SERVER_ERROR;
```

Now the credit card information needed to process the order is stored, then waits for automatic or manual action. The status of 'Unprocessed' indicates that no action has yet been taken. The details of the order move out of the shopping cart and into LineItem:

```
  $sth = $dbh->prepare_cached
    ('select Bin, Quantity from Carts ' .
     'where Username = ?') or return SERVER_ERROR;
  $sth->execute($username) or return SERVER_ERROR;
  my $u = $dbh->prepare_cached
    ('insert into LineItem ' .
     '(OrderN, Username, Bin, Quantity) ' .
     'values (?,?,?,?)') or return SERVER_ERROR;
  my $d = $dbh->prepare_cached
    ('delete from Carts where Username = ? ' .
     'and Bin = ?') or return SERVER_ERROR;
  while (my ($bin, $quantity) = $sth->fetchrow_array) {
    $u->execute($order, $username, $bin, $quantity)
      or return SERVER_ERROR;
    $d->execute($username, $bin)
      or return SERVER_ERROR;
  }
}
```

Note the use of three statement handles here: $sth is the handle for the select statement which the while loop uses to retrieve records, $u is the handle for the insert statement for moving records to the LineItem table and $d is the handle for deleting records from the Carts table. We could also delete the Carts records en masse with one statement like this:

```
delete from Carts where Username = ?
```

By either road the cart is now empty, and the order is ready for someone in the store to process and ship. Figure 10.5 shows a sample confirmation:

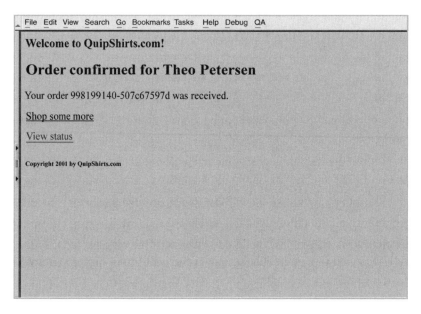

Figure 10.5 Confirmation page

The anxious user is left to await the arrival of his prized T-shirts. What can they do in the meantime?

10.2.5   Tracking shipments

E-commerce customers like online status information about their orders, both for the way it keeps them informed and for the high-tech, connected feeling it gives them about conducting business on the Web. Business sites like it for the savings on calls to customer service personnel. More importantly, a customer who returns to the site for status information may look at other pages there as well. This is a terrific example of how giving your visitors more services facilitates repeat business.

For QuipShirts we'll have a simple status page that shows the users what orders they have in progress. There are links to this page on the order confirmation screen and the site's main catalog page. The code is in `orders/status.mhtml`:

```
<& ../qphead.mcmp, title => 'Order status' &>
% if ($username) {
  <H2>Order status for <% $session{'realname'} %></H2>
  <TABLE>
```

```
    <TR><TH>Order</TH><TH>Status</TH></TR>
%   foreach my $order (@orders) {
      <TR>
        <TD><A HREF="detail.mhtml?order=<% $$order[0].'-'.$username %>">
            <% $$order[0] %></A></TD>
          <TD><% $$order[1] %></TD></TR>
%   }
  </TABLE>
% } else {
  <FORM METHOD="POST" ACTION="detail.mhtml">
    Order number:
    <INPUT TYPE="text" NAME="order" SIZE=25>
    <BR>
    <INPUT TYPE="submit" VALUE="Show status">
  </FORM>
% }
<A HREF="../stockshirts.mhtml">Shop some more</A><P>
<& ../qpfoot.mcmp &>
```

The HTML section is simple enough that I didn't bother with a subcomponent for the table. If the user is logged in, we know his username and can thus retrieve all his records from the Orders table. Each line has a link to another component which will display the details for the order.

If the user isn't authenticated (or didn't create an account in the first place), the page provides a form to enter the order number shown on the confirmation page. The value he enters will be passed as an argument to the detail page. It works the same way via either section.

The Perl section merely builds up the array used for the table as usual:

```
<%init>
  my $username = $session{'username'};
  my @orders;
  if ($username) {
    my $dbh = DBI->connect('DBI:mysql:QuipShirts:localhost',
                           'web','nouser')
      or return SERVER_ERROR;
    my $sth = $dbh->prepare_cached
      ('select OrderN, Status from Orders ' .
       'where Username = ?') or return SERVER_ERROR;
    $sth->execute($username) or return SERVER_ERROR;
    while (my ($order, $status) = $sth->fetchrow_array) {
      push @orders, [$order, $status];
    }
  }
</%init>
```

If the customer clicks on an order for more details, he gets the detail page:

```
<& ../qphead.mcmp, title => 'Order status detail' &>
% if (defined($status)) {
  <H2>Order <% $order %> for
```

```
    <% $session{'realname'} || 'you' %></H2>
  Status as of <% scalar(localtime()) %>:<P>
  <% $status %><P>
  <FORM METHOD="POST" ACTION="shiptrack">
    Enter the ShipExpress ID here to track it:<BR>
    <INPUT TYPE="text" NAME="id" SIZE=50><BR>
    <INPUT TYPE="submit" VALUE="Track shipment">
  </FORM>
% } else {
  <H2>Unknown order</H2>
  There is no <% $order %> in our database.<P>
  Please verify the order number and enter it again.
% }
<P><A HREF="../stockshirts.mhtml">Shop some more</A>
<& ../qpfoot.mcmp &>
```

This page features a (bogus) link to ShipExpress, QuipShirt's package shipping company of choice. As the order is processed and shipped, the store worker will enter the shipment ID into the status field along with other updated information. The customer can then proceed to track his T-shirts via the shipping company's site.

The Perl section implements that logic:

```
<%args>
 $order
</%args>

<%init>
  my ($ordern, $username) = split('-', $order);
  my $dbh = DBI->connect('DBI:mysql:QuipShirts:localhost',
                          'web','nouser')
      or return SERVER_ERROR;
  my $sth = $dbh->prepare_cached
      ('select Status from Orders where OrderN = ? and ' .
      'Username = ?') or return SERVER_ERROR;
  my ($status) = $dbh->selectrow_array
                  ($sth, undef, $ordern, $username);
</%init>
```

This breaks up the $order argument into an order number and username, and then retrieves that record from the table. If no such record exists, $status is left undefined. That causes the error message in the HTML section to be displayed instead of the order details.

QuipShirts now has a bare-bones site that shows products, takes orders, and provides some simple user services. Missing from all this is the employee side—the applications to let workers add or move inventory, fill orders, contact customers, and so on. Remember that employees have to be happy with the site too, so follow the same guidelines of easy navigation and helpful defaults in creating their pages.

We wish the good folks at QuipShirts the best of luck with their clothing line, but what can they do to get more business?

10.3   FEEDBACK

While many companies caught on to the possibilities of online catalogs, few made their sites into great successes. Some early entrepreneurs realized that they could combine the catalog's ease of presentation with the features of a community site: open feedback sections for product reviews and discussion of service and future needs. The community aspect keeps customers returning, even if they aren't buying directly. With those repeat page views, the site can also advertise its own specials or other features, or display links to sell products from other sites.

In chapter 8 I mentioned the Internet Movie Database, http://www.imdb.com/. This is an example of customer feedback selling products, although it grew in reverse (it started as a community site and was acquired by Amazon to add e-commerce features). Movie fans log in to post reviews about films, exchange stories, and vote for their old favorites. New users arrive to search out information on a movie they saw, then get hooked on following links about actors and titles. Finding an old film you love in the database gives a nice moment of nostalgia, and you can buy it right there before the warm glow fades.

Amazon and other book sites capitalize on the volunteer efforts of customers in a number of ways. Let users review books and you'll make each one a salesman. Negative feedback isn't really a problem—if I find myself agreeing with a reviewer's low opinion of a work, I'll seek out the books they praised.

Allowing customers to openly rate (or rant about) your service adds to the community feeling of a site, as does a proper response to criticism when it occurs. Remember too that people who come back to your site with complaints came back—proving that they are people who want to buy from your site.

How you provide for customer feedback depends on the scope of your site. Given a small product line, a simple web forum like those suggested in chapter 8 can supply all you need. Each product can have its own board or topic, and the built-in search features take care of the rest. A larger site would do well to have a feedback section on each product page. The IMDB site presents the opposite organization, leading with the feedback and tying in the products. That's a great approach where the scope of the site is (potentially) the whole range of merchandise in its field.

For the next sections I'll assume the middle approach, and we'll see how to add feedback to the previous section's QuipShirts site.

10.3.1   Product reviews

User comments can include ratings, free-form text, links to other products, or all of the above. For this example we'll handle text comments by adding another table to the QuipShirts database and another Mason component to the site.

The table is called Reviews:

```
CREATE TABLE Reviews (
    Username VARCHAR(10) NOT NULL,
```

```
Bin VARCHAR(10) NOT NULL,
RevTime INTEGER,
Comments TEXT,
PRIMARY KEY (Username, Bin)
);
```

I'm using MySQL, and have taken advantage of the database TEXT type to store text of any length (up to 64 kilobytes). Perl's DBI interface handles TEXT columns as simple scalars, making this trivially easy to work with. The table records the user, time, and product identifier.[6] Requiring a user to identify himself isn't an unreasonable requirement here (and the form will make it easy, as we'll see) and adds to the community nature.

The table's key is the username and bin, limiting a customer to one review per item. If the user brings up the same shirt for review again, he will be able to update his comments. The way we construct the form makes that easy.

Here is the new component, reviews/dhandler:

```
<& ../qphead.mcmp, title => $quiptitle &>
% if ($path) {
  <IMAGE src="<% $path %>"><P>
% }
% if (@comments) {
  <H2>Comments on <% $quip %></H2>
%   foreach my $c (@comments) {
      <% $$c[0] %> on <% $$c[2] %>:<BR>
      <% $$c[1] %><P>
%   }
  Please <% $found ? "update" : "add" %> your comments!
% } else {
  No comments to date, please enter your own below.
% }
% if ($username) {
  <FORM METHOD="POST">
    <TEXTAREA NAME="newcomments" ROWS="6" COLS="40"
    ><% $newcomments %></TEXTAREA>
    <P>
    <INPUT TYPE="submit" VALUE="Save comments">
  </FORM>
% } else {
  <P><A HREF="../account.mhtml?goto=reviews/<% $bin %>">
  Please log in</A> to enter your comments.<P>
% }
<A HREF="../cart/<% $bin %>">Add this shirt</A>
  to your shopping cart.<P>
<A HREF="../stockshirts.mhtml">Return to the catalog</A>
<& ../qpfoot.mcmp &>
```

---

[6] Using the inventory bin is showing itself as a bad plan here. If a product moves between bins, we need to move the comments in the database as well. Lucky for me it's only an example.

The HTML section displays the graphic if there is one, then the existing comments if there are any in the database. If the user has reviewed the product before, we offer to let him change or add to his views.

Note the section that checks $username. If the user isn't logged in, it presents a link to the accounts page with a parameter that will bring the user back to this page after he has been authenticated. For a validated user, the form presents a text area input for writing comments. Remember that any white space between the opening and closing tag of the text area will be present in the form!

The Perl section borrows from the shirt detail component, so I'll skip to the part which handles comments:

```
$sth = $dbh->prepare_cached
       ("select Username, Comments, RevTime " .
        "from Reviews where Bin = ? " .
        "order by RevTime desc" )
    or return SERVER_ERROR;
$sth->execute($bin) or return SERVER_ERROR;
my (@comments, $found, $username);
$username = $session{'authenticated'} ?
              $session{'username'} : '';
while (my ($name, $comment, $time) = $sth->fetchrow_array) {
  if ($name eq $username) {
    if ($newcomments) {
      $comment = $newcomments;
    }
    else {
      $newcomments = $comment;
    }
    $found++;
  }
  push @comments, [$name, $comment, scalar(localtime($time))];
}
```

This portion reads the Reviews table, sorted to present the most recent reviews first. It builds an array of comment entries and checks along the way to see if the current user entered comments previously.

Note that this code will show all the comments. It would be a better idea to limit the records retrieved and offer a navigation link to move between pages of comments in a larger database. More importantly, the code doesn't screen the text being displayed for HTML or JavaScript code. While it is a good idea to let savvy users format their comments via highlighting and other tags, such text needs to be filtered before sending it to browsers. Malicious users could try JavaScript exploits or other techniques to get data from other customers' browsers, or just make the site look awful with bad or buggy HTML.

We also need to check whether the user added a comment:

```
$newcomments =~ s/^[\s\n]+//;
$newcomments =~ s/[\s\n]+$//;
```

```
        if ($username && $newcomments) {
          if ($found) {
            $sth = $dbh->prepare_cached
              ("update Reviews set Comments = ?, RevTime = ? " .
               "where Username = ? and Bin = ?")
              or return SERVER_ERROR;
          }
          else {
            $sth = $dbh->prepare_cached
              ("insert into Reviews " .
               "(Comments,RevTime,Username,Bin)" .
               "values (?,?,?,?)")
              or return SERVER_ERROR;
            unshift @comments, [$username, $newcomments,
                                scalar(localtime)];
            $found++;
          }
          $sth->execute($newcomments, time(), $username, $bin);
        }
</%init>
```

If a previous entry was found, the current text replaces it. Otherwise we add a record to the table with the current timestamp. The latter branch adds the text to the beginning of the array of comments, as if it were retrieved in the first place. That might seem odd, but remember that this code is running after the array is built, while the user sees the net effect of all the records.

This page is a stand-alone component for purposes of the example. A better solution would be to make it a subcomponent and incorporate it into the product detail page, so that prospective buyers can see both store and customer information. Let your users sell the good products for you, and weed the unpopular ones from your inventory.

There is ongoing debate over whether any site should edit or delete product reviews. Certainly a store proprietor has a right to verify that discussions are germane and conducted in reasonable language. Beyond that, in my opinion it hurts the community aspect of a site to strip out negative reviews or other feedback. Customers will discuss your products and your business somewhere—letting them do so freely in your store gives you credit for honesty and keeps you aware of what is being said.

If a product gets more bad reviews than good, do you want your store to be associated with it? If reactions are mixed, find out why, and try to arrange your store so that people can find merchandise they like without wading through things they don't. When an otherwise successful product gets a strong bad reaction from a buyer, ask privately what went wrong and satisfy them with something else.

10.3.2 Customer feedback and other services

It would be a simple matter to implement a customer comments page in the same way as the product reviews in the previous section. But this kind of feedback is different from rating and reviewing catalog items. You want your users to discuss your business more than your product line.

A threaded forum serves this need better than a flat text system like we had in the last section. Building one is more complex too, but there's no reason to do it ourselves. Chapter 8 covered products like mwForum that are perfectly suited to the job. You can install and customize one in far less time than it would take to implement something new.

Threaded messages allow users to easily respond to others' comments and follow a discussion. Set up message boards for each aspect of customer service, as well as new product lines and other directions. Give your employees strong guidelines on how and when to respond to customer comments. No one who runs a business believes that "the customer is always right," but successful businesses keep in mind that the customer is always the one paying the bills. Reasonable complaints should be addressed apologetically in public. Angry customers should get private responses if possible, along with a public statement that the matter is being handled.

If you want to build the community aspect of your site, allow the customers to run some of your message boards. Promote some regular visitors to administrate forums on topics of interest, and don't worry too much about keeping things on topic. Everyone coming to your site is a potential buyer, even if they mostly drop in to browse gossip.

Let customers add pages to your site. If you sell collectibles, let them write about their collections, or talk about their pets if you sell pet food. Even a limited form of this can really make your site take off, as your hosted pages become a kind of directory and search engine for your community.

Should your community areas become more popular than your store, you could consider switching the site around. Host the forum as the main site, offering discreet links to the storefront on each page. Promote other sites in your virtual community and offer them hosting or hire the site builders and get their help in drawing more customers to your store.

Following any of these directions will take your site out of the realm of "brochure-ware" and into the ideal interactive world of the Web. Letting your customers add content to your site involves a loss of control and an investment in monitoring and responding to forums. In exchange you can get a good community name and loyal user base that sets you apart from competing sites.

10.4   OPEN SOURCE E-COMMERCE TOOLS

Building your own web storefront from scratch is a mighty task, and full of pitfalls. Buggy or short-sighted code can lead to lost customers or worse, security breaches that can expose sensitive data. The grind of the project may wear you out just as your energy is needed for the newly opened business.

Fortunately, this is an area that is well-trafficked by generous programmers, and searching a few sites will turn up a number of packages that can meet your needs. Restricting the search terms to "Perl" and a catch phrase such as "shopping cart" will locate most of the contenders, from CGI scripts that implement an order-taking application similar to my example to full-fledged site builders.

In looking for free e-commerce tools, expect to encounter a good deal of "promotion-ware," software that exists in part to build sales of a related service. Merchant accounts and credit card processing are the most typical of these services, where a free application is built to use a particular company's order handling. This may be ideal for those who have a small operation and don't want to be bothered with the details of credit card processing. If your needs are greater or you already have the financial issues handled, look for a more complete solution.

If you have partially implemented a site (or inherited one that was half-built by someone else) you may be looking for a solution to complete the site and get into business. Many tools exist (in Perl and other languages) for various e-commerce tasks—user management, order fulfillment, and so on. You may also be able to take the pieces you need from one of the site builders discussed in the next two sections.

The missing pieces you need are quite likely in credit card processing and other payment systems. This special area gets its own section later in the chapter. Be warned that there are no free solutions here. The companies that handle credit card transactions have good reasons to be picky in accepting requests.

In this section I'll cover complete site-building tools (and discuss how complete they are), rather than trying to put together sites from different products. By creating a site from scratch (or rebuilding it from the data and documents you already have) you will know at least that the resulting site doesn't have any gaps resulting from trying to glue together different pieces. I recommend that you consider a fresh start with any of these tools, and let the applications work as the developers intended rather than trying to fit them into another model.

The two products I'll discuss here are Interchange and AllCommerce. Both have long histories of Open Source development with good choices for underlying databases and Perl tools. Either one can get your site operational with a good effort, so let's get on with it to see how they differ.

10.4.1   Interchange

In 2000 two of the more popular Open Source e-commerce packages, MiniVend and Tallyman, were merged, as Akopia (the owner of Tallyman) acquired MiniVend and hired its lead developer. MiniVend had a long history (long for the Web—it debuted in 1995) among e-commerce builders and brought a loyal user base to the relatively new Akopia products. This proved attractive to RedHat, which acquired the company and product line at the end of the year and made Akopia its e-commerce division. That company has kept Interchange under the protection of the GPL license while integrating it into its suite of business products and consulting opportunities.

Interchange is available from its web site, http://www.akopia.com/, or as part of a bundled package from RedHat. The company sells training, consulting, site hosting, and other service packages for the product.

Interchange requires Linux or a Unix-variant OS to run. It can use its own data manager or a selection of DBI-compliant databases, and works with a number of payment systems. The product has its own HTML template processing system but employs a number of Perl modules along the way, easily installed via a CPAN bundle.

Web server requirements are minimal: Interchange can work with any server that handles CGI, so Apache isn't strictly required and mod_perl never becomes an issue. The reason is that all dynamic data comes from a separate server. The web host runs a small CGI application which forwards requests to the Interchange server and hands the results back to the browser. That provides considerable flexibility. You could have multiple web front-ends talk to a single secured machine running the store, for instance.

Akopia brags that Interchange runs on any hardware that will run the OS and web server. That may be true, but for good performance you'll need a respectable machine. Interchange consumes a hefty 14 MB of memory on my Linux machine, more than twice the size of an Apache/mod_perl process, so think twice about running Interchange and your web applications together. The main Perl script has some comments about how to reduce memory usage.

Installation and first catalog

The configuration script that comes with the installation handled my setup without a problem. Interchange wants to run as its own user, although any nonroot account will do. I told it to use a MySQL database instead of its own data manager, and I defaulted the rest.

The installation compiles a few C programs such as the CGI interface mentioned earlier, but supplies Perl implementations also should that be a problem. I installed the software in /usr/local/interchange and proceeded to the site-building step.

By Interchange terminology, a site is a catalog, and creating one is most easily accomplished by running the makecat script. This is quite a lengthy procedure, and if you aren't paying attention it will appear that you are answering the same questions over and over.

In the course of creating the catalog, Interchange will offer to scan your httpd.conf file to determine the answers to some of these questions. This confused me since it then went on to offer defaults that ignored my Apache setup. Be warned also that the configuration file scanner doesn't use Apache's parser at all, and so it doesn't understand conditional sections such as <IfDefine>, resulting in error reports about directives being found twice.

Interchange can build a new catalog from an existing template, which is terrific if you are planning to do this kind of thing a lot. It ships with one such template, its demonstration catalog called construct, and mentions that others are available elsewhere (although I never found them). The `makecat` script confusingly refers to the template as a demo (which it is, but I found it odd that it wanted to know what demo I wanted to use).

The script also asks for URLs for the new catalog and its static files. This is where you decide if Interchange will be the whole site (the top URL, or perhaps top of a virtual host) or just a path on your existing site. `makecat` will deposit an appropriate `index.html` file in the directory corresponding to the chosen URL.

You'll also be prompted to give an administration user name—this is a user within the Interchange system, not a shell account nor a database user. You will use that account to start customizing the site. Customers can create their own accounts through a simple form interface.

Following my previous example, I created a QuipShirts catalog and gave it the URL http://localhost/QuipShirts/. This added a new directory (`/usr/local/inter-change/catalogs/QuipShirts`) that received all the template files for the site, another directory (`/usr/local/apache/htdocs/QuipShirts`) for static files, a new MySQL database, and a copy of the CGI interface program in Apache's `cgi-bin` directory.

After creating the first catalog, you must start the Interchange server before trying to browse the site. The script prompts you to do this (and gives you the command line for a convenient cut and paste), but you'll need to add it to your boot scripts yourself if you want to start Interchange automatically.

Customization

One of the selling points of Interchange is its full web interface. Administration and site building are all performed via the browser. Log in as the admin user for your catalog and you'll receive a menu of configuration and editing pages: create items for your catalog, set up specials and discounts, edit the page templates, and so on. You can view orders and other user activity from this page as well.

Interchange uses its own templating system to build pages from templates and database entries. You can modify the templates from the administration page mentioned earlier or locate them under the catalog directory and edit them in your favorite text editor. The Interchange server checks for template modifications as it generates pages, so your changes will be reflected immediately.

Reworking the construct something demo catalog into a new store is quite a lot of work, most of it deleting categories and items that don't apply (unless you happen to have a hardware store). Fortunately, newer versions of Interchange will feature a new foundation store that will have less to remove. In the meantime, expect a few wrenches and hammers to turn up in your store until you've tracked them all down.

Adding items and categories to a store is a snap: bring up the Items menu and click the link to add an item, then fill in the page. Upload new graphics for the item, type in a description and its shipping characteristics, and you are done. Reload the customer interface and you can search for your item or browse to it immediately.

Features

Interchange has a very rich library of tags for building pages. The documentation lists more than 90, from simple database substitutions to display logic to embedded Perl code. Once you've learned your way around the template system you'll find yourself building nonstore pages with Interchange too. If you have existing pages for your store, you can link in Interchange pages for checkout—and more—without rebuilding everything; add new pages via Interchange and replace the old ones as you have time. Internationalization is available at multiple levels, via separate pages, separate sections within a page, currency symbols, and so on.

I hate sites that require cookies, so I appreciate that Interchange's session handling leaves them optional. Users can navigate the site via unique URLs instead, and Interchange will fix up internal links along the way.

Interchange also makes customer accounts optional, as I discussed in my example. Confidential information in orders can be encrypted via PGP if desired, and SSL mode works fine. Secure the whole site or just the order pages as you wish.

Interchange offers extensive handling for shipping services and costs. The shipping cost database can handle any number of different services, and cost calculation can be anything from a constant, UPS rules, or a Perl subroutine.

There are a number of great features for store builders: Interchange will scan the order database to build a list of products that tend to get ordered together, then add them to product pages with the usual "people who bought this also bought..." display. Cross-selling adds links to an item to the pages for related items, while up-selling offers the viewer a choice of superior items. You can also create promotion pages for special prices, items newly added to the catalog, and so on.

The affiliate manager allows you to maintain links from other sites to your catalog, and track the number of referrals and purchases you get from those sites. When a customer arrives from an affiliate site you can display alternate pages or sections created for that affiliate.

Interchange includes two different search engines and five search methods for helping users find pages of interest. It uses yet more template pages that let you customize the look of the results and tie in other information about specials and so on. Searches can operate on the text of pages or the rows of database tables with quite a few options for limiting and refining results.

Rather than tying to any specific payment handler, the order routing system is used to program how an order is handled. The default method is to mail the order to a specified address. Interchange will encrypt the order (or just the credit card data) before transmission if you wish (certainly recommended if the mail is delivered somewhere other than the server machine itself). The current product includes routing to resolve payment via CyberCash, and the developer promises the next version will handle a number of credit card gateways including a verification system and popular commercial services.

Nonfeatures

Interchange is not a product for a small store or a casual maintainer. The documentation recommends against using it for catalogs with fewer than 100 items. If half the entries in the earlier feature list made you shrug, then you will be taking on a great deal of complexity that is more than your site requires.

The product doesn't implement any form of user feedback. Adding this to pages isn't difficult, but you will be doing the programming yourself. Given the richness of other features I kept thinking I must have missed the feedback options.

The documentation is there, but it can be very hard to find something you are looking for. Admittedly, it would be amazing to find adequate documentation for a product this size. If you are looking for a tag, database table, or administrative feature you'll find what you need quickly, but for the rest, expect to do a lot of digging—you'll want to quickly locate the mailing list archive.

Support

Interchange has free support via its mailing list. This is a very active group with a lot of helpful members and regular appearances by representatives of the product owner. Most of what is missing from the documentation can be found by searching through old messages.

RedHat offers consulting based on the product, and it offers a number of other support packages. Check the product web page for more details.

10.4.2 AllCommerce

Zelerate's AllCommerce system has been available since 1998. It doesn't have the bumpy history of Interchange, having stayed with one company (and presumably one set of developers) since its inception.

The product is available from SourceForge. (Zelerate's development site, http://www.zelerate.org/, is now a pointer to http://allcommerce.sourceforge.net/, so pick whichever is easier to remember.) It consists of Perl tool scripts and CGI applications; there is no separate server to start. The documentation claims that AllCommerce is optimized for Apache (although I found no indication that is uses anything other than plain CGI scripts) and runs on Linux, Unix, and Windows. Some Linux distributions have AllCommerce preloaded.

AllCommerce can work with a range of DBI databases, although it warns that only MySQL is tested by the developers. You'll need to have DBI and the required DBD modules installed already. The installation script will set up databases for you.

No hardware suggestions were given in the documentation. If I were running a busy site with AllCommerce I'd want a fast machine with generous memory limits, where I could get everything working in Apache::Registry to avoid the CGI compilation overhead.

AllCommerce generates pages through (you guessed it) its own template processing system. The documentation discusses where and how the various templates are used, but there doesn't seem to be a reference guide to building your own. Expect to do a lot of digging to take advantage of this product.

Installation

The distribution comes as a tar file that has everything already laid out. Just unpack it under your Apache root directory. There are no compiled programs, and so no configuration or make steps for creating them.

AllCommerce comes with an installation script that will automatically set up a site running a default Apache installation with MySQL. I happen to have one of those handy, but I found the script a challenge to use. It failed mysteriously until I faked the directory to be `/home/httpd/os_allcommerce` (instead of the default Apache compiles with) and manually ran another script, `sepmdir.pl`, to create missing files.

It did create the MySQL database correctly, although before that it scanned through all installed DBD modules to build a list of possible databases to use. If you have nonfunctional DBD modules this will cause the script to again fail mysteriously.

AllCommerce prefers to run as a virtual host for each store. The script offers to add a virtual host entry to `httpd.conf` for you, but after my previous experiences I decided to do this manually.

The next step is to load shipping data into the database. The script can't possibly handle this step unless you've loaded the required files already as explained in the manual installation instructions. At this point I started to wonder if the automatic script weren't meant for updates rather than a new installation. Loading the shipping data manually isn't hard, however, and the instructions were all correct.

Customization

When all this is done, you can log in as the administrator and start building the site. My frustrations didn't end there, however, as I found a large number of wrong links and bad assumptions, and had to do a lot of finding and fixing before getting an example to work.

AllCommerce doesn't come with a standard set of files for building a new site as Interchange does (although you can create your own site template once you know what you are doing). I liked the fact that I had something working immediately with Interchange even though it looked nothing like the site I wanted to build, but when I started working with AllCommerce I found that I liked it more, despite the fact that I was starting from scratch.

The documentation suggests creating a product line and then adding to it. I followed the links on the admin page and re-created the QuipShirts product line in a few minutes. Each item has a few attributes to set (title, short description, long description, weight, and so on). Generate the pages for them (using buttons available as you go) and you can start viewing your store immediately.

AllCommerce doesn't have an online template editor, so you'll need to track down the template files and edit them yourself. In my case I found the easiest method was first to create a few products and examine the generated HTML files to figure out what templates are used.

Features

AllCommerce allows articles to coexist with products and categories. These are text pages that can be massaged through the template system to keep the look and feel of your site while educating customers. I liked the fact that the product helps to organize those pages at the same level as the product information.

Inventory management is more explicit and flexible in AllCommerce than with Interchange. Before trying out your store you must define a warehouse (future versions may handle multiple warehouses, although the current product allows only one), and then associate products with it. Pricing is controlled by inventory entries instead of at the product level, and prices in different currencies can be maintained separately.

Although I complained about the shipping data step in the automatic installation script, it was easy to load the relevant tables manually. Once I did, shopping carts all showed the available shipping options and prices correctly as pull-down menus. The interface is very clean and easy for the customer.

Order processing is very simple, with email as the default method of handling credit card information. One option is to configure AllCommerce to send part of the credit card number via mail and store another part in the database. The product has experimental support for CCVS credit card processing, but I didn't try it.

The user management features in AllCommerce are again simple and easy. Users can set up any number of addresses in their address books and use them automatically when filling out an order. Cookies are optional for users, but required for administrator access.

The promotion management features in AllCommerce aren't as rich as those in Interchange, but it is easy to set up gift offers, shipping specials, and so on. Products can be linked, but there is no automatic creation of the "also purchased …" data nor any up-sell feature.

My overall impression of AllCommerce is good for a small store, in spite of my complaints. It is easy to create and maintain a small catalog and inventory, and the customer interface is clean and clear.

Nonfeatures

AllCommerce expects you to create your own front page for your store, or use the page for a product line. I kept looking for some tool to generate this from one of the many templates but there doesn't seem to be one.

The documentation is in PDF files rather than HTML or POD. That would be fine if there weren't so many broken links in the documents, making internal navigation rather iffy. I never did find a reference for the template processing system. The developer seems to consider the tutorials sufficient for making a store.

Like Interchange, AllCommerce doesn't have direct support for any kind of customer feedback. Without a good reference for the template system it isn't as clear to me how I would add one myself.

Support

Zelerate offers commercial support (its own and from certified installers) for AllCommerce, as well as free support on the development-site message boards and mailing lists. The mailing list archives (linked on the development site) may offer answers to some of the questions and problems I had in getting started. Unfortunately, they reside on a slow site, and I was unable to reach them while working with the product.

Would I build a store with either of these products? Certainly. Interchange is a good choice for a large operation (or a consultancy that is creating a number of stores) while AllCommerce would work fine for a casual shop. If you haven't made a strong commitment to other tools then you won't mind learning a new template processor and fitting into their way of doing things.

If you would rather do it yourself, using one of these site builders is still a good way to get started. Create a prototype of your store, and use it to explore what you like and what you need that is different than the products provide. You may end up convincing yourself to take advantage of the considerable development effort that goes into these tools.

10.5 CREDIT CARD PROCESSING

E-commerce has spawned a number of new ways to move money over the Internet—micropayments, debit accounts, and so on. Exciting as those new prospects are, you will need credit card processing if you are building a web site for consumer purchases. Credit card transactions are the norm for e-commerce, and no other method is as pervasive. Requiring your customers to register for another online payment mechanism will certainly cost you business.

The first requirements for accepting credit card payments are the same for web stores as for brick-and-mortar establishments: you will need a merchant account and a regular business bank account. The two are not the same, which confuses some people who are doing this for the first time. Credit card transactions are processed via the merchant account, which then transfers money to the business bank account. You may be able to open both accounts with one bank, but there is nothing wrong with setting up a merchant account with a card processing service and a business account with a convenient local bank.[7]

---

[7] If you have no idea how to open a merchant account, don't worry—any number of card processing services will be happy to do this for you. Ask your banker first to find out whether he has any recommendations.

Plenty of stores (and web store fronts) process credit card orders entirely on paper. This requires very little start-up cost and is simple to handle. Your store's bank may handle all of the transactions for you, just by dropping off the paper receipts, or you may need to get a merchant account and handle some of the steps yourself. Paper processing is more prone to fraud and error, however, and usually has a higher cost per transaction, limits on the amount, or both.

Paper processing transactions for your web site requires only that you collect and store the credit card number, expiration date, name, and (possibly) billing address as part of your acceptance process. As shown in the site building products of the previous section, e-commerce applications typically email this information along with an order number (or all the order details) to whomever is responsible for processing orders, and that person does so manually through the paper system.

To get lower transaction fees and better security you'll need to process credit card transactions online. In a regular store, online card processing is handled either via a swipe box or a cash register tied to a computer which has the same functionality built in. Most of us are familiar with the small terminals that consist of a phone line jack, a card swipe slot, and a numeric key pad. The cashier enters the amount on the pad, runs the card down the slot, waits half a minute or so, and gets an approval or denial for the transaction (or not). The swipe box includes a modem which has been configured to dial the number of a transaction clearinghouse which handles the merchant account. The clearinghouse performs the transaction and credits the account. After a few more accounting steps the credited amount is transferred to the store's business bank account.

As stores opened for business on the Internet, so did many transaction clearinghouses, offering software for web merchants to process their orders over the network. The store application sends a transaction over a secure channel to the card processor of choice, which then performs the same steps—some of these services actually use a modem to dial another clearinghouse and process the card exactly as before. The approval is sent back to the store over the same channel, and the customer gets a confirmation.

Like much of the rest of the e-commerce world, these services have undergone a shakeup and consolidation phase during the time of my writing. You can find an online processor in a number of ways. The company that hosts your web site may have a deal with one, or you could ask the same person who is setting up your merchant account. The documentation for the site-building products discussed in section 10.4 has pointers to the services each program handles.

Working with such a service generally involves installing a program on your server, so be clear about your hardware and OS when talking to a provider. Some sites run the card processing service on a dedicated machine, allowing maximum security both from the network and internal users.

10.5.1 CCVS

CCVS turns up in discussions of many Open Source e-commerce packages. The letters stand for Credit Card Verification System, a software tool for interacting with card processing services.

CCVS was developed by Hell's Kitchen Systems in 1997, then acquired by RedHat (notice a trend here?) in 2000 to add to Interchange as part of its e-commerce suite. Despite its frequent presence in Open Source discussions, CCVS is *not* Open Source or free in any other sense. This is a commercial product with substantial licensing costs.

The product's popularity is owed in part to the developer's generous array of platforms and language interfaces. CCVS runs on most brands of Unix and most popular Linux distributions, with libraries and support modules for C, Java, Perl, PHP, Python, and TCL. Compared to the Windows focus of so many card processing services, this makes CCVS an automatic choice for many web builders.

I think the architecture of CCVS appeals to technical types too. The product emulates a credit card swipe box, using a modem on the host machine to dial a transaction processing service. The web application creates a transaction with CCVS, fills in the required details (an invoice number or other identifier, card number, expiration date, and amount) and optional billing address. It then tells CCVS to run the transaction and waits for the return authorization (or goes about other business and checks in now and then).

CCVS meanwhile uses the modem to dial the card processing service, and then performs the same protocols as a swipe box over that link. The documentation lists modems that will work with the service (older is better—these companies don't connect at faster than 1,200 baud anyway), and RedHat's support group will help you set up another modem if you don't have a supported one.

While CCVS is costly to license, you can download it free and try it in a demo mode. The support libraries and CCVS server will work as normal, but it won't dial the modem or attempt a real approval. Evaluate the system at your leisure.

Most CCVS users recommend setting up the modem and server on a protected machine, just as you would with other card processing software. This allows security measures as mentioned before. It doesn't take much machine to do this, and chances are you have an old PC with a modem anyway.

I hope that these guidelines and tools help you build a successful web store. And if you are successful, you'll need help maintaining the system and managing increased burdens on your server, which leads us to the final chapters.

# PART 4

Site management

Once your site is operational you face the exciting challenge of keeping it that way. Here are two chapters on tools and techniques for managing an active web site.

Chapter 11 covers content management: adding new documents and applications and keeping your site in sync with a development system. It covers tools for managing the site content and recovering from an accident.

Chapter 12 discusses performance issues, especially how to start your site on the right foot and how to monitor it for signs of slippage.

CHAPTER 11

Content management

When you start your first web site project, the process of setting up the server and providing content may seem daunting and mysterious. Once you have served up a few documents and have an application or two working, the mystery fades and the next steps look easy—just add more content, more apps, and more features.

Those who have watched other projects grow know what can happen next: as you add interdependent files and change documents and applications, errors almost inevitably creep in. Initially a simple manual check can verify that your site is still working properly. As you (or perhaps a group of others) add more content, you need a link-checking program to get through the site, or you simply fix problems as regular users report broken links and other failures.

While automated tools and manual tests are always a good idea, a developing site often needs more help than just that to keep working. Software developers know the need for code-management tools in any nontrivial project, and writers and artists have other methods for managing groups of files. In the web world we have *content management* to describe the tools and methodologies used to control the publishing and presentation of sites under development.

Content management can be as simple as a script that copies an entire site from a development system to the running version (and that's what most of us did first). Some commercial web server products have content-management tools built in, while other products integrate with Apache, including many Open Source options. Integrated packages like Slash have their own tools, which may make them more attractive for many sites.

The temptation is great for Perl programmers to write their own content managers, and many have. Before you announce your own new and improved wheel, consider some of the tools and packages discussed here. You'll find many pieces you need, and you might decide on a full solution.

11.1 DEVELOPMENT LIFE CYCLE

But before getting excited about solutions, let's discuss the problem.

It's common when first creating a site to work directly on the server (which may or may not be public) and one copy of the configuration and content files. If you are a programmer who is used to code-management systems such as CVS then you may have a repository for these files to preserve history and provide a backup copy. I will hazard a guess that most of us created our first sites on the bare network, edited files in place, and left the niceties for later—possibly when a screw-up signaled it was time for something better.

When that server starts generating value (in terms of money or reputation), the usual move is to a dual system. This might be two separate directory trees on one server or on different machines. The idea is the same, however, to have a place for testing code and configuration changes before moving them to the public system. When things look good, a simple batch upload or copy script moves the new files into production use.

If you are part of a development group you'll want even more diversity—letting each developer have his own copy of the system perhaps, or dividing the system up so that a developer's code can work in a stand-alone fashion. (Chapter 2 has some suggestions on how to configure this.) Now the uploading gets more complicated. It's likely that developers will need to change files in tandem, especially configuration files that tell Apache how to run their code. Letting developers upload directly to the production server will almost certainly result in a public failure somewhere along the line. Instead we need a safeguard system, a place where changes from different sources can be placed together and verified before going public.

Even if you work alone, multiple phases and systems are a good idea. If your server handles more than a moderate level of traffic you'll want to separate your CPU and bandwidth usage from public consumption. When your site becomes a big success you'll want to move the server to a better operational environment, or your development system to a comfortable spot for working long hours. And you'll want to check out the whole site in a test area before moving things to production, so you'll still need the safeguard phase, whether it resides on a development machine or the production system.

11.1.1 Development, staging, production

The most commonly discussed regimen for developing and publishing a web site is the three phase system of development, staging, and production.

Software, documents, and configuration changes start out in the development phase, on a developer's workstation or a shared machine or both. When development is complete and tested in place, accepted files are carried over to the staging area.

The staging phase is used to test changes in an environment configured as close to the production system as possible—the same OS and web server versions, bandwidth, and so on. Any databases used in testing the staging phase should be copies of production data.[1] In many cases the staging area is a virtual host on the production system itself, or just a different document tree, and uses the production databases directly. Changes are tested here again, where the new code can encounter a complete system. Preferably the person making the changes tests them first, then someone unrelated to the work tries out both the changes and other portions of the system. If the site passes its tests in the staging phase, it can be moved fully into production.

The production phase should always reflect a complete copy of the staging area. Not all tools enforce this, but if the production phase receives partial updates, it is possible to miss dependencies (especially as the staging area gets updated multiple times) and leave behind a crucial change. One simple technique for handling this is to use a symbolic link to point to the production phase root directory and switch that link from the old software to the staging area, making it the production version. The prior directory remains available as-is, and can be switched back if something goes wrong. Meanwhile, a new directory becomes the next staging area.

11.1.2 A staging area on your production server

Regardless of how you decide to move staging to production, there are a number of ways to set up a staging area on the server you use for production traffic. By sharing the production server, you don't have to worry about problems caused by different versions of Apache, Perl, and the OS on different machines. It also makes cutting over to production quick and simple.

There are a few different approaches you can take to setting up a staging area. The simplest is to create a mirrored directory tree and tell Apache about it. For example, I created /usr/local/apache/staging and loaded it with a backup of my examples. To have Apache serve files from this directory I added these sections to httpd.conf:

---

[1] If your system acquires sensitive data from customers, this may not be appropriate. In that case you'll need to build a large enough test database yourself, or use a procedure to copy production data and remove the sensitive information along the way.

```
# Staging area (directory/alias method)
<Directory "/usr/local/apache/staging">
    # Only allow local folks
    Order deny,allow
    Deny from all
    Allow from 192.168.
    AuthUserFile data/staging
    AuthName "Staging area"
    AuthType basic
    require valid-user
</Directory>

Alias /staging/ "/usr/local/apache/staging/"
ScriptAlias /staging/cgi-bin/ "/usr/local/apache/staging/cgi-bin/"
```

This uses the familiar `Directory` block to set up a protected zone. You can allow access by network address or a file of authorized users (or both as shown, if you are sufficiently paranoid). After telling Apache about the directory tree, an `Alias` and `ScriptAlias` pair tell Apache how to map URLs onto the files.

The unfortunate side effect of this approach is that all URLs have to start with "staging/" to work. While you should be using relative URLs in every place possible, applications and other code will likely break or (worse) send a browser to the production site instead of the staging area.

Virtual hosts

To keep uniform URLs while still using one server, use a *virtual host* instead of a directory alias. The whole idea behind virtual hosts is to allow one Apache server to handle multiple sites, differentiating between them either by name or by IP address. We can set up the staging area to use a different name, such as staging.example.site, and have all the URLs remain the same.

Obviously this scheme will require a little more setup, since we have to add a new name to the routing service that tells browsers how to find hosts. If you do all your work on one machine, you can just add an entry in your `/etc/hosts` file or equivalent. If your staging area is to be accessible only to local machines, you can add a new name and IP address to your local DNS database. A publicly accessible staging area needs a publicly accessible name, so in that case you'll have to get a new DNS entry from your service provider.

The original virtual host mechanism in Apache required a unique IP address for each named site. Since version 1.1 of the HTTP protocol, servers can distinguish between hosts just by name. This allows a machine with one IP address to host any number of sites directed to it by DNS aliases.[2] Apache supports either mechanism.

---

[2] CNAME aliases can provide any number of alternate names for a given IP address. See your DNS provider for more information.

If you need only one extra site and have a spare IP address (no problem at all if your staging area serves only a protected network) then I suggest using IP-based virtual hosting, as it doesn't require many changes to your configuration. It's also the mechanism recommended by the Apache Group due to various concerns they express in the server documentation.

I added staging.example.site to my machine with address 192.168.6.66, then told Apache to virtual host it via this block in `httpd.conf`:

```
# Staging area (IP virtual host method)
<VirtualHost staging.example.site>
    DocumentRoot /usr/local/apache/staging/htdocs/
    ServerName staging.example.site
    ErrorLog staging/logs/error_log
    CustomLog staging/logs/access_log common
    ScriptAlias /cgi-bin/ /usr/local/apache/staging/cgi-bin/
</VirtualHost>
```

After creating the log directory (`/usr/local/apache/staging/logs`) and making it writable for Apache, I restarted the server and browsed to http://staging.example.site/ to see the main index page as expected.

If you can't add IP addresses to your server, you'll need to use name-based virtual hosts. This requires more changes, since you'll have to make your production server a virtual host too, so that Apache can distinguish between the different traffic sent to the single IP address. Here is a simple configuration:

```
# IP to use for named virtual hosts
NameVirtualHost 192.168.6.66

# Main site's virtual host
<VirtualHost 192.168.6.66>
    DocumentRoot /usr/local/apache/htdocs/
    ServerName www.example.site
    ErrorLog logs/error_log
    CustomLog logs/access_log common
    ScriptAlias /cgi-bin/ /usr/local/apache/cgi-bin/
</VirtualHost>

# Staging area's virtual host
<VirtualHost 192.168.6.66>
    DocumentRoot /usr/local/apache/staging/htdocs
    ServerName staging.example.site
    ErrorLog staging/logs/error_log
    CustomLog staging/logs/access_log common
    ScriptAlias /cgi-bin/ /usr/local/apache/staging/cgi-bin/
</VirtualHost>
```

The `NameVirtualHost` directive tells Apache that any IP traffic sent to this address should be interpreted via the virtual host protocol. That is, it will check the request headers for the server name and use that to determine which virtual host receives the information. Then we have two virtual host blocks, one for www.example.site and one for staging.example.site, each with the same basic declarations of server name, log file locations, and aliases for the script directory.

I said this was a simple configuration. If you've created any more complex applications, alias schemes, etcetera, they'll all need to be replicated between the two virtual hosts, distinguishing between directories as appropriate. The same applies to any mod_perl applications you have, which leads us to the next section.

Staging mod_perl applications

If you have mod_perl applications (including scripts that run under Apache::Registry and its relatives) you need to take a few more factors into consideration.

The first matter to address is the security concern of handling production and staging data in one server. Remember that each Apache process has a single Perl interpreter. Any information kept globally in the server would be available to applications in any virtual host. Perl doesn't protect one package's variables and code from others, and generally assumes good behavior on the part of all scripts and modules.

If your applications cache data through a database or file mechanism, make sure each virtual host has its own cache. For example, suppose you maintain a list of users who have active sessions and display that on a status page. Store the user's virtual host in the list so that you can separate staging activity from production use.

Code has to be kept separate too.[3] Apache::Registry takes care of this for you, so long as you configure different directories for your staging and production areas. For instance, if we add this configuration to the virtual host sections, Apache::Registry will compile different versions of scripts in different phases:

```
# Main site's virtual host
<VirtualHost 192.168.6.66>
    DocumentRoot /usr/local/apache/htdocs/
    ServerName www.example.site
    ErrorLog logs/error_log
    CustomLog logs/access_log common
    ScriptAlias /cgi-bin/ /usr/local/apache/cgi-bin/
    Alias /perl/ "/usr/local/apache/perl/"
    <Directory "/usr/local/apache/perl">
        SetHandler perl-script
        PerlHandler Apache::Registry
        Options ExecCGI
        PerlSendHeader On
    </Directory>
</VirtualHost>

# Staging area's virtual host
<VirtualHost 192.168.6.66>
    DocumentRoot /usr/local/apache/staging/htdocs
```

---

[3] Different versions of code for different phases, that is. If you have multiple production virtual hosts, you'd probably want to share production code among them.

```
    ServerName staging.example.site
    ErrorLog staging/logs/error_log
    CustomLog staging/logs/access_log common
    ScriptAlias /cgi-bin/ /usr/local/apache/staging/cgi-bin/
    Alias /perl/ "/usr/local/apache/staging/perl/"
    <Directory "/usr/local/apache/staging/perl">
        SetHandler perl-script
        PerlHandler Apache::Registry
        Options ExecCGI
        PerlSendHeader On
    </Directory>
</VirtualHost>
```

Since Apache::Registry caches compiled scripts based on path name, having different paths to the scripts takes care of the problem.

It's more complicated for mod_perl applications loaded as modules however. Once the embedded Perl interpreter has loaded a module, it won't load it again for a different virtual host. We can't have a User::Login module in both a staging directory and in a production directory and have mod_perl load both. The Apache::PerlVINC module can handle unloading and reloading modules for different virtual hosts, but that behavior isn't desirable in a production server. We don't want Perl recompiling a module each time it is loaded.

One unsatisfying solution is to preface modules in the staging area with a prefix such as Staging:: so that Perl will load both sets correctly. This is just as balky and error-prone as changing URLs however, and will almost certainly result in a public failure. The only real solution for this problem is to have different servers for staging and production.

Separate servers

While keeping everything running in one set of Apache processes has its appeal, there are good reasons for making the staging and production servers separate:

- If testing the staging area is a part-time operation, the staging server can be shut down when not in use or when the system becomes too busy.

- The production server processes are never weighed down by nonproduction code.

- Resource use of the staging server can be monitored more easily. If you see a memory bloat or an infinite CPU loop, you know it's the new code.

- Persistent code such as mod_perl applications is easier to manage.

- If the server configuration is being tested, starting and stopping a staging server is likely preferred to shutting down the production server.

How do we run two different Apache process trees on one machine? If you have (or can add) multiple IP addresses for your system, it's a simple matter to have your production server listening to one address and your staging server on another.

For example, suppose our system has addresses 192.168.1.1 and 192.168.1.2. We'll use the first address for the production server and the second for the staging server. In the production server's `httpd.conf` we tell Apache to listen to 192.168.1.1:

```
Listen 191.168.1.1
```

Then in the staging server's configuration we give it the second address:

```
Listen 191.168.1.2
```

In both configurations we need to remove any `BindAddress` directives. If a server needs to respond to requests on more than one address, add `Listen` directives as necessary.

By assigning www.example.site to the first address and staging.example.site to the second (in DNS for a network, or the hosts file for a single machine setup) we now have essentially the same situation created with virtual hosts in the previous section. URL paths and other internal details will be the same, so application code doesn't have to be changed to work in one or the other.

If for some reason you can't assign multiple addresses to one machine, you can separate the servers by telling them to listen on different ports. The configuration is almost identical. We'll assume the production server should listen on port 80, the default. We'll assign the staging server to port 8080 like so:

```
Port 8080
```

We can also use `Listen` to assign a port, or even an address and a port together:

```
Listen 8080
Listen 192.168.1.1:8080
```

If you use ports to separate your servers, you'll need to specify the port number in the site part of the URL. For example, if both these servers are running on www.example.site, then the staging server on port 8080 would be http://www.example.site:8080/.

I've assumed the two servers would use two separate configuration files, and that's the simple method I prefer. Call one `staging.conf` and the other `production.conf` (or let it keep the default name if you prefer). When starting Apache, you'll need to tell it which configuration file to use. Do so by running `httpd` directly and using the `-f` switch rather than going through `apachectl`.

```
$ cd /usr/local/apache && bin/httpd -f conf/production.conf
```

or

```
$ cd /usr/local/apache && bin/httpd -f conf/staging.conf
```

Take the sections which are common to both files (which should be most of the text) and move it to a common file, then use the `Include` directive to use it in each. That way you can keep the bulk of your configuration in a file which is kept in whatever source control system you use and is moved out to production with other changes.

If having two configuration files doesn't appeal to you, there's another method: Apache's `IfDefine` directive lets you specify conditional sections and choose between them when starting the server. For example, we could have both the `Listen` directives in one `httpd.conf` file like so:

```
<IfDefine !staging>
    Listen 191.168.1.1
</IfDefine>
<IfDefine staging>
    Listen 191.168.1.2
</IfDefine>
```

Similarly to the C compiler's `#ifdef`, `<IfDefine staging>` applies its directives if we tell Apache that we are starting the staging version, and `<IfDefine !staging>` applies otherwise. That leads us to the `-D` command line switch:

```
$ cd /usr/local/apache && bin/httpd -Dstaging
```

This command will start the server with the staging definitions active. Omitting the switch (or just running `apachectl`) will start it normally.

If you have only a few of these sections in the global area of your configuration file, you might consider taking all of the site-specific directives and moving them to separate files, then including those files via `IfDefine`:

```
<IfDefine !staging>
    Include conf/production.conf
</IfDefine>
<IfDefine staging>
    Include conf/staging.conf
</IfDefine>
```

That will reduce the probability of errors from typos in the parameter name (such as `<IfDefine stagin>`). If compartmentalizing by files results in bad structure for your configuration file, don't do it, and keep an eye out for duplication of sections that are common to both servers.

Regardless of which method you use, remind everyone that configuration changes need to be tested promptly for both servers. At a minimum, check the syntax using Apache's `-t` switch:

```
$ cd /usr/local/apache && bin/httpd -Dstaging -t && bin/httpd -t
```

This performs the same check on the configuration file as `apachectl configtest`, and allows you to pass along other command line switches.

11.2   TOOLS FOR CONTENT MANAGEMENT

With those deployment scenarios in mind, let's consider some actual content-manager tools.

The Open Source project repositories and search sites have quite a large selection of choices in this area, ranging from simple batch upload scripts to graphical remote file managers. Many of these are built on FTP, and thus on its inherent insecurities. If this is a concern for you (as it should be for any site you don't want cracked), the field narrows considerably, but the quality of choices remains high.

Before we get to the Open Source options I'll mention support for the most asked about commercial tool, Microsoft FrontPage. The two tools I'll focus on in this section, rsync and Mason CM, represent opposite ends of the interface spectrum, but both are full-featured tools and in fact can be used together to form a more complete content-management kit. Then in the following section we'll go on to even more possibilities.

11.2.1   FrontPage

If you work with content developers and mention tools for uploading files to your web site, chances are good someone will bring up FrontPage. This popular page-creation and editing tool works with server-side extensions that allow the developer to publish pages, that is, send them to the web server from within the application.

This kind of integration is very convenient. Updating the server isn't much more complicated than saving the file locally. It is actually a little too convenient in that there is no enforcement of rules and no interdependency checking, making it too easy for a content developer to upload one file without sending other required updates. But assuming you can get everyone to agree to good development policies, it's not difficult to add support for FrontPage uploads to your site.

Whether it is advisable is another matter. Both the products I'll mention here come with security warnings, either in their own documentation or reports at other sites. Both require setuid execution or an equivalent wrapper program to give the uploader permission to write to the file system. I haven't been able to investigate either for other vulnerabilities, so as always you should ask around among other developers and check recommendations from current sites.

Ready-to-Run (RTR) software publishes a solution blessed by Microsoft at, http://www.rtr.com/fpsupport/. It's not Open Source at all—you'll need to agree to Microsoft's license to even download a free trial. RTR does offer commercial support, however, with versions for Apache and other servers on many platforms. They also stay current with new releases of FrontPage. The software comes with an installation script and instructions, and the web site's FAQ covers many common installations and issues.

For an Open Source solution, mrs.brisby provides a Perl CGI version at http://www.nimh.org/fpse.shtml. In spite of incomplete code and documentation when it was first published, the script got so many downloads that he set up a mailing list and

FAQ for it. The script also implements the WebDAV protocol, which we'll discuss more in the next section.

There was some discussion of implementing a mod_perl version of the Perl script on the mod_perl mailing list to provide more complete support. Check the list archives at http://perl.apache.org/ for information on whether that went anywhere after this book was published.

11.2.2 rsync

rsync is a remote file comparison and upload tool, available at http://rsync.samba.org by its authors, Andrew Tridgell and Paul Mackerras. It can be used to upload files or whole directory trees to a web site using an efficient, bandwidth-conserving algorithm that is good news to those of us whose development systems are on different networks than their production sites.

rsync is written in C and published under the GPL. It can move files via rcp, scp or its own transfer layer—more on that later in this section. If you have trouble with rsync or simply prefer to tinker with Perl code, fsync is an alternative. It is written entirely in Perl and shares many of rsync's features, although it requires either rcp or scp to transfer files.

I had no trouble installing rsync on three test systems. It's available in source form and in binaries for a variety of platforms; I installed it via RPM on RedHat and Mandrake Linux, and built it on a Windows system via the CygWIN package.

rsync's syntax is familiar to those who have used rcp or scp. If you haven't, get familiar with them now, as it will take only a moment. rcp is a simple file-copying tool that uses the authentication rules of rsh to establish permissions to copy files between systems. As I've preached in previous chapters, rsh (and rcp) are security risks and should be disabled on systems that are exposed to the Internet. That's why you're using ssh instead, and thus scp here.

Suppose we have updated HTML files on a development site, dev.example.site, that we want to copy to a production system, top.example.site, into /tmp/updates. After settling down in the directory with the files to move, the command using scp would be:

```
$ scp *.html user@top.example.site:/tmp/updates/
```

where *user* is the name of the user ID to own the files on the receiving side. If the username is the same on both sites, it isn't required here. ssh will do its usual authentication checks and prompt for a password if needed, and then move the files.

The syntax for specifying the remote site looks like an email address. Any file specification containing a colon is assumed to be remote, with the user and host indicated on the left side of the colon and the file path on the right.

Copying works in either direction. To pull the files back, just switch the order:

```
$ scp user@top.example.site:/tmp/updates/*.html .
```

For that matter, you can move files between two different machines from a third:

```
$ scp user@dev.example.site:cgi-bin/*.pl www@top.example.site:/usr/local/
apache/cgi-bin/
```

Note that this example copies files using a relative path. That path will be relative to the home directory of user@dev.example.site, wherever that may be, and has nothing to do with the directory where the command was typed on the controlling machine.

rsync uses the same syntax, and in fact can use rcp or scp to copy files. To enforce use of scp, set the environment variable RSYNC_RSH to ssh or use the -e or --rsh switch to specify this behavior when needed (if you have a mixed installation, say). rsync adds a great many other switches to control its behavior, but we'll need only a few for these examples.

Rather than operating blindly on files as rcp and scp do, rsync uses its own algorithm to examine files and determine what is out of sync. Ordinarily it ignores files that have the same size and date on the sending and remote system, although that can be turned off. If files appear different by size or date, rsync uses a system of checksums to compare the files without sending the full contents either way, and updates the remote file by section, thus (possibly) sending only a portion of the total file size across the network. rsync's -z switch can be used to compress the transferred bytes and save even more bandwidth.

New files (those present on the sending system but not the remote site) have to be sent in their entirety, of course. You can exclude files from consideration via options that specify pattern matches or through the same mechanism as CVS (the CVS-IGNORE environment variable and any .cvsignore files present in the sending directories). You can also have rsync delete remote files that aren't present on the sending system.

That bandwidth-conserving algorithm makes rsync faster than FTP or other batch file copies when updating sites between networks or over slow links. While a human can do smart transfers too, rsync isn't forgetful or error-prone. After the transfers have finished, you can be completely confident that all the changes are in place. rsync will also set file permissions if you like, so that scripts which are executable on the sending side will be executable on the receiving side and so on. The -a switch tells rsync to match all file attributes and ownership as well, although it can only set the ownership if running as the superuser on the remote side. (That's not a problem if you send the files via the remote account which will own them anyway, as you should.)

Returning to our scenario, suppose we want to move a development system's document tree and CGI directories to a testing phase on the production server. From Apache's root directory, we want to send the htdocs and cgi-bin directories. On the receiving side we want to put the files in /usr/local/apache/test/. The command to do that (assuming we're in the root directory already) is:

```
$ rsync -azC htdocs cgi-bin www@top.example.site:/usr/local/apache/test/
```

The switches (-azC) tell rsync to copy directories recursively and match file modes on the receiving side (-a), compress files in transit (-z), and ignore files that CVS would ignore (-C). rsync will compare the dates and sizes of files in the receiving directory at top.example.site, and will update each file that doesn't match, sending as small of an update as possible. It will also transfer any new files from the development site, unless we exclude them via the --existing switch, but will not delete files from the receiving side. To have rsync do that, we have to add the --delete switch.

If you are running rsync interactively and want to track its progress, add the -v switch to have it output a line for each file transferred. If you are updating one site from multiple sources, you might want to use the -u switch, which tells rsync not to transfer a file if the receiving side has a newer copy. You can also have it create backup copies of each file replaced on the receiving site. The -b switch moves existing files away by adding a ~ suffix (although you can control that too), or to another directory specified via --backup-dir. By specifying backup directories by date, you can use rsync to perform incremental backups of a site, with changes for each day in their own area.

If your system clocks don't match closely, you can help rsync in comparing dates. The --modify-window switch takes a number of seconds and tells rsync that files are the same if their sizes match and their times are less than that many seconds apart. Or you can have it ignore dates and check only sizes via the --size-only switch, or compare every file regardless with -c.

Ordinarily, if the rsync process on the receiving site loses its connection to the sender during a transfer, it deletes the partially sent file in progress. When sending large updates over a dial-up link, you may want to use the --partial switch to tell rsync not to lose the portion you've sent. You can then resume a transfer in place after restoring a broken connection. You can improve rsync's behavior in such cases with two more switches: --temp-dir tells rsync where to store partial files until they've been assembled completely, leaving the existing file in place until the transfer is complete, and --compare-dest indicates a directory to check for files besides the destination directory. By transferring files to a separate directory, you'll avoid errors on the remote system caused by partial files in transit, and you can save the progress in those files using the second switch.

When sending whole directory trees of files, there will inevitably be things you don't need or want to transfer to the remote site. I've mentioned the -C switch in this context, which ignores files as CVS does. See the rsync main page for a list of files ignored by default. The CVS mechanism is highly configurable. rsync will check each directory for a .cvsignore file, and if found, rsync will read it for a list of file patterns and suffixes to ignore in that directory and in its children (unless a child directory has its own file).

If the CVS behavior is overkill or you don't want to mess with extra files, the --exclude switch can be used to provide patterns of files that shouldn't be transferred. Specify it multiple times, once for each pattern. If a file that matches the pattern should be sent anyway, then use `--include` to specify file names or matching patterns that avoid the exclusion rules. If your inclusion and exclusion patterns are complex, you can store them in files and use the `--exclude-from` and `--include-from` switches to tell rsync where to find them. But in that case, consider using the CVS rules instead.

Running an rsync server

rsync uses other programs (rsh or ssh) to run itself on a remote system and copy files. If that isn't convenient for your systems, you can set up rsync in a server mode that allows you to connect without them. rsync in this mode can also work through a web proxy—important for systems protected by firewalls which will almost certainly cut off remote shell execution.

In this mode, rsync can either run all the time (as a web server does) or can start as needed via inetd. The latter mode is more convenient, but of course if you've disabled inetd for other reasons then full-time service is the only option.

For either mode, you'll need to tell rsync (and/or inetd) what port to listen on. The default is port 873; check your `/etc/services` file, and add a line for rsync's port if it isn't already there:

```
rsync   873/tcp  # rsync
```

To run rsync as a full-time server, start it up in your system's boot script (`rc.local` or one of its relatives) with the `--daemon` switch:

```
/usr/bin/rsync --daemon
```

rsync's path may be different on your system. You can specify any default options you want to set on the command, as well as the path to rsync's configuration file via the `--config` switch. The default location is `/etc/rsyncd.conf`.

Starting via inetd is just as simple. Add a line to your configuration (usually `/etc/inetd.conf`) like this:

```
rsync stream tcp nowait root /usr/bin/rsync rsyncd --daemon
```

And here again you can specify other default options and a different path to the configuration file. Remember to send the HUP signal to inetd after changing its configuration.

After setting up either mode, you'll need to tell rsync what directories are available for transfer via *module* definitions in its configuration file. When running as a daemon, rsync honors only paths that begin with a module name, and the module controls how the path is interpreted.

A typical `rsyncd.conf` file might read like so:

```
# PID file for shutting down servers
pid file = /var/log/rsyncd.pid

# Global password file
```

```
secrets file = /etc/rsyncd.secrets

[apache]
    path = /usr/local/apache
    comment = Apache root directory
    auth users = theo, www

[theo]
    path = /home/theo
    comment = Theo's directory
    auth users = theo
```

The syntax of the configuration file will be familiar to SAMBA administrators, which isn't surprising considering rsync's origins among SAMBA developers. The top section contains global options that apply to all modules. Each line containing bracketed text starts a module definition which continues to the beginning of the next module.

In this case, the global options specify the location for the PID and secrets files. The PID file simply holds the process ID of rsync. It is convenient if you want to stop rsync in a controlled manner in a system shutdown script or monitor daemon processes through other means such as WebMIN. The secrets file contains username and password pairs to control access to the modules. Each module can have its own secrets file if you prefer.

The first module definition creates the *apache* module, used to transfer files to and from Apache's root directory. The definition has these parameters:

- `path` sets the root path for the module. All file paths sent to rsync with this module name are interpreted relative to this path. Thus rsync will translate a path such as `apache/htdocs/products.html` from the client to `/usr/local/apache/htdocs/products.html` on the server.

- `comment` sets a one-line description sent back when an rsync client browses the server (by specifying the server name but no module).

- `auth users` limits what users are allowed to browse the module or transfer files. Each user must have a corresponding line in the secrets file.

The second module is similar, allowing access to a developer's home directory, with a stricter limit on users.

Before trying a transfer, make sure that rsync can read the configuration file (which shouldn't be a problem, as rsync will run as root unless you set it up otherwise). You don't need to HUP or restart rsync after changing the configuration file; the daemon process rereads the file each time a client connects. You'll also need to create the PID file if you're using one, and make it writeable. Then create the secrets file with the users specified in each module.

The format of the secrets file is very simple. Each line is a user and password, separated by a colon:

```
www:webwork
```

You can add comments if you wish. Set the secrets file so that root can read and write it, and no other user has access. If the file is readable by anyone else, rsync will refuse to process it.

Once the files are ready and rsync is running (or inetd is listening on its behalf), you can try browsing your server from other machines. To connect via rsync's daemon service instead of the usual rsh or ssh, specify the host name with a double colon instead of a single one as shown in previous examples. This command will browse the modules on the production site:

```
$ rsync top.example.site::
```

rsync will print a list of module names and the comments associated with them. To browse the files and directories in a module, specify the module name with no receiving path on the client:

```
$ rsync top.example.site::apache
```

This time you'll be prompted for a password, matched against the secrets file. rsync will assume the username is the same as the user running the client, unless you specify it in the site name. That is, use www@top.example.site instead to force connection as www. Assuming the user and password check out, rsync will send back a directory listing for the root directory given in the module's path. Use the -r switch to see a recursive listing.

Transferring files works as in previous examples, with appropriate changes to paths. Suppose once again we want to send the document and script directories from a development site to the production machine in a test subdirectory. The new command would be:

```
$ rsync -azC htdocs cgi-bin www@top.example.site::apache/test/
```

Note the double colon in the site name and the new path relative to the module.

If you are going to use rsync in a script, you need a way to specify a password without being prompted each time. You can set the password in the RSYNC_PASSWORD environment variable, or store your password in a file and tell rsync to use that via the --password-file switch.

If the sending system is behind a firewall that cuts off general Internet access, you can still use rsync's server mode by connecting via a web proxy. You'll need to add rsync's port to the proxy's rules so that it will connect to the remote site properly. Then set the RSYNC_PROXY environment variable on the sending side to the hostname and listening port of the proxy.

There are quite a few more options for servers and modules when running an rsync service. See the documentation on the rsyncd.conf config file that comes with the rsync distribution for more information.

We'll discuss more uses for rsync in other sections. Meanwhile, now that we can safely and easily transfer files, we need a way to manage them on our servers.

11.2.3   Mason-CM

While rsync makes it easy to move files across the network, it provides only the clumsiest sort of remote file management. That's okay, however, as there are a number of reasonable web-based file managers available to take over the job.

Chapter 9 presented some file managers you can use for the job, but it's nice to have a tool that does more. Mason-CM is such a tool: its file management is tied into a staging mechanism that allows files to be moved easily from a test area to production, and it also provides extra services to sites that use HTML::Mason components. In addition, it has a CGI-based editor for fixing files on the remote site, Perl test compiling, and spell-checking.

The Mason-CM project was started by Mark Schmick. Michael Alan Dorman and Jaron Rubenstein are continuing the work as of this writing. It is available on Source-Forge at http://mason-cm.sourceforge.net/, or you can follow the link from Mason Headquarters (http://masonhq.com/). It requires mod_perl and HTML::Mason to be installed. You might consider setting up a server just for Mason-CM requests, for reasons we'll get into shortly.

Mason concepts

Let's review how HTML::Mason works before getting into the content manager. Chapter 7 has much more discussion, as well as an example installation.

Mason is a tool for building web pages from components, individual files that can contain Perl code, HTML content, or (generally) both. A Mason top-level component sets up the general structure of a page, with references to subcomponents that yield headers, footers, articles, and the like. When Apache routes a request through Mason, a handler maps the request to a top-level component and the Mason Interpreter processes the special tags that indicate Mason sections and Perl code. Along the way it also invokes and interprets subcomponents and merges the output of each into a finished page.

While Mason provides the tools for all these steps, the actual handler that mod_perl invokes is custom written at each site.[4] The handler loads Perl modules used by itself and components, and initializes the Parser, Interpreter, and Handler objects that will do the bulk of the work. Part of that initialization tells Mason where the component root and data root are, and how to spot a top-level component.

The component root is the path to the directory that holds Mason component files, and is treated by Mason in much the same manner as Apache treats its document root. Absolute paths to components are rooted there, as the name suggests. Relative paths are relative to the current component, and can't reach outside the component root.

---

[4] The handler's author probably starts with one of the examples shipped with the product, as I did for my own session-handling variant.

The data root is the directory where Mason stores its cache of compiled components and other files. Mason gains considerable performance by translating components into Perl functions which are in turn compiled into live code by mod_perl in the Apache server processes. When Mason detects that a component is newer than its cache it recompiles the cache automatically. Mason-CM can help with that, as we'll see shortly.

Setting up Mason-CM

Installing Mason-CM is a simple, but manual, process. Download the distribution and unpack it into your Mason component directory (not the server's document root, as at least one version of the instructions suggests, unless your server serves only Mason documents). Using the example installation from chapter 7, that would be /usr/local/apache/mason; I unpacked the tar file there and renamed the resulting directory mason-cm.

Mason-CM requires HTTP authentication on the application's URL to identify the user and limit access. Here are the directives I added to mod_perl.conf to enable it:

```
PerlRequire /usr/local/apache/lib/perl/mason_handler.pl
Alias /mason/ "/usr/local/apache/mason/"
<Location /mason>
    SetHandler perl-script
    PerlHandler HTML::Mason
    DefaultType text/html
</Location>

# Mason CM authentication
<Location /mason/mason-cm>
    order deny,allow
    deny from all
    allow from 192.168.
    AuthUserFile data/masoncm_users
    AuthName "Content Manager"
    AuthType basic
    require valid-user
</Location>
```

If you have only a few users for Mason-CM, a regular text password file will be fine. Higher intensity sites will want something faster, as discussed in chapter 6.

After adding the new section you'll need to create the password file with htpasswd:

```
/usr/local/apache/bin/htpasswd -c /usr/local/apache/data/masoncm_users user password
```

where *user* and *password* are the ID and password of your first developer.

Configuring Mason-CM's configuration file is the next step. cmConfig is in the top directory of the distribution (mason-cm here in the example). The configuration file is a subcomponent used by the Mason-CM top-level to load in the site specific information. You'll need to set the following variables in the initialization section:

```
my $CM_HOME = '/usr/local/apache/mason/mason-cm';
my $CM_DATA = '/usr/local/apache/mason/mason-cm/data';
```

These identify the directory where Mason-CM resides and where it should store its data respectively. The data directory should be owned by Apache's user. Create and change the ownership if the data directory is not there.

Below those variables the component creates a hash, %cm_config, which contains the bulk of the configuration data. Browse through this and change the obvious items:

- *admin*—This should be a mail address where errors can reach you or a responsible party, not necessarily on this machine.

- *use_cookies*—Can be set to zero if you don't want Mason-CM to store state information in cookies.

- *prod_data_dir*—Change this to the path of the Mason object directory for your production server's components, not Mason-CM. For the example installation the path is /usr/local/apache/data.

- *use_reload_file*—Set this to 1 to speed up Mason in your production server, but we'll discuss that more shortly.

- *ftp_area*—If users are restricted to uploading files to a particular directory, set this item to that path. It doesn't matter if they are or not using FTP.

- Titles and error messages, if you prefer other text.

Then go to the section that begins with branches. This is where you tell Mason-CM what directories it manages. Each branch is really a section of files, unlike the usual meaning of the term in revision management. You could have a branch for your static documents, one for your Mason components, one for image files, and so on. Within a branch you can specify a staging and production directory and other attributes. Each section is managed separately.

The example configuration file calls the sample branches Content and Components which I found a little confusing at first. I named mine HTML and Mason to make it clear that the first section was for plain HTML files and the second was for Mason components.

If you have your branches in mind you can enter them now. The path for each branch is the top level directory for those files. Within that directory it expects two more directories which I suggest calling staging and production. As you would guess, those subdirectories are for the staging mechanism. The files in the first should be visible only to your developers, while the second directory contains the public files for your site.

Branches don't have to be separate. You can have a branch for the top of your directory tree and also have subdirectories listed as branches of their own. Use the configuration that lets you and your developers work most easily.

We'll get back to the branches so don't worry about getting everything right just now. To finish the other configuration tasks, look to the section that begins with get_privs. This is the user security configuration and it bears some explaining.

The get_privs element is a function that receives a branch and path, and returns a hash of privileges for the current user in that directory. The example function is rather simple, and can be used as-is to set the privileges of all users that are in the htpasswd file used to control access to Mason-CM. You can add lines for specific users to allow some to read files but not write them, or you can discard the example function altogether and implement as complex a scheme as you like. If you want to write your own, just invoke it via a shorter function in cmConfig, like so:

```
get_privs => sub { return MyModule::get_privs($user, @_) },
```

where MyModule is a module containing your function, which is loaded by your Mason handler.

The final configuration step is to add the modules Mason-CM needs to your handler. The INSTALL file included in the distribution will give you the current list of requirements. Add them to the block of modules that your handler loads for components to use. The section in my handler ended up like this:

```
{ package HTML::Mason::Commands;
  # Modules and variables that components will use.
  # Include Constants again here to give components
  # its exported values.
  use vars qw($dbh %session);
  use Apache::Constants qw(:common);

  # Modules used by Mason-CM
  use Fcntl;
  use IO::File;
  use MLDBM;
  use Image::Size;
  use URI::Escape;
  use File::PathConvert;
  use File::Copy;
  use File::Find;
  use IO::Handle;
  use IPC::Open2;
}
```

Now that you've configured things, you should be able to restart Apache (if you haven't since adding the Location directive for Mason-CM) and test the interface. Let's get into the meat of Mason-CM by exploring what we can do with branches.

Managing files with Mason-CM

If the configuration steps have gone well, after restarting your server you can start a Mason-CM session. You'll have the usual dialog box for HTTP authentication, then the top-level page. My example installation and setup is shown in figure 11.1.

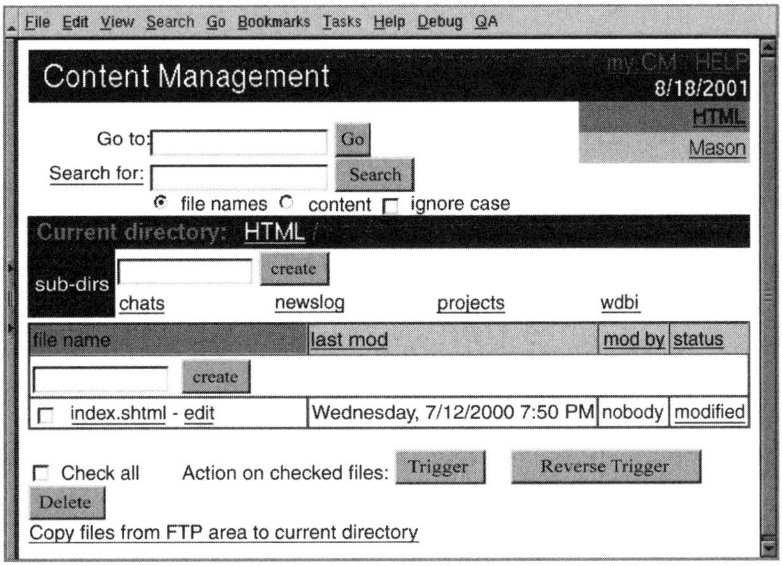

Figure 11.1   The first screen

In the upper-left corner there is a link (via the juggler image, or what ever logo you care to supply for your site) to return to this page from any other Mason-CM page. On the right side there are links for the customization page (my.CM) and the Help. The date is also supplied, for those developers who have been struggling with their site for so long they can't remember what day it is.

Under the standard links in the upper corner there is a list of branches that you configured in the earlier steps. By default the first branch in the list is also displayed on the main page. Mine isn't terribly interesting since I keep everything in the staging and production directories. To see more of what Mason-CM does, browse to a directory by clicking its name. I loaded a set of files from Apache's online documentation into my HTML staging directory (figure 11.2) to play with it.

This is the basic working screen for Mason-CM. The directory's file list is displayed (under a list of links for subdirectories, if any) in a table with data and links for each file. The column headings are themselves links which sort the page by the respective column. To see files by modification date click the header over that column.

The file name is a link that leads to a listing of the file. Next to it is an edit link (if the user's privileges allow writing to the directory) and a version link for displaying revision data (if you've configured RCS to store that data). Try those links in your own site to see how they work. I wouldn't want to use Mason-CM as my primary text editor, but it does the job fine for quick fixes. Figure 11.3 shows a file in the edit page.

The status section at the end of each file line and the check box at the beginning are tied to Mason-CM's method of moving files from staging to production. If a file has been uploaded to the staging area but isn't in the branch production directory, its

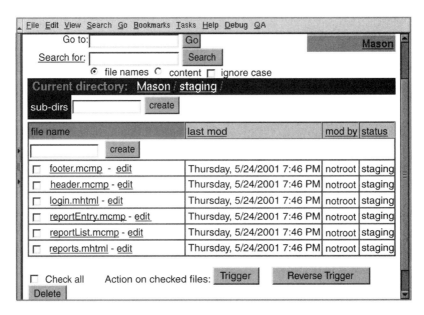

Figure 11.2   Staging directory

status is *staging*. If the file exists in both directories and is the same, the status is *prod*; otherwise the *modified* status indicates a change from staging to production. Sort the listing by the status column to see quickly what files might need to move.

Figure 11.3   A file in the edit page

And how do we move those files? That's where the check boxes in the left column come in. Check off each file that should be transferred from staging to production, then scroll to the end of the page. Click Trigger and the selected files will be copied over, then the directory view page will refresh with updated status values.

While that's very neat, I still think it is safer to transfer all of the files in staging to production at once. For that task there is yet another check box at the bottom of the page for selecting all of the files on the page without browsing through them individually. To perform a mass transfer, check that check box then click the Trigger button.

If you configured an FTP upload directory in cmConfig, there will be a link for it also at the bottom of the page. Follow that link to a browser of files and directories in your upload area. Once you've selected a directory, a dual selection box, shown in figure 11.4, allows you to choose files to copy from the upload to your previously selected branch and directory.

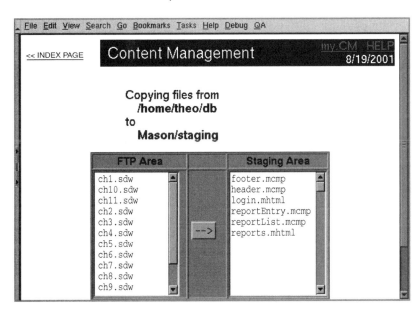

Figure 11.4   Upload area selection box

Remember that you don't have to use FTP to get files to this directory; scp or rsync will work just fine. Also, with a bit of trickery in cmConfig you could have Mason-CM display a different upload directory for each user:

```
ftp_area => "/home/$user/upload",
```

That quick walk-through shows the features Mason-CM brings as a visual file manager for a web site, but there is a lot more to see. Return to the listing of your staging area and choose the edit link for a file. Mason-CM displays the file in a text box along with buttons for changing the file's name or copying it to another file. (You can delete and create files from the directory listing.) If you've configured in spell checking you can have Mason-CM verify the file—it will automatically strip out the HTML tags before sending the buffer to your program of choice (as long as your program of choice works as `ispell` does), then use a JavaScript program to display words that aren't in the dictionary.

Make a change to your file and click the Save & Exit button to return to the directory listing. The file will be highlighted and selected automatically, so if you haven't copied it to production yet you can do so just by clicking the Trigger button at the bottom of the page.

Things are little more interesting if you change a file whose status is *prod*, that is, already exists in the production directory. Trigger a few files if you haven't already, then edit one of those (from the staging index page, remember) and save a change. The status is now *modified*, and you'll notice also that the status value is a link—it will take you to a page listing the differences between the staging and production versions. Figure 11.5 shows the differences between a staging file and a production file.

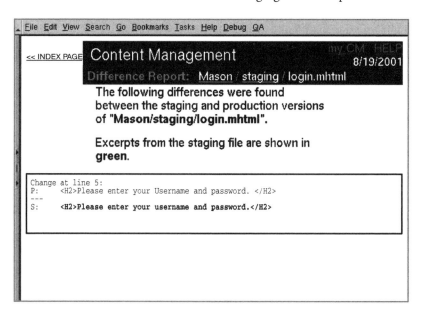

Figure 11.5   Staging and production file differences

When you start to edit a file, Mason-CM reserves that file for you to prevent simultaneous edits by other users. If you cancel or save your changes the reservation is released. Otherwise the reservation is held and noted in the list of reserved files at the top of the directory listing. You can release your locks via the links on that page. A user configured with admin privileges for the directory can release any locks.

If you need to copy a file back from production, that's a "Reverse Trigger" in Mason-CM terms. Deleted files can also be retrieved from the trash if you configured one in `cmConfig`.

Mason-CM provides a pair of entry fields at the top of each directory listing. The top field is for quick navigation if you know the path to the directory or file you wish to see. It's very convenient for cutting and pasting your way to files. The second entry box is the search field, which allows you to look for files by matching name or content. Enter a word and click the search button to see a list of matching files. While it doesn't advertise it much, you can enter a regular expression pattern as well; enter `[Aa]pache` to find instances of "Apache" and "apache".

Managing Mason components

While you can use Mason-CM on a site that doesn't otherwise use Mason, there are some special features to consider in managing a site with Mason components.

Looking back at the branch definitions in `cmConfig`, there is a branch attribute that activates these features, helpfully called `components`. Here's the definition of my Mason branch:

```
Mason => {    path => '/usr/local/apache/mason',
           trg_from => 'staging', trg_to => 'production',
        components => 1,
          obj_dir => '/usr/local/apache/data/obj' },
```

I copied the Mason examples from chapter 7 into the staging directory of this branch to serve as tests for the special component features.

When working with a component branch, Mason-CM precompiles each file as you save or trigger it. If you are changing the file via the editor, Mason-CM will show you syntax errors immediately when you save a file with problems. For example, I edited `login.mhtml` and put in a bad argument in the `<%args>` section. When I saved it, Mason-CM brought up the error page that is shown in figure 11.6:

You can force Mason-CM to accept the file as-is by clicking the Check button to ignore errors. This allows one developer to pass the duty of fixing an error to another, for instance.

The same error checks apply when you trigger files to production. If any triggered files fail the test, Mason-CM brings up a list of problem components with links that will allow you to edit each one and fix the problems. If the file isn't a component (or has problems that you know won't affect production use) you can force the triggering operation to complete with the current state.

In chapter 7 I mentioned a performance enhancement for Mason's component cache. As Mason processes components it compiles them into Perl functions and caches the code in the configured object directory. Since Mason can be running in a number of Apache child processes, each one needs to check the cache for each

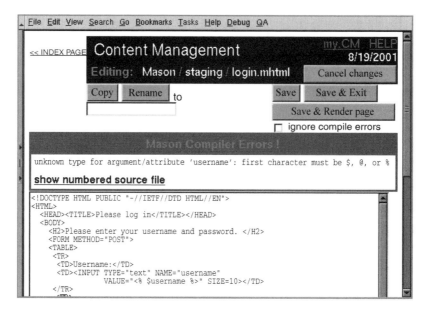

Figure 11.6   Compilation errors in login.mthml

component to know if its internal code is up to date. This results in a directory lookup and `stat` call for each component of a request.

The fix is to enable the reload file feature in your Mason handler: a flag that tells the interpreter not to check the individual component files for changes, but rather to look in a single file that contains a line for each component that needs to be reloaded. Thus only the reload file is checked for each request.

Mason-CM takes over the chore of maintaining that file for you. Enable it in `cmConfig` like so:

```
        prod_data_dir => '/usr/local/apache/data',
        use_reload_file => 1,
```

where prod_data_dir points to the same data directory as given to the interpreter object in your handler:

```
# Set up Mason interpreter.
my $interp = HTML::Mason::Interp->new
  ('parser' => HTML::Mason::Parser->new,
   'comp_root' => '/usr/local/apache/mason',
   'data_dir' => '/usr/local/apache/data',
   'use_reload_file' => 1,
  );
```

With those changes in place, Mason-CM will inform the Mason interpreters of changed files automatically.

11.2.4   WebDAV

Content management is ultimately about shipping files to web servers and managing them in place. During all this discussion it may have occurred to you to ask if the web server couldn't do this itself.

We view the Web in terms of serving documents to browsers, but according to many sources, the original vision of the Web was a distributed authoring system in which a server's business included accepting and managing files from (appropriately identified and privileged) users as well. That vision has been restored in WebDAV. The following is from the project's home page at http://webdav.org/:

> What is WebDAV?
> Briefly: WebDAV stands for "Web-based Distributed Authoring and Versioning". It is a set of   extensions to the HTTP protocol which allows users to collaboratively edit and manage files on remote web servers.

A brief look at the site shows that WebDAV goes far beyond simple file transfer issues. This is the basis of considerably more, a distributed file system that includes locking facilities and extensive document attributes. Locks are long-term entities that allow an author to reserve access to given files, preventing overlapping updates as a basic function and maintaining privileges in the longer run. Document attributes are stored and retrieved as XML, allowing arbitrary information to be associated with files—lists of authors, history information, and so on. The WebDAV protocol suite includes methods to search for files via matching metadata and other criteria.

In the present time frame, however, WebDAV is mostly about file management via HTTP, replacing FTP, scp, rsync, and other file-transfer systems. There are advantages to building this kind of thing into the web server:

- WebDAV uses SSL for secure transfers if you have one of the Apache SSL modules built in.

- Users and passwords are defined via htpasswd (or a compatible authentication scheme) and validated via HTTP authentication. That means they don't require shell accounts on the server machine, and thus can't be used to crack the system via telnet, FTP, or ssh exploits.

- By replacing other services, the system has fewer open ports and thus fewer security holes.

The main disadvantage is that WebDAV is built into the web server. Any security holes mean the server itself is breached. It also adds its weight to the memory footprint of each Apache child process. The simple answer to both those objections is to run a separate Apache just for WebDAV use, thus allowing stricter configuration controls on the management server and keeping its code out of the busy production server. That spoils the simplicity offered by the initial view of WebDAV somewhat, but it is a perfectly reasonable solution. Configuring an extra Apache server isn't necessarily any more trouble than configuring other content management tools, and if access can be limited to a protected network (nodes behind your firewall or in your VPN) then SSL isn't necessary and other security concerns largely vanish.

Building WebDAV into Apache is as simple as any other add-on module: mod_dav has been available from the WebDAV site since mid-2000, and configures and builds similarly to mod_ssl. There are source distributions at the site as well as binary add-ons for Windows versions. The Apache Group has also announced that WebDAV protocols will be incorporated into the core distribution of Apache 2.0, which will make this even easier.

WebDAV has spawned some new tools and is being built into many existing products, both commercial and Open Source. The strong momentum shown here indicates that WebDAV is very likely to be in your content-management future, and possibly your present as well.

If your site developers use a commercial product with WebDAV support, you should consider adopting it now. Nothing beats a familiar tool that integrates into the server you already have. The Open Source products I looked at were all at early stages when I took my first look at WebDAV, and they haven't matured enough as of the time of writing for me to recommend them. Things are moving quickly though, so check the web site for more news as these products get up to speed.

I think the final decision on using WebDAV or a separate transfer/management mechanism depends on criteria we discussed earlier in the chapter. If you have a large content-development group which includes people who need to send updates regularly to the server but who should not have access to a shell, then WebDAV ought to appeal strongly to you. WebDAV can be configured to limit users to exactly what you want them to be able to do, and it offers a variety of features that will help your users manage content on their own (as those features are incorporated into their tools).

On the other hand, a smaller group will probably find WebDAV to overlap other services they need. If your developers also have administrative duties (that is, they have to have a shell account anyway) then giving them an extra password encourages bad practices (or bad passwords). They'll still need other file-copying services to handle their tasks. Chances are the whole group will need access to all the files, so there won't be any advantage to WebDAV's additional privilege layers. If that sounds like you, then keep using the tools you prefer. But keep an eye on newer tools anyway. It seems likely that as WebDAV client services are built into more software, it will also get configured into more sites.

So what are those new WebDAV tools? Here are a few that work closely with the new services.

sitecopy and cadaver are two programs that could replace rsync in my list of recommended content management products. sitecopy can use WebDAV or FTP to transfer files, so you can consider it for use on protected networks even if you aren't a fan of WebDAV. Both have good comparison features for deciding what needs to be uploaded to the remote site, and use the move and copy capabilities of WebDAV to manage files on the remote site. cadaver also lets you read files on the remote site without going to a browser.[5] sitecopy has a twin product, xsitecopy, which adds a graphical front-end that makes it easier to configure the local and remote directories of a site.

The PerlDAV project is part of WebDAV, and provides administrators with the HTTP::DAV module to handle file transfer and remote management from scripts. This project is at an early stage, but the close relationship of the product to the main WebDAV effort makes it promising. WebDAV functionality will find its way into other Perl tools quickly as the module matures. Compiled programs can use the neon library, which offers a high-level API.

Rumors and tidbits of WebDAV abound in other projects. One of the most interesting is the fact that the GNOME project's file system abstraction, gnome-vfs, does or will include a handler for WebDAV so that a remote site can be managed through the Nautilus file manager (among others). Keep an eye on WebDAV's home page for developments.

11.3 MANAGING A PRODUCTION SITE

Now that we've seen some good tools, let's put them to work in a sample configuration.

We'll cover the directory layout for a machine that hosts the staging and production phases. Development lives elsewhere, possibly on individual workstations. The configuration of a pair of Apache servers comes next, followed by the role of content-management tools.

As you work through this section, remember that content management has to be flexible in order to meet users' needs—and in this case, the users are your developers, creative people who are possibly under a lot of pressure to make the site work. I've talked about enforcing rules and laying out guidelines, but in reality, people will do what works, and different things work for different people. Where there are multiple tools and methods, consider implementing and offering them all. Find out what your users like and then make the rules work the way they do.

Draw the line at security holes and system sanity; protect sensitive data and customer privacy. For anything else, let the users have their way if at all possible, so that content management is a tool for them instead of a restriction to get around.

11.3.1 Configuration

It's time to put together that production system. If you already have a system in place, perhaps this section will give you ideas on how to migrate to an environment that is better for content management.

---

[5] It might be worth it just so you can drop lines like "we use cadaver for remote viewing."

Our system will run two instances of Apache: one for staging and one for production. The development stage exists virtually on various workstations as described elsewhere. The staging and production web servers will share Apache binaries and static files. Each has its own subdirectory of the Apache root, like so:

```
/usr/local/apache
    conf
    logs
    data
    lib/perl
    staging
    production
```

The `conf` directory has both shared and phase-specific configuration files (if any); since we have to arbitrate ports and addresses here, we can't move the staging configuration to production. Within the server directories (staging and production) we have the files that are maintained by content management:

```
staging
    cgi-bin
    data
    htdocs
    lib/perl
    mason
    perl
```

The `htdocs` directory contains static documents, while `cgi-bin`, `perl`, and `lib` contain applications. These files should represent the whole site content, so that we can update the site by copying the entire contents of the staging directory tree to production. The `mason` and `data` directories are for Mason components and cache files. If you use only Mason-CM, then only staging will need them.

The configuration in `httpd.conf` is largely standard, with a few phase-specific sections. At the beginning of the global environment setup I added these directives:

```
<IfDefine !staging>
  SetEnv PhaseRoot /usr/local/apache/production
</IfDefine>
<IfDefine staging>
  SetEnv PhaseRoot /usr/local/apache/staging
</IfDefine>
```

The `PhaseRoot` environment variable can be read by CGI scripts and other applications that need to keep different data by phases. The other sections manage the directories and files that need to be different for separate servers:

```
<IfDefine !staging>
  PidFile /usr/local/apache/logs/httpd.pid
</IfDefine>
<IfDefine staging>
  PidFile /usr/local/apache/logs/staging.pid
```

```
</IfDefine>

...

<IfDefine !staging>
  Port 80
</IfDefine>
<IfDefine staging>
  Port 8080
</IfDefine>
```

Note the use of ports to separate the servers. Insert `Listen` directives here to sort them out by address if you prefer. If you do use the port method, you should block access to the port from outside your network.

```
<IfDefine !staging>
  DocumentRoot "/usr/local/apache/production/htdocs"
</IfDefine>
<IfDefine staging>
  DocumentRoot "/usr/local/apache/staging/htdocs"
</IfDefine>

...

<IfDefine !staging>
  ErrorLog /usr/local/apache/logs/production_error_log
</IfDefine>
<IfDefine staging>
  ErrorLog /usr/local/apache/logs/staging_error_log
</IfDefine>

...

<IfDefine !staging>
  CustomLog /usr/local/apache/logs/production_access_log common
</IfDefine>
<IfDefine staging>
  CustomLog /usr/local/apache/logs/staging_access_log common
</IfDefine>

...

<IfDefine !staging>
  ScriptAlias /cgi-bin/ "/usr/local/apache/production/cgi-bin/"
</IfDefine>
<IfDefine staging>
  ScriptAlias /cgi-bin/ "/usr/local/apache/staging/cgi-bin/"
</IfDefine>
```

Most of the configuration remains global. We can handle permissions in both servers' document roots with one `<Directory>` block, with the help of a wildcard in the path:

```
<Directory "/usr/local/apache/*/htdocs">
    Options Includes Indexes FollowSymLinks MultiViews
```

```
        AllowOverride None
        Order allow,deny
        Allow from all
</Directory>
```

And the same treatment takes care of the CGI directory:

```
<Directory "/usr/local/apache/*/cgi-bin">
        AllowOverride None
        Options FollowSymLinks
        Order allow,deny
        Allow from all
</Directory>
```

That's enough to get both servers running and to test with static documents and scripts. Apache::Registry scripts need a similar treatment in mod_perl.conf:

```
<IfDefine !staging>
  Alias /perl/ "/usr/local/apache/production/perl/"
</IfDefine>
<IfDefine staging>
  Alias /perl/ "/usr/local/apache/staging/perl/"
</IfDefine>
<Directory "/usr/local/apache/*/perl">
    SetHandler perl-script
    PerlHandler Apache::Registry
    Options ExecCGI
    PerlSendHeader On
</Directory>
```

Handlers and other applications are a little more complicated. We want mod_perl to load modules from the phase-specific lib/perl directory in preference to any other location, so our staged code can move cleanly from one phase to the next. A short <Perl> section accomplishes that:

```
<IfDefine !staging>
  <Perl>
    use lib '/usr/local/apache/production/lib/perl'
  </Perl>
</IfDefine>
<IfDefine staging>
  <Perl>
    use lib '/usr/local/apache/staging/lib/perl'
  </Perl>
</IfDefine>
```

Now PerlModule and other directives will behave as we like, finding the module in the phase library directory. Just as importantly, any Perl use statements in those modules will look in the right place first. Third-party mod_perl code can still live in /usr/local/apache/lib/perl; that directory remains in the search path for modules. Our configuration change affects only items that should be under content management.

Any handlers we load by path have to be managed for each phase, such as this section for loading the Mason handler:

```
<IfDefine !staging>
  PerlRequire /usr/local/apache/production/lib/perl/mason_handler.pl
  Alias /mason/ "/usr/local/apache/production/mason/"
</IfDefine>
<IfDefine staging>
  PerlRequire /usr/local/apache/staging/lib/perl/mason_handler.pl
  Alias /mason/ "/usr/local/apache/staging/mason/"
</IfDefine>
```

And the directory paths inside the handler need to be changed too, of course, so that Mason caches components independently by phase. Since the handler is under content management control, we don't want to hard code a path there. Here's a trick that figures out the directory using Perl's special __FILE__ constant:

```
my $dir = $1 if __FILE__ =~ /^(.*)\/lib\/perl\/mason_handler\.pl/;
die "Can't initialize Mason directory path" unless $dir;
my $interp = HTML::Mason::Interp->new
  ('parser' => HTML::Mason::Parser->new,
   'comp_root' => "$dir/mason",
   'data_dir'  => "$dir/data",
  );
```

Perl translates __FILE__ to the path of the currently parsing file during compilation. The pattern match extracts the leading directory from the part that will remain constant to determine what phase it is in, and passes that path along to the initialization of the Mason interpreter.

The server is configured, and the structure is in place for content management. Now to deploy the tools discussed earlier.

11.3.2   Development to staging

We haven't discussed the development phase much in the configuration discussion. A typical scenario has each developer on his own workstation, with an Apache server set up more or less like the original single-server machine the rest of the book has used. Alternatively, each could have his own subdirectory of a shared server although that makes mod_perl much harder to use.

Developers can use rsync to load files to the staging area. Remember that we want Apache's user (www in this case) to own the files on the receiving server. To send over the directories with CGI applications and associated documents, the developer would move to his Apache root directory and fire up the transfer:

```
$ rsync -azC cgi-bin htdocs www@top.example.site:/usr/local/apache/staging/
```

This works fine if there is only one developer. With multiple people working on the site, chances are good that someone will overwrite a file uploaded by another developer. It's wise to first find out what rsync thinks needs transferring:

```
$ rsync --dry-run cgi-bin htdocs www@top.example.site:/usr/local/apache/
staging/
```

Alternatively the -u switch will tell rsync to skip files that are newer on the receiving side than the sender. That might work if your clocks are all in sync, but I'd probably throw in the -b switch to make backup copies also.

CVS check-in

When you have multiple developers, you should also have a code repository.[6] CVS dominates the scene, but plenty of sites still use RCS directly or other packages. CVS is available for most development platforms, including clients for proprietary desktops. Learn more about CVS at the product home page, http://www.cvshome.org/.

If your group uses CVS, then uploads should always be from the repository. Developers check in their code, then use cvs export to extract the files to a directory (or tree). The exported files are then transferred to the staging area.

More adventurous project administrators can use CVS check-in hooks to transfer files to the staging area as developers return them to the repository.

Once the staging area is set up, thorough testing can begin. If everything passes, we can move to the next phase (literally).

11.3.3   Staging to production

When the files in the staging area have been approved, the whole set moves to production. Resist all temptation to move individual files or directories—things that were tested together move together.

The fastest way to do this is to rename directories. Move the old production directory to another name, rename staging to production, and everything will be in place. I recommend giving Apache a fresh start if you have mod_perl applications. If you use Mason, the running servers will pick up the changes as they process requests, so you can leave them alone if restarting is unwise.[7]

If moving the directories is problematic, you can use rsync to copy all the changed files between phases. You don't even need to be on the server to do this, as I showed in a previous example with scp:

```
$ rsync www@top.example.site:/usr/local/apache/staging/* \
        www@top.example.site:/usr/local/apache/production
```

This is also a good role for Mason-CM. The example configuration earlier in the chapter was set up for this task. You can make each subdirectory of staging and production a branch (and thus take advantage of the special features for your Mason components, if any) or treat each phase as a branch for simpler triggering.

---

[6] If you are a solo developer, you should also have a code repository. I used one for examples while writing this book.

[7] If you use a reload file, you'll have to trigger the changes there of course.

If you are using Mason-CM, remember that you don't have to configure it for both servers; setting it up just in the staging server is sufficient. Modify your mod_perl configuration like so:

```
<IfDefine staging>
  Alias /mason-cm/ "/usr/local/apache/staging/mason/mason-cm/"
  <Location /mason/mason-cm>
    order deny,allow
    deny from all
    allow from 192.168.
    AuthUserFile data/masoncm_users
    AuthName "Content Manager"
    AuthType basic
    require valid-user
  </Location>
</IfDefine>
```

Since I use Mason for other files in the staging phase, I've placed Mason-CM there too. If you are using Mason only for content management then it should live separately from the phase directories. We won't copy Mason-CM files to production however.

Now we set up cmConfig in staging/mason/mason-cm:

```
my $CM_HOME = '/usr/local/apache/staging/mason/mason-cm';
my $CM_DATA = '/usr/local/apache/staging/mason/data';
...

                    All => {    path => '/usr/local/apache/',
                            trg_from => 'staging',
                              trg_to => 'production',
                          components => 0 },
                    CGI => {    path => '/usr/local/apache/staging/cgi-bin',
                            trg_from => '/',
                              trg_to => '../../production/cgi-bin',
                          components => 0 },
                   HTML => {    path => '/usr/local/apache/staging/htdocs',
                            trg_from => '/',
                              trg_to => '../../production/htdocs',
                          components => 0 },
                  Mason => {    path => '/usr/local/apache/staging/mason/',
                            trg_from => '/',
                              trg_to => '../../production/mason',
                          components => 1,
                             obj_dir => '/usr/local/apache/data/obj' },
               Mod_perl => {    path => '/usr/local/apache/staging/lib/perl',
                            trg_from => '/',
                              trg_to => '../../production/lib/perl',
                          components => 0 },
                   Perl => {    path => '/usr/local/apache/staging/perl',
                            trg_from => '/',
                              trg_to => '../../production/perl',
                          components => 0 },
```

This is more complicated than it seems because of the structure of a Mason-CM branch. If we had separate production and staging directories for each subdirectory (instead of the other way around) then it would match Mason-CM's expectations. As it is, our sample configuration is good for mass copies via rsync, not so simple for Mason-CM.

If you are using Mason in production, you can enable the reload file features for greater performance. Be sure to tell Mason-CM about it too:

```
prod_data_dir => '/usr/local/apache/production/data',
use_reload_file => 1,
```

You should now be able to browse and trigger files from your staging server.

11.4 BACKUP AND RECOVERY

Systems need to be built with maintenance in mind. If you are a hardware failure survivor, you know this lesson already, and perhaps you've already taken steps indicated in this section. If you haven't formulated a recovery plan, start on it now, even if your site is in early development stages. You'd hate to waste your time with a messy system cleanup (or worse, recreating lost configurations and code) at any point in your development.

While this section is mostly concerned about the production system, you need backups and recovery plans for all of your machines. In the case of development workstations, a daily backup of the code repository is a good first step. The techniques discussed next for remote backup of a server can also be used for development systems. Perhaps you need only to archive developer's home directories (or wherever daily work is performed) on a regular basis.

Here's an inexpensive recovery plan for developer workstations, where each developer has his own web server and other resources:

1 Replace failed hardware, if any.

2 Reinstall the operating system.

3 Create the user account and apply user-level backups.

4 Copy a working version of development resources (database, web server, applications) from another development system.

5 Let the users perform other configuration tasks personally (just as they did when they first started to work at the machine).

While this plan may get you grumbled at by people who want the computer equivalent of a magic resurrection spell, it is easy on the administrator and doesn't tie up a lot of media (tapes, duplicate disks, or what have you) in perfect copies. It works fine for my own business.

If your production site is busy enough, chances are you will move it to a hosting service which provides backup and recovery, unless you already have. That's a great idea, but review the plans carefully, with an eye toward issues I raise in the following sections. Physical copies may not be sufficient, and data security may call for other measures.

11.4.1 Backup

Somewhere in your collection of machines and hardware, you need devices and media for archiving files. This can be a tape drive on the production machine, duplicate disks elsewhere in the network, or combinations and multiples of these.

If you are buying a hefty server system from a vendor, chances are you're getting backup capabilities built-in. When building your own system, don't leave out a cheap way of archiving files. In either case, consider the points in this section for both price and manageability.

Media

While backups bring tapes (or other removable media) to mind, that's not the only way, nor is it advisable to depend solely on tapes as we'll discuss.

Tape backups should be used for long-term storage (where long-term may mean a month or so) and for data that is not critical to your recovery plan such as user directories. It's good to have a complete backup in a separate location, but that can be accomplished via remote backups instead of the old method of carting tapes around.

Critical backups should stay on duplicate disks if at all possible. Use a remote backup technique to copy archives to a separate system. When disaster strikes, you'll appreciate the fast access and quick searching this method affords. If a business partner or other party demands backup to removable media, then make those physical copies at the remote site.

Automation

A backup plan has to be automated to work. If your system requires many manual steps, then someone will skip a step the night before a key component catches fire.

Any backup to removable media requires an operator to change that media regularly. That's an acceptable level of manual intervention. Just make sure that the operator has a backup too, so someone handles the task on sick days. If possible, have your procedure detect if the media has changed and report an error when it doesn't.

Backing up to duplicate disks has the advantage here as it can run unattended. Your procedure needs to know when to delete old archives as new ones demand room.

Remote or local

Proximity generally means faster recovery, but of course a backup that is close to the server is vulnerable to site catastrophes. Removable media for local backups can be moved to another site for safekeeping, introducing more management hassles in the process.

Remote backup involves using rsync, scp, or other tools to send an archive over a network link to another system. This is the method I prefer in almost all cases, if recovery time is acceptable. Once you've sent the archive to the remote machine, you can perform an additional backup to removable media if necessary.

A favorite trick among ssh fans is to use ssh to run tar on a remote machine and pipe the output back through the secure channel to a local file. Your ssh man pages should have documentation (or at least similar examples). rsync does this for you in a recursive directory copy.

Capacity

Capacity planning for your server must also include backup capacity. If you are using removable media, buy a system that allows a full recovery from one tape if at all possible, and make that backup every day, recycling tapes after a month or so. You don't want to have to cycle through several tapes in an emergency recovery.

Remote systems need the same capacity, but not all of it has to be online at once. Spool older backups to removable media. Bandwidth is a more important concern here: you don't want backup traffic to interfere with a high-volume site. Once you have a procedure in place, check that the network usage plus the user traffic are within acceptable levels. rsync has an option (`--bwlimit`) for limiting bandwidth usage, making it more useful on busy links.

Recovery time

How long will it take to restore a full backup after a system failure? Compare the cost of downtime to the cost of a better backup system. You may be saving money in the wrong place.

Local media recovers faster than remote backups, assuming the disaster didn't also take out the local media. One good solution is to have the same hardware for removable media at a local and remote site. Perform remote backups and spool them to tape, then carry the tape to the production system for faster recovery when needed.

Is a copy enough?

Copying files is fine for program binaries and configuration files, but that may not work reliably for relational databases, DBM files, and other high-level storage systems. Some products require the database to be at a safe point before copying files. In other cases you might need the base files plus a transaction log or other journal system to recover the data.

As you evaluate tools for use in your system, check into their backup requirements. Make sure your procedure for a full backup handles all of these (or you won't have a full backup).

Security

This is one point that is often overlooked in backup planning. If your site hosts sensitive data, you know you have to protect it from general public snooping, but what about your backups?

If you are using a remote backup system, it needs to run over a secure channel. Once received, the files need the same protection on the remote site as they had on the production system.

Backups to physical media need physical security. This can be very hard to implement at a site with a large operations staff. One option is to encrypt files en route to the media, so that a pass phrase or other key is required to restore the backup.

11.4.2   Recovery

Recovery planning is (in my experience) more difficult than backup planning, as it involves more high-level business decisions. If your site is an e-commerce business, you may have the funding for a full site backup. News and community sites are more likely to make server-swapping deals or other accommodations.

A recovery plan should consider the worst (total site loss) and proceed from there, marking clear stages along the way. In the far more likely event of a disk, memory, or network failure, you need only to start the plan from the failure point and follow along to a working system.

Hardware recovery

Sites that absolutely depend on up-time for survival will need solutions (live fail-over and other technologies that keep a system running when individual pieces aren't) beyond the scope of this chapter. See the next chapter on web farms and load-balancing services to learn how to accomplish this.

For purposes of discussion, we'll assume a single server is running the site. Budget allowing, have a duplicate (or at least comparable) machine available to stand in the place of a failed server. A ready system in working order is far better than an array of spare parts. I value the working system at ten times the cost of parts during an emergency recovery.

Whether you have a system standing by or just a set of replacements for key components, make sure that everything is compatible—same manufacturer, model, drivers and so on—so that you aren't taken by surprise at a bad moment.

Backup sites

If your budget doesn't allow for duplicate hardware, perhaps you can move your site to another location when trouble strikes, then come home again when you are ready. This is a good option for community and news sites. Chances are you can make a deal with someone else in your community to share servers during failures. Exchange backups with each other regularly, thus achieving two goals in one.

Commercial sites that host their own systems should have an option to move to a network-provider site when necessary. You can use remote backup procedures to maintain a panic-ready system, to establish a procedure in advance for borrowing hardware and connections.

Rebuilding the system

Once you have hardware to work with, you need to know how to recreate your working server.

Again, if budget allows, the best way to do this is to keep a working version of the system elsewhere. As you install software, upgrade the operating system and so on, keeping your backup machine in sync.

The next step down from there is a working machine with the correct OS and products already installed. Take your backup and apply it to the system. If your backup really is comprehensive then you are back in business.

If that isn't viable, then you need either a good upgrade log or a very good memory, along with OS media and backup copies of the product distributions. The problem here is that it is far too easy to miss a step, forget something crucial, and end up wasting hour or days in frustration over software that you know worked on another system. The potential cost of this time should have you rethinking your budget for a backup server.

Returning to work

The final steps of the process are the same as getting the server online in the first place. Your recovery plan should document what those steps were so you can recreate them quickly. Once the system is secured, connect it to your network. Tell your router about it, adjusting DNS accordingly if necessary. Start the web server and other network services, then monitor closely.

Don't be shocked if you've forgotten something. Your recovery plan should include the phrase "Don't Panic" at regular intervals.

The best way to avoid panic in an emergency recovery is to have a plan and practice it. That takes us to the final section.

11.4.3   Test and verify!

You test your software, your network, your database. But, do you test your operational procedures?

If your answer is not a firm yes then chances are very good that your next emergency will be a major one. No matter how proud you are of your backup procedures and your stand-by systems, you don't really know that things will work until you try them.

Test your recovery plan at least once during development, and then again before your site goes live. Verify the following points:

- You have (or can quickly get) a machine with the right OS, sufficient disk space, and correct product versions handy.
- You can load your backup onto that system. Do you have duplicate drives for removable media?
- Once you've loaded the backup, the products work correctly. Carefully verify your database here, as well as any user authentication systems.
- The resulting system boots correctly and is accessible to the network. Applications run correctly.
- The system reboots without manual intervention. If disaster strikes once, it may come by again soon.

You have your system running, with good tools for managing growth and a plan to handle any mishaps that come your way. Congratulations, your system is under control!

Or is it? This discussion has completely ignored performance issues that are likely to come up as your site grows—because that is next chapter's topic.

Performance Management

Whether your site is a community information source or a store front, chances are good your traffic will rise dramatically in the first year or so in business, then at a slower but steady rate after that. You'll be adding features as you determine what your users want, and those users will be sending more viewers your way. Search engines will publish your location, getting you more hits. Simple web demographics come into play also as the number of potential visitors increases with each month.

While no one can guarantee the success of a web site, anecdotal evidence among developers indicates a one year rule: if your site survives its first year of business it will outgrow bandwidth, hardware, or both. That's not a bad plan—why pay for expensive resources until your business is proven? But it does mean you need to budget for the fruits of your success.

A large part of performance management is monitoring and analyzing—knowing when you are approaching a problem point, and what that problem is. You should begin this analysis before your site starts accepting public traffic, and make performance reviews part of your maintenance regimen.

When you see a problem developing, the traditional solution is to buy hardware. This is often the right solution, but always bear in mind that it doesn't scale well. Adding memory is fine until you reach the capacity of your system, and getting a faster CPU becomes expensive when you cross the price/performance boundary.

Knowing your software and how it consumes resources helps you to put off the limits of hardware solutions. Web applications can eat up memory at a fierce rate, especially when Perl is involved. You may find a cheap solution in reducing the number of processes while increasing the number of requests they handle, a seeming paradox that we'll explore in a few different ways.

If your software is well behaved and hardware upgrades are no longer affordable, you have little choice but to move from a simple configuration to a web farm of several specialized machines. This step is a complicated one, requiring more analysis and planning than a CPU or memory upgrade, making it particularly important that you know when the time is approaching.

12.1 VICTIMS OF SUCCESS

Performance management is all about properly assigning system resources, but just what resources does a system have? In chapter 2 I mentioned the basics: CPU, memory, network bandwidth, and storage bandwidth.

When most of us think of monitoring a system, CPU utilization is what first comes to mind, possibly with visions of graphical system monitors pegged out when a favorite application is running. If your CPU is saturated, starting a shell or a new command may be sluggish. Web applications and background processes will take longer to complete, and thus will hold on to other resources.

CPU saturation is easy to spot. `top`[1] or almost any other monitoring program examine CPU resources by default. The obvious cure is to upgrade the processor, but a little analysis may save you an expensive chip:

- Is a single process always hogging the machine? If the system is otherwise satisfactory, consider a move to multiple processors instead of multiple machines. You can effectively give the culprit its own CPU and save on other resources and administration.

- Are there application issues—sections of code that swamp the CPU for long enough to peg your monitor? Perhaps those can be rewritten to use another mechanism (or another language). If those applications are generating dynamic content, consider caching the results. That might be less dynamic, but possibly more affordable and better for viewers who are waiting patiently for a page.

---

[1] `Top` is a program that will give continual reports about the state of the system, including a list of the top CPU using processes. To avoid confusion, the term is set in fixed-width font

- If groups of unrelated processes are in contention for the CPU, it's time to move to separate machines. Upgrading a single resource is likely to just delay this move and add expense in the long run.

When you get rid of CPU contention, you may also free other resources, especially memory. Temporary processes will come and go faster, releasing what they've used to the general pool. If you use mod_perl applications or other means to make Perl persistent, memory saturation can become your chief problem. Systems that are out of physical memory may be slow to start new processes, as the OS is busy swapping pages to and from disk. If out of swap space, the system may grind to a halt.

Diagnosing a memory shortage isn't hard, as long as you haven't reached the "crawl off and die" point. The same tools that monitor CPU usually have a memory display as well. Learn the difference between the total size of a process and its use of shared and private pages. A group of httpd processes with mostly shared pages is a good thing, even if the total size is large. We'll discuss sharing more memory later in this chapter.

If memory contention comes from processes that run different applications (and thus are unlikely to be able to share more pages), you may be facing a migration to a web farm. If Apache's children are the culprits, however, tune your configuration first by reducing the number of server processes. Fewer processes may be able to get more work done, at least in part because they won't wait around for memory.

Even if you don't have memory contention, make sure your system has ample swap space. This is a hard lesson most of us learn after a frustrating incident involving the aforementioned death crawl. There isn't a whole lot the OS can do about this other than to let processes die and hope things get better. In the meantime you'll be in the dark about what is causing the problem. Head it off by having an ample swap partition and you'll at least be able to diagnose what is wrong.

It seems odd to say, but network bandwidth is seldom a problem for web sites. Broadband access at home provides casual sites with more than enough pipe, while commercial sites have plenty of other incentives to locate their servers close to a backbone. Overloading the network connection is mostly a problem for sites that primarily serve binaries—software, graphics, or sound files—not application hosts.

Temporary network overloads do occur at many sites, however. If your router or other hardware monitor reports a problem, first find out if the problem is you. Remote backups, content uploads, and other internal usage can swamp a network for extended periods. If that is the cause of your problem, consider tools such as rsync (discussed in the previous chapter) that will limit bandwidth used by transfer. Perhaps your router can also restrict bandwidth usage from particular networks or hosts.

When no other culprit turns up, you still have some software options available. If your web site serves up large HTML pages, chances are you can reduce the size of each transfer by optimizing and/or compressing them. Apache supports various filter modules to handle this. In mod_perl, you can run the output through HTML::Clean, Apache::GzipChain, or both. The first module removes extra white space and performs other optimizations on HTML, while the second checks to see if the client browser accepts compressed output and uses the gzip compression scheme if so. Either of these modules will add CPU overhead to your system, and uncompressing on the client side will delay the rendering of your pages somewhat, but together these two modules can save considerable bandwidth on large pages. You can save CPU expense for the server by precleaning HTML pages and caching compressed results.

You can trade some bandwidth for the maximum number of connections, allowing those who connect to your system a chance to get what they came for while possibly turning away viewers at peak times. No one wants to lose customers, but users who get a "try again later" message may in fact try again later, while some, fed up with pages that never finish loading, might not come back.

I didn't list disk space as a resource problem because it so seldom is any more. Capacity per unit cost increases every year, making storage a problem only for sites that have vast databases. Storage bandwidth can catch site builders by surprise, however. This is your hardware's ability to get bits to and from the disk at a pace that keeps up with application demand. If you have ample memory and CPU capacity available but your applications are still sluggish, it could be that there is too much contention for storage hardware. You can resolve this by trading memory for disk space, either by caching more pages or putting high demand data on a RAM disk. You can also reduce contention by reducing the number of application processes. Beyond that, you're facing a migration of one sort or another, to faster disk drives or more servers.

12.1.1   Monitoring system loads

As I've said before, you don't want to wait until you have a problem to start learning what to do about it. Once your basic system is functional you should find out what monitoring tools you have available and learn to use them (and get more if they aren't sufficient to give you confidence in finding a problem). Your development schedule should include testing for performance problems.

The most common system resource monitor in the Unix world is `top` (and its endless relatives and variations). This simple utility displays the vital statistics of a system in a banner at the top of the screen (number of processes, CPU states, memory, and swap consumption) followed by a list of processes and their statistics. The default is to sort the process list so that the top CPU consumers appear first, but you can have `top` sort by memory usage, total CPU time used, or other attributes.

`top` shows a lot of information at once, and it can be confusing initially. Keep a copy of the man page handy so you have a legend to decipher the display. Once you are familiar with it you can see at a glance if your system is healthy, and if not what the likely contenders are.

Since various failure modes make it difficult to start new processes, I like to keep `top` running all the time on a problem system. That of course helps only if someone is there to see it when trouble strikes. Fortunately, `top` can also be used noninteractively to catch a snapshot of resource usage and save it to a file. Build a profile of your system by running `top` during peak periods, perhaps catching a culprit in the act.

Many implementations of `top` are built on libgtop, a library of functions for gathering system resource information. Doug MacEachern (the same Doug who is primarily responsible for mod_perl) has provided a Perl interface in the GTop module, which makes it possible to write your own script for recording resource utilization in a database, displaying it on a web page or what have you. The module includes some examples that will get you started. If libgtop isn't ported to your operating system yet, perhaps you can get resource consumption information via BSD::Resource.

Apache::VMonitor

Of course, running `top` or its relatives requires a shell account and a logged in session. You may be thinking that a web interface would be preferable. Others have thought so too, as can be seen in the selection of tools to choose from. One that I like is Apache::VMonitor, Stas Bekman's implementation of `top` as mod_perl application. Not only does it implement the usual `top` displays, but it adds one specifically for Apache children that can help you quickly spot problems in your applications (or your clients). It can also display mount status and file system information with color-coded alerts about overfull disks.

Install Apache::VMonitor from CPAN, along with GTop and Time::HiRes. To get the Apache-specific status info you'll also need Apache::Scoreboard and the mod_status module for Apache (it's compiled by default in a static build). Turn on mod_status in your `httpd.conf` file:

```
ExtendedStatus On
```

Status reporting does impact Apache's performance by adding system calls to get the beginning and ending processing time for a request. That shouldn't be enough to notice, but if you are squeezing every drop out of your server, squeeze here. (You'll also want to use something other than Apache::VMonitor, which is not a lightweight either.)

Choose a URL for the status display and configure it as a `<Location>` block in your mod_perl configuration (`mod_perl.conf` for me):

```
PerlModule Apache::VMonitor
<Location /sys-monitor>
    SetHandler perl-script
    PerlHandler Apache::VMonitor
    order deny,allow
    deny from all
    allow from 192.168.
    AuthUserFile data/admin_users
    AuthName "Administrator functions"
    AuthType basic
    require valid-user
</Location>
```

```
<Perl>
  $Apache::VMonitor::Config{PROCS} = 1;
  $Apache::VMonitor::PROC_REGEX = ".";

</Perl>
```

This block loads the module and tells Apache that it will handle requests to /sys-monitor. It protects the page in the same way that we showed protecting status information in previous chapters, by restricting access to the local network and requiring a user and password from an htpasswd database. That's rather paranoid, and either mechanism could be used by itself.

The `<Perl>` section sets package variables used to configure Apache::VMonitor. The `Config` hash tells which sections to display when the page first comes up. The system summary and Apache child sections are on by default, so they don't need to appear here. I added the PROCS section which shows a list of processes by CPU consumption. PROC_REGEX further tells which processes to display, via a regular expression match; I want to see all processes, since a problem could come from a cron job or a logged-in user. See the documentation for further configuration options.

Restart Apache and visit the page for a quick status update. Figure 12.1 shows the VMonitor display:

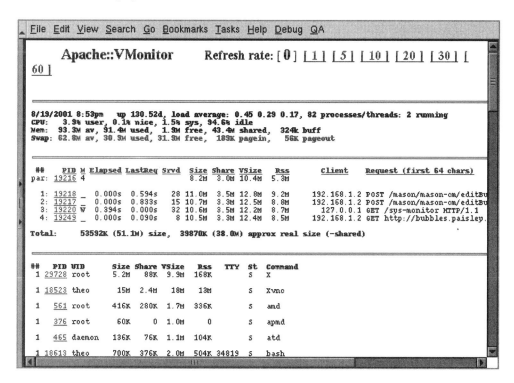

Figure 12.1   VMonitor

You can tell the page to refresh automatically at any of the intervals (in seconds) displayed by clicking the appropriate link. Be warned, however, that Apache::VMonitor has considerably more impact on the system than *top* does, so you probably don't want to leave it running once per second on a busy server.

Other links allow you to add or remove sections from the display. In the process list or Apache child section you can click a process ID to get detailed information on that process. The latter is very helpful in identifying problem clients or application code.

12.1.2 Stress-testing your server

Now that you have monitoring tools ready, you'll want to load up your system and see what happens. Most of us try the usual have-everybody-click-on-a-bunch-of-links method first, and while that's fun, it's not much of a methodology.

To automate loading a server with requests, we need to automate web clients. There are a number of tools for this, including a good many in Perl, and with good reason: Perl's LWP library and HTML handling modules make it easy to script web clients. Simulating page hits is trivially easy with programs such as ab (short for Apache Bench), which comes with Apache and is probably sitting in the same directory as your httpd binary. Automating sessions for more complex applications requires a little coding, but is still easy with these tools.

Suppose you want to simulate a user browsing through the static pages of your site. Here is a quick script using the LWP::UserAgent module which requests a series of pages (using documents from the Apache manual as an example):

```perl
#!/usr/bin/perl -w

use strict;
use LWP::UserAgent;
my $ua = LWP::UserAgent->new;
my @docs = qw(
        bind.html cgi_path.html content-negotiation.html
        custom-error.html dns-caveats.html dso.html
        ebcdic.html env.html footer.html handler.html
        header.html index.html install-tpf.html
        install.html invoking.html keepalive.html
        location.html man-template.html multilogs.html
        );
foreach (@docs) {
  print;
  my $req = HTTP::Request->new
    (GET => "http://localhost/manual/$_");
  my $res = $ua->request($req);
  if ($res->is_success) {
    print " succeeded\n";
  }
  else {
    print ' failed, ', $res->status_line, "\n";
  }
  sleep 1;
}
```

We could make the script smaller by using LWP::Simple instead, but that wouldn't give us any error information if a request failed. The example creates the list of documents to fetch, then loops through that list and requests each one. Doing so consists of creating a request object (typically called `$req` in the documentation and examples) and supplying it with a URL and an action—GET in this case, although you could fill in forms via POST, among other things. The request is sent to the web server via the `request` method, which yields a response object (`$res` by similar convention). If we were interested in the contents of the page, we could get that from `$res->content` here, although we need to know only if the request succeeded or failed, along with the error code for the latter case.

Run this script with your favorite monitoring program working in another window, and you'll see Apache handling the document requests. You can add URLs and/or wrap the document handling in an outer loop to provide more of a load. It should take quite a lot to make Apache busy with static document requests.

Once you start loading up your system, you'll want to tune your configuration and make other changes to improve performance, but how do you measure the improvement? My simple example doesn't record how long a theoretical user waited to receive a document, and it doesn't simulate a client very well anyway (unless your clients are usually located on the fast local network). Before you start adding statistics to the script, look for better tools. There's one as close as your CPAN mirror site.

HTTPD::Bench::ApacheBench

I've already mentioned ab, the program for sending rapid-fire requests to a web server. It comes with Apache and is compiled automatically when you build from sources.

Ling Wu decided to take the core ab code and implement it as a Perl module, allowing more complex benchmarks while retaining most of the efficiency of the original. Adi Fairbank took over the project later, yielding the current HTTP::Bench::ApacheBench module. I'll refer to it as ApacheBench from here on.

ApacheBench is a toolkit for creating benchmark scripts. As a sample and verification tool, the authors reimplemented ab using ApacheBench; you'll find it in the distribution, although it doesn't get installed by default. The documentation contains examples of more complex benchmarks, including cookies, filling in forms, and other options.

Install ApacheBench via CPAN. It contains its own copy of the required ab code, so you don't need the other sources handy. ApacheBench is a tool for sending Apache traffic, but isn't an Apache module itself, so you don't need to reconfigure or restart.

Here is `bench.pl`, an example script I set up to try out three areas of service, presented in sections:

```perl
#!/usr/bin/perl -w

use strict;
use HTTPD::Bench::ApacheBench;
my $b = HTTPD::Bench::ApacheBench->new;
```

```
$b->concurrency(7);
$b->priority("equal_opportunity");
```

The code sets up the required benchmark object ($b) and sets global configuration
options. The `concurrency` method establishes how many simultaneous requests
the benchmark will try to run, seven in this case. The `priority` setting
`equal_opportunity` means that those concurrent requests will be taken from all
scheduled runs, the batches of requests that we'll configure next:

```
# Exercise mod_perl apps...
my $mod_perl_apps =
  HTTPD::Bench::ApacheBench::Run->new
  ({urls  => [
        "http://localhost/create",
        "http://localhost/todo",
        "http://localhost/mason/reports.mhtml",
        ],
    order  => "depth_first",
    repeat => 400,
  }) or die "initializing mod_perl_apps";
die "adding mod_perl_apps"
  unless defined $b->add_run($mod_perl_apps);
```

This section creates a run that stresses mod_perl applications (two handlers and one
Mason component). Each request will be made 400 times in the order given. If we
change the `order` parameter to `breadth_first` then the run would perform the
first request 400 times, then the second, then the third.

The script sets up two more runs, one for CGI requests and the other for static
documents:

```
# And some CGI requests...
my $cgi_apps =
  HTTPD::Bench::ApacheBench::Run->new
  ({urls  => [
        "http://localhost/cgi-bin/addrbook.pl",
        "http://localhost/cgi-bin/tableform4.pl",
        "http://localhost/cgi-bin/hello-web.pl",
        "http://localhost/cgi-bin/checkdata.pl",
        ],
    order  => "depth_first",
    repeat => 20,
  }) or die "initializing cgi_apps";
die "adding cgi_apps"
  unless defined $b->add_run($cgi_apps);

# And static documents.
my $static_docs =
  HTTPD::Bench::ApacheBench::Run->new
  ({urls  => [
        "http://localhost/manual/index.html",
        "http://localhost/manual/sections.html",
```

```
          "http://localhost/manual/windows.html",
        ],
     order  => "depth_first",
     repeat => 1000,
   }) or die "initializing static_docs";
die "adding static_docs"
   unless defined $b->add_run($static_docs);
```

Now that the benchmark has plenty to do, we tell it to run via the `execute` method. When the requests are all complete, the script gets some statistics and prints results:

```
$b->execute or die "executing";
my $seconds = $b->total_time/1000;
print $b->total_requests, " requests sent\n",
  $seconds, " seconds elapsed\n",
  $b->total_requests/$seconds, " requests per second\n";
```

There are a couple of reasons for splitting requests into different runs, besides a compulsive need for pigeonholing things. The repeat count of requests is set in each run, so if we want (say) a balance of static documents with some applications thrown in we have to create different runs for each. ApacheBench can also give detailed statistics about each run after the whole batch executes, so you might group your requests by the way you want to analyze performance.

ApacheBench allows you to vary some information within a run. For example, you can supply an array of cookie values to go with a run, such that ApacheBench will cycle through the cookies and send one along with each request. Suppose your site's main page displays user-configured information depending on a user ID cookie. You could set up a run with the URL of the page and an array of 1,000 cookie values to simulate 1,000 different user views. You can similarly supply an array of data to go along with POST requests to simulate users filling in forms.

Of course you wouldn't ordinarily run this code on the same machine as the Apache server if you were trying to determine the maximum throughput of your system—the client script will take up considerable resources. Modify the URLs and run the script from a fast workstation, or more than one to get enough CPU power to swamp the web server.

If you are looking for a list of URLs to feed to your benchmark, you can extract typical usage from Apache's `access_log` file. Save a copy after a busy day, then run through it with your favorite text editor and extract the visited URLs. If you wanted to be fancy you could even get the access times and feed both into an LWP script to simulate the day's business.

Scripting or log-mining both make it possible to simulate users, but we'd like it to be easier. A promising product along this line is Deluge (http://deluge.source-forge.net/), which has (among other tools) a web proxy that records your requests in full to a server, so that it can play back your traffic multiple times to put the server under load. Deluge is at an early stage as I'm writing this, without enough documentation to be used easily, but I hope the project improves.

Another scriptable stress tester is Hammerhead (http://hammerhead.source-forge.net/), which offers a few more nice features to the mix, including the ability to use different IP aliases for its simulated users. It is also useful for regression testing as you can specify expected responses to any request and report errors when you don't get them.

Autobench (available via FreshMeat) is a Perl front-end to another popular load generator, httperf. This tool's forte is to generate requests at a starting rate, and then gradually increase that rate until a specified maximum is achieved. The data it stores are easily imported to graphing packages so that you can spot trends and saturation points. Another useful feature is Autobench's ability to work with two servers at once, so that you can compare hardware or software changes more easily.

Now you can load and monitor your system—let's find out what to do inside it to improve performance.

12.2 TUNING YOUR SERVER

Calling the incremental process of change and analysis tuning brings up images of stringed instruments and their aficionados to some, grease-covered overalls to others. Like piano or engine tuning, performance tuning seems like a mix of art and science to those who haven't done it themselves. The artistry comes from familiarity with how networks and software function, so that one sees a problem and has a good guess as to what is causing it. But this is an artistry you can (and should) develop from science, by spending the time it takes to get to know your system.

Tuning a system without understanding calls to mind various old engineering stories, in which an apprentice hits a stuck machine with a wrench in an attempt to get it working. The master sees the apprentice and upbraids him for trying something without knowing why it works. He then picks up the wrench and hits the machine with it himself, which of course sets everything in motion.

That said, most of us learn system tuning through a combination of research and experimentation. Following a tip sheet or list of guidelines is a good way to start, as is searching mail archives and documentation. Some good places to look for help with Apache and mod_perl are Dean Gausdet's tuning notes (part of the manual that is distributed with the source) and mod_perl's home page (http://perl.apache.org/) where you'll find Stas Bekman's extensive mod_perl guide, Vivek Khera's performance guide, and pointers to other good resources.

Once you have some guidelines, it's time for the experimentation part. This is always a little scary at first, and shouldn't be tried on a production server if you can help it, although in a pinch it's better to try something than do nothing. When you try something that works but you don't know why, make sure you learn what has happened before making other changes to your system.

12.2.1 Apache configuration

The directives in the `httpd.conf` file allow you to largely control the responsiveness of your system and cost of a request. By far the most important issue is the number of server processes you have available for handling users. After that, the issue becomes one of how much extra work Apache has to do per request. We'll discuss some of these issues again in the section 12.2.3.

Recall that when the Apache parent process starts up, it spawns a number of children set by the `StartServers` directive. As the children handle requests, the parent process checks to see how many are free to receive incoming traffic. If there are fewer than `MinSpareServers` children available, the parent process spawns more until that many servers are free, unless it reaches the limit set by `MaxClients`. If more than `MaxSpareServers` are loitering with nothing to do, Apache kills some for the good of the cause.

This flexibility is nice, but one school of thought is to discard it completely. Why waste time starting and stopping processes when you want your system to be ready for peak throughput at all times? To those in this school, all four parameters should be set to the same large value, representing the approximate memory limits of the machine. Apache will start up and create a systemful of children, ready for something to do.

The reason why this isn't the standard practice lies in implementation details of the current Apache code and the way child processes wait for a request. Suppose there are several dozen idle servers when a request arrives. Each of those servers is in a wait state, listening for a message on one or more sockets. The incoming request ends the wait state, and several dozen idle children try to read the socket. Only one actually gets the message; the others find the cupboard is bare, and return to their wait state.

The actual implementation on most OS is better than the simple scheme I describe here, but it always includes a group of processes waking up and (mostly) going back to sleep. Depending on your version and OS, the attempt to grab the incoming message may be visible as process activity (you'll see all the idle processes become computable on *top* or Apache::VMonitor), or may be hidden in system calls that show up as kernel activity (shown in the system CPU state with *top*). In network application parlance this phenomenon is called *starvation*, but some articles use the more descriptive *idle thrash* which certainly characterizes the problem.

Apache's architecture is shifting (on some operating systems) to handle this better in future versions by using threads instead of (or in addition to) multiple processes. In a threaded server, one thread[2] listens on sockets while other threads process

---

[2] A thread is a sort of miniprocess within a process. Programs built with threads can have multiple lines of execution, so that, for example, one thread updates a GUI interface while another searches a database. Writing threaded code is tricky, however, and adding threads to an existing program is a great way to discover hidden assumptions that make threading a challenge.

requests. This kind of minischeduler will reduce idle-thrashing considerably, as only the listening threads will awaken when a request arrives.

Should you care about idle thrash? Some say that if you can measure it, either your system isn't very busy in the first place, or is woefully underpowered. Tuning can help in the latter case, but ultimately you need better hardware. In the first case, though, why not give the off-hours user the best response you can by reducing unnecessary overhead?

To reduce idle thrash and configure the right number of servers, you first need a reasonable estimate of the number of server processes your system can handle. Observe the system under load and see how much total memory your Apache processes use—shared size plus the private usage of each child.[3] Also determine how much physical memory your machine has left. If you are swapping at all, then you are already overloaded. Divide the remaining memory by the average private usage, subtract a reasonable margin of error (a process or two, depending on how much memory you have to start with), and add that many more children to MaxClients. Restart, load up the system, and monitor it again to see how close your margin is.

If that results in too few processes to handle your expected peak traffic, you need to either get more memory or reduce the load on the machine. Does this server also run your database or other services? Time to start migrating to a multiserver configuration. Are you measuring it while there is unusual user activity?[4] If there isn't anything to remove (or this isn't the time to do so) then you need some way to lighten Apache. The following sections offer several ideas.

While you can set MaxClients empirically, you have to choose StartServers from experience with your site. The value should represent the number of servers you typically need to handle business. There is no advantage in starting fewer if you are going to reach that number soon anyway. I think the same value is reasonable for MinSpareServers (again, why have less than what you'll soon need?) but some argue for half that value to reduce process retention overhead (explained shortly).

You can arrive at the value for MaxSpareServers empirically also: start Apache on a system with little or no load, so that the usual StartServers are running, then send a single request to the server while observing with your monitor (*top* would be a better choice than Apache::VMonitor in this case). See any evidence of idle thrash? If not, set a larger value for StartServers, restart, and measure again, increasing until you can either measure the overhead or you are convinced that it isn't a problem for your configuration. MaxSpareServers should be less than the number of servers

---

[3] Unsure on how to calculate memory usage? Not to worry, Apache::VMonitor will do this for you. Fire it up and look at the last line of the Apache section.

[4] Possibly defined as "someone running Emacs," but during development periods you might expect more user logins and activity than normal. If you built your system with a graphical user environment, you should get rid of it before going to production (or at least disable X-windows and such from the system startup).

that cause overhead, `MaxClients` if you can't measure any, or halfway between `StartServers` and `MaxClients` if process retention is a problem (or you just like the symmetry of it all).

What is process retention overhead? This is the cost to your system for having processes sitting round doing nothing. It is usually a cost in memory, though it could also be figured in database connections if your servers use Apache::DBI or other methods to save on initialization time. For the moment we'll worry only about memory cost, the real memory used by processes.

Having configured `MaxClients` to be the maximum number of Apache children your system can handle without swapping, you may be wondering what the issue is with having them sit around. The answer is that those processes may have a tendency to grow with time (as many developers do) in spite of the fact that they don't seem to be doing anything more than usual. Memory leaks exist in many OS libraries and sometimes in Apache itself (although it is thoroughly analyzed for this), causing each process to grab a little more memory with each request. If you have mod_perl or other persistent applications, your chances of having problems increase enormously as application programmers may not be aware of the conditions that cause a leak.

Should you have memory leaks for any reason, you will eventually start swapping when you are running the maximum number of servers and each is bloating up—that's process retention overhead. To cure it you need server suicide, where processes give their all for the cause and then die (secure in the knowledge of a job well done) to release their memory and other resources back into the pool. The simplest way to invoke server suicide is to set `MaxRequestsPerChild` to a positive value; when a child process has handled that many requests, it will die after finishing its business with the last client. The main Apache process will notice the child shutdown and start a new one if required to maintain `MinSpareServers`. You should configure a lower minimum and maximum spare set if you are seeing overhead here.

If you are using an operating system known to have leakage problems, Apache will configure a default value for `MaxRequestsPerChild` automatically. If not, this value defaults to zero, meaning that server suicide is disabled (at least by this means). The analysis to determine the correct value here is tricky unless your leak is obvious and dependable (in which case you are probably fixing the leak now instead of reading this). Fortunately it isn't critical to get an exact value. If a child can process a few hundred requests without exceeding a reasonable size then go ahead and set the limit there. Conversely, if your child can't process that many requests, you have a serious problem on your hands, but you can still set a lower value for `MaxRequestsPerChild` to handle the situation. Creating child processes isn't that expensive on most of Apache's OS, and it is certainly cheaper than pushing other needed memory out to the swap file.

The downside of using `MaxRequestsPerChild` is that it is completely arbitrary—a child process may still be well within its memory limits when it expires. If you have mod_perl built into your system for application or monitoring purposes you can configure server suicide based on real analysis as we'll see in the next section. Process retention overhead also comes up again a little later when we discuss Keep-Alive.

Per-request costs

Some Apache directives add to the overhead of processing a request. These usually identify themselves in the configuration file, but it's often the case that a developer will change one of them for debugging purposes and then not set it back. If you are looking to squeeze maximum performance out of a production server that handles static documents, then check the items in this list.

Most applications are expensive enough on their own to push this kind of savings into the noise level, so I wouldn't worry about these directives for a server that primarily handles mod_perl or other dynamic pages. If you have very lean code that is otherwise well-behaved, you might get some savings here.

The following are in the order you'll see them in the default config file:

- *ExtendedStatus*—As mentioned previously, this adds system calls to each request. If Apache::VMonitor is your system monitor of choice, then you could consider turning `ExtendedStatus` on and sending Apache a USR1 signal to reload the configuration file while you monitor. Beware however, that if you forget to make the switch and run Apache::VMonitor with `ExtendedStatus` off you may see stale information displayed.

- *AllowOverride*—Use of .htaccess files (or whatever the name you've configured happens to be) makes it easy to divide configuration information up into logical sections by directory. Unfortunately, it also adds a good bit of overhead when processing requests, as Apache has to check each permitted directory along the way to the document for an override file. Thus if overrides are enabled on /userfiles and a request comes in for /userfiles/bob/hobbies/cds.html, Apache has to check three directories for .htaccess files (and then parse them if they exist). You should either turn off overrides entirely, or restrict their use to low-traffic areas of your site.

- *Symbolic links*—Oddly enough, request overhead increases if you *don't* set the `FollowSymLinks` option, since Apache has to check each component of a file path to see if it is a link. The cheapest option thus is to set `Option FollowSymLinks` and just control your document directories properly. If you add `SymLinksIfOwnerMatch`, then Apache still has to check for links and verify ownership, so no savings result.

- *HostnameLookups*—If set, this requires Apache to perform DNS lookups for each client connection so that it can log the hostname with the request instead of the IP address. Should you require that information, you are better off doing the lookups later in a log analyzer script rather than slowing down your production server. Specifying a domain instead of an IP address in `allow` or `deny` also causes DNS traffic and delays.

- *Old links*—If you are rearranging your site and need to maintain old URLs, do so via `Alias` directives, symbolic links in the file system, or rewrite rules so that Apache handles the request in one shot. Redirection doubles your pain as the client sends you one request for the old URL and one for the new version.

So much for the Apache basics. If mod_perl is present it brings its own list of issues, so we'll cover that next.

12.2.2　mod_perl issues

Perl and Apache go great together, and mod_perl is an excellent tool for developing Web applications. That doesn't mean every Apache server should have Perl built in, however, even if a site uses Perl applications extensively.

The most obvious issue with mod_perl is the large memory footprint of the Perl interpreter. Start up a stock Apache build and one linked with mod_perl and you'll immediately see what I mean. You will have to drastically cut back on `MaxClients` if your main server uses mod_perl. Other potential problems arise too, as Apache mixes its static document work load with Perl applications. Servers that mostly send files to clients will also hold on to database connections and other resources.

The solution for this is to separate the work load into two servers, one built with mod_perl and one kept as lean as possible to handle static documents (and perhaps lightly used CGI scripts and other occasional tasks). The default server should listen to your site's main address and port—probably the static server, unless your main page is a mod_perl application. The mod_perl server gets a separate port if both processes run on the same machine. If they don't, they get a separate address;[5] modify your documents and applications to use full URLs for all links, specifying the static server for simple files and images and the mod_perl server for applications.

The best thing about this configuration is that it frees you from many hard choices in setting Apache configuration directives and other parameters. You can set different values for `MaxClients` and the other process constraints, then you should monitor the system to see if either the static or application servers are topping out and trade off servers between them. It also leaves you ready for a migration to a web farm as soon as that's required.

Running multiple Apache servers isn't very difficult. The previous chapter has some examples that share most of their configurations, but those were using the same httpd binary. In this case we want different servers, but they can share the bulk of the configuration files if desired. You can use `<IfModule mod_perl.c>` sections to provide separate `Port` or `Listen` addresses (or `IfDefine` if you prefer), and guard the mod_perl configuration similarly.

---

[5] Using a port instead of an IP alias will save your clients a DNS lookup for the second server. If using a separate address and your IP numbers are unlikely to change, use IP addresses instead of host names in your links for the same reason.

If running on one machine, the two servers can share `access_log` and `error_log` files if desired. In that case, you might want to modify the log format to include the port number so that you can tell which server processed what request. You'll need to assign a PID file to each and use `kill` to shut them down directly.

Suppose we have two Apache binaries, `bin/httpd` and `bin/httpdmp`, the latter built with mod_perl. We can set them up with one configuration file arranged similarly to the staging and production servers of the previous chapter:

```
<IfModule mod_perl.c>
  Port 8080
  PidFile /usr/local/apache/logs/httpdmp.pid
</IfModule>
<IfModule !mod_perl.c>
  Port 80
  PidFile /usr/local/apache/logs/httpd.pid
</IfModule>
```

The settings for `MaxClients` and other process constraints would be separated out in the same way.

To modify the log messages so that the port number is included we modify the `LogFormat` directive:

```
LogFormat "%h %p %l %u %t \"%r\" %>s %b" common
```

The `%p` will be replaced with the port number in `access_log` messages. If you are using one of the other formats (as indicated by your `CustomLog` directive, which generally follows the `LogFormat` sections) then change that format instead.

Start both servers:

```
cd /usr/local/apache && bin/httpd && bin/httpdmp
```

To shut down either server individually, use `kill` with the contents of the appropriate PID file:

```
kill `cat logs/httpd.pid`
kill `cat logs/httpdmp.pid`
```

Or take out both at once with

```
kill `cat logs/*.pid`
```

This configuration is common for a number of different sites: one stripped-down Apache binary for static content and a fully loaded application server for dynamic work. The usual term for the static server is *thin Apache*; we'll see more uses of it in later sections.

The server for static content doesn't have to be Apache, of course. In chapter 2 we discussed alternatives such as thttpd, which can outperform Apache for static content in the right circumstances. I like the convenience of the single configuration file mentioned earlier, but don't reduce your options for the sake of convenience.

After setting up the two servers, you'll have to monitor both to set reasonable values for `MaxClients` and other parameters. Before you go dividing your system memory, however, consider how to get more out of each mod_perl process.

Sharing (more) memory

There isn't much we can do about the size of Perl. Those mod_perl processes are going to be large. But if you check your system monitor right after starting Apache, you'll notice that a good portion of the size of each process is shared. All of the interpreter's code is in shared memory (as is Apache itself, of course), used equally among the servers. If we can keep the ratio of shared pages to private memory high then we can run more processes and increase throughput.

On Linux and Unix systems, Apache processes share memory through a mechanism called *copy-on-write*. As the parent process forks off children to handle requests, each child shares the pages of the parent—for that brief moment, everything is shared. As soon as either process modifies a page, the page clones itself so that each process has its own copy. It remains private from then on.[6]

Now consider a single mod_perl process: it loads modules, does any other initialization, and then waits for business to arrive. Loading a Perl module involves reading the file, compiling the code (into *bytecode*, the readily executable form), and running any global initialization as well. At the end of this process, the Perl interpreter is unchanged (perl doesn't modify itself at run-time, although Perl code can). However, various internal data has been set (the namespace structures and the `%INC` hash, for instance), and the bytecode is sitting in memory.

As soon as the Perl code executes, we start losing shared pages. Perl mixes code and data freely, so setting a variable can cause a page copy even if the page is mostly bytecode. But we still get a higher number of shared pages by initializing modules and global data in the parent, then copying those pages to children. For a given module's code, a child process might never trigger a page copy.

To get more sharing out of mod_perl then, we want to do as much as we can in the parent process before forking any children. In chapter 5 I mentioned that it is a good idea to load all the modules we're likely to use at initialization time (via `Perl-Module`, `<Perl>` sections, or a handler setup script). Modules such as CGI.pm and DBI (or Apache::DBI if it isn't causing your scripts trouble) should be loaded in your mod_perl configuration file if they are used by any of your applications.

Recalling the discussion of CGI.pm in chapter 5, remember that Apache has its own modules for parsing parameters and handling cookies (Apache::Request and Apache::Cookie). If you are using the CGI modules for just those functions, consider

---

[6] There are utilities for resharing pages that are identical among processes. On Linux you can try mergemem (http://mergemem.ist.org/), which will sweep through the system and collect pages in just this fashion. It's considered experimental at this time, so use with caution.

switching to save size. CGI.pm also has its large library of helper functions for writing correct HTML, but recall that many of those functions are generated on demand—that's great for CGI scripts, since it puts off compiling what would be a large number of subroutines until they are actually needed, but bad for mod_perl. Tell CGI.pm to precompile the HTML tag functions when you load it:

```
use CGI qw(-compile :standard);
```

This compiles the HTML tag functions, CGI helper functions, and form tags; use :all if there are any features you need that aren't on the list (such as CGI.pm's support for browser-specific tags). If your code uses the CGI object interface instead of the functions, you'll need to do this in two lines:

```
use CGI;
CGI->compile(':standard');
```

If you are using DBI, check to see if your driver allows shared database connections (none that I'm aware of do at this writing). If not, then don't bother connecting to the database at initialization time. However, do preload your DBD modules. DBI will take care of this and perform other useful setup work when you call the DBI-> install_driver method, so use that instead of loading the module directly:

```
DBI->install_driver('mysql');
```

DBI's prepare_cached method saves a copy of the statement handle in the database handle's data. Use that in your code to save on request compilation time. But unfortunately, you can't copy these prepared statements between processes (just as you can't share a database connection), so you can't prepare in advance in the parent process. You can have Apache::DBI establish the child's database connections when it is created via the connect_on_init method. If you wish, you can also call prepare_cached in an initialization section for the child, but I prefer just to call that method in the code and thus ensure that the child builds only statements it is using.

If you use Apache::Registry to speed up CGI scripts, you can have it preload them in the parent process. Apache::Registry ordinarily compiles a script when it first encounters it, via its internal Apache::RegistryLoader module. You can have this module do the loading in advance in a <Perl> section or required script instead:

```
use Apache::RegistryLoader;
my $load = Apache::RegistryLoader->new;
my @scripts = qw(hello-mod_perl.pl addrbook.pl);
foreach my $s (@scripts) {
    $load->handler("/perl/$s");
}
```

Call the handler method for each URL that corresponds to a preloaded script. The example shown here assumes that all the scripts are in one directory, and that directory has an alias of the same name in Apache's configuration file. That is, it assumes the configuration I gave for Apache::Registry in chapter 5:

```
Alias /perl/ "/usr/local/apache/perl/"
<Directory "/usr/local/apache/perl">
    SetHandler perl-script
    PerlHandler Apache::Registry
    Options ExecCGI
</Directory>
```

Assuming that `ServerRoot` is /usr/local/apache, Apache::RegistryLoader will find the scripts and map them to the appropriate URLs. If your file-mapping scheme is more complicated, you can supply your own mapping function to Apache::RegistryLoader, or just supply the file name that goes with each URL as you call the `handler` method.

Initialize everything else you can: add a script with `PerlRequire` (or a `<Perl>` section) to set up any global state, and preload common Mason components, template files, and other such embedded Perl tools. Since I'm a Mason fan I'll show how it's done for that case:

```
my $interp = HTML::Mason::Interp->new
  ('parser' => HTML::Mason::Parser->new,
   'comp_root' => '/usr/local/apache/mason',
   'data_dir' => '/usr/local/apache/data',
   'preloads' => [qw(/header.mcmp /footer.mcmp)],
  );
```

The new `preloads` parameter to the Mason interpreter can be a list of components (by absolute path) or file-matching patterns (using shell-style globs, not Perl regular expressions). You can thus preload all the components in a directory with a simple `'*.mhtml'` or what ever extension you use. Remember to preload only regularly-used components that are unlikely to change.

We maximize shared memory by doing everything we can in the parent process, but as mentioned, those shared pages become private as soon as a Perl variable scribbles on them. Long-running mod_perl applications will have fewer and fewer shared pages, so the next question is how to get the most out of those processes without configuring for the worst case of maximal private memory.

Server suicide, mod_perl style

Assuming mod_perl has a server to itself, you need to configure `MaxClients` and the other process constraints correctly. The same methods discussed previously work, but remember to keep your server under load for a while before measuring memory use (or just add a much larger margin for error).

Given that a mod_perl process is eventually going to become a memory hog, we need to decide when children should return their pages to the pool and give a new player a start. One option is to use `MaxRequestsPerChild` as before, setting it to the number of requests where we think the child will become too large. But that's an arbitrary limit, and we could shut down some processes that aren't a problem and keep others that are oversized.

You'd think a versatile combination like Apache and Perl could do better, right? The tools are right at hand, as usual—a pair of them, Apache::SizeLimit and Apache::GTopLimit. They conveniently implement the same interface, differing only in their underlying implementation (the first requires BSD::Resource, while the second uses GTop as implied). Apache::SizeLimit comes with mod_perl, while Apache::GTopLimit is available on CPAN.

Suppose we've decided that 12 MB is enough for anyone. In a required startup script add these lines:

```
use Apache::SizeLimit;
$Apache::SizeLimit::MAX_PROCESS_SIZE = 12 * 1024;
$Apache::SizeLimit::CHECK_EVERY_N_REQUESTS = 10;
```

This tells Apache::SizeLimit to check resource usage every tenth request, and kill the process *after* the request if the process size has reached or exceeded 12 MB (the process size limit is in kilobyte units).

Individual processes can change their limits programmatically via Apache::SizeLimit's `setmax` method, which is a reasonable move if you have one process that is managing some large resource on behalf of the others.

Note that Apache::SizeLimit doesn't care about shared and private pages, just total process size. With Apache::GTopLimit, you can tell a process to die if its shared page count drops, or if its total size is too large.

```
use Apache::GTopLimit;
$Apache::GTopLimit::MAX_PROCESS_SIZE = 12 * 1024;
$Apache::GTopLimit::MIN_PROCESS_SHARED_SIZE = 5 * 1024;
$Apache::GTopLimit::CHECK_EVERY_N_REQUESTS = 10;
```

Those settings will shut down the server if it isn't sharing at least 5 MB. You'll want to monitor your system carefully after setting MIN_PROCESS_SHARED_SIZE. Too low a value will cause quite a high suicide rate, which is counterproductive.

Should you still use MaxRequestsPerChild? Some authors think so, with a value in the neighborhood of several hundred requests. Personally I set the value to zero, unless I'm also using other limits, as we'll see next.

With application code running inside of Apache, we need to guard against bugs that can tie up valuable server resources. Testing is certainly the best way to do that, but safeguards will help us rest more easily at night. An infinite loop will consume a large proportion of available CPU time until someone notices it. Worse still, if such a loop leaks memory, it will swell the server process and possibly induce system swapping before the OS shuts it down.

The memory-limiting modules mentioned previously can't help us here, since they check a process only after it has completed a request, and in the case of a bug the request won't complete. We need to be able to shut down a server midrequest when it starts behaving in a way that threatens the rest of the system. That means the request that invoked the bug isn't going to get a response, but drastic measures are called for here.

The solution is already waiting in your mod_perl distribution: Apache::Resource, which uses the BSD::Resource module mentioned in an earlier section. The module uses a Perl interface to the `setrlimit` routines (which your OS will need before you can use BSD::Resource) to enforce resource consumption limits on processes.

Suppose we want to cover the two primary bug issues, severe memory leakage, and infinite loops. We want to shut down a process if it reaches 20 MB in size, or runs up a 10 minute CPU time charge. To set those limits we add the following to our `mod_perl.conf`:

```
PerlModule Apache::Resource
PerlSetEnv PERL_RLIMIT_CPU 600
PerlSetEnv PERL_RLIMIT_AS 20
PerlChildInitHandler Apache::Resource
```

The two environment variable settings establish the limits we want, in CPU seconds for the first and megabytes for the second. Memory would usually be limited by PERL_RLIMIT_DATA, but Linux doesn't honor that setting, while PERL_RLIMIT_AS (limiting the size of the address space) works on Linux and other platforms. BSD::Resource allows us to work with other restrictions handled by `setrlimit` too, such as the maximum file size a process can create.

We probably don't want the same memory limit here as used with Apache::Size-Limit or Apache::GTopLimit. Remember that those modules check a process after it has finished a request, while `setrlimit` will cause a process to shut down when it tries to exceed a resource limit. If a server process goes a little bit over the memory limit but does complete the request, we want the response sent back to the client before terminating the process to reclaim memory.

That same issue makes setting the CPU limit a difficult problem. Since `setrlimit` can't tell the difference between an infinite loop and a process that is just very devoted to its job, setting any CPU boundary will almost certainly kill off some processes that are otherwise well behaved. If a server handles a large number of requests but never exceeds the memory boundary, it may rack up a lot of CPU time, and will eventually hit the infinite loop guard. When that happens it will die in midrequest, which is very undesirable for our clients.

The solution takes us back to the issue of `MaxRequestsPerChild`. If we set a value for that limit which is well within the CPU time check, then processes will get shut down cleanly after processing a final request. Should the arbitrariness of that mechanism still bother you, consider coding your own cleanup handler and using BSD::Resource to check whether a process is approaching the point where it needs to shut down voluntarily.

Congratulations on getting mod_perl up to speed, but keep reading—you still need to protect yourself from network oddities.

12.2.3 Socket tricks

When your server is under load, you may notice some strange behavior in the way Apache assigns work to processes. With a thin server handling static documents it may be unnoticeable, but in a mod_perl server we want to get a lot of work out of a few processes, and when the system is busy your processes could be sitting around doing nothing (other than holding on to memory and other resources).

Two of the causes of this slacker behavior are built into the network: *Keep-Alive* is part of the HTTP 1.1 protocol, and *lingering close* is an option for any TCP/IP communication.

Keep-Alive

The original HTTP protocol was written mostly with text in mind, and in that scenario it made sense that a socket would be used for a single request: the client opened a socket to the server, asked for a document, received it and closed it. As soon as text mixed with graphics became the norm, this protocol was seen to be extremely inefficient, and the Keep-Alive option was added in version 1.1 to allow a client to make more than one request on a socket. This conserves the overhead and delay involved in opening sockets and makes transfers of complex documents far more efficient.

Apache enables Keep-Alive via the directive of (almost) the same name, `KeepAlive`. Set to on by default, this directive works with two others to tell Apache how to handle the wait for additional requests: `KeepAliveTimeout` sets the number of seconds a server process should wait for requests (after completing the current one) before closing the socket, and `MaxKeepAliveRequests` limits the number of requests that Apache will accept on a connection. The defaults are 15 seconds and 100 requests respectively; setting `MaxKeepAliveRequests` to 0 allows unlimited requests.

All this is fine and sensible so far, and wouldn't cause a problem were it not for two issues:

- Have you ever noticed how your browser loads multiple images simultaneously? That's because browsers tend to run separate requests in parallel on different sockets; if a browser used only one socket plus Keep-Alive to request a complex document, you'd see each graphic arrive individually.

- A server which is waiting for extra requests on a socket is not serving anything else. The browser keeps its sockets open until it has satisfied all requests. We can hope it will close its connections quickly when it has all the requests it needs, but this isn't necessarily the case.

Putting those two together means that a client can tie up multiple server processes and leave them idle for the time limit in `KeepAliveTimeout`. In practice it should be shorter than that, but a bunch of clients on slow network links can really gum things up for you.

Apache isn't completely naïve about Keep-Alive. It uses the protocol only for fixed-length documents (those which supply a Content-Length header), which excludes most dynamic content systems, and of course offers it only to browsers that support the protocol. However if you have a single Apache server which handles both static content and mod_perl apps, or your mod_perl server takes care of fixed-length documents, then you could have valuable server processes waiting for extra requests.

If you have a separate mod_perl server, I suggest you set `KeepAlive Off` to disable the protocol entirely. If sharing a server for static and dynamic content, set a short expiration time and limit the number of requests to the maximum used by your high-traffic documents.

There are other solutions to Keep-Alive slacking, including the one in the next section. This issue will come up again when we look at reverse proxies.

Lingering close

To correctly handle communications with the client and verify that all sent data has been received, Apache implements a lingering socket close (sometimes called malingering close for reasons that are about to become clear). This means that Apache closes both "directions" of a socket before releasing related buffers and going on with useful work, a process that takes a second or so if all network connections are well behaved.

This malingering time creates the same kind of problem for a high-traffic server that Keep-Alive timeouts generate, as large application processes sit idle while cleaning up the network. Roger Espel Llima of iAgora Software resolved the problem by creating lingerd, a separate server that takes over sockets from Apache processes when they finish their work. Thus lingerd does the lingering close and suffers any delays while Apache goes back to useful tasks. This server (and its required patches for Apache) is available at the company's web site, http://www.iagora.com/.

There are some compelling advantages to using lingerd to unburden Apache. It is far easier to set up and run than a proxy front end, it takes very few system resources itself, and it doesn't slow down communication as a proxy can when handling large documents. However, it also performs none of the tasks a reverse proxy can, so read the upcoming "Reverse proxies" section before forming a strong opinion as to which approach makes the best sense.

Always remember that the price of well-tuned servers is eternal vigilance. Well, perhaps not that much, but still, the more closely you tune your system the more closely you need to monitor it and verify that it is performing well. A system that is optimized for one scenario may perform very badly should the situation change.

12.3   WEB FARMING

I've mentioned a number of times that your site may need to grow beyond a simple, single machine. Moving to a group of systems is not trivial, but it doesn't have to be all that tough either. Good tools are at hand, as always.

The basic web farm is a group of specialized machines that maximize the benefits of division of labor:

- *Front-end server*—The site's domain address is assigned to a fast web server that handles static content, a thin Apache server, thttpd, or other speedy system. It has enough memory to keep all the needed processes running without any swap activity, disk space to cover the content, and room to grow, and utilities to analyze traffic and manage the log files and other overhead.

- *Application server(s)*—Applications run on one or more application servers, which handle all of the site's dynamic content. Each server has its own URL and links in static content from the front page or a database. If there are more than one, the servers could be homogenous for ease of maintenance and administration. The best performance would come from further specialization however, so that each app loads and compiles only the code it needs. Specializing along applications further benefits traffic analysis and resource management—you know where to put your next hardware acquisition.

- *Database server(s)*—The databases live on their own machine (or machines, again to take advantage of division of labor) which has a fast I/O subsystem and reflects emergency planning—redundant disk arrays, removable media that matches your backup system, and so on. If the applications use flat-files or a database system that reads the disks directly from the application[7] then this entry would be replaced by a fast network storage mechanism.

- *Other*—Add any other specialized servers as required—ad servers, media streamers, and so on.

This configuration is very manageable, in that problems are localized and if, for example, an application bug causes a process to swamp the CPU or memory resources it takes out only that machine, not the database and static content too. A hardware failure won't shut down the whole site at once. Good emergency planning will allow you to move the affected services to one of the other machines while you get a solution or a backup into place.

The two complaints about it that come up first in most discussions are the use of multiple public URLs and the related problem of securing multiple machines. Each of the application servers (and any other service that has to talk to a browser) has to be

---

[7] Most relational and object databases have a separate server (or servers), providing their own tuning issues and, we hope, guidelines for good performance.

on a machine with a direct route to the Internet at large, and so each is vulnerable to attack and needs the same kind of protection and monitoring the front page machine has. Since your application servers have unique URLs, users can, and will tend to, bookmark them instead of your front page, leaving either broken links or rewriting headaches when you move things around. Users who type in or modify URLs to their browser will get the wrong machine if they change the path to cross over service lines. You can fix that with a set of redirection rules for each service, which means more administration hassles.

Working around these issues adequately requires another layer between the browser and the web farm, forming both a unified virtual server to the user and a single public contact point for security management. The security issues for the machine are the same as those discussed in chapter 2 for a single server, so I won't cover them again here. I will instead concentrate on the unifying layer.

Here's the new web farm with an intermediate layer added:

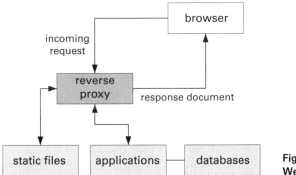

Figure 12.2
Web farm with a proxy

The intermediary accepts the incoming request (and any POST data) from the browser, then forwards it to the responsible party for processing. That server (again) receives the request and data, processes it and generates a response, which it sends to the intermediary. The middle layer then moves the response back through the user's connection to his browser.

As you can see, there is a loss of performance here as the intermediary introduces latency: the time taken to forward the request, plus the time taken to buffer the response before sending it on to the user. The actual implementations mitigate this as we'll see in the next sections.

12.3.1   Reverse proxies

The generic name for the kind of intermediary described in the previous section is a *reverse proxy*, so-called because it behaves in the opposite fashion to the kind of web proxy used by firewalls and ISPs to buffer content and shield internal network systems. A regular proxy accepts outgoing requests and stands in place of the user to the server, receiving the content response and handing it back to the browser (and perhaps caching it to save on network traffic also). A reverse proxy stands before the actual server and performs the same buffering role at the far end of the network connection from the user's system.

The proxy acts as a unifying front-end, taking the output of the various back-end servers and feeding it to the client while the back-end processes move on quickly to other work. The buffering induces latency, but it shields the application processes from slow client links and other network delays. All interaction with the application servers happens on a high-speed internal network. Since the proxy is kept thin we don't mind having a large number of its processes waiting on malingering and Keep-Alive waits, and overall throughput of the system is improved.

A proxy can also act as a cache for some of a site's dynamic content, where such content is not unique to the requesting user or exact time of day. For example, suppose a news site stores articles in a database. When a request for an article comes in, it retrieves the article and builds a page around it, then ships that back to the user. A caching proxy could hold onto that page for its expected lifetime and shield the application server from additional requests.

In order for caching to be useful, the dynamic content server needs to tell the proxy how long to keep documents around by setting an Expires header in each one. In the case of our news server, we could set the expiration to the time when the article database is updated, or to an interval representing when we want to refresh the headlines and other faster-changing elements of the generated page. Also set a Last-Modified header representing how old the article is, which the cache will use in turn should a browser send it an If-Modified-Since request. Some proxies consider only documents that arrive with Content-Length headers, which means you'll need to generate the document before sending the headers back. This induces more latency for that request, but hopefully with better overall performance via the cache.

Given the place Apache has in the heart of the Open Source community and its diverse group of developers, it's not surprising that it has the needed capabilities to serve as our reverse proxy (or a regular proxy for that matter). Apache can serve as the front-end server for static content, be the intermediary for application servers, and also cache documents from the back-end if desired (although you can still split those functions among other servers if you prefer). We'll discuss implementations of Apache proxies using mod_proxy, mod_rewrite and mod_perl. There are undoubtedly many other combinations and possibilities, so as always it is a good idea to keep an eye on new developments.

After covering those implementations we'll bring in one example from outside the Apache world with the Squid cache, which for years has been unobtrusively speeding up browsing sessions from both the front and back ends of connections.

Apache with mod_proxy

The core functions to implement an Apache proxy are in the aptly named mod_proxy, which has been in the set of add-ons since version 1.1 (reverse proxying capabilities arrived with version 1.3). mod_proxy is not compiled in by default, so chances are good you'll need to rebuild your server for this role.

Once you've enabled proxying you can configure Apache to dispatch traffic to background servers based on URLs. For example, suppose we have three application servers: news.example.site handles dynamic news content and searches, store.example.site handles a catalog, and perl.example.site for miscellaneous scripts that run under Apache::Registry. Here's how we tell the front-end server (www.example.site) to divide the traffic:

```
ProxyPass /news/ http://news.example.site/
ProxyPassReverse /news/ http://news.example.site/
ProxyPass /store/ http://store.example.site/
ProxyPassReverse /store/ http://store.example.site/
ProxyPass /perl/ http://perl.example.site/
ProxyPassReverse /perl/ http://perl.example.site/
```

When our main server gets a request for http://www.example.site/news/headlines it will convert the URL to http://news.example.site/headlines and forward it along to the news server. It also proxies the request, so that news.example.site sends the response back to www.example.site, which then rewrites the Location headers to show the document as http://www.example.site/news/headlines again.

Note that the URL paths on www.example.site don't match those on the application servers—the path in the example becomes /headlines on the back-end server, instead of /news/headlines. If that is confusing, just add the missing part of the path to the target URLs in the proxying directives.

Why two sets of directives? The `ProxyPassReverse` set handles the Location change on the return trip from the application server to the proxy. Without that set, the user will see the application server's site and URL in his browser. If you want further requests to go directly to the application server (or you have a clever redirection scheme in place for traffic from outside your local network) that may be fine with you. It's also useful if you want your front-end server to look like several different machines, or if you are temporarily hosting another site's services.

That kind of one-to-one mapping is fine if each back-end server handles a single function, but what about the homogenous case, where all (or some) of the servers can handle any of the applications? Put another way, what if a single server can't handle the load for store.example.site?

To map URLs onto multiple servers we need a scheme that tells Apache which server to pick. By invoking the powerful mod_rewrite engine we can use a random choice or write our own function to perform the mapping. Other solutions appear in the load balancing discussion to follow.

The random solution may seem puzzling at first, since it's, well, random; some heuristic-based method which takes load and capability into account would be better, right? But actually, random selection is a good method for handing out requests to a list of busy servers. Consider the simplicity: the server needs no information about the network, traffic level, or resources of the target servers. If the traffic load is high enough, random choice will apportion requests about equally to all servers, and all should stay busy. To make a better choice than random selection requires considerably more information, as we'll see later.

mod_rewrite's random selection method works like so: make a list of servers which can all handle a given request. It is important that the servers in the list all have roughly equal capabilities, or at least that no one of them will be swamped by its proportion of the requests. Put the list into a text file like so:

```
news      news1.example.site,news2.example.site,super.example.site
catalog   store1.example.site,store2.example.site,store3.example.site
```

We'll call the file maps.txt. Each line has a map name and the list of servers that can handle a particular set of requests. There are three in each list here, but there isn't any need for different maps to have the same number of entries. Now we tell the main server (which must have mod_rewrite compiled in) to use those maps to handle the news and catalog URLs:

```
RewriteEngine On
RewriteMap backend rnd:maps.txt
```

The first directive activates mod_rewrite (and can appear anywhere before your first Rewrite directive), and the second loads the map file. Now we can use the maps in substitution rules:

```
RewriteRule ^/news/(.*)$ http://${backend:news}/$1 [P,L]
ProxyPassReverse /news/ http://news.example.site/
RewriteRule ^/catalog/(.*)$ http://${backend:catalog}/$1 [P,L]
ProxyPassReverse /store/ http://store.example.site/
```

The RewriteRule directive takes a regular expression which is used to match against the URL of an incoming request. When a match comes in, the substitution is made according to the second pattern. That is the place where the selection of an application server happens, as mod_rewrite looks up the back-end map, sees that it is a random selection mapping (specified by rnd: in the RewriteMap directive), and picks a member of the indicated group (news or catalog). The substitution is made, and then mod_rewrite applies the postprocessing directives (the characters in brackets at the end, [P,L]), which tell it to run the request through mod_proxy (P) and stop rewriting it (L).

The ProxyPassReverse directives do the same thing they did previously, fixing up the response on its way back to the client.

After you've convinced yourself that this works, you'll probably want to turn off rewrite logging:

```
RewriteLogLevel    0
```

If we want some scheme other than random selection, we can still use mod_rewrite in more or less the same way. The engine allows an external program to do the mapping and return a choice to Apache. This isn't as slow in practice as it sounds, since Apache starts the program when the server starts and keeps it running until its own shut-down. The mapper can be a Perl script or almost anything else that can read its input and write a selection to output.

Tell mod_rewrite to use an external mapping program via the `prg:` map type, and pass the full path to the executable (not relative to Apache's root):

```
RewriteEngine On
RewriteMap backend prg:/usr/local/bin/weekday.pl
```

Here's `weekday.pl`, a script that directs traffic based on the day of the week:

```perl
#!/usr/bin/perl -w

use strict;
$| = 1;
my @news = qw(
                sunday.example.site
                monday.example.site
                tuesday.example.site
                wednesday.example.site
                thursday.example.site
                friday.example.site
                saturday.example.site
                );
my @store = qw(
                grocery.example.site
                shoe.example.site
                book.example.site
                );
my %classes = (news => \@news, store => \@store);
my $day = (localtime)[6];
while (<>) {
    chomp;
    if ($classes{$_}) {
        print $classes{$_}->[$day]
            || $classes{$_}->[0], "\n";
    }
    else {
        print "NULL\n";
    }
}
```

The script reads from input and verifies that it has a matching class; if so it returns the array element corresponding to the day of the week for that class, or the first element if the array is short. When the input doesn't match a class it returns NULL so that Apache will know there is an error and return an appropriate page.

Of course, if we're going to use Perl for this, why not do it inside of Apache?

Apache with mod_perl

In chapter 8's discussion of mod_rewrite I mentioned that some Perl programmers don't like learning another regular expression engine when they have such a powerful one at hand. That's the case here too, where mod_perl can take the place of mod_proxy and mod_rewrite to handle proxying.

This brings up the question of whether the thin front-end server can stay lean and fast enough if it has a Perl interpreter built into each Apache process. My answer is a lukewarm "maybe" depending on the circumstances. If your front-end needs mod_perl tools for other purposes, there's no reason you can't use it for proxy handling also, but it probably wouldn't be my first move if the server is otherwise bare Apache.

The fact that many Perl developers use a mod_perl proxy is shown in the number of modules already written for this task:

- If you want to use mod_proxy and mod_perl together, Apache::Proxy provides a Perl interface to the proxy module's functions.

- Apache::ProxyPass will take care of the functions of the `ProxyPass` directive in Perl if you don't want mod_proxy (or you are looking for a good place to start on your own version).

- Either Apache::ProxyRewrite or Apache::RewritingProxy can take care of the `ProxyPassReverse` tasks, modifying the returned document so that it appears to have come from the front-end machine. Apache::ProxyRewrite has interesting options for whether HTTP authentication is handled by the back-end or front-end machine.

And of course you can just write it yourself. Chapter 8's examples of URL rewriting in Perl can be extended to handle any kind of mapping scheme you like, from heuristic-based balancing systems to link of the day, hour, or minute. After you've munged the URL to your satisfaction, use Apache::Proxy to hand off the rest of the work to mod_proxy and let it take care of the actual proxying part, or write your own with Perl's LWP library.

By whatever implementation you choose, Apache remains a good choice for this task, especially if the front-end machine is also handling static content. You can turn on Apache's caching functions as well to save documents from the back-end servers (and save processing time on busy systems) for a complete solution in one box.

But it's not the only solution, as we'll see next.

12.3.2   Squid accelerator

The Squid cache split off from the Harvest project, a much larger Internet document search and cross-linking system. Duane Wessels started development of Squid as a cache server which could cooperate with peer- and parent-servers in localizing frequently requested documents. Currently the Squid Team maintains the server, although Duane is still the lead developer. The product is available on its home page, http://www.squid-cache.org/.

Most sites use Squid as a web proxy, either to forward requests through a firewall, cache documents, or both. It also has a reverse-proxy mode that it calls an HTTPD accelerator, in which it performs all of the proxying functions mentioned previously. Enabling this mode will turn off the regular proxying features by default. You can still enable both, although the Squid documentation recommends running two separate servers for this.

Unlike Apache, Squid runs as a single process which manages all requests. As such it is somewhat easier to configure and tune, since there is only one server to monitor. The impressive volume of documentation that comes with it can be daunting to a first time user, but as with Apache, you can ignore most of the options at first and learn what you need as you go. If Squid has the front-end machine to itself, you can assign the bulk of the system's memory and disk space to the cache. If not, consider your memory allocations carefully, as Squid uses more cache memory than you get from just looking at the configuration file. Squid's documentation and configuration file both advise you of this in the proper places.

The accelerator mode runs in one of two configurations: the single server mode proxies requests to one back-end server as you would guess from the name, and the virtual mode proxies any number of systems. Single server mode is unlikely to be useful to a web farm, although there is the possibility of putting Squid in front of what had been a front-end Apache server and proceeding with the implementations given in the previous chapter.

It is more likely, that you'll want Squid to handle the whole back-end mapping itself. This requires a *redirector* which looks at a URL and tells Squid where to send a request. It is in fact the same kind of script (or program) that mod_rewrite can use, with the same behavior and interface. Any Perl script will do, reading URLs on its standard input and writing the new location back out. Squid will start the redirector program at startup (or more than one, according to configuration) and keep it around for its own lifetime.

When Squid is running as an accelerator you have to configure it to listen on port 80 (and any other ports where you expect web traffic). If you are going to run an Apache server on the same machine, you can tell it to use a different port, or bind the Apache server to the localhost loopback address (usually 127.0.0.1) via a `Listen` directive. Then tell Squid (or the redirector) to use localhost for the Apache server on the same machine.

12.3.3   Load balancing

For smaller web farms, specialization is the way to go. Each machine has its role, and each is tuned to capacity. As the farm grows however, you'll need to build pools of machines, perhaps for each role or within roles.

Such a pool of machines requires maintenance and monitoring, and we want to ensure that our customers are getting the most out of the investment. Random server assignment can produce the occasional anomaly that spikes one server while others sit waiting. Luck of the draw might also assign several hard-hitting searches to one server while the others get status reports. After some such incidents, chances are you will go looking for better algorithms for balancing the work load across servers.

DNS round-robin

In any load-balancing discussion, round-robin assignment comes up as the simple case against which other methods are measured. In case it isn't obvious from the name, this method passes out requests to servers in turn. It thus avoids the random assignment problem of luckily handing three or four requests in a row to one server. If the entity which passes out the requests uses no other information, however, there is still just as much chance of one server getting swamped with difficult tasks while others get lightweight jobs, so round-robin doesn't solve much more, it's just cheap.

The usual way to implement a round-robin in a web farm is to set up the reverse proxy using the simple `ProxyPass` + `ProxyPassReverse` style shown earlier for Apache, as if the server were handling one machine for each role. However, that "machine" is really a special DNS address that corresponds to two or more names. When BIND encounters a request for the round-robin address it returns the first address in the list, then moves that address to the end of its list so that it won't be used again until the list is exhausted.

Thus suppose we had these records in the DNS database for our web farm:

```
news1   IN   A      192.168.10.1
news2   IN   A      192.168.10.2
news    IN   CNAME  192.168.1
news    IN   CNAME  192.168.2
```

You might prefer using CNAME records for the virtual address and address records only for the individual machines. Don't forget reverse-lookup records for the 192.168 namespace:

```
10.1   IN   PTR   news1.example.site
10.2   IN   PTR   news2.example.site
```

Now when the reverse proxy sends requests to http://news.example.site/, they will be parceled out alternately between the two servers.

One advantage in doing this at the DNS level is that a proxy isn't required at all. We could make news.example.site a public address and clients will get distributed more or less evenly among the machines. The problem with this approach is that client OS and browsers may cache DNS requests and thus send all their requests to one member of the round-robin. With enough clients that's not likely to be a problem, but it may cause anomalous spikes now and then.

DNS round-robins are also used to implement backup and fail-over. When a system is taken down for maintenance, just remove it from the round-robin (preferably beforehand). You can also have a script check for the presence of each server and remove it automatically if an emergency shutdown occurs.

As a balancing mechanism, round-robins are cheap and simple, but they don't give us the real balancing that a smarter method does. If you need more, keep reading.

mod_backhand

The Backhand project began in 1998 at the Johns Hopkins University, as a study of ways to balance server loads. The project progressed from academic interest to deployed program as the creators (Yair Amir and Theo Schlossnagle) progressed similarly through their studies. The deployed form is the Apache module of the same name, mod_backhand, which handles communication among servers to choose which is best suited to handle a request. The Backhand project has a page at http://www.backhand.org/.

Backhand-enabled servers send each other status messages on a regular basis to indicate how heavily loaded they are. This adds some overhead and internal traffic to the network, but it doesn't have to be much. You could configure the status updates to happen every several seconds and not notice the load at all. Of course, the more frequent your status updates happen the better the system will function.

After building mod_backhand into the relevant servers (both front- and back-end), you need to enable it for handling URLs in a fashion similar to the `ProxyPass` methods above, choosing groups of servers to receive requests for given URL matches. The difference lies in the way the dispatching to the back-end works: in the `Location` directive for the matching URL you enter a series of *candidacy functions*, each of which applies a heuristic to the list of available servers and decides whether or not to reduce the list based on that heuristic.

The first candidacy function for a URL receives a list of all the mod_backhand servers available. Thus a good heuristic for the first test is to eliminate all the servers that don't implement the required service (assuming your back-end servers are grouped by role—if they are all homogenous, this step is unnecessary). The suggested method is to name your servers such that a regular expression match can find the ones which handle the request (i.e., the news and stores groups given previously), though you can write any method you prefer.

mod_backhand provides functions for eliminating servers from the list by:

- `Age`—Eliminate servers that haven't responded to Backhand status requests within a certain time.

- `Load`—The method you would expect from a load balancing discussion. This method doesn't eliminate servers. It just sorts the list so that the least busy servers appear first.

- *Busy (as in Apache children)*—Almost the same as load. A server moves to the head of the list if it has no busy Apache processes, or if it has fewer than the other servers.

- *Cost*—You can assign costs to requests and servers, and sort the list by lowest cost.

- *LogWindow*—A function that cuts the list down by the log base 2 of the size of the list. After sorting the list by one of the load methods mentioned earlier, this function cuts all but the few least loaded servers out of the running.

After cutting the list down, you can either have Backhand send the request to the first entry, or choose one from the list at random.

Backhand understands some forms of session handling, which is terrific if you need to have a particular user's requests always return to one server. The request must have a recognizable session ID in the form of a cookie or a part of the URL. mod_backhand provides a candidacy function which will find the server indicated by the session ID and make it the only candidate left in the list.

You can write your own candidacy functions (and indeed you must if you don't have a homogenous back-end) in Perl if you like (or C if you don't), with the help of the Apache::Backend module, which also provides a Perl interface to the internal information on servers that mod_backhand collects.

Backhand has clear advantages for real load balancing needs within Apache. If you need load balancing outside of Apache (because you use other servers or other services), read on.

Linux Virtual Server

Load balancing at the TCP/IP level has advantages over any mechanism built into a web server, most obviously because it will work for FTP and other Internet services, but also because it separates the administration and maintenance of the balancing functions from the web functions.

A number of TCP/IP balancing mechanisms exist, but one of the most complete and usable is the Linux Virtual Server (LVS) Project, described at its home page (http://www.linuxvirtualserver.org/). As the name implies, this project is a modification of the Linux OS to create a balanced, high-availability virtual server out of a number of physical machines. The load balancing server (the *director* in LVS terminology) must run Linux. Depending on the balancing mechanism, the back-end servers might need Linux, but this is not required.

The simplest implementation of LVS is via network address translation (NAT). The director acts as a reverse proxy for all services, accepting and redirecting incoming requests and rewriting the responses so that they appear to come from itself. This method adds the usual latency to the system, but allows any OS to run in the back-end. The director can become a bottleneck for a large back-end if its network interfaces can't handle the merged load.

In the IP Tunneling implementation, the directory accepts incoming requests on behalf of the back-end and redirects them as usual, but the back-end servers reply directly to the client. This gets rid of the bottleneck problem of the first implementation, but of course it brings back all the problems that prompted the need for a reverse proxy—lingering closes, slow network interfaces, and so on. Also, the machines in the back-end all need to implement the IP Tunneling protocol which (so far as I know) is unique to Linux.

If the director and the back-end servers are all on a single physical network, the director can act as a router for the back-end services and thus skip the IP Tunneling mechanism. This relieves the requirement for Linux everywhere, but has the same problems on the back-end as the previous implementation.

For very large web farms, LVS or some other form of virtual server becomes almost a given. Virtual servers provide scalability and high availability that is difficult or impossible to achieve otherwise, being able to remove and replace hardware without shutting down the system at large. Check the site above for further reading and links to other projects.

I hope these guidelines and pointers will help you keep your system running smoothly, and that this chapter and this book leave you with confidence and ideas for perfecting your web server.

references

BIBLIOGRAPHY

I couldn't possibly list all the books I've read to learn what I know, even in an area as (comparably) focused as web development. However, I take advantage of two facts to list the most influential books I have in this area:

1. My bookshelves are right next to my desk.

2. I organize my books in a way that I tell people is "conceptual," but which is actually the simple method of putting any book I take down in the place that is closest at hand.

That means the books I use the most tend to be right next to me. Not all of these were used in writing this book, but I recommend them heartily to anyone who wants to master Perl and Apache. Glancing over at them, I can see that (in "conceptual" order) they are:

Apache: The Definitive Guide, by Ben Laurie and Peter Laurie (O'Reilly and Associates, 1997) and *Writing Apache Modules with Perl and C*, by Lincoln Stein and Dough MacEachern (O'Reilly and Associates, 1999)—these two represent the best printed material I know of on Apache and mod_perl. I tend to use online information for reference, but turn to these books when I need to put the details into larger context.

Object Oriented Perl, by Damian Conway (Manning Publications, 1999)—my Perl reference of choice whenever I have a question about objects or methods. It has lots of good things to say about coding in general.

Dynamic HTML, The Definitive Reference, by Danny Goodman (O'Reilly and Associates, 1998)—even in a book that does as little HTML as this one, it's helpful to have a strong reference when you are trying to remember how tables work.

Programming Perl, (also known as the "Camel Book") by Larry Wall, Tom Christiansen, and Jon Orwant (O'Reilly and Associates, 2000), *Perl: The Programmer's Companion* by Nigel Chapman (John Wiley and Sons, 1997) and *Advanced Perl Programming* by Sriram Srinivasan (O'Reilly and Associates, 1997)—don't venture too far in the Perl world without the Camel Book, along with one or more of the many other good Perl programming aids.

Official Guide to Programming with CGI.pm, by Lincoln Stein (John Wiley and Sons, 1998)—an essential starting point for those learning CGI and the premiere Perl module. After getting started you'll want to switch to online sources however, unless a more up-to-date version is now available.

The Perl Journal, Jon Orwant's quarterly magazine, is always a pleasure to read and the breadth of articles will help broaden your horizons and see new approaches and solutions to your Perl problems.

ONLINE RESOURCES

Many of the most commonly used sources on my "bookshelf" are online. I consider these sites as important as the books in learning and growing with Apache and Perl:

perlmonks.org
> Simply the best place to go for Perl support and community. Questions and discussions there range from basic script and CGI problems to profound questions of programming. Look me up when you get there.

http://www.perl.com/ and http://www.perl.org/
> The primary news sites of the Perl developers.

http://www.apacheweek.com/, http://apachetoday.com/
> News and updates for the Apache world.

http://www.apache.org/
> Apache development and module news.

http://perl.apache.org/ and http://take23.org/
> mod_perl news and discussions of new modules and tools.

http://search.cpan.org/
> The online CPAN search engine. Find great Perl modules here.

http://slashdot.org/
> My favorite news site, with sections for my favorite language and web server.

http://freshmeat.net/ and http://sourceforge.net/
> Great places to look for Open Source software.

index

C

use_reload_file 335, 342, 352
user 193
    authentication, HTTP 144
    data 133
user management 132
    Apache::DBI 155
    CGI.pm 153
    CreateUser.pm 152
UserDir 31–34, 36, 262

V

validation
    headers 144
    tools 67
values 80
VARIABLES 193
version 123
virtual host 29, 36, 309
    configuration 142
    for staging and production phases 319–320
virtual private network (VPN) 269–270
virtual server 383
VMonitor 363
VPN 271
VPN_HOWTO 271
vulnerabilities 25

W

-w (Perl command line switch) 66, 114
WDBI 97
    Delete 102
    Delete function 102
    FDF 98–99
    installation 98
    Update 102
    Update function 102
    using 100
web farm 274, 359, 382–383
web mail reader 243
Web Projects 250
web proxy 383
web rings 235

web server
    Apache 25
    Apache configuration 28
    apachectl 35
    bandwidth requirements 21
    database 21
    development server 33
    disk space 22
    graphics files 21
    hardware 21, 23
    operating system 22
    performance analysis 22
    production server 30
    securing the site 24
    static pages 21
    thttpd 37
Web-based Distributed Authoring and Versioning.
    See WebDAV
WebCal 248
WebClock.pm 119
WebDAV 327, 343
Web-FTP 256
WebMIN 257, 331
WebPass 255
WebRFM 255
WebRSH 255
weekday.pl 387
WHERE (SQL) 94, 96
wide area networks (WAN) 270
Windows 26, 43
WING 247
WITH_APXS 111
World Wide Web Consortium 63
WWWThreads 210, 215

X

XBitHack 165
XML 28, 202, 343
    AxKit 203
xsitecopy 345

Z

Zope 41